TAKING SIDES

Clashing Views in

Food and Nutrition

SECOND EDITION

Selected, Edited, and with Introductions by

Janet M. Colson
Middle Tennessee State University

Mc Graw Hill

Connect
Learn
Succeed™

TAKING SIDES: CLASHING VIEWS IN FOOD AND NUTRITION,
SECOND EDITION

1 2 3 4 5 6 7 8 9 0 DOC/DOC 1 0 9 8 7 6 5 4 3 2 1

MHID: 0-07-351447-0
ISBN: 978-0-07351447-5
ISSN: 1547-1802 (print)

Managing Editor: *Larry Loeppke*
Senior Developmental Editor: *Jade Benedict*
Senior Permissions Coordinator: *Lenny J. Behnke*
Senior Marketing Communications Specialist: *Mary Klein*
Senior Project Manager: *Jane Mohr*
Design Coordinator: *Brenda A. Rolwes*
Cover Graphics: *Rick D. Noel*
Buyer: *Nicole Baumgartner*
Media Project Manager: *Sridevi Palani*

Compositor: MPS Limited, a Macmillan Company
Cover Image: © The McGraw-Hill Companies, Inc./John Flournoy, photographer

Editors/Academic Advisory Board

Members of the Academic Advisory Board are instrumental in the final selection of articles for each edition of TAKING SIDES. Their review of articles for content, level, and appropriateness provides critical direction to the editors and staff. We think that you will find their careful consideration well reflected in this volume.

TAKING SIDES: Clashing Views in

Food and Nutrition

Second Edition

EDITOR

Janet Colson
Middle Tennessee State University

ACADEMIC ADVISORY BOARD MEMBERS

Editors/Academic Advisory Board continued

Preface

As humans, we must eat to live. However, determining what to eat has become very perplexing for many of us. We are bombarded with advertisements for newly formulated products that claim to be healthier than the foods humans have thrived on for years. Reports of the latest scientific studies cast doubt on many things we have always considered to be wholesome. Controversy continues when the nutrient content of foods are considered. Nutrition researchers throughout the world continue to investigate the impact that specific nutrients have on health, and each discovery leads to another question. One thing they have agreed on is what we consume does impact health. But is that impact positive, negative, or neutral?

The purpose of this book is to present some of the most hotly debated current issues on food and nutrition as related to health. The issues are presented as yes/no questions. For each question, two previously published selections that present clashing views on the topic are included; one selection says "yes" to the question and the second that supports the negative position. *Taking Sides: Clashing Views in Food and Nutrition* is designed to challenge students to do just that—take a side and decide if they agree with one of the views—or to think beyond the two sides to formulate their own opinion. A class of 30 students may yield 30 different opinions on the same issue.

The book is divided into six units with each containing related issues. Units 1 and 2 deal with nutrition guidelines and recommendations and their relationships to health. The next unit focuses on diet as related to weight management and obesity. Units 4 and 5 examine the food supply and food and nutrition policies that govern what we eat. The last unit centers on nutrient concerns for the life cycle.

Each issue begins with background information that lays the foundation for the topic. Questions are included at the end of each issue; instructors may assign the questions as a written assignment for submission or simply use them as a springboard for in-class debate and discussion.

Acknowledgments

Many thanks to my colleagues and students at Middle Tennessee State University for all their helpful suggestions. A special thank you to Tracy Morris, Rachel Harris, Debbie Goddard, and Jennifer Parham for all the help they provided in narrowing down the issues and selections. Without the editorial staff at McGraw-Hill Contemporary Learning Series this book would not exist. Thank you for all your suggestions, guidance, and help. And, of course, I owe everything to my two wonderful children, Heather and Beau. Without them my world would not exist.

Contents In Brief

Contents

Preface   v

Correlation Guide   xv

Introduction   xvii

Writer Lindsey Getz describes orthorexia, the condition that makes a person strive for a perfect diet. People with orthorexia avoid sugar, trans fat, cholesterol, sodium, and anything they believe is "unhealthy" and take pride in eating a perfect diet. Health and medical writer Chris Woolston believes the typical American diet is excessive in calories, fat, and sugar. He says we would be much healthier if we ate more "fish, poultry, cruciferous vegetables (i.e., cabbage and broccoli), greens, tomatoes, legumes, fresh fruits, and whole grains." He also believes we should "skimp on fatty or calorie-rich foods such as red meats, eggs, high-fat dairy products, french fries, pizza, mayonnaise, candy, and desserts."

UNIT 2   NUTRITION AND HEALTH   51

Health writer Lindsey Getz applauds restaurants and the food industry for eliminating the trans fat in foods and stresses how it will improve the health of the nation. Physician Joseph Mercola strongly disagrees and points out that food manufacturers are replacing trans fat with interesterified fat. He claims these are worse than trans fats.

Osteopathic physician Joseph Mercola considers that high fructose corn syrup (HFCS) is more deadly than sugar and explains how the body converts fructose to fat. He accuses the Corn Refiners Association of trying to convince us that their HFCS is equal to table sugar. The Corn Refiners Association claims that HFCS has no adverse health effect and is the same as sucrose and honey. They also emphasize the benefits that HFCS provides to food.

The Silk Soy Nutrition Center claims that scientific studies show that soy lowers cholesterol and reduces the risk of heart disease. They also claim that "populations eating diets high in soy-based foods have a lower incidence of breast cancer, prostate cancer and menopausal problems." Representing Cornucopia, Charlotte Vallayes and colleagues consider isolated soy proteins to be highly overrated, and possibly hazardous to the health of women and infants. They say that the heart health claim "is a direct product of corporate boardrooms searching for ways to sell more soy products—and to turn the soy 'waste' soy-products of soybean oil extraction into profits."

UNIT 3   DIET, PHYSICAL ACTIVITY, AND WEIGHT MAINTENANCE   103

Journalist Jeremy Singer-Vine points out that "the circumference around a person's waist provides a much more accurate reading of his or her abdominal fat and risk for disease than BMI." But "waist measurements require slightly more time and training than it takes to record a BMI." Since BMI is cheap and easy to use, physicians and the medical community will continue using it. Mathematician Keith Devlin, who is classified as "overweight" by his physician, since Keith's BMI is 25.1, despite his 32-inch waist, considers that BMI is "numerological nonsense." While he applauds the knowledge that physicians have about the human body and health issues, he feels that the mathematics behind the BMI calculations are used irresponsibly and says BMI should not be used in medical practice. He calls for mathematicians to demand responsible use of math.

Best-selling author Jane Brody says that a huge part of the population is deficient in vitamin D and that studies indicate deficiency increases risk of cancer, heart disease, arthritis, and a host of other conditions. She also reports that the "experts" recommend a supplement of 1,000–2,000 IU each day. The 14-member committee appointed by the Institute of Medicine (IOM) of the National Academy of Sciences to set the Recommended Dietary Allowance (RDA) disagrees. After reviewing over 1,000 studies and listening to testimonies from scientists and other stakeholders, the committee set the RDA for people up to age 70 years at 600 IU and at 800 IU for those over age 70. They conclude that few people are deficient in vitamin D and the only health benefit is the vitamin's role in bone health.

and help ensure a safe food supply. Ed Hamer and Mark Anslow argue that GM foods cost farmers and governments more money than they are worth, that they are ruining the environment, and point to the health risks associated with GM foods.

Issue 12.   Are Probiotics and Prebiotics Beneficial in Promoting Health?   178

YES: **Anneli Rufus**, from "Poop Is the Most Important Indicator of Your Health," *AlterNet* (March 27, 2010)   *181*

NO: **Peta Bee**, from "Probiotics, Not So Friendly After All?" *The Times* (London) (November 10, 2008)   *186*

Journalist Anneli Rufus describes how chemicals added to today's food supply destroy the good bacteria (probiotics) and various ways to restore the bacteria to the body. She also encourages us to start looking for prebiotic-fortified foods, since it is hard to get an adequate amount from foods. Health and fitness journalist Peta Bee is skeptical of probiotics and counters that some products that claim to contain probiotics may not actually have bacteria that are still "live and active" by the time we eat it. She points out that some bacteria added to foods may even be harmful.

Issue 13.   Should Energy Drinks Be Banned?   191

YES: **Chad J. Reissig, Eric C. Strain, and Roland R. Griffiths**, from "Caffeinated Energy Drinks—A Growing Problem," *Drug and Alcohol Dependence* (January 2009)   *194*

NO: **Ellen Coleman**, from "Back to the Grind: The Return of Caffeine as an Ergogenic Aid," *Today's Dietitian* (March 2009)   *205*

Chad Reissig, Eric Strain, and Roland Griffiths, medical researchers at Johns Hopkins, say there are increasing reports of caffeine intoxication from energy drinks and predict that problems with caffeine intoxication may be on the rise. California sports nutritionist and exercise physiologist Ellen Coleman is not concerned about the potential side effects of caffeine in energy drinks and bars. She writes that "substantial research suggests that caffeine enhances endurance performance."

UNIT 5   FOOD AND NUTRITION POLICY   215

Issue 14.   Is Hunger in America a Real Problem?   216

YES: **Joel Berg**, from "Hunger in the U.S.: A Problem as American as Apple Pie," *AlterNet* (February 4, 2009)   *220*

NO: **Sam Dolnick**, from "The Obesity-Hunger Paradox," *The New York Times* (March 12, 2010)   *227*

Hunger advocate Joel Berg says that 35.5 million Americans either suffer from hunger or struggle at the brink of hunger, which results in stunted growth in millions of American children. As the executive director of New York City Coalition Against Hunger, he points out that hunger is becoming a significant problem in the suburbs and is no longer only seen in poor inner city and isolated rural areas. New York journalist Sam Dolnick says that few Americans are hungry, if you picture hunger as a rail-thin child with nothing to eat. But he points out that Americans are "food insecure," which he describes as people "unable to get to the grocery or unable to find fresh produce among the pizza shops, doughnut stores and fried-everything restaurants." In fact, obesity often results from this type of food insecurity, where there is little access to affordable fresh produce and other lower calorie foods.

Kelly Brownell and colleagues propose a "fat tax" targeting sugar-sweetened beverages. They feel a tax will decrease the amount of sugary drinks people consume and ultimately help reduce obesity. They also suggest that the tax has the "potential to generate substantial revenue" to help fund health-related initiatives. Daniel Engber disagrees with a fat tax on sugary beverages since it will impact poor, nonwhite people most severely and they would be deprived of the pleasures of drinking palatable beverages. He says that the poor would be forced to "drink from the faucet" while the more affluent will sip exotic beverages such as POM Wonderful, at about $5 a pop.

First Lady Michelle Obama says that the *Let's Move* campaign can correct the health problems of the upcoming generation and realizes that the problem cannot be solved overnight. She thinks that "with everyone working together, it can be solved." The "first ever" Task Force on Childhood Obesity was formed to help implement the campaign. Public health attorney Michele Simon claims that *Let's Move* is just another task force and there is more talk than action. She questions if it's realistic to be able to reverse the nation's childhood obesity epidemic in a generation.

Science writer Phyllida Brown maintains that even a small amount of alcohol can damage a developing fetus and cites new research indicating that any alcohol consumed during pregnancy may be harmful. Food and nutrition journalist Julia Moskin argues that there are almost no studies on the effects of moderate drinking during pregnancy and that small amounts of alcohol are unlikely to have much effect.

Haley Stevens and Mardi Mountford, representing the International Formula Council (IFC), point out that "the available evidence strongly supports benefits of adding DHA and ARA to infant formula." They point out that "a large database exists concerning not only the safety but also the efficacy of infant formula containing both ARA and DHA. These facts, together, support the addition of both ARA and DHA when LC-PUFAs [long-chain polyunsaturated fatty acids] are added to formula." Food writer Ari LeVaux is more skeptical. He says the oils are produced from lab-grown algae and fungi and extracted with the neurotoxin hexane. He also is concerned that some "parents and medical professionals believe these additives are causing severe reactions in some babies, and it has been repeatedly shown that taking affected babies off DHA/ARA formula makes the problems go away almost immediately."

Pat Thomas, the editor of the London-based *The Ecologist*, believes that breast-feeding is the best and healthiest way to feed babies and contends that advertisements from formula companies are jeopardizing the health of infants and children around the world. *The Atlantic* editor Hanna Rosin claims the scientific data on benefits of breast-feeding are inconclusive and, as an experienced mother of three, suggests a more relaxed approach to the issue.

Correlation Guide

The *Taking Sides* series presents current issues in a debate-style format designed to stimulate student interest and develop critical thinking skills. Each issue is thoughtfully framed with an issue summary, an issue introduction, and challenge questions. The pro and con essays—selected for their liveliness and substance—represent the arguments of leading scholars and commentators in their fields.

Taking Sides: Clashing Views in Food and Nutrition, 2/e is an easy-to-use reader that presents issues on important topics such as *Dietary Guidelines, Food Supply,* and *Obesity.* For more information on *Taking Sides* and other *McGraw-Hill Contemporary Learning Series* titles, visit http://www.mhhe.com/cls.

This convenient guide matches the issues in **Taking Sides: Clashing Views in Food and Nutrition, 2/e** with the corresponding chapters in three of our best-selling McGraw-Hill Nutrition textbooks by Wardlaw/Smith and Schiff.

Taking Sides: Food and Nutrition, 2/e	Contemporary Nutrition: A Functional Approach, 2/e by Wardlaw/Smith	Contemporary Nutrition, 8/e by Wardlaw/Smith	Nutrition for Healthy Living, 2/e by Schiff
Issue 1: Can All Foods Fit Into a Healthy Diet?	**Chapter 2:** Guidelines for Designing a Healthy Diet	**Chapter 2:** Guidelines for Designing a Healthy Diet	**Chapter 3:** Planning Nutritious Diets
Issue 2: Is the Dietary Guideline for Sodium Realistic?	**Chapter 2:** Guidelines for Designing a Healthy Diet **Chapter 8:** Nutrients Involved with Fluid and Electrolyte Balance	**Chapter 2:** Guidelines for Designing a Healthy Diet **Chapter 9:** Water and Minerals	**Chapter 3:** Planning Nutritious Diets
Issue 3: Can an Overemphasis on Eating Healthy Become Unhealthy?	**Chapter 13:** Eating Disorders: Anorexia Nervosa, Bulimia Nervosa, and Other Conditions	**Chapter 11:** Eating Disorders: Anorexia Nervosa, Bulimia Nervosa, and Other Conditions	**Chapter 3:** Planning Nutritious Diets
Issue 4: Does "Trans Fats-Free" Mean a Food Is Heart-Healthy?	**Chapter 5:** Lipids	**Chapter 5:** Lipids	**Chapter 2:** Evaluating Nutrition Information **Chapter 6:** Fats and Other Lipids
Issue 5: Does a Diet High in Fructose Increase Body Fat?	**Chapter 7:** Energy Balance and Weight Maintenance	**Chapter 7:** Energy Balance and Weight Control	**Chapter 5:** Carbohydrates
Issue 6: Does Eating Soy Improve Health?	**Chapter 6:** Proteins	**Chapter 6:** Proteins	**Chapter 2:** Evaluating Nutrition Information
Issue 7: Should Physicians Use BMI to Assess Overall Health?	**Chapter 12:** Nutrition: Fitness and Sports	**Chapter 10:** Nutrition: Fitness and Sports	**Chapter 10:** Energy Balance and Weight Control

(Continued)

Taking Sides: Food and Nutrition, 2/e	Contemporary Nutrition: A Functional Approach, 2/e by Wardlaw/Smith	Contemporary Nutrition, 8/e by Wardlaw/Smith	Nutrition for Healthy Living, 2/e by Schiff
Issue 8: Do Americans Need Vitamin D Supplements?	**Chapter 7:** Energy Balance and Weight Maintenance	**Chapter 7:** Energy Balance and Weight Control	**Chapter 10:** Energy Balance and Weight Control
Issue 9: Does Obesity Cause a Decline in Life Expectancy?	**Chapter 7:** Energy Balance and Weight Maintenance	**Chapter 7:** Energy Balance and Weight Control	**Chapter 10:** Energy Balance and Weight Control
Issue 10: Are Organic Foods Better than Conventional Foods?	**Chapter 1:** What You Eat and Why	**Chapter 1:** What You Eat and Why	**Chapter 3:** Planning Nutritious Diets
Issue 11: Does the World Need Genetically Modified Foods?	**Chapter 15:** Food Safety	**Chapter 13:** Safety of Food and Water	**Chapter 12:** Food Safety Concerns
Issue 12: Are Prebiotics and Probiotics Beneficial in Promoting Health?	**Chapter 11:** Nutrients Involved with Energy Metabolism and Blood Health	**Chapter 3:** The Human Body: A Nutrition Perspective	**Chapter 4:** Body Basics
Issue 13: Should Energy Drinks Be Banned?	**Chapter 15:** Food Safety	**Chapter 13:** Safety of Food and Water	**Chapter 12:** Food Safety Concerns
Issue 14: Is Hunger in America a Real Problem?	**Chapter 14:** Undernutrition Throughout the World	**Chapter 34:** A World Without Borders	**Chapter 13:** Nutrition for a Lifetime
Issue 15: Should Government Levy a Fat Tax?	**Chapter 7:** Energy Balance and Weight Maintenance	**Chapter 7:** Energy Balance and Weight Control	
Issue 16: Can Michelle Obama's "Let's Move" Initiative Halt Childhood Obesity?	**Chapter 7:** Energy Balance and Weight Maintenance	**Chapter 7:** Energy Balance and Weight Control	**Chapter 13:** Nutrition for a Lifetime
Issue 17: Is It Necessary for Pregnant Women to Completely Abstain from All Alcoholic Beverages?	**Chapter 16:** Pregnancy and Breastfeeding	**Chapter 14:** Pregnancy and Breastfeeding	**Chapter 13:** Nutrition for a Lifetime
Issue 18: Should Infant Formulas Contain Synthetic ARA and DHA?	**Chapter 17:** Nutrition from Infancy Through Adolescence	**Chapter 15:** Nutrition from Infancy Through Adolescence	**Chapter 12:** Food Safety Concerns **Chapter 13:** Nutrition for a Lifetime
Issue 19: Is Breast-Feeding the Best Way to Feed Babies?	**Chapter 16:** Pregnancy and Breastfeeding	**Chapter 14:** Pregnancy and Breastfeeding	**Chapter 13:** Nutrition for a Lifetime

Introduction

Janet M. Colson

When I was growing up in rural Mississippi during the 1960s, eating was very simple. Summer meals consisted of vegetables from my father's garden served with meat or fish. My father kept the freezer filled with beef or pork that he had slaughtered from his farm and fish from the river. We had three meals a day with the entire family sitting around the kitchen table. And for snacks, my mother very patiently taught us to use a knife to peel oranges, making sure the rind stayed in one continuous coil. Winter meals consisted of hot vegetables, the product of hours spent picking and freezing produce harvested during the warmer months. School lunches were "meat and three" cooked from scratch by some of the best cooks in the county. The only beverages available in school were plain white milk and water from the fountain. In other words, we had real food. The first time I saw pizza, tacos, chicken nuggets, and chocolate milk in a school cafeteria was when I had lunch with my daughter in the 1980s.

So what has happened over the last 50 years? Most people don't have time or space for a family garden, so we rely on what the local grocer decides to stock. Some of us, including many college students, opt for whatever is on sale. And eating out, especially at fast food restaurants, can actually be cheaper and is definitely easier than cooking at home. Most of us are aware that the substances we consume will eventually impact our health. But is that impact positive, negative, or neutral? This is where the confusion, controversy, and discussion begin.

Each year, thousands of articles appear in professional journals, magazines, newspapers, and blogs about the latest discoveries and claims about food and its impact on the body. In most instances, if you read three articles on the same topic, you'll get three different opinions. The authors may agree on some aspects, but vary on others. Not only is it mind-boggling to the general public, but health and nutrition professionals are often confused on whom to believe. This book presents 19 of the most current and debated issues about food and nutrition and challenges students to analyze the issue and form his or her individual opinion. Each issue is presented as a yes/no question with two previously published selections, one answers "yes" to the question and the second "no." While this book only presents two sides of each issue, it is important for students to realize that there may be more than two sides; each person must carefully evaluate the issue and figure out what he or she believes and what is best for him or herself. The issues are designed to help the reader work through the process of thinking analytically and critically—to compare, analyze, critique, and justify.

Our Food Supply

As humans, we must eat food to stay alive. Fortunately, our food supply is plentiful. In 2008, the Food Marketing Institute reported that the average grocery store carries close to 47,000 different items. While the immense number of products gives us vast variety, it also makes selecting food very confusing. Many people base their food choices on the claims they see in food advertisements or what is written on food labels. Virtually all advertisements promote the beneficial aspects of the food they are promoting, and these ads do influence our decision to buy the product. The nutrition facts on food labels also influence many people's choices. The Food and Drug Administration (FDA) has tracked food label use since 1982. Based on results of their 2008 Health and Diet Survey, 54 percent Americans report they read food labels, compared to only 44 percent in 2004. Most are looking at calories, fat, or salt content. Additionally, the FDA study found more Americans say they know about the heart-health benefits of omega-3 fatty acids and negative aspects of trans fats than in earlier years. However, less people recognize the benefits of eating fruits and vegetables and heart disease reduction. This could be related to less advertising by the vegetable and fruit industry compared to the billions spent by the processed food and beverage industry.

Our food supply is changing and becoming very complex. Because of the advances in food chemistry, hundreds of natural chemicals in foods have been identified. They include nutrients—proteins, carbohydrates, fats, vitamin, and minerals—plus live microorganisms and hundreds of phytochemicals. Nutrition scientists investigate the impact that these natural substances have on health status. Results of their investigations impact our diets in two ways. First, the food industry promotes the health benefits of the foods that contain the substances, which increases sales. Second, food manufacturers extract the substances from its natural source, and add it to newly created products. Some food producers use synthetically produced versions of the nutrients. After products are developed, the manufacturer spends millions marketing the new food to the public. For example, the health benefits of omega-3 fatty acids (such as DHA and EPA) have been studied for last few decades. They are naturally found in fatty fish and breast milk. Today, members of the fish industry promote the DHA and EPA that are found naturally in their products. Other manufacturers, especially infant formula and baby food companies, add synthetic versions of DHA or EPA to their products. When the public sees the DHA or EPA claim on the label, they purchase it because of the perceived health benefits.

Debate begins when people question the safety and benefit of these nutrients, or other substances from food. And many people question the safety of how the synthetic versions are made and speculate that fake versions may be harmful to humans. For example, some groups are skeptical of the synthetic DHA in infant formula; critics claim that synthetic oils, which are derived from lab-grown algae, may be hazardous. Other groups, including the FDA, say it's no different than natural sources.

Complexities of Our Diets

If foods we eat are complex, our diets are even more so. Southerners have a totally different diet than people from New York or California. And what we eat varies based on the season; most of us eat more fresh fruits and vegetables in the summer months and more candy and other sweets beginning at Halloween continuing until New Years Day. Culture, traditions, and religion also impact our diets. As the world's population becomes more transient, dietary practices change. Not only do immigrants bring their native foods and dietary preferences to the new country, they also adopt dietary practices of the culture. The United States Department of Agriculture (USDA) has evaluated acculturation of immigrants to the United States and found that dietary quality decreases as immigrants become more "Americanized" and give up their native lifestyles. Religion also impacts the diet. Some of the healthiest populations are those with strictest religious dietary practices. For example, Seventh-Day Adventists (SDA) who follow vegetarian diets and avoid alcohol and tobacco are healthier than the general population. According to a recent SDA Dietetic Association report:

> SDAs in general have 50% less risk of heart disease, certain types of cancers, strokes, and diabetes. More specifically, recent data suggests that vegetarian men under 40 can expect to live more than eight years longer and women more than seven years longer than the general population. SDA vegetarian men live more than three years longer than SDA men who eat meat. Researchers believe this added length of life and quality of health is due in particular to the consumption of whole grains, fruits and vegetables as well as the avoidance of meat, alcohol, coffee and tobacco.

Our diets are made up of foods that are composed of hundreds of nutrients and other chemicals. However, many studies that examine the impact of nutrition on health focus on single nutrients. For example, many reports suggest that eating fructose increases triglyceride levels in the body. They may base this observation on studies that show laboratory animals that are fed high levels of plain fructose become obese and develop obesity-related diseases. But few of us have a diet that is predominately fructose. Do our bodies handle free fructose differently than natural fructose found in fruits and vegetables? Or is fructose that is eaten with other foods handled differently than pure fructose? Some people say "yes" to both of these, while others claim there are no differences. Many people believe that the total diet should be considered instead of focusing on a single food or a single nutrient.

Organization of the Book

The book consists of 20 issues, each with two previously published selections. Some of the selections are reprinted from scientific journals and others are excerpts from books, government or industry press releases, magazines, newspapers, and blogs. The selections encompass debates about matters affecting the entire food chain, from production to advice about a healthy diet. The book is divided into six units with each containing related issues:

- Unit 1: Nutrition Guidelines and Recommendations
- Unit 2: Nutrition and Health

- Unit 3: Diet, Physical Activity, and Weight Maintenance
- Unit 4: Our Food Supply
- Unit 5: Food and Nutrition Policy
- Unit 6: Nutrition Concerns of Pregnant Women and Infants

Each of the 19 issues begins with an introduction, which sets the stage for the debate and provides the historical context and timeline. For each selection, the affiliation and education of the author or authors are included. (A more detailed background is available in the back of the book.) The authors include nutrition scientists, physicians, pharmacists, attorneys, dietitians, nurses, sports nutritionists, award-winning journalists, and even one mathematician. Consider who the authors are, their areas of expertise, and their stake in the issue as you critique what they write. Question their position on the issue and if they may profit from their opinions or if their position is totally altruistic. Ask yourself, "What does the author (or who pays the author) stand to benefit from his position?"

Who Writes About Food and Nutrition?

Authors of the selections represent one of five main groups as outlined below. Each of the groups has a different stake in the issue. Consider their stake in the issue as you read.

1. Food, Nutrition, and Health Professionals

Professionals in this category include people who have the academic training and credentials needed to conduct research and to interpret the scientific evidence behind nutrition recommendations. They include professionals such as dietitians, physicians, chiropractors, nurses, and food and nutrition researchers. Some of the professionals work directly with the public and have first-hand experience with delivering dietary advice, while others work in research. Some research is laboratory based and other is done with large clinical trials. Many of the selections are written by registered dietitians (RDs) who describe their experiences advising the public about nutrition. For example, the authors for both sides of Issue 1 are all RDs; the "YES" article is written by two RDs on behalf of the American Dietetic Association, while the author of the "NO" selection is also an RD who speaks on the basis of her experience working with the public. Even though they have the same education and credentials, they disagree on topics in their areas of expertise. Other selections are written by food and nutrition researchers, many of them are recognized internationally for their research. For example, Issue 15 (fat tax) was coauthored by seven of America's leading experts on the impact that sugar-sweetened beverages have on health.

2. Representatives of Government Agencies

The two main U.S. agencies that publish reports, policies, and recommendations related to food and nutrition are the USDA and the Department of

Health and Human Services (HHS). The two agencies work together to develop the *Dietary Guidelines for Americans,* but have specific functions in other areas. The main responsibility of the UDSA is to promote sale and consumption of American agricultural products, but it also houses units that work on nutrition policies and advise the public about diet and health with tools such as MyPyramid. Interestingly, one section of the USDA promotes agricultural products such as beef, pork, eggs, dairy products, and oils made from soy beans, peanuts, and corn, whereas another section recommends to limit saturated fats (found in meats, eggs, and dairy) and total fat intake. These different functions can, and do, generate debate. The USDA also oversees the following food and nutrition assistance programs: the Supplemental Nutrition Assistance Program (SNAP, formerly Food Stamps); the Supplemental Nutrition Program for Women, Infants, and Children (WIC), and the National School Lunch Program.

The HHS consists of several subagencies and several of these deal with food, nutrition, and health. The FDA is a subagency that regulates the safety and labeling of the food supply. The Centers for Disease Control and Prevention (CDC) conducts research and sponsors programs to prevent diet-related diseases. They track the health status of the nation through National Health and Nutrition Examination Survey (NHANES) and sponsor Healthy People 2020. The National Institutes of Health (NIH) conducts and sponsors research on many areas of nutrition and health. NIH consists of 20 institutes including the National Cancer Institute; National Heart, Lung, and Blood Institute; and the National Institute on Drug Abuse.

Several other government, or government-sponsored, agencies investigate food and nutrition matters. For instance, the General Accounting Office conducts research in response to congressional queries. In 2010, they investigated the safety of herbal dietary supplements and provided the report to Congress. The Institute of Medicine (IOM) of the National Academies is a private, nonprofit group. The government contracts with IOM to conduct research related to health. The "YES" article for Issue 2 is a report from the IOM on sodium reduction in American foods. The government announces programs through press releases. The "YES" selection for Issue 16 is based on a government press release.

3. Representatives from the Food Industry

The food industry is the term that describes groups involved in growing, harvesting, processing, transport, and sale of food and beverages. They have the biggest impact on what we eat. According to the Food Industry Center of the University of Minnesota:

> Few industries reach as many consumers on a daily basis or are as fundamental to their lives as the food industry. Americans spend more than $1 trillion annually for food, accounting for nearly 10 percent of our Gross Domestic Product (GDP). The food system employs over 16.5 million people. . . .

We must eat; therefore, the food industry impacts everyone. Food must be produced, processed, distributed, and prepared before we eat it, and each stage is represented by its own segment of the food industry with its own special interests in influencing dietary advice and government regulations. Advice to avoid a particular food, or component in a food, can decrease sale of that item, and result in loss of profit for that segment of the food industry. Therefore, the food industry hires food and nutrition researchers, either paid directly or through grants, to conduct studies that support the benefits of their products. They also hire lobbyists to make sure laws and government regulations do not interfere with production, sale, or use of their products.

Four of the selections are from special interest groups. In Issue 5, the Corn Refiners Association claims that eating high-fructose corn syrup (a refined corn product) is the same as eating honey or regular table sugar. The Silk Soy Nutrition Center touts the health benefits of soy protein in Issue 6; and the International Formula Council, which represents the leading formula manufacturers, promotes safety of synthetically produced fat added to infant formulas in Issue 18.

4. Advocacy Groups and Individuals

Advocacy may come from an individual or by an advocacy group such as the Center for Science in the Public Interest (CSPI) or from national organizations such as the American Heart Association (AHA) or the American Cancer Society. Groups, such as these, attempt to promote the nutritional health of the public, and sometimes point out problems of the food industry or petition the government to strengthen policies. Advocacy can also take the form of media campaigns, public speaking, commissioning and publishing research or polls, or filing lawsuits. And many individuals and groups who advocate for healthier food get results.

For instance, in 1993, the CSPI recommended that the trans fat content of foods should be included on food labels since they had recognized that trans fats are linked to elevated blood cholesterol. However, it took 13 years before the FDA agreed to require trans fat content on the nutrition facts labels of processed foods. In 2003, California attorney Stephen Joseph filed a lawsuit ordering Nabisco to stop selling Oreo cookies to children in California, because the cookies were high in trans fat. The suit did not actually go to trial since Nabisco agreed to reformulate their Oreos. Joseph dropped the suit. More recently, the AHA suggested to the USDA that the sodium intake recommendation should be lowered to 1,500 mg of sodium each day. Authors of the new *Dietary Guidelines for Americans* for 2010 have agreed to include the lower sodium recommendation for the entire adult population, based, in part, on the strong recommendation from the AHA.

Issues in this book include those from people who advocate against pesticide use and genetic modification to seeds, while others question the safety of man-made products such as high-fructose corn syrup, synthetically made fats, and other food-processing practices.

5. Food and Nutrition Journalists

Many of the selections in this book are written by journalists who write about other people's opinions on the topic or simply report results of recent developments related to food and nutrition. Some of the journalists have academic training in food and nutrition, while others have developed expertise through personal interest. Time and again journalists are criticized about what they write; some people accuse journalists of sensationalizing the story. Stories about controversial issues attract readers and enhance the careers of journalists as well as of the researchers or groups that they write about. Research about the effects of food, nutrients, or agricultural practices on health often grabs front-page attention, and many leading journalists issue press releases on studies likely to gain attention. Reporters writing about food and nutrition issues of unusual interest win prizes and book contracts for their work. Because controversy makes news, media attention tends to focus on the differences rather than the similarities in points of view.

Ruth Kava, the director of nutrition at the American Council on Science and Health, warns journalists about good stories and bad sciences in "Good Stories, Bad Science: A Guide for Journalists to the Health Claims of 'Consumer Activist' Groups." She stresses the need for journalists to be skeptical of reporting information from consumer activist groups about the alleged hazards in our food supply. She concludes:

> Often these claims are coupled with suggestions for specific actions to reduce the purported risk of disease or premature death by avoiding or reducing exposure to the allegedly harmful substance. Supposedly, the public claims and warnings that these activist groups make are based on scientific evidence. But, in general, there is no independent peer review of their claims or recommendations. The groups publish the reports themselves, often via press release or paid advertisements. Often, the claims are extrapolations from small studies or animal studies, and lack strong supporting evidence. This is not the way mainstream science works.

In some instances, an author's affiliation may fit into two or more of these categories. For example, time and again food, nutrition, or health professionals will be employed by a government agency or in the food industry. The professionals must promote the interest of their employer, whether they personally agree with it or not. And some work as freelance journalists or begin their own blogs on nutrition and health issues in an effort to voice their own opinions. Others work for advocacy groups or are simply very vocal in their opinions.

Internet References . . .

Center for Nutrition Policy and Promotion (CNPP)

This Center for Nutrition Policy and Promotion (CNPP) Web site provides recent United States Department of Agriculture (USDA) publications on diet and health, including the USDA Pyramid graphic, brochure, and the history of its development; the Food Guide Pyramid for Children; the Dietary Guidelines for Americans; the Healthy Eating Index (a 10-component index of foods and nutrients designed to measure overall dietary quality); and data on the dietary intake of Americans. Click on the *Nutrition Insights* button to see especially, Insight 2, Escobar A., "Are All Food Pyramids Created Equal?" (April 1997).

http://www.usda.gov/cnpp/

Economic Research Service (ERS)

This Economic Research Service (ERS) research reports site offers the complete text of *America's Eating Habits: Changes & Consequences.* The site also offers a large range of USDA publications on food and nutrition policy.

http://www.ers.usda.gov/Publications/

The American Dietetic Association

The American Dietetic Association site is primarily designed for members, but it also offers information for the public about dozens of issues in nutrition, resources for studying those issues, legislation affecting food and nutrition, and nutrition careers.

http://www.eatright.org/Public/

Nutrition Guidelines and Recommendations

*F*or years, professional organizations, government agencies, and many health and nutrition researchers have advised the public about what to eat and what to avoid. Their advice is designed to help promote health and reduce risk of major chronic diseases. Nutrition and health organizations typically develop and publish position papers related to topics within their realm of expertise. The federal government, through the United States Department of Agriculture (USDA) and Department of Health and Human Services (HHS) provides guidance for the general population. Many food-related policies and laws are based on their recommendations. A third area of advice comes from the private sector, frequently from people who are leaders in cutting-edge nutrition research and those who write about or critique the latest developments. The researchers may not agree with existing guidance from other groups, which often provokes debate and controversy.

    The authors of the first two issues represent one of these areas. In Issue 1 centers around a disagreement between the American Dietetic Association, which claims that all foods can fit into a healthy diet, and a professor from the University of North Carolina at Chapel Hill, who disagrees saying that some foods should be considered good and others bad. The second issue includes recommendations from the ION to FDA and HHS about the need for reduction of sodium in processed foods. A health journalist describes problems that the food industry claim they will encounter if they try to comply with the stringent recommendations. The third issue deals with complications that may arise when people take dietary advice and guidelines to the extreme. It asks if avoiding sugar, trans fat, salt, and other "bad" foods can actually become unhealthy and describes the health condition known as orthorexia.

- Can All Foods Fit Into a Healthy Diet?
- Is the Dietary Guideline for Sodium Realistic?
- Can an Overemphasis on Eating Healthy Become Unhealthy?

ISSUE 1

Can All Foods Fit Into a Healthy Diet?

YES: Susan Nitzke and Jeanne Freeland-Graves, from "Position of the American Dietetic Association: Total Diet Approach to Communicating Food and Nutrition Information," *Journal of the American Dietetic Association* (July 2007)

NO: Suzanne Havala, from *Good Foods, Bad Foods: What's Left to Eat?* (Chronimed Publishing, 1998)

As you read the issue, focus on the following points:

1. Reasons that ADA thinks that the "total diet approach" to eating is better than the "good food, bad food" approach.
2. The influence the food industry (dairy, beef, sugar, wheat, pork, etc.) has on nutrition messages from ADA and USDA.
3. Benefits and problems associated with using terms such as "moderation," "balance," and "variety" when describing desirable diets.

ISSUE SUMMARY

YES: Nutrition professors Susan Nitzke and Jeanne Freeland-Graves represent the position of the American Dietetic Association (ADA) when they write that there are no "good" foods or "bad" ones, since all foods can fit into "a healthful eating style." ADA emphasizes the total diet that a person eats is more important than any one particular food. They stress moderation and portion control. As the world's largest association of food and nutrition experts, ADA "emphasizes a balance of foods, rather than any one food."

NO: Nutrition professor, and author of *Good Foods, Bad Foods: What's Left to Eat?*, Suzanne Havala counters that some foods are better than others and that saying otherwise is just a way to "rationalize the dietary status quo and protect the commercial interests of the food industry."

American Dietetic Association (ADA) is the world's largest association of food and nutrition experts and currently has close to 70,000 members. The association publishes "position papers" that describe ADA's opinions on various topics. Positions are developed by a small committee of ADA members who have expertise on the particular topic. Key leaders of the association vote on the adoption of the position. If adopted, it is then published in the *Journal of the American Dietetic Association* and posted on their Web site. Positions are reviewed every few years, and updated as needed based on evidence of research findings.

ADA members are not required to agree with each and every position. In fact, Suzanne Havala is an active ADA member and strongly disagrees with ADA's claim that "Any food fits into a healthful eating style." To counter ADA's claim, she wrote the book *Good Foods, Bad Foods: What's Left to Eat?*

The "good food" concept evolved from foods that had been identified as "the best sources" of vitamins or minerals. In the early 1940s, the first Recommended Dietary Allowances (RDAs) were published, which recommend we eat specific amounts of vitamins, minerals, and protein to prevent nutrient deficiencies. Since malnutrition was common at that time, recommendations focused on the nutrients considered to have very positive health benefits. For example, people were told to eat oranges to treat or prevent scurvy. Oranges, because of the high amount of vitamin C, were promoted as being "good for you." Eventually, oranges became known as a "good food." Milk was put into the "good food" category since it provides substantial amounts of calcium, and carrots, because of the vitamin A, as beta-carotene.

Nutrition messages continued to focus on the positive things foods provide until the 1970s when reports showed that eating certain foods increase the risk of heart disease. In an effort to correct the problem, the public was advised to eat less cholesterol and saturated fat. Since eggs, liver, and processed meats are high in both of these lipids, the public got the message that these foods are "bad." By 1980, the first Dietary Guidelines for Americans were published that told us to decrease the amounts of fat, sugar, and sodium that we ate. This resulted in the public adding French fries, potato chips, candy bars, and sodas to the "bad" list. Some refer to this as the beginning of the "negative nutrition" era.

More recently, many books, Web sites, and bloggers have published lists of good and bad foods. Even the well-respected Center for Science in the Public Interest has the "Ten Worst and Best Foods." Foods that are included as "best" or "good" are unprocessed fruits, vegetables, whole grains, and nonfat dairy, while processed foods high in fat, sodium, and added sugar are on the "worst" or "bad" category. So what is the problem with this type of labeling? Susan Nitzke and Jeanne Freeland-Graves stress that "no single food or type of food ensures good health, just as no single food or type of food is necessarily detrimental to health." In contrast, Suzanne Havala bases her opinion on her work as a nutrition counselor. She writes that "people want specific advice about what they should and should not eat. . . . They want concrete examples of good foods." So what is your opinion? After reading the two selections, you decide if foods should be labeled "good" or "bad" or if "all foods can fit."

1941	First Recommended Dietary Allowances (RDAs) are established.
1996	"Any food in today's diverse marketplace fits in a healthful eating style" was key message for ADA National Nutrition Month.
1997	Dietary Reference Intakes replace the RDA.
1997	"All Foods Can Fit" is ADA's National Nutrition Month Theme.
1998	*Good Foods, Bad Foods: What's Left to Eat* is published.
2001	ADA adopts the original position on the "Total Diet Approach" for healthful eating.
2007	ADA publishes updated position on the "Total Diet Approach."

YES

**Susan Nitzke and
Jeanne Freeland-Graves**

Position of the American Dietetic Association: Total Diet Approach to Communicating Food and Nutrition Information

Position Statement

It is the position of the American Dietetic Association that the total diet or overall pattern of food eaten is the most important focus of a healthful eating style. All foods can fit within this pattern, if consumed in moderation with appropriate portion size and combined with regular physical activity. The American Dietetic Association strives to communicate healthful eating messages to the public that emphasize a balance of foods, rather than any one food or meal.

Over the past 4 decades, Americans have become more conscious of diet and nutrition. Although nearly all consumers believe that body weight, diet, and physical activity influence health, diet surveys suggest that their food habits are not always commensurate with knowledge and beliefs. Only half describe their diet as healthful, and 14% eat five or more servings of fruits and vegetables per day. One third classify themselves as sedentary and do not engage in physical activity. Even though more than half of consumers say they are making dietary changes to improve their health, approximately two thirds are overweight or obese. It is clear that practical guidance by food and nutrition professionals is needed to promote positive lifestyle changes that are sustainable.

According to the Shopping for Health 2004 study, nearly six in 10 consumers are trying hard to eat healthfully so they can avoid health problems later in life. More than half of food shoppers strongly agree that eating healthfully is a better way to manage illness than medication. Unfortunately, this trend toward increasing awareness has been accompanied by widespread confusion with complaints that nutrition education is focused on what NOT to eat, instead of what TO eat. These conflicting messages make it difficult to know what to do.

Eating is an important source of pleasure. As food and nutrition professionals strive to improve the quality of Americans' dietary and lifestyle choices, challenges are exacerbated by the widespread perception that individuals must choose between good taste and nutritional quality. In fact, no single food or type of food ensures good health, just as no single food or type of food is necessarily detrimental to health. Rather, the consistent excess of food, or absence of a type of food over time, may diminish the likelihood of a healthful diet. For example, habitual, excessive consumption of energy-dense foods may promote weight gain and mask possible underconsumption of essential nutrients. Yet small quantities of energy-dense foods on special occasions have no discernible influence on health.

In most situations, nutrition messages are more effective when focused on positive ways to make healthful food choices over time, rather than individual foods to be avoided. Unfortunately, the current mix of reliable and unreliable information on diet and nutrition from a variety of sources is confusing to the public and elicits negative feelings such as guilt, worry, helplessness, anger, fear, and inaction.

The total diet approach is based on overall eating patterns that have important benefits and health consequences and that provide adequate nutrients within calorie needs. This includes the concept that foods are not inherently "good" or "bad." Over the years, the American Dietetic Association has consistently recommended a balanced variety of nutrient-dense foods eaten in moderation as the foundation of a health-promoting diet.

Federal Nutrition Guidance Supports the Total Diet Approach

The *Dietary Guidelines for Americans,* which are the centerpiece of federal food, nutrition education, and information programs, are based on a total diet approach to food guidance. The DASH (Dietary Approaches to Stop Hypertension) Eating Plan from the US Department of Health and Human Services is one of many resources that are available to assist consumers in implementing these recommendations."

The MyPyramid Food Guidance System is another example of a dietary pattern that uses a total diet approach to ensure nutritional adequacy and healthful food choices. MyPyramid was released in 2005 as an updated graphic to replace the Food Guide Pyramid. The developers of the *Dietary Guidelines for Americans* and MyPyramid found that consumers and educators preferred dietary guidance that enables consumers to eat in a way that suits their individual tastes and lifestyles. The concept of monitoring discretionary calories (solid fats, added sugars, alcohol) was introduced to allow consumers to choose small amounts of less-nutrient-dense foods while meeting nutrient needs within caloric limits. For example, consumers can balance a small amount of low-nutrient or high-energy-density food or beverage (eg, fried food, butter/margarine, jelly, alcohol) with nutrient-dense foods (vegetables, whole grains, nonfat milk) to achieve an overall healthful dietary pattern. However, the discretionary calorie values can be quite low (150 kcal/day), such that if an individual ate a fried chicken entree, it would be impossible to stay within the recommended limits with the addition of other high-energy foods. Thus, large servings of foods or beverages high in solid fats, added sugars, or alcohol are not compatible with the *Dietary Guidelines for Americans,* but limited quantities would be acceptable, provided that nutrient-dense foods comprise the bulk of the day's choices. This message of the total diet approach must be communicated to consumers by food and nutrition professionals.

Nutrition Labels

Nutrition labels are a third tool that consumers can use to choose and compare foods. The Nutrition Facts label was developed by the Food and Drug Administration and its collaborating agency partners as a consumer information system. Food and nutrition professionals have found the label to be an effective educational tool that helps consumers plan their diets. For example, 48% of survey respondents reported that they had changed their minds about buying or using a food product after reading the nutrition label in 1995, as compared with 30% in 1990.

Nutrient Intake Recommendations

The Dietary Reference Intakes (DRIs) are reference values that are used to plan and assess diets for healthy populations. The DRIs replaced the Recommended Dietary Allowances, which had been revised periodically since 1941. The new dietary standards emphasize the prevention of chronic diseases and promotion of optimal health. A positive emphasis was implemented, rather than "focusing solely on the prevention of nutritional deficiencies." In addition to the Recommended Daily Allowances (RDAs), DRI categories include Estimated Average Requirements (EARs), Adequate Intakes (AIs), and Tolerable Upper Intake Levels (Uls). Each type of DRI refers to average daily intake over time—at least 1 week for most nutrients. For macronutrients, recommendations are stated as Acceptable Macronutrient Distribution Ranges (AMDRs). The AMDRs show that there is not just one acceptable value, but rather a broad range within which an individual can make diet choices based on their own preferences, genetic backgrounds, and health status. This concept of adequacy of nutrient intakes over time supports the need to help consumers understand the importance of the total diet approach.

Successful Communication Campaigns and Programs

Teaching consumers to make wise food choices in the context of the total diet is not a simple process. Depending on the audience and the situation, a variety of nutrition information, communication, promotion, and education strategies may be needed for an appropriate and effective nutrition intervention. It may be necessary to suggest a change to a more healthful lifestyle in terms of small steps that are achievable in increments, so that these can build to broader successes in improving fitness or dietary quality. In addition, successful campaigns often include the coordinated efforts of a number of agencies and organizations with similar health promotion goals.

A growing body of evidence supports the recommendation to design behavior-oriented food and nutrition programs that are targeted to help learners adopt a total diet approach that is sustainable and fits individual preferences. Nutrition education research supports the identification of components that are effective across various types of interventions.

Psychosocial Consequences of Good and Bad Food Messages

Categorizing foods as good or bad promotes dichotomous thinking. Dichotomous thinkers make judgments in terms of either/or, black/white, all/none, or good/bad and do not incorporate abstract or complex options into their decision strategies.

The Magic Bullet Approach

Thinking in terms of dichotomous or binary (either/or) categories is common in childhood. Almost all elementary-age and half of middle school children believe that there are good and/or bad foods. Although the ability to think in more abstract and complex modes is prevalent among adolescents and adults, consumers of all ages tend to rely on dichotomous thinking in certain situations.

An example of dichotomous thinking is the quick fix or "magic bullet" approach to weight control. As long as one stays on the diet (target behavior) the person feels a sense of perceived control (self-efficacy). However, when an individual encounters a high-risk situation such as a tempting food (e.g., a cookie), loss of control may occur, depending on the individual's emotional state, interpersonal conflict, and social pressure.

In this scenario, a cookie would be regarded as a forbidden food and a dieter who yields to a desire for a cookie would tend to say, "I ate the cookie. I have blown my diet. I might as well finish the rest of the box." This pessimistic approach becomes self-fulfilling, as the subject believes that there is not much that can be done once a loss of control occurs. A skilled nutrition counselor might reduce the probability of relapse by increasing awareness of nutrition (knowledge), teaching coping skills (alternative behaviors), incorporating personal favorites in individualized eating patterns, and promoting acceptance of personal responsibility and choice ("I can refuse to eat it" or "I can occasionally enjoy a small portion"). The option of providing simple, one-size-fits-all decision rules may be an expedient approach to education and counseling, but it often misleads consumers into thinking that a given type of food is always a positive or negative addition to the diet. The alternative of offering more comprehensive and targeted education involves context-based judgment. This type of educational message is more difficult to address in language that is easy to understand and apply, but it is more likely to help the consumer to make well-reasoned food choices and adopt behavior patterns that are sustainable over time.

All-Good or All-Bad Foods?

Problems occur when a food or food component is oversimplified as all good or all bad. The increased risks for cardiovascular disease associated with ingestion of *trans* fat produced during processing of foods might lead to the classification of all *trans* fat as bad. However, a type of *trans* fat that occurs naturally from ruminant animal sources (dairy and meat), conjugated linoleic acid, has far different effects on metabolic function, genetic regulation, and physiological outcomes. In contrast to the atherogenic nature of most synthetic forms of *trans* fat, conjugated linoleic acid has been shown to have beneficial effects on cardiovascular disease, diabetes, immune response, energy distribution, and growth. To avoid this confusion, the Food and Drug Administration has excluded the naturally occurring *trans* fat that is in a conjugated system from its definition of *trans* fat for nutritional labeling.

Conversely, even foods associated with a healthful diet such as egg whites and soybeans should not be oversimplified as being perfect. Egg whites are low in cholesterol and high in protein, yet they are also so low in zinc that they can induce a zinc-deficiency when used as a primary or sole source of protein in the diet. Similarly, soybeans have n-3 fatty acids, flavonoids, and phytoestrogens with health-promoting properties, but soy also contains phytates that diminish absorption of zinc and iron and the health benefits of adding soy to the diet have not been consistently supported by research. For example, animal studies in which soy intake was higher than that found in Asian diets found an *increase* in tumor growth. Thus, foods such as egg white and soy cannot be classified as completely good or bad, but rather their value is determined within the context of the total diet. Furthermore, lists of good and bad foods were considered one of the "Ten Red Flags of Junk Science" by the Food and Nutrition Science Alliance, a collaboration of seven scientific professional organizations.

With over 45,000 food items in the average supermarket and an infinite array of recipe combinations, the futility of attempting to sort all food items into dichotomous categories becomes evident, leading to confusion and frustration. Thus, the total diet approach, with its emphasis on long-term eating habits and a contextual approach to food judgments such as discretionary calories, provides more useful information to guide long-term food choices.

Controversies with the Total Diet Approach

One concern with the total diet approach is that it may be viewed as permitting unlimited inclusion of low-nutrient-density foods and beverages or encouraging overconsumption of foods with marginal nutritional value. In a study using a Dietary Guidelines index as a measure of healthful diet quality, heavy consumption of savory, high-fat snacks was associated with poor diet quality. In addition, three national surveys of the US population have documented that portion sizes and energy intakes have increased substantially over time both inside and outside the household. Nutrition education is critical because individuals tend to eat more calories when served large portions of foods, especially energy-dense foods. Yet foods low in nutrient density can fit as part of the total diet, if these foods are consumed as discretionary calories in combination with appropriate quantities of other recommended foods.

Another controversy with the total diet approach is the emphasis on variety. Choosing a variety of foods has been a cornerstone principle in the *Dietary Guidelines for Americans,* but that emphasis has changed from overall variety to varying choices within the food groups. Choosing a variety of nutrient-dense foods helps to ensure adequate intakes of more than 50 nutrients that are needed for growth, repair, and maintenance of good health. However, an increase in food availability and variety in food choices may be a cause of overeating, especially when applied to energy-dense foods. For example, the multitude of choices at a buffet and the temptation to taste each food can result in a greater intake of calories than from a plated or family-style meal. When McCrory and colleagues analyzed 1999 food consumption data, increases in energy intakes and body fatness were associated with ingestion of a high variety of sweets, snacks, condiments, entrees, and carbohydrate foods, coupled with a limited variety of vegetables. KrebsSmith and colleagues observed that a variety of foods was associated with nutrient adequacy to a point, beyond which there was no improvement. When nutrient needs are satisfied, eating additional foods provides excess calories without added health benefits. . . .

Reducing Nutrition Confusion

To reduce confusion from the high volume and apparent inconsistencies of nutrition advice, the following should be considered when designing nutrition education for the public:

- Promote *variety, proportionality, moderation,* and *gradual improvement.* Variety refers to an eating pattern that includes foods from all MyPyramid food groups and subgroups. Proportionality, or balance, means eating more of some foods (fruits, vegetables, whole grains, fat-free or low-fat milk products), and less of others (foods high in saturated or *trans* fats, added sugars, cholesterol, salt, and alcohol). Moderation may be accomplished through advice to consumers to limit overall portion size and to choose foods that will limit intake of saturated or *trans* fats, added sugars, cholesterol, salt, and alcohol. To make gradual improvement, individuals can take small steps to improve their diet and lifestyle each day.
- Emphasize *food patterns*, rather than individual nutrients or individual foods, as key considerations in evaluating and planning one's food choices. Be aware of the social, cultural, economic, and emotional meanings that may be attached to some foods and allow for flexibility whenever possible. Understand that social and cultural aspects of food consumption are essential for planning educational programs to help correct nutritional problems of individuals and population groups.
- Acknowledge the importance of *obtaining nutrients from foods,* rather than relying on nutrients from supplements or fortified foods. Although nutrient modifications are recommended when food intake is inadequate to meet specific needs (e.g., iron, folic acid, vitamins B-12 and D for some population groups), it is important to stress that a diet based on a wide variety of foods remains the preferred overall source of nutrients. Numerous bioactive compounds in foods such

as phytochemicals and ultra trace elements have been identified that have potential health benefits. Yet the precise role, dietary requirements, influence on other nutrients, and toxicity levels of these dietary components are still unclear. Furthermore, foods may contain additional nutritional substances that have not yet been discovered. Thus, appropriate food choices, rather than supplements, should be the foundation for achieving nutritional adequacy.

- Stress that *physical activity* complements the total diet approach because it permits individuals to help manage weight and lowers the risk of premature diseases. The minimum amount recommended for health benefits by MyPyramid and the *Dietary Guidelines for Americans* is 30 minutes, preferably each day. To avoid weight gain, 60 minutes per day may be necessary, and this may increase up to 90 minutes to maintain weight loss.

Role of Food and Nutrition Professional

Food and nutrition professionals have a responsibility to communicate unbiased food and nutrition information that is culturally sensitive, scientifically accurate, medically appropriate, and feasible for the target audience. Some health and nutrition experts and many "pseudo-experts" promote specific foods or types of food to choose or avoid in order to improve health. A more responsible and effective approach is to help consumers understand and apply the principles of healthful diet and lifestyle choices. Unless there are extenuating circumstances (e.g., individuals with severe cognitive or physical limitations such as dementia or renal failure), the total diet approach is preferred because it is more consistent with research on effective communication and inclusive of cultural/personal differences. To achieve this goal, the Board of the American Dietetic Association approved the objective to focus nutrition messages on total diet, not individual foods. . . .

Suzanne Havala  **NO**

Good Foods, Bad Foods: What's Left to Eat?

Talking Politics

The Politics of Your Plate

. . . It never really bothered anybody, say, back in the 1940s and 1950s, when the National Dairy Council produced its "Guide to Good Eating," which was used by elementary schools everywhere for decades to teach the fundamentals of nutrition. Based on the Basic Four Food Groups dietary model, it depicted dairy products—milk, cheese, ice cream—as one of the four cornerstones of a "balanced" diet. Never mind that the concept was the ultimate marketing tool for the dairy industry. The focus then was on preventing dietary deficiencies, and the nutritional merits of dairy products were emphasized exclusively. Recognition of and concerns about excesses in the American diet—too much fat, cholesterol, and protein—were many years away. Besides, milk was as American as apple pie. Who could find fault with that?

Fast forward to 1980, the year that the U.S. Departments of Agriculture (USDA) and Health and Human Services (HHS) jointly published the first Dietary Guidelines for Americans. Targeting every person over the age of two years, the Dietary Guidelines give advice about food choices that promote health and lessen the risk for disease. Revisions of the report were published in 1985, 1990, and 1995 [and 2000, 2005, and 2010].

The Dietary Guidelines are the cornerstone of federal nutrition policy. As of 1990, legislation requires that the report be published every five years by the secretaries of USDA and HHS. The information is directed to the general public, must be based on the preponderance of scientific and medical knowledge current at the time of publication, and is to be promoted by USDA, HHS, and other federal agencies.

So the USDA is in the business of giving dietary advice to the American public. That's a sideline, however. The USDA's primary reason for being is to support American agriculture. The biggest players—and the most powerful, given their financial clout—are the meat and dairy industries. A conflict of interest? You bet. Does it influence what the Dietary Guidelines say? Absolutely. . . .

It has long been in industry's interest to support dietary guidelines that are relatively vague and "open to interpretation." The meat, dairy, and egg industries, in particular, would stand to lose if dietary guidelines were more specific and people began eating fewer of their products. It's that very ambiguity, however, that vexes the public and annoys consumer advocates. Without clearcut guidelines that name names and give specific recommendations that get to the nitty-gritty of what people should eat, everyone is left standing at square one saying, "I've read the guidelines, and that's all well and good, but *what do I eat for dinner tonight?*". . .

The 1995 Dietary Guidelines Advisory Committee acknowledged that consumers have not been successful overall in translating the Dietary Guidelines into lifestyle changes and recommended that future revisions of the Dietary Guidelines take this problem into consideration. To investigate the issue further, the USDA and HHS sponsored consumer-based research in the spring of 1995. The findings: Consumers want straightforward advice with specific directions. Consumers do not have the time, energy or inclination to learn nutrition science before they can begin to eat a healthful diet. No surprise here.

In the meantime, an alliance of food industry and health organizations, in liaison with the federal government, was formed in 1996 to develop materials that will help consumers translate the Dietary Guidelines and put them into practice. Called the Dietary Guidelines Alliance, the group includes, along with the USDA and HHS, the American Dietetic Association, the food Marketing Institute, the International Food Information Council, the National Dairy Council, the National Food Processors Association, the National Cattlemen's Beef Association, the Produce Marketing Association, the Sugar Association, the Wheat Foods Council, and the National Pork Producers Council.

Once again, that's the politics of your plate. . . .

No Good Foods, No Bad Foods

When nutritionists say there are "no good or bad foods, only good or bad diets," they often add the caveat that one cannot assign moral qualities to foods. Okay, so the salami isn't guilty of clogging your arteries. It was you who put it on your menu. As opponents of gun control will tell you, the hand that pulls the trigger is the guilty party, not the gun itself.

I look at the issue a little differently. Personally, when I say that a food is "good" or "bad," I am referring to the food's relative value in terms of health. A "good" food is one that promotes health. A "bad" food is one that is comparatively worse for you. A bad food is a food that, eaten in sufficient quantities, either contributes to nutritional excesses or displaces more valuable foods from the diet.

As Marian Burros, food writer for *The New York Times,* once opined, "Regarding good foods/bad foods: There are some foods that are better than others. If you don't want to use the term 'bad foods,' then there are foods and there are good foods. The good foods you can eat anytime and the foods you can eat occasionally."

Over the many years that I have been counseling people on diet and nutrition, one need has always risen above all others. That is, people want specific advice about what they should and should not eat, preferably with the emphasis on the good choices. They want to know what they can have for dinner tonight. They want concrete examples of good foods to order at restaurants, and they want lists of good snack ideas.

One of the ADA's "key messages" for National Nutrition Month 1996 was, "Any food in today's diverse marketplace fits in a healthful eating style." The theme for 1997 was "All foods can fit."

Sure. A chocolate chip cookie can be worked in each day if the rest of the diet is up to snuff. Dietary recommendations don't have to be strictly black or white, eat this and don't eat that. There is some gray area, some room for play and for individualizing the diet.

But most Americans are light years away from meeting current dietary recommendations. There are certainly some very specific tips that could be given that would be relevant to the majority. That means identifying some foods as being better choices than others. If the vague statements that are now the norm are not backed up strongly with specific recommendations that name names and define terms, then people will not be able to make the kinds of dietary changes that they need to make in order to see significant health benefits.

An article by Marian Burros in the November 15, 1995 issue of *The New York Times* explored the sticky issue of health professional associations accepting industry monies and in-kind services. She quoted Joan Gussow, Ph.D., a former head of the nutrition education program at Columbia University's Teachers College, who stated that the American Dietetic Association's dependence on industry money meant that "they never criticize the food industry." The ADA won't finger any particular food as being bad, unhealthful, or a poor choice. Even candy bars and soft drinks have a place, according to the ADA. "Actually, we could put our name on any McDonald's meal," said Dr. Doris Derelian, who was the current president of the American Dietetic Association.

In the same article, Dr. Gussow also stated, "If health professionals are led to agree that there are no 'good' or 'bad,' 'healthy' or 'unhealthy' foods, then we can't object to any food product that's put on the market, however wasteful or useless it may be."

She added, "The food critics of the '60s and '70s have been silenced, which is, of course, the point. The food industry prefers it that way."

"Variety, Balance, and Moderation Are the Keys"

Another of the ADA's key messages for National Nutrition Month 1996 was, "An eating style with food variety as well as balance and moderation maximizes life-long fitness." What does this mean?

The statement that there are no good or bad foods is often followed by the equally vague concept that variety, balance, and moderation are the keys to a healthful diet. What does this mean to a person for whom breakfast is a sausage-egg-and-cheese biscuit, lunch is a Big Mac and a Coke, and dinner consists of a "balanced" meal of a pork chop, mashed potatoes with gravy, iceberg lettuce salad with bleu cheese dressing, and a glass of milk? Does the salad balance the pork chop? Is moderation having a small Coke instead of a large? Does variety mean having chicken for dinner one might and beef the next?

The reality is that these terms mean little to anyone. We are a culture with such extremes in diet that a little tweaking here and there does not result in changes substantial enough to promote significant health benefits.

Politics enters into the frequent use of these terms as well. Take the term "moderation."

Bonnie Liebman, Director of Nutrition for the Center for Science in the Public Interest, has said, "I never use the term because it's too vague, and the food industry uses it as a smoke-screen to make people think whatever they're eating is okay."

Moderation. It seems so reasonable. So sane. It's a pacifier, especially when someone has the audacity to suggest that there might be something wrong with a steak at Morton's.

It bears repeating: If we were at the point of fine-tuning our diets, the term "moderation" might be relevant. But given the starting point for most people in our culture—such extremes in diet composition—the term loses its meaning.

Then there are "variety" and "balance." Increasingly, these words come into play when discussions about dietary recommendations get close to "naming names" and citing specific advice about food choices.

Why? Because the science is becoming difficult to ignore, and as research overwhelmingly points to the need for Americans to move to a more plant-based diet, this creates serious conflict. A move to a plant-based diet is a threat to the American way. Not only do we have an animal-based agricultural system, with many who stand to lose if meat and dairy products are relegated to the side of the plate or are pushed off all together, but we have a tradition of a certain way of eating.

Traditions are hard to shake. Ask anyone who has tried to overhaul his or her diet how difficult it is to change. Try eating out at a restaurant, inviting guests over for dinner, or being the guest in someone's else's home. Try finding a replacement for Aunt Dee's cream cheese brownies or simply letting go of the idea that a meal has to center around a piece of meat.

Changing lifelong habits and replacing old traditions with new ones is tough. It's uncomfortable. No wonder we all resist. We bargain. We rationalize. We grieve. We get angry. Ultimately, however, if we want to lose weight, to lower our cholesterol levels, and to be healthy, most of us will have to make the change.

So the terms "balance" and "moderation" are ways to resist, bargain, and rationalize.

"Sure, you can eat a cheeseburger. Just balance it with lower-fat foods the rest of the day."

"Extra-sharp cheddar cheese melted over your broccoli? Sure. All of that fat can be balanced with lower-fat choices elsewhere in the meal."

And so it goes. The idea is that by balancing high-fat foods with low-fat foods, it all evens out and everything is fine. The reality, of course, is that most people don't do a good enough job of the balancing act. They eat too much of too many high-fat foods. They don't eat enough plant matter—fruit,grains, vegetables, legumes. Most importantly, though, by not making more fundamental changes in the way they eat, they perpetuate a way of life that undermines their dietary goals and their health.

With the trend in dietary recommendations toward a more plant-based diet, the concept of "variety" is a trump card played by many in the food industry and in certain nutrition circles. "Eat a variety of foods" is often followed by warnings not to "omit entire food groups." The danger here, of course, is that people might get it into their heads that meat, eggs, cheese, and other dairy products should be limited. That wouldn't be good for business for many in the food industry, nor for their friends.

When all is said and done, "no good foods, no bad foods" and "variety, balance, and moderation" are words that sound like advice but don't actually have a useful meaning. They don't step on toes, they don't offend. They're friendly, feel-good words that don't disappoint. They don't elicit change. They perpetuate the status quo. . . .

Putting the Politics Into Perspective

The "politics" within groups of health professionals or government agencies are dynamic. Positions or statements made by organizations reflect what the current leadership thinks but may not be consistent with the opinions of some individuals or small groups within the organization. If those individuals and small groups persevere, they can eventually influence and change the voice of the organization as a whole.

. . . [E]xamples can be seen within groups of health professionals, such as the American Dietetic Association. The ADA leadership has a long history of protecting its relationships with industry groups, in part by not making any negative statements about particular foods. However, in recent years, a vegetarian nutrition dietetic practice group—a subgroup within the ADA—was organized by ADA members who want to explore nontraditional, plant-based diets. The practice group has worked to produce nutrition education materials that promote plant-based diets for the public and encourage people to consume fewer foods of animal origin. The group sponsors conference sessions at the ADA's annual meeting that focus on vegetarian diets, and the group produces a newsletter that is circulated among members.

The ADA is a large organization, and choices made by the leadership do not always speak for individual members or subgroups of the parent organization, some of which "politic" within the association for changes.

The point is, dietary recommendations are what they are, in part, because of politics. Because "politics" is the result of interactions among individuals and groups, the outcome is always changing. For now, though, you need to be aware of how the current political climate has influenced the dietary recommendations that you are hearing today. You need advice that has your best interests at heart—not the interests of industry groups or professional associations.

Let's peel back the layers of confusion produced by the politics of your plate and expose the truths behind recommendations about how you should eat. . . .

Summary: The Simple Truth . . .

Simple Keys to an Optimal Diet

The healthiest diet? That's the easy part. Remove the overlay of politics and cultural bias, and here you have it:

Eat a variety of foods Make the bulk of the diet consist of whole-grain breads and cereal products, legumes such as beans and peas, vegetables, and fruits.

Get enough calories in your diet to meet your energy needs Burn enough calories through regular physical activity to allow you to eat a reasonable volume of food, which, in turn, will help ensure that you will get all of the nutrients you need.

If you eat foods of animal origin, such as dairy products, eggs, and meat, make them no more than a side dish or minor ingredient in a dish Animal products should be eaten as condiments rather than as a primary component in a meal. Most people would do best to weed these foods out of their diets, if not entirely, then considerably.

Limit the sweets and fatty, greasy, junk foods Soft drinks and French fries are vegetarian, but they don't make for a nutritious diet. The more "empty calorie" foods you eat—foods that give you little nutrition for the calories—the more of the "good stuff" you displace or push off your plate. Most people can't afford to eat much junk without seriously compromising the nutritional quality of their diets.

Go easy on added fats in your diet, especially in the form of oils, margarine, butter, salad dressings, mayonnaise, fried foods, and fats that are added to foods in processing or preparation. Avoid them altogether if you can, particularly if weight control is an issue for you. A few nuts and seeds are fine if they are used as a garnish or very minor ingredient in a dish—a sprinkling here and there. This is especially true for children or people who are very physically active and need more calories. In these cases, added calories from plant sources of fat may be appropriate and desirable.

Choose foods as close to their natural state as possible Processed foods are typically inferior to whole foods, since they have had fiber and nutrients removed or destroyed and often contain more sodium and other additives. Buy locally grown and organically grown produce when you have the choice.

If you feel uncertain about the nutritional adequacy of your diet or need individualized assistance, see a registered dietitian I strongly advise you to find one that is familiar with plant-based or vegetarian diets. Call the American Dietetic Association's referral service (800-366-1655) to locate a vegetarian friendly dietitian in your area. You can also call your health care provider, local vegetarian society, or community hospital for a referral.

CHALLENGE QUESTIONS

Can All Foods Fit Into a Healthy Diet?

1. Describe what ADA means by "total diet approach" for healthful eating.
2. Explain why the food industry agrees with using moderation and balance when educating the public about diet planning.
3. In many states, the National Dairy Council has helped pay for milk vending machines in schools. The machines dispense flavored milks (chocolate, strawberry, etc.), with most sold in 16-oz containers. The flavored milk averages about 30 g (~8 teaspoons) of added high fructose corn syrup or sugar per container. Based on the ADA position, should a 16-oz serving of flavored chocolate milk be considered a food that "fits in a healthful eating style?" Explain your answer. Why do you think these milks are sold in schools?
4. Your roommate reads an article that says "all foods fit into a healthful diet" and claims that she can make the 32-oz soda with a King Size Snickers her lunch each day. What advice would you give her about her lunch?
5. You have been asked to give a nutrition lesson to a kindergarten class on healthy snacks. The teachers said most children typically bring cup cakes or brownies for snack each day with a container of fruit punch. Outline a lesson for the class on healthy snacks. Include the narrative you would use to define what a healthy snack is and comments you would make on eating cup cakes or brownies each day for snack.

Additional Internet Resources

American Dietetic Association

National association for food and nutrition professionals. Contains ADA position papers and other resources related to food and nutrition.

http://www.eatright.org

ISSUE 2

Is the Dietary Guideline for Sodium Realistic?

YES: **Institute of Medicine**, from "Strategies to Reduce Sodium Intake in the United States: Brief Report," *The National Academies Press* (April 2010)

NO: **Michael Moss**, from "The Hard Sell on Salt," *The New York Times* (May 29, 2010)

As you read the issue, focus on the following points:

1. The Institute of Medicine's recommendation to FDA.
2. Stakeholders that need to be involved to reduce sodium content of the American food supply and the steps each stakeholder needs to take.
3. Barriers the food industry will encounter if sodium is reduced in their products.

ISSUE SUMMARY

YES: Jane Henney, Christine Taylor, and Caitlin Boon, editors of the Institute of Medicine's report on sodium, recommend the FDA set mandatory national standards for sodium content of foods and require the food industry (including manufacturers and restaurants) to gradually lower the sodium they add to processed foods and prepared meals.

NO: Health writer Michael Moss describes the numerous problems the food giants such as Kellogg, Frito-Lay, and Kraft will face if they attempt to lower sodium in foods they make.

For years, Americans have been advised to eat less sodium, and many people think they are doing so. They claim that they never use a saltshaker at the table or salt when cooking. (And some people don't even have a box of Morton's salt in the kitchen.) What most people don't realize is that close to 80 percent of the sodium we consume is added by the food industry in packaged foods we buy at the grocery store and salt added by cooks in restaurants. People are so concerned about calories and fat grams that they seldom look at

19

the sodium content listed on food labels. A cup of canned spaghetti sauce is packed with 1,203 mg of sodium. And Subway's 6" meatball sub has 1,530 mg, and that's without adding chips or a cookie. So, unless you're a Martha Stewart or Rachel Ray and make everything from scratch—including breads, crackers, soup, pizza, taco sauce, and salad dressing—it's hard to eat less salt.

For the last 40 years, dietitians, physicians, and the government have been warning people to cut back on salt. Because of our increasing dependence on cheap, processed foods and the convenience of eating out, our sodium intake is steadily increasing. Michael Jacobson, the executive director of the Center for Science in the Public Interest, reports, "Salt is the single most harmful element in our food supply, silently killing about 100,000 people each year." Excessive sodium not only raises blood pressure, but also increases risk for stroke, coronary heart disease, kidney disease, and osteoporosis. Recent evidence shows the adverse effects begin during childhood.

Cutting back on sodium has been a part of the *Dietary Guidelines for Americans* since they were introduced in 1980. Every 5 years, as a new advisory committee reviews the latest scientific data, changes evolve. These changes have largely been based on the escalating rate of hypertension (HTN) and death rates associated with the disease.

In 1980, when 17 percent of Americans had HTN, the recommendation was simply to "avoid too much sodium." Even though HTN rate climbed to 25 percent, the 1985 message did not change.

In 1990, when 33 percent of the nation had HTN, the message changed to "Use salt and sodium only in moderation." Finally, in 1995, the *Dietary Guidelines* put a number with the recommendation. They advised us to eat less than 2,400 mg each day. This continued in 2000.

In 2005, when it was predicted that 90 percent of Americans would develop HTN at some time in their lives, the recommended amount was lowered to 2,300 mg. And for people with HTN, blacks, and middle-aged and older adults, the aim was to consume no more than 1,500 mg. At that time, the committee realized that it would be hard to change people's taste preferences for salt, but cited studies that showed it is possible to kick the salt habit after eating low-salt foods for 8–12 weeks.

Finally, the 2010 committee, after realizing that the majority of Americans, including children, need less sodium, changed the goal to 1,500 mg per day for the general population. In their summary report, they conclude:

> Given the current US marketplace and the resulting excessively high sodium intake, it will be challenging to achieve the lower level. In addition, time is required to adjust taste perception in the general population. Thus, the reduction from 2,300 mg to 1,500 mg per day should occur gradually over time. Because early stages of blood pressure–related atherosclerotic disease begin during childhood, both children and adults should reduce their sodium intake.

The two selections on the following pages look at sodium from the food industry standpoint. After all, food manufacturers and the restaurant industry dictate what we eat since they make the vast majority of foods that are available to us. After reading the articles, you decide if it's possible for Americans to slash sodium intake to the recommended 1,500 mg per day. The editors representing the Institute of Medicine say it is possible, but it will require a coordinated approach including cooperation by the food industry. Journalist Michael Moss is realistic and points out the problems the food manufacturers will encounter if they cut salt out of their recipes and the impact it will have on their sales and profit.

TIMELINE FOR DIETARY GUIDELINES ON SODIUM

1980	Avoid too much sodium
1990	Use salt and sodium only in moderation
1995	Eat less than 2,400 mg sodium each day
2005	Eat less than 2,300 mg sodium each day
2010	Eat less than 1,500 mg sodium each day (Proposed by the IOM)

YES

Strategies to Reduce Sodium Intake in the United States: Brief Report

Americans consume unhealthy amounts of sodium in their food, far exceeding public health recommendations. Consuming too much sodium is a concern for all individuals, as it increases the risk for high blood pressure, a serious health condition that is avoidable and can lead to a variety of diseases. Analysts estimate that population-wide reductions in sodium could prevent more than 100,000 deaths annually.

While numerous stakeholders have initiated voluntary efforts to reduce sodium consumption in the United States during the past 40 years, they have not succeeded. Challenges arise because salt—the primary source of sodium in the diet—and other sodium-containing compounds often are used to enhance the flavor of foods, and high amounts are found in processed foods and foods prepared in restaurants. Sodium also is added to enhance texture or to serve as a preservative or thickener. In fact, very little of the sodium in foods is naturally occurring most of it is added as it is being processed or prepared by the food industry. The actual sodium levels in food may surprise consumers, especially if the food does not taste salty.

In 2008, Congress asked the Institute of Medicine (IOM) to recommend strategies for reducing sodium intake to levels recommended in the Dietary Guidelines for Americans—currently no more than 2,300 mg per day for persons 2 or more years of age. This amounts to about 1 teaspoon of salt per day, while the average American consumes about 50 percent more than that—more than 3,400 mg of sodium per day. The IOM committee that authored this report concludes that a new, coordinated approach is needed to reduce sodium content in food, requiring new government standards for the acceptable level of sodium. Manufacturers and restaurants/foodservice operators need to meet these standards so that all sources in the food supply are involved and so that the consumer's taste preferences can be changed over time to the lower amounts of salt in food. The goal is to slowly, over time, reduce the sodium content of the food supply in a way that goes unnoticed by most consumers as individuals' taste sensors adjust to the lower levels of sodium.

Identifying the Problem

Despite efforts to reduce sodium intake in the United States, consumption levels remain high. [There is] an upward trend in sodium intake since the early 1970s. Further, in recent years, consumers have not focused nearly as much on reducing sodium intake as they have on other nutrients of concern such as fat. One reason for high sodium consumption is that consumers have become accustomed to high levels of sodium in processed and restaurant foods and have difficulty adjusting to foods with healthier levels of sodium. However, the preference for salty taste can be changed. What is needed is a coordinated effort to reduce sodium in foods across the board by manufacturers and restaurants—that is, create a level playing field for the food industry. All segments of the food industry would be carrying out the same reductions and none would be at a disadvantage.

No one is immune to the adverse health effects of excessive sodium intake. While some may have the impression that sodium reduction is only necessary for individuals with hypertension or for groups with a higher risk of developing hypertension (for example, African Americans and older adults), in reality, it is necessary for all populations in order to avoid high blood pressure and cardiovascular disease.

Recommended Strategies to Reduce Sodium Intake

As its primary strategy for sodium reduction, the committee recommends that the FDA set mandatory national standards for the sodium content in foods—not banning outright the addition of salt to foods but beginning the process of reducing excess sodium in processed foods and menu items to a safer level. It is important that the reduction in sodium content of foods be carried out gradually, with small reductions instituted regularly as part of a carefully monitored process. Evidence shows that a decrease in sodium can be accomplished successfully without affecting consumer enjoyment of food products if it is done in a stepwise process that systematically and gradually lowers sodium levels across the food supply.

The Food, Drug, and Cosmetic Act specifies that substances added to foods by manufacturers must be proven safe under the conditions of their intended use, unless the substance is generally recognized as safe, known in the industry as GRAS. Currently, the manufacturers' addition of salt and a number of other sodium-containing compounds to foods is considered a GRAS use of the substance, but no standard level that constitutes a "safe use" has been set. Therefore, the committee recommends that the FDA modify the GRAS status of such compounds added to processed foods—that is, change the level to which the use of such compounds is considered safe. This change, when carried out in a stepwise manner, will reduce the sodium content of the food supply slowly, in a way that should avoid making food unpalatable to consumers.

A range of stakeholders, including public health and consumer organizations and the food industry, will need to work together in order to successfully reduce sodium intake among Americans. In order to implement these new food standards, leadership and coordination at the national level [are] essential. Specifically, the Secretary of Health and Human Services (HHS) should act in cooperation with other government and non-government groups to design and implement a nationwide campaign to reduce sodium intake and should set a timeline for achieving the sodium intake levels established by the *Dietary Guidelines for Americans*. Consumers do not have direct control over how much sodium is added to foods, but they have an important role to play in reducing their sodium intake by making healthy food choices and selecting lower-sodium foods. In addition, government agencies, public health and consumer organizations, health professionals, the health insurance industry, the food industry, and public–private partnerships should support the implementation of the sodium standards for foods and also support consumers in reducing their sodium intake. Finally, better monitoring of sodium intake and of the progress toward changing salt taste preference are essential so that the reduction efforts can be tracked and evaluated, and improvements can be made as needed.

Implementation and Research Needs

The implementation of these important changes will require preliminary data-gathering, dialogue among stakeholders, and careful analysis of food supply data. Further, if carried out in a stepwise manner, the process can be informed by the continual monitoring of the impact of the steps. In other areas, the committee identified three topics that require research:

- Understanding how salty taste preferences develop throughout the life span
- Developing innovative methods to reduce sodium in foods while maintaining palatability, physical properties, and safety
- Enhancing current understanding of factors that impact consumer awareness and behavior relative to sodium reduction

Conclusion

In the face of chronic disease risks associated with sodium intake, the current level of sodium in the food supply—added by food manufacturers, foodservice operators, and restaurants—is too high to be "safe." The recommended strategies in this report set a new course for reducing sodium intake with an innovative and unprecedented approach to gradually reducing sodium levels in foods. The patchwork of voluntary approaches that have been implemented over the years [has] not worked and [has] not created the level playing field deemed critical to any successful effort to reduce the sodium content of the overall food supply. While these efforts are laudable, they are not sustainable. The current focus on instructing consumers to select lower-sodium foods and making available reduced-sodium "niche" products cannot result in intakes consistent with public health recommendations. Without major change, hypertension and cardiovascular disease rates will continue to rise, and consumers, who have little choice, will pay the price for inaction.

Report at a Glance

Released: 4/20/2010

Primary Strategies

Recommendation 1: The Food and Drug Administration (FDA) should expeditiously initiate a process to set mandatory national standards for the sodium content of foods.

- FDA should modify the generally recognized as safe (GRAS) status of salt added to processed foods in order to reduce the salt content of the food supply in a stepwise manner.
- FDA should likewise extend its stepwise application of the GRAS modification, adjusted as necessary, to encompass salt added to menu items offered by restaurant/foodservice operations that are sufficiently standardized so as to allow practical implementation.
- FDA should revisit the GRAS status of other sodium-containing compounds as well as any food additive provisions for such compounds and make adjustments as appropriate consistent with changes for salt in processed foods and restaurant/foodservice menu items.

Interim Strategies

Recommendation 2: The food industry should voluntarily act to reduce the sodium content of foods in advance of the implementation of mandatory standards.

- Food manufacturers and restaurant/foodservice operators should voluntarily accelerate and broaden efforts to reduce sodium in processed foods and menu items, respectively.
- The food industry, government, professional organizations, and public health partners should work together to promote voluntary collaborations to reduce sodium in foods.

Supporting Strategies

Recommendation 3: Government agencies, public health and consumer organizations, and the food industry should carry out activities to support the reduction of sodium levels in the food supply.

- FDA and the U.S. Department of Agriculture (USDA) should revise and update—specifically for sodium—the provisions for nutrition labeling, related sodium claims, and disclosure or disqualifying criteria for sodium in foods, including a revision to base the Daily Value for sodium on the Adequate Intake.
- FDA should extend provisions for sodium content and health claims to restaurant/foodservice menu items and adjust the provisions as needed for use within the restaurant/foodservice sector.

- Congress should act to remove the exemption of nutrition labeling for food products intended solely for use in restaurant/foodservice operations.
- Food retailers, governments, businesses, institutions, and other large-scale organizations that purchase or distribute food should establish sodium specifications for the foods they purchase and the food operations they oversee.
- Restaurant/foodservice leaders in collaboration with other key stakeholders, including federal, state, and local health authorities, should develop, pilot, and implement innovative initiatives targeted to restaurant/foodservice operations to facilitate and sustain sodium reduction in menu items.

Recommendation 4: In tandem with recommendations to reduce the sodium content of the food supply, government agencies, public health and consumer organizations, health professionals, the health insurance industry, the food industry, and public-private partnerships sbould conduct augmenting activities to support consumers in reducing sodium intake.

- The Secretary of Health and Human Services (HHS) should act in cooperation with other government and non-government groups to design and implement a comprehensive, nationwide campaign to reduce sodium intake and act to set a timeline for achieving the sodium intake goals established by the *Dietary Guidelines for Americans*.
- Government agencies, public health and consumer organizations, health professionals, the food industry, and public–private partnerships should continue or expand efforts to support consumers in making behavior changes to reduce sodium intake in a manner consistent with the *Dietary Guidelines for Americans*.

Recommendation 5: Federal agencies should ensure and enhance monitoring and surveillance relative to sodium intake measurement, salt taste preference, and sodium content of foods, and should ensure sustained and timely release of data in user-friendly formats.

- Congress, HHS/CDC (Centers for Disease Control and Prevention), and USDA authorities should ensure adequate funding for the National Health and Nutrition Examination Survey (NHANES), including related and supporting databases or surveys.
- CDC should collect 24-hour urine samples during NHANES or as a separate nationally representative "sentinel site" type activity.
- CDC should, as a component of NHANES or another appropriate nationally representative survey, begin work immediately with the National Institutes of Health (NIH) to develop an appropriate assessment tool for salt taste preference, obtain baseline measurements, and track salt taste preference over time.
- CDC in cooperation with other relevant HHS agencies, USDA, and the Federal Trade Commission should strengthen and expand its activities to measure population knowledge, attitudes, and behavior about sodium among consumers.

- FDA should modify and expand its existing Total Diet Study and its Food Label and Package Survey to ensure better coverage of information about sodium content in the diet and sodium-related information on packaged and prepared foods.
- USDA should enhance the quality and comprehensiveness of sodium content information in its tables of food composition.
- USDA in cooperation with HHS should develop approaches utilizing current and new methodologies and databases to monitor the sodium content of the total food supply.

Michael Moss

The Hard Sell on Salt

With salt under attack for its ill effects on the nation's health, the food giant Cargill kicked off a campaign last November to spread its own message.

"Salt is a pretty amazing compound," Alton Brown, a Food Network star, gushes in a Cargill video called Salt 101. "So make sure you have plenty of salt in your kitchen at all times."

The campaign by Cargill, which both produces and uses salt, promotes salt as "life enhancing" and suggests sprinkling it on foods as varied as chocolate cookies, fresh fruit, ice cream and even coffee. "You might be surprised," Mr. Brown says, "by what foods are enhanced by its briny kiss."

By all appearances, this is a moment of reckoning for salt. High blood pressure is rising among adults and children. Government health experts estimate that deep cuts in salt consumption could save 150,000 lives a year.

Since processed foods account for most of the salt in the American diet, national health officials, Mayor Michael R. Bloomberg of New York and Michelle Obama are urging food companies to greatly reduce their use of salt. [The] Institute of Medicine went further, urging the government to force companies to do so.

But the industry is working overtly and behind the scenes to fend off these attacks, using a shifting set of tactics that have defeated similar efforts for 30 years, records and interviews show. Industry insiders call the strategy "delay and divert" and say companies have a powerful incentive to fight back: they crave salt as a low-cost way to create tastes and textures. Doing without it risks losing customers, and replacing it with more expensive ingredients risks losing profits.

When health advocates first petitioned the federal government to regulate salt in 1978, food companies sponsored research aimed at casting doubt on the link between salt and hypertension. Two decades later, when federal officials tried to cut the salt in products labeled "healthy," companies argued that foods already low in sugar and fat would not sell with less salt.

Now, the industry is blaming consumers for resisting efforts to reduce salt in all foods, pointing to, as Kellogg put it in a letter to a federal nutrition advisory committee, "the virtually intractable nature of the appetite for salt."

The federal committee is finishing up recommendations on nutrient issues including salt. While its work is overseen by the Department of Agriculture, records released to *The New York Times* show that the industry nominated a majority of its members and has presented the panel with its own research. It includes two studies commissioned by ConAgra suggesting that the country could save billions of dollars more in health care and lost productivity costs by simply nudging Americans to eat a little less food, rather than less salty food.

Even as it was moving from one line of defense to another, the processed food industry's own dependence on salt deepened, interviews with company scientists show. Beyond its own taste, salt also masks bitter flavors and counters a side effect of processed food production called "warmed-over flavor," which, the scientists said, can make meat taste like "cardboard" or "damp dog hair."

Salt also works in tandem with fat and sugar to achieve flavors that grip the consumer and do not let go—an allure the industry has recognized for decades. "Once a preference is acquired," a top scientist at Frito-Lay wrote in a 1979 internal memorandum, "most people do not change it, but simply obey it."

In recent months, food companies, including Kellogg, have said they were redoubling efforts to reduce salt. But they say they can go only so far, so fast without compromising tastes consumers have come to relish or salt's ability to preserve food. "We have to earn the consumer's trust every day," said George Dowdie, a senior vice president of Campbell Soup. "And if you disappoint the consumer, there is no guarantee they will come back."

Case Study: The Cheez-It

The power that salt holds over processed foods can be seen in an American snack icon, the Cheez-It.

At the company's laboratories in Battle Creek, Mich., a Kellogg vice president and food scientist, John Kepplinger, ticked off the ways salt makes its little square cracker work.

Salt sprinkled on top gives the tongue a quick buzz. More salt in the cheese adds crunch. Still more in the dough blocks the tang that develops during fermentation. In all, a generous cup of Cheez-Its delivers one-third of the daily amount of sodium recommended for most Americans.

As a demonstration, Kellogg prepared some of its biggest sellers with most of the salt removed. The Cheez-It fell apart in surprising ways. The golden yellow hue faded. The crackers became sticky when chewed, and the mash packed onto the teeth. The taste was not merely bland but medicinal.

"I really get the bitter on that," the company's spokeswoman, J. Adaire Putnam, said with a wince as she watched Mr. Kepplinger struggle to swallow.

They moved on to Corn Flakes. Without salt the cereal tasted metallic. The Eggo waffles evoked stale straw. The butter flavor in the Keebler Light Buttery Crackers, which have no actual butter, simply disappeared.

"Salt really changes the way that your tongue will taste the product," Mr. Kepplinger said. "You make one little change and something that was a complementary flavor now starts to stand out and become objectionable."

Salt started out more than 5,000 years ago as a simple preservative. But salt and dozens of compounds containing sodium—the element in salt linked to hypertension—have become omnipresent in processed foods from one end of the grocery store to the other.

For example, salt makes 10 appearances on the label for the Hungry-Man roasted turkey dinner, made by the Pinnacle Foods Group, with nine additional references to sodium compounds. The label for Roasted Chicken Monterey, a ConAgra Healthy Choice product, has five references to salt. It makes its most surprising cameo in the accompanying peach dessert, which is flavored with whiskey mixed with salt.

"Without adding the salt, we would be required to carry a liquor license," explained a ConAgra spokeswoman, Teresa Paulsen.

The food industry releases some 10,000 new products a year, the Department of Agriculture has reported, and processed foods, along with restaurant meals, now account for roughly 80 percent of the salt in the American diet. The rest comes from the kitchen saltshaker or occurs naturally in food. In promoting cooking with salt, Cargill and its star chef, Mr. Brown, said they recognized the health concerns and recommended "smarter salting."

Making deep cuts in salt can require more expensive ingredients that can hurt sales. Companies that make low-salt pasta sauces improve the taste with vine-ripened tomatoes and fresh herbs that cost more than dried spices and lower grade tomatoes.

Food companies say that reducing salt by 10 percent or so is easy, but that going further is difficult.

Take smoked ham sold by Kraft Foods under its Oscar Mayer label. Three slices have 820 milligrams of sodium, more than half of the daily intake recommended for most Americans. Kraft said it was releasing a version with 37 percent less sodium, but when it tried to eliminate an additional 3 percent, consumer testers failed it on flavor, texture and aroma. "We often fall off a cliff, and that's what we did here," said Russell Moroz, a Kraft vice president.

Campbell says it has reduced salt in over 100 soups through a variety of changes, including using a sea salt with half the normal sodium. But some soups present bigger challenges.

"It feels unfinished," Dr. Dowdie, the Campbell vice president and scientist, said while tasting vegetable beef soup that the company prepared with less sodium for *The Times*. "The sweetness of the carrots isn't pronounced. The broth, you don't get an explosion of flavors."

Chicken noodle soup has been especially vexing, he said. With only 150 calories, a single can of the condensed soup has more than a whole day's recommended sodium for most Americans.

"It's a very unique recipe," Dr. Dowdie said. "Consumers of chicken noodle, they love it and they know it and they have a strong bond with it. And any slight change they will recognize."

Dr. Howard Moskowitz, a food scientist and consultant to major food manufacturers, said companies had not shown the same zeal in reducing salt as they had with sugars and fat. While low-calorie sweeteners opened a huge market of people eager to look better by losing weight, he said, salt is only a health concern, which does not have the same market potential.

"If all of a sudden people would demand lower salt because low salt makes them look younger, this problem would be solved overnight," he said.

Diversionary Tactics

In 1978, Michael F. Jacobson, an M.I.T.-trained microbiologist, was studying food additives when he noticed the growing research linking sodium to hypertension. "I realized that conventional ingredients like salt were probably far more harmful," said Dr. Jacobson, who directs the Center for Science in the Public Interest, a consumer group.

He petitioned the Food and Drug Administration to reclassify salt from an ingredient like pepper or vinegar posing no health concerns to a food additive that the agency could regulate by mandating limits or warning labels.

The broadside on the food industry was taken seriously by the F.D.A. and touched off a scramble by producers to head off regulation, confidential company records and interviews show.

Robert I-San Lin, who was then overseeing research and development at Frito-Lay, said in an interview that he had been caught between corporate and public interests.

"The public's concern over high sodium intake is justifiable," Dr. Lin wrote in a 1978 memo. A handwritten memo titled "Salt Strategy" shows that his staff worked on ways to reduce sodium, including adjusting the fat in potato chips as a way of lowering the need for salt and using a finer salt crystal.

But the company adopted few of his recommendations and joined the industry's resistance.

Scientists testifying for the snack industry at a government hearing warned that lower salt consumption could pose certain health risks to children and pregnant women. The food industry also challenged the link between salt and hypertension, emphasizing studies that found no significant correlation.

In what Dr. Lin says was an attempt to divert attention from salt, records show, Frito-Lay also financed research on whether calcium might negate the harmful effects of salt, even though Dr. Lin said he doubted it would really absolve salt. "An effective promotion of 'Calcium Antihypertension Theory' may release the pressure on sodium for the time being," Dr. Lin wrote in a memo at the time.

In 1982, Campbell sponsored an American Heart Association symposium that included a study on calcium, which is now seen as having only a small role in reducing hypertension, and another that asserted that only some people were susceptible to hypertension from salt.

That same year, the F.D.A. finally responded to Dr. Jacobson's petition. An advisory panel had concluded that salt should no longer have a blanket designation as safe, which "would normally trigger F.D.A. action," Michael R. Taylor, a current deputy commissioner at the agency wrote last year in analyzing salt regulation. But the agency decided to rely on consumer education and voluntary efforts by companies.

Sanford A. Miller, then director of the F.D.A.'s Center for Food Safety and Applied Nutrition, said agency officials had recognized the health effects of salt, but had believed that they did not have enough data to justify mandating sodium levels. "The salt people, especially, were constantly badgering us on that," Dr. Miller said. "There were little tidbits that people could challenge us on."

Dr. Lin, who works for a nutrition supplement producer, said Frito-Lay's response back then was a "macho show of force" by an otherwise responsible company. "I was employed at a time I couldn't do much about it," he said.

A Frito-Lay spokeswoman, Aurora Gonzalez, says the company has aggressively searched for solutions to nutrition issues. In March, its parent company, PepsiCo, announced it would cut on average 25 percent of the salt in its products. "We are proactive," Ms. Gonzalez said. One solution it recently embraced takes a page from Dr. Lin's old research: using a finer grade of salt.

Back in the 1980s, some companies began offering low-sodium products, but few sold well. Surveys by the Center for Science in the Public Interest have found little change in salt levels in processed foods.

Sugar and fat had overtaken salt as the major concern in processed foods by the 1990s, fueling the "healthy" foods market. When the F.D.A. pressured companies to reduce salt in those products, the industry said that doing so would ruin the taste of the foods already low in sugar and fat. The government backed off.

"We were trying to balance the public health need with what we understood to be the public acceptability," said William K. Hubbard, a top agency official at the time who now advises an industry-supported advocacy group. "Common sense tells you if you take it down too low and people don't buy, you have not done something good."

The Battle Broadens

On April 26, Mayor Bloomberg stood before a microphone at City Hall to announce an initiative to prod food companies to cut salt in earnest, with an initial target of 25 percent by 2014. The industry's resistance was readily apparent.

After two years of planning, nearly 30 other jurisdictions joined New York, which said it was acting because federal officials had not. But only 16 manufacturers and restaurants had signed on to the initiative, and records released to *The Times* through the state's Freedom of Information Law reveal a shift in industry strategy.

Rather than challenging salt's link to hypertension, industry representatives, in the private planning meetings with city officials, cited financial objections: the higher cost of other seasonings and the expense of new product labels and retooled production lines. In a Feb. 1 letter to a city health official, the Grocery Manufacturers Association wrote that "aggressive, short-term sodium reduction has the potential to further raise food prices."

Companies also warned that reducing salt might force them to increase sugar in foods like peanut butter, meeting minutes show.

Among those declining to join the initiative was Campbell. Chor-San Khoo, its vice president for global nutrition and health, said that the company would continue its own reduction plan, but that the city's pace "was overly aggressive."

In April, the independent Institute of Medicine said food companies were moving too slowly on their own and called on federal officials to set firm salt levels for food.

Dr. Margaret A. Hamburg, the F.D.A. commissioner, said in an interview that salt was a serious concern her agency would address in concert with other issues, like obesity. "We will use a variety of strategies, including education, voluntary reduction and potentially regulation," she said, adding that "we are really at the beginning of the process of shaping our blueprint for action."

One glaring issue before the F.D.A. concerns nutrient labels, which for years have overstated the amount of salt the government says is safe to consume. In calculating the percent of the daily recommended sodium intake in each serving, companies use the standard for healthy adults below middle age, a teaspoon of salt, or about 2,300 milligrams. But the recommendation for the vast majority of Americans—children, adults of middle age or older, all blacks and anyone with hypertension—is less than 1,500 milligrams a day.

The F.D.A. announced in 2007 that it was aware of that problem, but it has taken no action. The federal Dietary Guidelines Advisory Committee is considering adopting the lower standard for everyone as part of its review of nutrition standards.

The food industry has identified the guidelines as a battleground. The panel needs "to include expertise and perspective related to food product development," the Grocery Manufacturers Association wrote to the Agriculture Department in nominating 7 of the panel's 13 members.

Food companies then peppered the committee with their perspective on salt. In a letter, Kellogg said that lower salt guidelines were "incompatible with a palatable diet."

ConAgra, whose brands include Chef Boyardee and Orville Redenbacher, made a different argument to the panel. It submitted a study it commissioned that asserted that far more savings in health care costs—about $58 billion—could be generated if people simply cut 100 calories from their daily diets than if they consumed less salt.

The study put the savings from salt reduction at just $2.3 billion, compared with the $18 billion to $24 billion in savings cited by other analysts, including the Rand Corporation, the research giant. One scientist involved in the research, David A. McCarron, a longtime food industry consultant, said ConAgra's lower estimate stemmed from its more judicious use of hypertension data.

How the industry will fare in the fight over nutrition standards will not be clear until they are finalized later this year. But in committee meetings, some members nominated by the industry have voiced concerns about cutting salt.

Joanne L. Slavin, a committee member and nutrition professor at the University of Minnesota, told her colleagues that reducing salt in bread was difficult and warned of unintended consequences. It is an argument also made by food companies.

"Typically, sodium, sugar bounces around," she said. "So you take sodium down in a product and then sugar a lot of times has to go up just for taste."

CHALLENGE QUESTIONS

Is the Dietary Guideline for Sodium Realistic?

1. Describe the recommended steps that FDA will take to gradually reduce sodium in the American food supply.
2. Identify stakeholders that must be involved to successfully reduce sodium content of the American diet and the role that each will have.
3. Who do you think will have the greater challenge in reducing sodium content of foods they prepare, the food processors or chefs and cooks in restaurants? Explain your answer.
4. Prepare your favorite "from-scratch" baked product (cake, cookies, or bread) without using any sodium-containing ingredients such as salt, baking soda, baking powder, or any prepared mixed. Describe how it looks, feels, and tastes compared to a produce made using the traditional recipe.
5. Using a nutrient analysis program such as the MyPyramid Tracker, analyze the sodium content of the foods you ate in the last 24 hours. If the amount was greater than 1,500 mg, determine which foods could be changed to meet the 1,500 mg recommendation.
6. Is a compromise possible between the health professionals who promote lower sodium foods and the food industry? Based on the selections you read, do you think the Institute of Medicine is realistic in their recommendations for the food industry? Do you think the food industry, or part of it, will attempt to lower salt in their products? What needs to occur between all the stakeholders for American people to actually cut back on salt?

Additional Internet Resources

US Dietary Guidelines for 2010

The entire report of the Dietary Guidelines Advisory Committee on the *Dietary Guidelines for Americans 2010* may be found here.

http://www.cnpp.usda.gov/dietaryguidelines.htm

Strategies to Reduce Sodium Intake in the United States (Complete Report)

The entire 480-page report is available to read free online. Included is a link to a podcast on strategies to reduce sodium.

http://www.nap.edu/catalog.php?record_id=12818

The Salt Institute

North America–based nonprofit salt industry trade association dedicated to advocating responsible uses of salt to ensure quality water and healthy nutrition.

http://www.saltinstitute.org

ISSUE 3

Can an Overemphasis on Eating Healthy Become Unhealthy?

YES: Lindsey Getz, from "Orthorexia: When Eating Healthy Becomes an Unhealthy Obsession," *Today's Dietitian* (June 2009)

NO: Chris Woolston, from "What's Wrong With the American Diet?" *Consumer Health Interactive* (October 28, 2009)

As you read the issue, focus on the following points:

1. The messages that professional health and nutrition associations, government agencies like USDA, and registered dietitians promote about healthy eating.
2. What orthorexia is and what causes the condition.
3. How "healthy eating" messages may lead to orthorexia.
4. The differences between orthorexia nervosa and anorexia nervosa.
5. How to recognize a person with symptoms of orthorexia and the recommended treatment for the condition.

ISSUE SUMMARY

YES: Writer Lindsey Getz describes orthorexia, the condition that makes a person strive for a perfect diet. People with orthorexia avoid sugar, trans fat, cholesterol, sodium, and anything they believe is "unhealthy" and take pride in eating a perfect diet.

NO: Health and medical writer Chris Woolston believes the typical American diet is excessive in calories, fat, and sugar. He says we would be much healthier if we ate more "fish, poultry, cruciferous vegetables (i.e., cabbage and broccoli), greens, tomatoes, legumes, fresh fruits, and whole grains." He also believes we should "skimp on fatty or calorie-rich foods such as red meats, eggs, high-fat dairy products, french fries, pizza, mayonnaise, candy, and desserts."

The mid-1970s was the birth of the "negative nutrition" era when people were told certain foods are bad and to avoid eating them. During this time, reports hit the news telling people that foods high in saturated fat and

cholesterol cause heart disease; sugary foods increase chances of getting diabetes and cause cavities; salt increases blood pressure; and artificial flavors and
coloring increase the risk of cancer.

Adding to the negativism, the *U.S. Dietary Goals for Americans* were developed in 1977, and 3 years later, the first *Dietary Guidelines for Americans* were
published. Both convey messages telling us not to eat certain foods. At the
same time, organizations like the American Heart Association and American
Cancer Society published dietary recommendations with similar messages.

The organic food movement began in the late 1970s and has increased
dramatically since then, especially after the passage of the Organic Food Production Act of 1990. Proponents of organic foods say that it's better than conventionally grown foods since pesticides in conventionally grown products
cause health problems.

Today, we are bombarded with messages that tell us to eat better. Web
sites, newsletters, and newspaper columns are dedicated to the "right" way
to eat. Magazine covers stress healthy eating: and there's even one called
EatingWell. The Web address for the American Dietetic Association says it all,
"*http://www.eatright.org.*"

In 1997, after years of working with patients who were obsessed with
healthy diets, physician Steven Bratman wrote the article "The Health Food
Eating Disorder" (*Yoga Journal*, October 1997). In the article, he describes a
new condition where people are obsessed with healthy foods. He outlines his
definition and description as follows:

> Many of the most unbalanced people I have ever met are those who
> have devoted themselves to healthy eating. In fact, I believe some of
> them have actually contracted a novel eating disorder for which I have
> coined the name "orthorexia nervosa." The term uses "ortho," mean-
> ing straight, correct, and true, to modify "anorexia nervosa." Ortho-
> rexia nervosa refers to a pathological fixation on eating proper food.
>
> Orthorexia begins, innocently enough, as a desire to overcome
> chronic illness or to improve general health. But because it requires con-
> siderable willpower to adopt a diet that differs radically from the food
> habits of childhood and the surrounding culture, few accomplish the
> change gracefully. Most must resort to an iron self-discipline bolstered by
> a hefty dose of superiority over those who eat junk food. Over time, what
> to eat, how much, and the consequences of dietary indiscretion come to
> occupy a greater and greater proportion of the orthorexic's day.

Orthorexia is not considered a medically defined eating disorder by the
American Psychiatric Association (APA). Tim Walsh, who led the group of psy-
chiatrists that worked on the 2013 edition of APA'S *DSM*, a manual, told *Time*
magazine (February 12, 2010) that it will not be included in it.

"We're not in a position to say it doesn't exist or it's not important,"
Walsh told *Time* magazine (February 12, 2010). "The real issue is significant
data. Getting listed as a separate entry in the *DSM* requires extensive scientific knowledge of a syndrome and broad clinical acceptance, neither of which
orthorexia has."

More research about orthorexia has been conducted in Europe than in the United States. Donini and colleagues published a report in *Eating and Weight Disorders* (June 2004) where they found that 6.9 percent of 400 Italians have this condition.

Many nutritionists and other health professionals believe that it is a true disorder. So what has caused the condition? Have the messages to improve our eating caused some people to eat too healthful? Lindsey Getz describes orthorexia as a real condition that dietitians should be concerned about. Christina Pirello considers it to be the "most ridiculous disorder that the psychiatric industry has fabricated."

TIMELINE

1977 *U.S. Dietary Goals* are published that recommend limiting fat to 30 percent of total caloric intake.

1979 The first *Healthy People: The Surgeon General's Report on Health Promotion and Disease Prevention* is published.

1980 First *Dietary Guidelines for Americans* is published that recommended limiting fat, sugar, and sodium.

1990 Organic Food Production Act is passed.

1997 "Orthorexia" is first defined by Steven Bratman.

2006 The Alliance for a Healthier Generation and the American Beverage Association agree to eliminate high-calorie soft drinks from public schools by 2009–2010.

DEFINITIONS

Diagnostic and Statistical Manual of Mental Disorders (DSM) Manual published by the American Psychiatric Association that defines various mental disorders.

"Negative Nutrition" Harmful foods and practices.

Obsessive-compulsive disorder (OCD) Anxiety disorder characterized by recurrent unwanted thoughts (obsessions) and/or repetitive behaviors (compulsions).

Orthos Greek word meaning "correct or right."

Orexis Greek word meaning "appetite."

Orthorexia A fixation of eating only pure, healthy, and natural foods.

YES

Lindsey Getz

Orthorexia: When Eating Healthy Becomes an Unhealthy Obsession

*T*here's a fine line between including foods deemed healthy in your diet and eating nothing but! Teaching your clients the value of all foods can help them forge a healthy relationship with eating and may prevent them from taking their diet to a potentially dangerous extreme.

What could be wrong with a desire to eat healthy? After all, promoting healthy eating is part of a dietitian's job description. But when the urge to eat healthy foods becomes more of an obsession, there may be an eating disorder in the works—and the consequences can be dangerous.

Although it is not yet a clinically recognized term or disorder, orthorexia is gaining wider recognition as cases continue to emerge and capture media attention. Steven Bratman, MD, author of *Health Food Junkies—Orthorexia Nervosa: Overcoming the Obsession With Healthful Eating,* coined the term to denote an eating disorder characterized by an obsession with eating foods deemed healthy.

Bratman began studying the condition after personally becoming obsessed with health foods. "I suffered from a psychological obsession with food," he said in a *20/20* interview last year. "When I was involved with this, it took up way too much of my life experiences when there were other things I could have been doing."

Like other eating disorders, orthorexia starts to negatively impact many areas of an individual's life and, in some cases, can even lead to severe malnutrition or death, as the person increasingly eliminates food types from his or her diet.

"It's not an official diagnostic term, but I think it's something that's important for dietitians to know about," says Evelyn Tribole, MS, RD, owner of a California-based nutrition counseling practice and author of seven books, including *Healthy Homestyle Cooking* and *Intuitive Eating.* "If a client likes to always eat healthy, the question is whether it's helping or hurting them. Is it something that affects their social life? For instance, are they no longer seeing their friends because they can't go out to dinner? This is the type of indication that eating healthy is becoming an unhealthy obsession."

Orthorexia could easily begin as simple healthy habits but then spiral out of control, adds Sondra Kronberg, MS, RD, CDN, a national liaison for the

National Eating Disorders Association and the cofounder and nutritional director of the Eating Disorder Associates Treatment & Referral Centers and Eating Wellness Programs of New York. "The person takes something that's normally considered healthy and good for their body and takes it to the extreme," she says. "They wind up with disordered thinking and psychological torment. The behavior becomes restrictive to the degree that it begins to interfere with the person's quality of life. And what starts out as something they are controlling becomes something that controls them."

Unlike anorexia or bulimia, orthorexia is not about the desire to become thin. "The driving force seems to be a desire to eat a perfectly healthy or even 'pure' diet," says Deborah Kauffmann, RD, LDN, owner of Mindfulness Based Nutrition Counseling in Baltimore. "For instance, organically grown vegetables and fruits may be thought of as 'safe foods' [for both those with anorexia and orthorexia] because they are seen as healthy and low in calories. But artificial sweeteners and diet frozen meals, which usually seem acceptable to someone with anorexia, would not be seen as acceptable to someone with orthorexic tendencies. Conversely, expeller-pressed canola oil may be acceptable to someone with orthorexia but not someone with anorexia because of the fear of weight gain due to eating fat."

Impressionable Minds

Perhaps one of the most alarming trends associated with orthorexia is that children are picking up some of these tendencies. Kids who watch their parents obsess over certain foods may mimic that behavior. And well-intentioned parents who strictly limit their children's sugar intake or try to feed them only organic foods may instill a sense of fear in their children that other foods are "bad" or that scary things could happen if they eat them.

"A few years ago, I had a 10 year old who was terrified of trans fats," says Tribole. "Part of her treatment was me sitting down and eating a Ding Dong with her. Can you imagine a dietitian eating a Ding Dong with her client? But she needed a healthier relationship with food. She had to realize that you don't eat one Ding Dong and end up with a clogged artery."

"I believe many well-meaning parents, teachers, pediatricians, and even dietitians are passing on their beliefs about unhealthy foods to children," says Kauffmann. "This can create not only orthorexia but eating disorders like anorexia, bulimia, and compulsive eating. Recently, I have seen children in my practice afraid to eat all kinds of foods because of things they have learned at home or in school regarding foods being unhealthy or fattening. In my practice, I often use the program in the book *Preventing Childhood Eating Problems* [*A Practical, Positive Approach to Raising Children Free of Food & Weight Conflicts*] by Jane Hirschmann and Lela Zaphiropoulos to teach parents how to help their children become healthy, intuitive eaters. Parents also need to understand that healthy bodies come in all shapes and sizes. Ellyn Satter's book *Your Child's Weight: Helping Without Harming* includes a wonderful appendix which reviews the literature regarding the actual relationship between weight and health in children."

Parents must be especially careful with the behavior they exhibit around their kids and also keep an eye on whether they are too involved with their children's diet, says D. Milton Stokes, MPH, RD, CDN, owner of One Source Nutrition, LLC in Connecticut. Parents can easily make the transition from being helpful and healthy to giving their children a complex about what they're eating. "Kids have a natural appetite regulation," says Stokes. "They eat when they're hungry and stop when they're full. That gets interrupted when mom starts pushing more or less food. Everyone should rely more on that physiological hunger rather than turning eating into something emotional."

Developing a healthy relationship with food certainly seems to be a key to preventing these tendencies, and that means not tying words with heavy meaning to food. "In our society, food is constantly painted as this moral dilemma," says Tribole. "A low-fat food may be termed 'guilt free,' for instance. But eating shouldn't make you feel guilty. And we are constantly calling foods 'good' or 'bad.' Putting all of this weight onto what we eat, as though it actually affects who you are as a person, is where the problem is stemming from. And kids pick up on that."

Instead, parents should teach their children about moderation. Frequently eating trans fatty foods such as French fries or processed snacks is not healthy behavior, but neither is becoming obsessive about avoiding them or being scared to be around such foods.

Warning Signs

Because orthorexia is not an officially recognized disorder and is somewhat controversial, many dietitians may be unfamiliar with it. Some physicians and other health professionals say orthorexia does not require its own classification because they believe it is a form of anorexia or obsessive-compulsive disorder.

Still, regardless of what orthorexia is called or how it is classified, dietitians should be aware of potential warning signs that could indicate something is wrong with the way a client views and eats food. The "worry factor" is one of the biggest indicators, suggests Tribole. "If a client has too much anxiety over what they eat, then that stress may be worse for their health than what they're actually eating and can lead to these orthorexic tendencies," she says.

If you have a client who follows a particularly restrictive diet, try to gain a sense of their feelings about food and whether they're behaving obsessively. "In other words, if they go to a party and they're only serving fried foods, are they going to be devastated? Are they not going to eat all night? These are signs that their behavior is extreme," warns Tribole.

"Also look for any patterns that your client has become overly ritualistic when it comes to their diet," adds Stokes. "If you find out it takes them an extraordinary amount of time to shop for food, that could be another indicator."

Like other eating disorders, orthorexia may also have a lot to do with control. Those with orthorexia often want to be able to heavily regulate the health food they consume. Kronberg says this may be particularly true of clients who have an unmanageable illness and have become desperate to take control of their situation.

"If they have some illness or disease that medicine could not cure, they may become obsessed with their diet, something they feel they can control even when they can't control the disease," she explains. "Maybe they have cancer and they follow a macrobiotic diet extremely rigidly. Or maybe they have multiple sclerosis and they read a book that said to eliminate animal protein. These behaviors can start with good intentions but can lead to a restrictive diet, which isn't healthy for the client."

But a person's desire to gain control doesn't have to be the result of an illness. Orthorexia may stem from someone hearing about a negative effect of a food type or group and ultimately eliminating it from his or her diet. Fat is a good example, says Stokes.

"Some people may have this intense fear that fat is bad and will kill them, so they avoid it at all costs," he says. "But in fact, fat can be healthy, particularly unsaturated fats, [which] may actually be able to protect our heart and lower our cholesterol. We don't need much fat, but we do need some. It's important for the health of our skin and our hair. And we also have fat deposits throughout sensitive places in the body, such as on the temples to protect the skull from impact or around the kidneys to provide some cushioning" should someone fall.

Some with orthorexia are focused more on what they do eat than on what they don't. This could mean, for instance, eating only organic foods. But in many cases, orthorexic tendencies may drive a person to eliminate those foods that he or she believes to be bad—commonly carbohydrates, trans fats, animal products, dyes, and sugars. Doing so can ultimately lead to malnutrition.

A recent article on orthorexia that appeared in **The New York Times** reported on an 18-year-old girl who began her struggle with food when she started eliminating all carbohydrates, meats, refined sugars, and processed foods from her diet. By the time she had gotten rid of all of the foods that she thought were not "pure," she had brought her daily calorie intake down to only 500. Her weight fell to 68 lbs, and she was repeatedly hospitalized until she finally received help and restored her weight. Which food(s) your client may obsess over depends largely on his or her own experiences. "It's all based on information," says Kronberg. "People may have become carb restrictive because of the Atkins diet or fat phobic because of some various theories they've heard. It's all about what they read or what they hear, and the obsession differs from person to person."

How to Help

Dietitians who specialize in eating disorders are most likely the best match for someone dealing with orthorexia. However, all dietitians can learn to recognize early signs and perhaps even prevent orthorexic tendencies from developing. "In general, dietitians need to take the leading role in helping patients to 'legalize' all foods by educating about the nutritional value of all foods, as well as teaching mindful eating techniques and empowering individuals to use primarily internal cues when making eating decisions," says Kauffmann.

Tribole adds that it's important for dietitians to be careful that they do not generate or enable a client's fear of certain foods or food types. While the average person may take advice about avoiding trans fats and apply it meaningfully to the diet, an individual who is bordering on developing an eating disorder may distort that information. "You may be giving out very ordinary nutritional advice, but if they have an eating disorder brewing and you don't know it, then it could be taken the wrong way," says Tribole. "It's just important to pay attention to the way we give out orders to our clients."

"Dietitians can end up being an ally to the disorder without even recognizing it," agrees Kronberg. "Clients could come to you seeking assistance for their disorder, ways that they can be more obsessively healthy. It's our job to recognize when it's become a problem and balance things back out."

Orthorexia may be an emerging condition, but dietitians should realize that they have the power to prevent it from becoming a more widespread issue. Kronberg notes, "We're on the front line, so it's crucial that we're able to recognize early on when there's a problem."

Chris Woolston  **NO**

What's Wrong With the American Diet?

What's wrong with the typical American diet? This is what the experts have to say:

"Too many calories," says Marion Nestle, PhD, MPH, Professor of Nutrition and Food Studies at New York University.

"Too many calories," asserts Melanie Polk, registered dietitian and former director of nutrition education for the American Institute of Cancer Research.

Barbara Gollman, a registered dietitian who used to be the spokesperson for the American Dietetic Association, weighs in with her own theory: "Too many calories."

Perhaps it's time to stop talking about fatty foods and admit that we simply eat too many calories. Twenty-five years ago, the average American consumed about 1,850 calories each day. Since then, our daily diet has grown by 304 calories (roughly the equivalent of two cans of soda). That's theoretically enough to add an extra 31 pounds to each person every year. Judging from the ongoing obesity epidemic, many Americans are gaining those pounds—and then some.

Take the latest national surveys on weight. More than sixty-six percent of all Americans are considered overweight, according to the Centers for Disease Control and Prevention. (This means they have a Body Mass Index greater than 25.)

But calories don't tell the whole story. To truly understand what's wrong with the American diet, you have to know how we manage to consume all those calories. There are two possible ways to go overboard: You can eat too many calorie-dense foods, or you can eat too much food or beverages in general. Many people choose to do both.

Our fondness for fast food is taking a particularly heavy toll. Although the federal government recommends that we have at least two to five cups of fruits and vegetables a day, for example, surveys show that the average American eats only three servings a day, and 42 percent eat fewer than two servings a day.

Here's a closer look at our love affair with calories—and the health crisis it has created.

The Carnival Mirror

Of course, there is no single American diet. We all have our individual tastes, quirks, and habits. Still, experts see clear patterns in our food choices. In fact, most American diets fall into one of two broad categories: "Western" or "prudent."

The prudent diet is a nutritionist's dream. People in this category tend to eat relatively large amounts of fish, poultry, cruciferous vegetables (i.e. cabbage and broccoli), greens, tomatoes, legumes, fresh fruits, and whole grains. They also skimp on fatty or calorie-rich foods such as red meats, eggs, high-fat dairy products, french fries, pizza, mayonnaise, candy, and desserts.

The Western diet is the prudent diet reflected in a carnival mirror. Everything is backwards: Red meat and other fatty foods take the forefront, while fruits, vegetables, and whole grains are pushed aside. In addition to fat and calories, the Western diet is loaded with cholesterol, salt, and sugar. If that weren't bad enough, it's critically short on dietary fiber and many nutrients—as well as plant-based substances (phytochemicals) that help protect the heart and ward off cancer.

Put it all together and you have a recipe for disaster. In a 12-year study of more than 69,000 women, published in the *Archives of Internal Medicine,* a Western diet was found to significantly raise the risk of coronary heart disease. Other studies have shown that a high-fat, low-nutrient diet increases the likelihood of colon cancer, diabetes, and a host of other ailments.

Portion Distortion

The Western diet is nothing new. The typical American family in the 1950s was more likely than we are to sit down to a meal of pork chops and mashed potatoes than stir-fried tofu and broccoli. So why has the obesity epidemic exploded in the last 20 years? It's a matter of size. "Twenty years ago, the diet wasn't as varied as it is today, and people didn't eat nearly enough fruits and vegetables," Gollman says. "But the portions were more in line with what people really need."

From bagel shops to family restaurants to vending machines to movie theater concession stands to the dining room table, our meals and snacks are taking on gargantuan proportions. "Everyone in the food industry decided they had to make portions larger to stay competitive, and people got used to large sizes very quickly," Nestle says. "Today, normal sizes seem skimpy."

The hyperinflation of our diet is especially obvious away from home. "Look through the window of any of the big chain restaurants, and you'll see huge platters of food coming out of the kitchen," Polk says. One of those platters could easily pack 2,000 calories, enough to last most people all day.

Convenience Culture

Despite our national obsession with weight loss, the obesity epidemic continues to be a national health concern. The human craving for fats and sweets will never go away, and it's getting easier than ever to satisfy those cravings. With 170,000 fast-food restaurants and 3 million soft-drink vending machines spread across the country, huge doses of calories are never far away—especially when those soda machines are sitting right in the middle of public schools.

In 1978, for example, the typical teen-age boy in the United States drank about seven ounces of soda a day, according to *Fast Food Nation* author Eric Schlosser. Today, he drinks nearly three times that much, getting a whopping 9 percent of his daily calories from soda. Teenage girls are close behind.

Perhaps not surprisingly, studies show that childhood obesity has hit epidemic proportions over the last decade. One study, published in the *Journal of the American Medical Association,* notes that from 1986 to 1998 the number of overweight white children doubled. Among Latino and African American kids, there's a 120 percent increase. More recent data shows no significant changes in the past few years, though the number of overweight kids remains high. The main culprits, according to experts: high-fat foods, sodas, and too little exercise.

However, the obesity epidemic has moved some to take action. In 2006, the Alliance for a Healthier Generation struck a deal with the American Beverage Association to eliminate high-calorie soft drinks from public schools by the 2009–2010 academic year. While government agencies and private industry grapple with implementing new policies, ultimately it will be up to us individually to improve the way we eat and increase the amount of exercise we get.

Taking Control

Fatty, unbalanced, and oversized: That, in a nutshell, is the American diet. But it doesn't have to be your diet. "People think eating healthy is a difficult task, but small things make a big difference," Polk says. "You just have to employ some important strategies. It's called taking charge."

If you eat more than four meals away from home each week, you can start by making healthy choices as you dine. "As we eat at restaurants more and more, we have to take control of these outlandish meals," Polk says. Order foods that have been baked, steamed, or grilled instead of deep-fried. Have your salad dressing or other fatty toppings served on the side, and if mayonnaise isn't low-fat, skip it entirely. Consider ordering a salad and an appetizer instead of an entree. If you do order an entree, plan to take at least half of it home with you. For more information on portion control, see Downsize This!. ["Downsize This: The Fun of Smaller Portions" by Chris Woolston (updated on Sept. 18, 2009) is available at: http://www.cvshealthresources.com/topic/portions]

No matter where you eat, try to stick to a few basic guidelines. The amount you should eat depends on your age and activity level—teenage boys and men need to eat more than young children, for example. Aim for three to eight ounces of bread, cereal, rice, or pasta each day, the more whole grains the better. This isn't quite as daunting as it sounds—one cup of rice counts as two ounces, and a single slice of bread counts as one ounce. Two to five cups of fruits and vegetables each day will give you fiber and vital nutrients. (One serving is a medium piece of fruit, a half cup of chopped fruit, a half cup of chopped vegetables, or a cup of fresh greens.) Taken together, fruits, vegetables, and grains can satisfy your hunger and fuel your body without blowing your calorie budget.

Meat isn't forbidden, but try to think of it as a complement to your meals, not the main attraction. According to the U.S. Department of Agriculture (USDA) food pyramid, you only need two servings (up to six and a half ounces) from the "meat group" each day. The group includes meat, poultry, fish, dry beans, eggs, and nuts. It goes without saying that six ounces of salmon, pinto beans, or chicken breast is preferable to six ounces of marbled steak (a serving of meat, by the way, should be about the size of a deck of cards).

Much of the advice can be boiled down to one word: moderation. By eating different foods from every part of the pyramid and watching your portion size, you can make your own personal American diet healthy and nutritious. We have more choices and more temptations than ever before, but ultimately, we also have the final say over what we eat. Take control, and enjoy.

CHALLENGE QUESTIONS

Can an Overemphasis on Eating Healthy Become Unhealthy?

1. List eating habits of a person with orthorexia.
2. Compare a person with orthorexia nervosa to one with anorexia nervosa.
3. Outline the nutrition messages from USDA, professional health associations such as AMA and ADA, and registered dietitians as related to healthy eating.
4. Do you think the dietary messages and advice to "eat right" that *many* nutrition experts and government agencies encourage may cause orthorexia? Explain your answer.
5. Currently, the APA does not include orthorexia nervosa as a clinical mental disorder in their DSM. Why do you think it is not currently in their manual? Do you think it should be considered a clinical mental disorder. Explain your answer.

Internet References . . .

The General Accounting Office (GAO)

In response to congressional requests, General Accounting Office (GAO) investigators produce reports on many issues related to agriculture, food, nutrition, and health. They also testify before Congress on these issues. This site provides the full text of GAO reports and testimony.

http://www.gao.gov

The American Diabetes Association

The American Diabetes Association promotes research, education, and advocacy to prevent, cure, and treat people with diabetes mellitus, type 1 ("juvenile-onset") and type 2 ("adult-onset"). This site provides information about these conditions for health professionals and the public. It also provides access to the association's journals, many of which publish articles on aspects of diet and diabetes prevention and control, such as the glycemic index.

http://www.diabetes.org/homepage.jsp

Nutrition and Health

*E*veryone agrees that what we eat has an important effect on health, but arguments begin when the discussion focuses on the exact impact of specific foods or nutrients. The selections in this unit focus on the impact of diet on health. As you read the selection, keep in mind the possible motives of the authors. The opinions expressed are from health professionals, food industry associations, advocacy groups, or journalists.

The three issues deal with the macronutrients. Issue 4 asks if "trans fats-free" foods are really healthy and describes how the food industry is replacing trans fat with interesterified fats. Issue 5 is a debate between the makers of high-fructose corn syrup (HFCS) and a physician who says that HFCS is more deadly than sugar. Issue 6 questions if soy, as protein source, is as beneficial as the soy industry says it is.

- Does "Trans Fats-Free" Mean a Food Is Heart-Healthy?
- Does a Diet High in Fructose Increase Body Fat?
- Does Eating Soy Improve Health?

ISSUE 4

Does "Trans Fats-Free" Mean a Food Is Heart-Healthy?

YES: Lindsey Getz, from "A Burger and Fries (Hold the Trans Fats)—Restaurants Respond to Demand for Healthier Oils," *Today's Dietitian* (February 2009)

NO: Joseph Mercola, from "Interesterified Fat: Is It Worse Than Trans Fat?" *Mercola.com* (March 5, 2009)

As you read the issue, focus on the following points:

1. How and why restaurants and food manufacturers are either reducing or eliminating trans fat in foods, and the health implications of the changes.
2. How interesterified fats are formed and why food manufacturers use them.
3. Reasons why foods labeled "trans fats-free" may not be as healthy as people think.

ISSUE SUMMARY

YES: Health writer Lindsey Getz applauds restaurants and the food industry for eliminating the trans fat in foods and stresses how it will improve the health of the nation.

NO: Physician Joseph Mercola strongly disagrees and points out that food manufacturers are replacing trans fat with interesterified fat. He claims these are worse than trans fats.

Partially hydrogenated vegetable oils (and trans fats) were first developed in 1901 in Britain and introduced in the United States as Crisco shortening in 1911. During both world wars, when butter and other solid animal fats were scarce, people began using margarine and shortening as replacements. In the 1950s, after the first reports linking saturated fats to heart disease were published, the American Heart Association (AHA) recommended that people use margarine and shortening instead of solid animal fats to help lower saturated fat intake. Popularity of margarine and shortening increased until the late 1980s when early reports began to question the impact of trans fat on the body. In 1990, a highly publicized report from the Netherlands by Martijn Katan showed that high levels of trans fat increase low-density lipoprotein (LDL) cholesterol as much as saturated fats.

In 1993, the Center for Science in the Public Interest filed a petition requesting the Food and Drug Administration (FDA) take steps to add trans fat content of foods to nutrition labels. After inviting comments, the FDA concludes that research does not support this requirement. The following year, a Harvard report describes how trans fats are more damaging to heart health than saturated fats and are "likely responsible for at least 30,000 premature US deaths per year."

By the late 1990s, health and government groups begin to recommend people cut back on foods that contain trans fat. Finally, after 50 years of research and public education, the 2005 *Dietary Guidelines for Americans* include "Limit intake of fats and oils high in saturated and/or *trans* fatty acids." In 2006, the FDA requires food manufactures to include grams of trans fat on food labels.

The battle against trans fat continues. Some cities have banned trans fat foods sold in restaurants. Walter Willett, the chair of Harvard's Department of Nutrition, wants to see partially hydrogenated fats removed from the FDA "Generally Regarded as Safe" (GRAS) list, which would essentially eliminate their use. "Given that every major review of trans fats has concluded that intake should be as low as possible," he says, "it is indefensible that they be allowed as GRAS constituents of foods."

So how is the food industry responding? The food industry is engaging in a major effort to find new solid fats that have the same cooking properties as partially hydrogenated vegetable oils and animal fats like lard, beef tallow, and butter. Some are using "fully hydrogenated" fats since they technically have no trans fats, only high amounts of saturated fats.

Food companies have reformulated many products on the grocery shelves, and the edible oil industry has developed alternatives to partially hydrogenated oils. The June 2006 issue of the *Journal of the American Dietetic Association* contains a comprehensive article "New and Existing Oils and Fats Used in Products with Reduced *Trans*-Fatty Acid Content." One of the fats they mention is interesterified fat (IF) and many companies are switching to it. The article describes that interesterification "can be achieved chemically or enzymatically. It is usually done by blending highly saturated hard fats (e.g., palm oil, palm stearin, and fully hydrogenated vegetable oils) with liquid edible oils to produce fats with intermediate characteristics."

These fats are produced by taking a type of saturated fatty acid that is considered relatively healthy (such as stearic acid) and combining it with liquid vegetable oils. The term "interesterified" refers to the "ester" bonds that attach fatty acids to the glycerol backbone. The bonds are broken and the fatty acids are rearranged. For example, the fatty acids that are naturally on the first and second carbons may be forced to switch places or the fatty acid on one carbon of the glycerol is removed and another fatty acid is replaced. The combination produces a type of fat that has the stability and solidity of solid fats like partially hydrogenated vegetable oils, but technically has "no trans fat." The food industry hopes it will have the health benefits of unsaturated fats.

One of the few studies on the health implications of this new fat was published in the January 2007 issue of *Nutrition and Metabolism*. Results show that interesterified fats decrease the "good" high-density lipoprotein (HDL) levels, whereas they increase blood glucose. These results have made some nutritionists skeptical of the new fat.

The FDA allows food companies to label products containing these new fats as "high stearate" or "stearic-rich" fats, or as "interesterified fats," thus avoiding the politically negative buzz word, "hydrogenated," which is associated with trans fats.

So, we have a new fat in our "FDA-approved" food supply. Is it "heart-healthy?" Health writer Lindsey Getz applauds the food industry for eliminating the trans fat in foods but makes no mention of any of the new substitute fats. In contrast, physician Joseph Mercola claims that interesterified fats are worse than trans fats. After reading the two selections, decide for yourself if "trans fats-free" translates into "heart-healthy."

TIMELINE

1902 The first patent for hydrogenated vegetable oils is filed in Germany.

1911 Proctor and Gamble introduces Crisco shortening made with partially hydrogenated oil.

1920s Interesterified fats are introduced in Europe.

1939–45 During both world wars, butter is rationed so the public switches to trans fat-containing margarines made from vegetables' oils.

1957 Ancel Keys publishes first report linking saturated fats to heart disease (*Lancet*, 1957) and the American Heart Association (AHA) recommends replacing animal fats with margarine and shortening made from partially hydrogenated vegetable oils.

1985 The Center for Science in the Public Interest and *The New York Times* (November 14) report that many fast food restaurants use beef tallow to fry foods. Media attention prods restaurant chains to switch to hydrogenated vegetable oils, which are high in trans fats. FDA concludes that trans fats are probably similar to saturated fats in their cholesterol-raising properties, but more research is needed.

1990 The Netherlands scientist Martijn Katan and colleagues publish report in the August issue of *The New England Journal of Medicine* showing a diet high in trans fats increases LDL cholesterol as much as saturated fats.

1992 Trans fat-free margarines are introduced in the United States

1994 Harvard's Alberto Ascherio and Walter Willett wrote a commentary in the *American Journal of Public Health* (May) that describes how trans fats are more damaging to heart health than saturated fats and are likely responsible for at least 30,000 premature U.S. deaths per year. They call for a "regulated phase-out or strict limitation" of trans fats and request trans fat labeling requirements on all foods, including fast foods.

1996 The Center for Science in the Public Interest calls on restaurants and food manufacturers to disclose trans fat levels and switch to liquid vegetable oils.

1999 FDA proposes rules requiring that the amount of trans fat be listed on nutrition labels and advises consumers to cut their intake as much as possible.

2005 *Dietary Guidelines for Americans* includes "Limit intake of fats and oils high in saturated and/or trans fatty acids."

2006 FDA requires food labels to include the grams of trans fat.

2006 The AHA recommends that less than 1 percent of calories be from trans fats.

2010 California bans trans fat in restaurants.

YES

Lindsey Getz

A Burger and Fries (Hold the Trans Fats)—Restaurants Respond to Demand for Healthier Oils

Restaurants across the United States have been slowly making progress toward eliminating trans fats from their menus. Cities such as New York, Philadelphia, and Boston have already placed a ban on the use of these fats in restaurants, while California recently became the first to introduce a statewide ban. It's expected that such bans will continue across the country as consumers begin to recognize the importance of eliminating dangerous trans fats from their diets and demand a change in what restaurants are serving up.

"When California's Gov Schwarzenegger signed the bill banning trans fats as of January 1, 2010, I think restaurants got the message loud and clear that this change will most likely spread nationwide quickly," suggests Joanne "Dr. Jo" Lichten, PhD, RD, creator of *Dr. Jo's Eat Out & Lose Weight Plan*.

Trans fats are formed when liquid oils are converted into solid fat through hydrogenation. Consuming trans fats can lead to heart disease by raising LDL cholesterol and simultaneously lowering HDL cholesterol. A study published in *The New England Journal of Medicine* in 2006 estimated that approximately 228,000 coronary heart disease occurrences could be avoided by reducing trans fat consumption or eliminating these fats from the American diet. Unfortunately, many popular foods contain them, and many Americans consume these foods in excess. The FDA estimates that the average American consumes approximately 4.7 pounds of trans fats every year.

Trans fats are especially common in baked goods, as they aid with preservation. "I tell my clients that trans fats are essentially a man-made fat," says Sara Shama, RD, director of nutrition for Kingley Health in New Jersey. "It helps Twinkies stay on the shelf for six years without going bad. Baked goods are supposed to go bad!"

Stephanie Dean, RD, LD, coauthor of the book *Fit to Serve*, adds, "While trans fats were created to increase the shelf life of foods, consumers can increase their own 'shelf life' by eliminating trans fats from their diets."

A Change for the Better

Fortunately, many restaurants and chains across the country are making changes—even if they aren't located in a city with a ban. The Cheesecake Factory was one of the leaders pioneering these changes in the industry. "Nearly two years ago, our management team and kitchen staff began partnering with our foodservice manufacturers to work toward the elimination of trans fats from our menu," says Mark Mears, senior vice president and chief of marketing for the company.

The restaurants of Passion Food Hospitality, including DC Coast, TenPenh, Ceiba, and Acadiana, located in Washington, D.C., decided to seek alternatives to trans fats about two years ago. Since losing 125 pounds, chef/owner Jeff Tunks decided to prepare his light dishes even lighter and healthier by eliminating trans fats. "I am the first to admit I would eat a fried shrimp po'boy every day if I could," he says. "But when I take that first bite, it surely sets me at ease to know there is not trans fat in the oil."

Fast-food restaurants, which are one of the biggest culprits of foods high in trans fats, have been quick to follow. Chains such as Burger King, McDonald's, and Hardee's have announced a switch to zero trans fat oils for their cooking. Subway, a chain that had very little trans fats in its food in the first place, has completely eliminated it from its core menu as well. "We always look for ways to improve our products," says Les Winograd, a Subway spokesman. "We have a reputation for offering healthy alternatives to traditional, fatty fast foods. Eliminating even the small amount of trans fats we had was just another way of improving."

Even hotels are recognizing the importance of switching to a healthier alternative. Last year, Carlson Hotels Worldwide announced plans to eliminate shortening containing trans fats at the majority of its hotels. The Radisson Fort McDowell Resort & Casino in Scottsdale, Ariz., was one of the hotels that participated in the pilot program. The resort's restaurant, the Ahnala Mesquite Room, successfully eliminated trans fats from its menu in October 2006 and found that guests actually preferred the flavor of its healthier alternatives and appreciated the restaurant's effort to emphasize good health.

Many restaurants have reported no change in taste after switching to a healthier alternative. Of course, each restaurant has its own alternative formula. McDonald's, for instance, uses a canola oil cooking blend for its fried items, such as French fries, chicken, and its Filet-O-Fish sandwiches. The Cheesecake Factory reports using a blend of olive and canola oils to replace the oils previously used for cooking. "In making the switch to trans fat-free cooking oils, our guests have reported no discernable taste differences to our unique menu items," says Mears, who adds that the switch has not affected menu pricing.

The public has responded positively to increased healthy options—especially those with no trans fat. "Our customers rave about the freshness and selection of ingredients," says Thomas DuBois, CEO and founder of Tomato Tamoto, a new made-to-order salad bar restaurant that recently opened in Plano, Tex.

Of course, that's not to say there haven't been any complaints since these bans first took effect. Much of the initial resistance was due to the high cost of trans fat-free oils, says Lichten. "But as more and more restaurants switch over, this has increased the availability from the oil companies," she adds. "Many restaurants have found that the trans fat-free oils are the same price or even lower."

Some in the restaurant industry have also complained that it's not the government or any other agency's place to ban these fats. Dan Fleshler, a spokesman for the National Restaurant Association, was quoted in 2006 (when New York City's Board of Health voted to make it the nation's first city to ban trans fats) as saying, "We don't think that a municipal health agency has any business banning a product that the Food and Drug Administration has already approved."

However, most restaurants have willingly complied—or even made changes without being placed under a ban—and the general public has been happy with the changes. And dietitians surely agree it's been a change for the better. "Even though it's each person's individual right to choose what they want to consume, as a nation, I believe we should be looking out for the well-being of our people," says Shama. "Everyone's lives are busy and everyone is on the go, and there are times they have to rely on fast or convenient foods. They should be comforted in knowing that whatever they do pick up is something that's not going to give them heart disease because of having trans fats. We have to give people choice, but we still need to look out for their best interest."

Helping Your Patients

Regardless of whether your city has a ban, there seems to be a lot of confusion surrounding trans fats, especially since it's become such a hot news item in the last couple of years. Shama says her patients ask her many questions, but she tries to make it simple. "I call them the artery-clogging, heart disease-causing fats," she says. "That makes it pretty clear."

Elaine Pelc, RD, LDN, of Baltimore, gives patients a visual picture to help them get the point. "I tell my patients to think about what bacon grease does when it cools: It solidifies," she explains. "I tell them that trans fats do the same thing in your arteries. And when they solidify, they clog up the arteries."

Dietitians can help their patients make wiser choices when dining out, regardless of whether they reside in a city with a trans fat ban. Shama tells clients to check up on places where they plan to eat. "If they know where they're going to eat, they can look up the menu online," she says. "If they take the time to check out the menu beforehand and get a sense of what some of the healthier options are, they'll be less likely to opt for the colossal cheeseburger with fries."

"There are no health benefits of trans fats, and no level is considered to be safe," adds Janel Ovrut, MS, RD, LDN, who is based in Boston. "I tell my clients that when it comes to how much trans fats are in their diet, they should stick to zero."

Ovrut says that Boston's ban on trans fats has taken the guesswork out of which restaurant foods contain them. "Now we can all rest assured that the answer is 'none,'" she says. "I think that Boston residents take pride in the fact that we're part of a health initiative that will hopefully guide other cities and towns to make the same changes. The ban has also created more buzz about the harmful effects of trans fats, and consumers are starting to realize the negative impact after a unanimous vote that forbid trans fats from dining establishments. Consumers take notice and are hopefully making changes in their at-home eating habits as well."

Consumer habits are certainly an issue. Even if people live in an area where a ban is in place, they still may be consuming trans fats at home. That's why it's important to help clients be more proactive about their nutrition, not only when dining out but also when purchasing groceries.

"I advise my clients to read the ingredient list on foods," says Ovrut. "Just because a package says 'zero trans fats' per serving doesn't mean the product is completely void of partially hydrogenated oil. Products can be promoted as trans fat free as long as there is less than 0.5 grams per serving. But once you consume more than one serving of a product—which is easy to do with packaged snacks or baked goods—you're creeping up toward 1 gram or more of trans fats. Some food manufacturers are even decreasing the listed serving size of their product so that it meets the trans fat-free guidelines. Consumers are hungry for more and often eat double or triple the serving size."

However, as a result of consumers' interest in trans fat-free products, some manufacturers—just like many restaurants—have decided to eliminate it, says Lichten. "But remember, trans fat free still does not mean fewer calories. Most trans fat-free products have exactly the same amount of fat and calories as the original," she notes.

A Balanced Diet

Even without reading the ingredient list, patients can have a good idea of which foods might contain trans fat. These include premade desserts, butter spreads, convenience foods, and fried items, says Dean. These are the types of foods that clients should avoid in general.

They also tend to be the products that have a long list of ingredients, adds Stella Lucia Volpe, PhD, RD, LDN, FACSM, an associate professor and the Miriam Stirl Term Endowed Chair of Nutrition at the University of Pennsylvania School of Nursing in Philadelphia. "If you look at a packaged product and it has an extremely long list of ingredients, chances are it's probably not very good for you and may contain trans fats," she explains. "I advise clients to try to make pure food choices. Natural, unprocessed foods like lean meat, fish, fruits, or vegetables are always the best option."

While the increased awareness surrounding the dangers of trans fat has been wonderful, one potential problem with the focus on switching to "healthier alternatives" is that consumers may start to believe that certain foods are healthy just because they don't have trans fat. With or without trans fats, French fries are not a healthy choice. Clients need to know that trans fat-free items may be better for you than those with the dangerous fat, but they still aren't necessarily healthy. "It's important to make healthy choices in general," says Pelc. "People should be limiting their intake of these foods anyway in order to maintain a healthy lifestyle. Choosing trans fat-free foods does not mean that you are choosing healthy foods. It's important for clients to remember that removing trans fat from a food does not necessarily make it a healthy choice."

"Just because it says they have zero trans fat still doesn't mean those potato chips or French fries were the best option on the menu," adds Volpe. "I typically try to work on portion control with my clients. If they really love something like potato chips and won't give them up, we can at least work on limiting their portion."

The bottom line? Getting clients to eat a healthy, well-balanced diet may not happen overnight, but helping them eliminate or even simply cut down on trans fat is definitely a step in the right direction.

Joseph Mercola

 **NO**

Interesterified Fat: Is It Worse Than Trans Fat?

It was inevitable that food manufacturers and the edible oil industry would find a substitute for trans fats, now that consumer backlash is forcing the issue.

After all, we're talking big business here. Over 90 percent of the money Americans spend on food is spent on the processed stuff.

Now that the health dangers of trans fats have been clearly exposed, the food industry would do you a great favor by returning to the use of natural saturated fats for frying and in baked goods. But that would mean reversing their entirely unscientific, 50-year campaign to vilify saturated fats, and would bring an end to the enormously powerful edible oil industry.

Since that's not about to happen, it's time for a quick review of the bad news about trans fats, followed by an investigation into what seems to be a fast-growing substitute: interesterified fats.

Why Trans Fats Are Being Replaced in Processed Foods

Trans fats cause a host of health problems. Among the most serious, trans fats

- Raise your LDL ("bad") cholesterol levels and lower HDL ("good") cholesterol levels
- Are believed to contribute to auto-immune disease, cancer, heart disease, fertility problems, and bone degeneration
- Inhibit insulin receptors in your cell membranes and are the main cause of type 2 diabetes, characterized by high levels of insulin and glucose in your blood

The Trans Fat Replacement—Interesterified Fat

Interesterified fats have been an ingredient in foods in the U.S. since the 1950s. They were introduced in Europe even earlier—in the 1920s—and have been in widespread use there for the last 15 years as a substitute for partially hydrogenated oils (trans fats).

These fats are oils that have been chemically altered. They are hydrogenated and then rearranged on a molecular level.

Although technically not the same as partially hydrogenated oils, the unnatural manipulation of lipid molecules in interesterified fats raises similar health concerns to those caused by trans fats.

The Process of Interesterification

The interesterification process hardens fat, similar to the hydrogenation process, but without producing oils that contain trans fats. The end product, like trans fat, is less likely to go rancid and is stable enough to use to fry foods.

There are three ways to modify natural fat:

1. Fractionation
2. Hydrogenation (the process used in trans fat production)
3. Inter-*ester*-ification

Interesterification acts on compounds in oil known as *esters*. The process combines a natural vegetable oil with stearic acid and alkylinic catalysts. Either enzymes or chemicals are used to modify the molecular structure of the oil in order to make it perform like a fat. The end result is a fat rich in stearic acid.

Interesterification is similar to the process that creates trans fats. Like hydrogenation, which generates unnatural trans fats, interesterification also produces molecules that do not exist in nature.

The highly industrialized process of interesterification may result in a product that is trans-free, but that product will still contain chemical residues, hexanes, and other hazardous waste products full of free radicals that cause cell damage.

The Use of Interesterified Fat Is Already Raising Health Concerns

Studies show that interesterified fat raises your blood glucose and depresses insulin production. These conditions are common precursors to diabetes, and can present an even more immediate danger if you already have the disease.

After only four weeks consuming these fats, study volunteers' blood glucose levels rose sharply—by *20 percent*. This is a much worse result than is seen with trans fats.

Insulin levels dropped 10 percent on the trans fat diet used in the studies, and twice that on the interesterified fat diet. Study results conclude interesterified fat affects the production of insulin by your pancreas, as opposed to the insulin receptors in your cell membranes.

Interesterified fat also reduces levels of good (HDL) cholesterol.

The Problem with All Processed Vegetable Oils

Natural vegetable oils that have been altered create problems for your body at the cellular level. These fats are no longer in their natural state, and your body doesn't know how to handle them. Your system will try to make use of them and in the process, these fats end up in cell membranes and other locations where they can wreak havoc with your health.

If you are male, the danger of these man–made fats is an increased risk of heart disease. In men, these unnatural oils trigger an immune response as they enter your artery walls. As your body attacks this unknown intruder, your arteries become inflamed, leading to a dangerous buildup of plaque.

If you are a woman, your body will react somewhat differently. Processed vegetable oils don't appear to trigger an immune response in the arteries of women. Rather, they get deeper into your body and into fatty tissues like those of the breast, increasing your cancer risk.

Finally, a problem with processed vegetable oils no matter what your gender is the accumulation of the toxic by-products of the catalysts used to change the oils from their natural state. These catalysts are created from metals like aluminum and nickel. They build up in your nervous system, are difficult to eliminate, and can lead to neurological problems and other health concerns.

How to Recognize Interesterified Fats in Your Food

You'll find interesterified fats in the same types of processed foods that use trans fats. Products such as

- margarine and shortening
- fried foods like French fries and fried chicken
- doughnuts
- cookies
- pastries
- crackers
- processed foods like cereal and waffles
- salad dressings
- mayonnaise

Interesterified Fat Will Likely NOT Be on List of Ingredients

If you're in the habit of reading product labels, you may or may not see the word "interesterified" fat among the list of ingredients, even if it's in there.

The FDA has ruled that food manufacturers can use terms like *high stearate* or *stearic rich* fats in place of "interesterified." To confuse things even further, if you see the terms *fully hydrogenated vegetable oil*, *palm oil* and/or *palm kernel oil* on labeling, the product may or may not contain interesterified fat.

And beware eating out, because while restaurants and their suppliers are touting removal of trans fats from the foods they serve, very little is being said about the fats that are replacing them.

The bottom line is that if a processed food label includes "vegetable oil" as an ingredient, you can be absolutely sure you're about to consume either interesterified fats, or trans fats.

And if a processed food product is labeled "0% trans fats" or "no trans fats" but is made from vegetable oils, you can be certain it contains either interesterified fats or fully hydrogenated vegetable oils.

My Position on Interesterified Fats

Regular readers of my newsletter know that I'm a firm believer in eating foods in the *most natural unprocessed state* possible.

Foods that have been altered by an industrial process do not metabolize in your body the same way natural foods do, and eating them is an invitation to serious health problems.

My firm position is that you shouldn't knowingly put interesterified fats into your body. You can be virtually assured that no one knows at this time what the long-term health concerns of this product will be.

It took the mainstream medical community and food manufacturers 30 years to determine and admit that trans fats are dangerous to your health. It could take another 30 years for the truth to come out about interesterified fats—or any other substitute fat that does not exist in nature.

Options to Consider

Fortunately avoiding these fats is relatively easy as they are in virtually all the foods that trans fats are, so by avoiding trans fat you will also avoid interesterified fats.

If you're like most Americans, your diet consists predominantly of processed food. And eating processed foods, especially those with a long shelf life, means you're consuming interesterified fats, trans fats, or some other type of man-made ingredient that your body was not designed to metabolize.

- If you want to avoid dangerous fats of all kinds, your best bet is to eliminate processed foods from your diet.
- Use butter instead of margarines and vegetable oil spreads. Butter is a healthy whole food that has received an unwarranted bad rap.
- Use coconut oil for cooking. It is far superior to any other cooking oil and is loaded with health benefits.
- Following my nutrition plan will automatically reduce your modified fat intake, as it will teach you to focus on healthy whole foods instead of processed junk food.

CHALLENGE QUESTIONS

Does "Trans Fats-Free" Mean a Food Is Heart-Healthy?

1. Describe what trans fats are, how they are made, and the benefits of them to the food industry.
2. Explain what "zero trans fat" or "trans fat-free" on a food label means.
3. Compare the structure, uses, and health implications of trans fats to interesterified fats.
4. Walter Willett feels that trans fats should not be on the GRAS list, which would virtually eliminate it from the American food supply. First, decide if you agree or disagree with his position. Write a letter to your U.S. congressman supporting your position.
5. Trans fats were a big part of the American food supply for 50 years before the FDA decided to require food manufacturers to disclose the amount in a product on food labels. And it required years of research before "limit trans fat" was included in the *Dietary Guidelines for Americans*. Do you believe it will take 50 more years for the government to make a similar recommendation about new fats such as interesterified fats? Explain your answer.

Additional Internet Resources

Stop Trans Fats

"STOP TRANS FATS" is a campaign designed to educate consumers about trans fats and encourage them to eat less or no trans fat. It also contains a section on interesterified fat.

http://www.stop-trans-fat.com

Ban Trans Fats

Site that was highly influential in the national trans fat campaign. It was designed to encourage the food industry to reduce the trans fats in foods. Perhaps the most highly recognized effort was the lawsuit they filed against Oreo cookies "seeking an injunction against the sale and marketing of Oreo cookies to children in California." The lawsuit simply wanted Oreos with no trans fat. Ban Trans Fats won! Actually, they voluntarily dismissed the lawsuit when Oreo manufacturer (Kraft) announced they would reformulate their cookies.

http://bantransfats.com/theoreocase.html

ISSUE 5

Does a Diet High in Fructose Increase Body Fat?

YES: Joseph Mercola, from "This Harmful Food Product Is Changing Its Name—Don't Get Swindled," *Mercola.com* (October 1, 2010)

NO: Corn Refiners Association, from "Questions & Answers about High Fructose Corn Syrup" (August 2008)

As you read the issue, focus on the following points:

1. Differences between HFCS and sucrose (table sugar) and trends in consumption of the two.
2. How fructose metabolism differs from glucose metabolism and why fructose is "lipogenic."
3. Health effects of diets high in HFCS compared with health effects of eating regular sucrose.

ISSUE SUMMARY

YES: Osteopathic physician Joseph Mercola considers that high fructose corn syrup (HFCS) is more deadly than sugar and explains how the body converts fructose to fat. He accuses the Corn Refiners Association of trying to convince us that their HFCS is equal to table sugar.

NO: The Corn Refiners Association claims that HFCS has no adverse health effect and is the same as sucrose and honey. They also emphasize the benefits that HFCS provides to food.

Corn syrup has been on the market for about 100 years. It's made from breaking down cornstarch to free glucose. In the late 1950s, the enzyme called glucose isomerase was developed. The enzyme rearranges the carbons in glucose so it becomes fructose, changing plain corn syrup into high fructose corn syrup (HFCS). The name "high fructose" leads many to believe it's mainly fructose, but in reality, most HFCS is either 42 percent or 55 percent fructose with the other part glucose. In the mid-1970s, when the cost of sugarcane and sugar beet imports became very high, the food industry began looking for alternative sweeteners and realized that HFCS, made from American-grown corn, was the solution. Soft drink manufacturers quickly began to replace expensive sugar with cheap HFCS; by 1985 all nondiet soft drinks were sweetened with it.

With the help of U.S. government subsidies, corn farmers have managed to keep the price of corn (and HFCS) about 25–30 percent below production cost. This translates into a win–win situation for farmers and the food industry. And, since the price of HFCS is low, beverage manufacturers have been able to make large 20- and 32-oz bottles of pop while charging the consumer just a little more than for the typical price of the 12-oz can. And with the cheap cost, we're drinking more and more of it. HFCS is hidden in many other foods; even canned and frozen vegetables, cereals, and breads contain it. But what is this doing to our health?

The average American consumes 52 g of HFCS per day, which translates into about 200 kcal. And most of it is from HFCS-sweetened beverages. The increase in HFCS consumption has not only paralleled increase in diabetes, but also obesity, high blood lipids, and other metabolic problems common today. Should we blame these health problems on HFCS? In his article "Are Refined Carbohydrates Worse Than Saturated Fat?" Frank Fu predicts that "refined carbohydrates are likely to cause even greater metabolic damage than saturated fat" (*American Journal of Clinical Nutrition*, June 2010). HFCS is definitely a "refined" carbohydrate. As recent as 2008, the Corn Refiners Association of America considered HFCS to be a "natural" ingredient. They point out that "under FDA rules, 'natural' means that nothing artificial or synthetic has been included."

Researcher Chi-Tang Ho says since fructose and glucose in HFCS are "unbound" they form chemicals called "reactive carbonyls" that cause tissue damage which could lead to diabetes, especially in children. His studies found that these damaging chemicals are not found in beverages made with sucrose, since its glucose and fructose are "bound" (*Science Daily*, August 23, 2007).

Numerous other studies have been published on the health impact of HFCS. In the following selections, Joseph Mercola claims that HFCS is more deadly than sugar and that the Corn Refiners Association is trying to convince us that their product is equal to table sugar. The Corn Refiners Association claims that HFCS has no adverse health effect and is the same as sucrose and honey since all three have about the same one-to-one ratio of fructose to glucose. After reading the selections, form your own opinion.

TIMELINE	DEFINITIONS
1921 Corn syrup, made totally from glucose, is developed.	**Glucose isomerase** Enzyme that changes the structure of glucose to fructose.
1950s The enzyme glucose isomerase used to convert glucose to fructose is developed.	**Government subsidies** Money given by the government to an individual or business to support an enterprise regarded as being needed by the general public.
1970s High fructose corn syrup (HFCS) use in the United States began.	
1980s HFCS used in all non-diet soft drinks in the United States.	**Reactive carbonyls** An unstable carbonyl, which is a carbon double bonded to an oxygen; high levels are associated with diabetes.

YES

Joseph Mercola

This Harmful Food Product Is Changing Its Name— Don't Get Swindled

The Corn Refiners Association (CRA) has petitioned the U.S. FDA to allow manufacturers the option of using the term "corn sugar" instead of "high fructose corn syrup."

In their press release on the subject, they claim that "independent research demonstrates that the current labeling is confusing to American consumers."

They blame "inexact scientific reports and inaccurate media accounts" for the current stigma associated with high fructose corn syrup.

In reality, as opposed to the CRA's dream world, if you need to lose weight, or if you want to avoid diabetes and heart disease, high-fructose corn syrup is one type of sugar you'll want to avoid.

Part of what makes HFCS such an unhealthy product is that it is metabolized to fat in your body far more rapidly than any other sugar.

Source: PR Newswire September 14, 2010

Dr. Mercola's Comments

As I've stated on many occasions, the number one source of calories in the United States is high-fructose corn syrup (HFCS), mainly in the form of soda.

This dangerous sweetener is also in many processed foods and fruit juices.

Even seemingly "health-conscious" beverages like Vitamin Water, Jamba Juice and Odwalla SuperFood contain far more added sugar and/or fructose than many desserts!

The corn industry persistently claims that it is not much different than sugar and is perfectly safe, but we know otherwise.

The primary reason it's so dangerous is that it is quite cheap to produce, so it has been added to nearly all processed foods. The excessive consumption of fructose, such as HFCS, is a primary driving factor behind a number of health epidemics, including obesity, diabetes and heart disease.

Don't Get Confused By the Latest Smoke and Mirror Tactics

Americans' consumption of corn syrup has fallen to a 20-year low, probably due to consumer concerns that it is more harmful or more likely to cause obesity than ordinary sugar.

This is why the corn industry wants to sugar coat the fact that their product may be prematurely killing hundreds of thousands of Americans each year, and rename it to confuse people to keep using it—all in the name of trying to "clear up" confusion!

You have probably seen their new marketing campaign on television. Two new commercials try to alleviate shopper confusion, showing people who say they now understand that "whether it's corn sugar or cane sugar, your body can't tell the difference."

This is an absolutely brilliant marketing strategy and will work as the average consumer will not be smart enough to realize the difference.

However with your help, spreading the message through your Facebook accounts, your blogs and websites, and sharing it with your friends and family, we can sabotage their plans to manipulate and deceive you and the rest of the public.

Their latest strategy is aimed at seeking to defend their market and their profits, and your health depends on whether or not you buy into their smoke and mirrors routine.

The corn industry is still holding fast to the claim that all sugars are metabolized by your body in the same way, even though this outdated belief has been entirely SHATTERED in more recent years by a number of scientific studies.

This research has devastated the image of high fructose corn syrup which is why they are doing this massive makeover, to do an end around the science.

The CRA claims that "a continuing series of inexact scientific reports and inaccurate media accounts about high fructose corn syrup and matters of health and nutrition have . . . increased consumer uncertainty."

Folks, there's nothing inexact about the evidence against fructose. It's very clear. If you want to improve your health, you need to avoid fructose in all its forms, especially HFCS, which is a highly processed, unnatural form of fructose.

Why the ADA's Support of Fructose as 'Safe and Equivalent to Other Sugar' Means NOTHING . . .

The industry has one ace up their sleeve that they pull out again and again— the 2008 report by the American Dietetic Association (ADA), which concluded that HFCS is "nutritionally equivalent to sucrose (table sugar)."

But, could that report possibly have had anything at all to do with the fact that the ADA partnered with Coca-Cola Company earlier that same year?

The press release declaring this unholy union states:

> "The Coca-Cola Company's Beverage Institute for Health & Wellness team of physicians, PhD-level nutrition scientists and registered dietitians serve as a resource for health professionals and others interested in the science of beverages and their role in health and living well.
>
> The Coca-Cola Company will share research findings with ADA members in forums such as professional meetings and scientific publications, to augment the body of knowledge around consumer motivation and health behaviors. To improve understanding of consumer behavior and motivation around healthy living, The Coca-Cola Company will also share its consumer research and expertise with ADA members."

How nice. I'm sure we can all sleep better knowing that one of the authorities for dietary recommendations in the US is getting their scientific information from such a health-minded group of corporate scientists.

And while we're at it, who are some of the *other* ADA sponsors?

Let's see . . . there's PepsiCo . . . and sugary-snack giants Hershey and MARS Inc . . . oh, and SoyJoy, along with a couple of sugary-cereal giants.

All in all, I'm not impressed. In fact, it's downright frightening to see how many corn syrup-reliant companies support the ADA.

Financial alliances such as these are a major part of why it is virtually impossible to get honest, impartial, factual information about health from conventional media, medicine, and government health agencies.

The Truth about High Fructose Corn Syrup

The truth is, scientists HAVE linked the rising HFCS consumption to the epidemics of obesity, diabetes and metabolic syndrome in the U.S., and medical researchers HAVE pinpointed various health dangers associated with the consumption of HFCS specifically, compared to regular sugar.

This is why the corn industry is now scrambling to save face and profits—NOT because it's *really okay* to consume an average of 59 pounds of HFCS a year.

If you haven't yet read the impressive scientific analysis on fructose in one of my favorite nutritional journals, I would strongly encourage you to do so as it will open your eyes to some of the major problems with this sweetener. [Sharon S. Elliott and colleagues, from "Fructose, Weight Gain, and the Insulin Resistance Syndrome," *The New England Journal of Medicine* (November 2002)]

And for an in-depth review of just how different fructose and HFCS really is from regular sugar, please read through this article [Joseph Mercola, from "This Common Food Ingredient Can Really Mess Up Your Metabolism," *Mercola.com* (January 26, 2010)] and watch the lecture given by Dr. Robert Lustig. ["Sugar: The Bitter Truth" is available on the UCTV site at http://www .uctv.tv/search-details.aspx?showID=16717

If you have not yet taken the time to see it, you owe it to yourself to do so. It's a real eye-opener!

Another expert on fructose is Dr. Richard Johnson, who has also written the best book on the market on the dangers of fructose, called *The Sugar Fix*.

The information presented by Drs. Lustig and Johnson is exactly why I am so passionate about educating you about the dangers of fructose!

I am thoroughly convinced it's one of the leading causes of a great deal of needless suffering from poor health and premature death.

If you received your fructose only from vegetables and fruits (where it originates) as most people did a century ago, you'd consume about 15 grams per day—a far cry from the 73 grams per day the typical adolescent gets from sweetened drinks today. And, in vegetables and fruits, the fructose is mixed in with fiber, vitamins, minerals, enzymes, and beneficial phytonutrients, all which moderate its negative metabolic effects.

The main factor that makes fructose so dangerous is the fact that people are consuming it in absolutely MASSIVE DOSES. This is largely related to technology advances in the mid 70s that made it so cheap to produce. The vast majority of processed and restaurant foods are now loaded with it, so it is very difficult to avoid.

How Fructose Wrecks Your Health

Contrary to industry claims, your body does NOT recognize and treat all sugars the same.

HFCS is a *highly processed* product that contains similar amounts of unbound fructose and glucose.

Fructose and glucose are metabolized in very different ways in your body.

Glucose is metabolized in every cell of your body and is converted to blood glucose, while all fructose is metabolized in your liver, where it's quickly converted to fat and cholesterol. (When a diet includes a large amount of fructose, it can therefore create fatty liver, and even cirrhosis.)

Sucrose, on the other hand, is a larger sugar molecule that is metabolized into glucose and fructose in your intestine.

Fructose is metabolized to fat in your body far more rapidly than any other sugar, and, because most fructose is consumed in liquid form (soda), its negative metabolic effects are further magnified.

Why does it turn to fat more readily than other sugar?

Most fats are formed in your liver, and when sugar enters your liver, it decides whether to store it, burn it or turn it into fat. However, researchers have discovered that fructose *bypasses this process* and turns directly into fat.

According to Dr. Elizabeth Parks, associate professor of clinical nutrition at UT Southwestern Medical Center, and lead author of a recent study on fructose in the *Journal of Nutrition*:

> "Our study shows for the first time the surprising speed with which humans make body fat from fructose. Once you start the process of fat synthesis from fructose, it's hard to slow it down. The bottom line of this study is that fructose very quickly gets made into fat in the body."

It is also this uncontrolled movement of fructose through these metabolic pathways that causes it to contribute to greater triglyceride [i.e. fat] synthesis.

There are over 35 years of hard empirical evidence that refined man-made fructose like HFCS metabolizes to triglycerides and adipose tissue, not blood glucose.

The metabolic pathways used by fructose also generate uric acid. In fact, fructose typically generates uric acid within minutes of ingestion. When your uric acid level exceeds about 5.5 mg per dl, you have an increased risk for a host of diseases, including:

- Hypertension
- Kidney disease
- Insulin resistance, obesity, and diabetes
- Fatty liver
- Elevated triglycerides, elevated LDL, and cardiovascular disease
- For pregnant women, even preeclampsia

Other specific health problems associated with excessive fructose consumption include:

- Metabolic Syndrome
- Diabetes
- High blood pressure
- Obesity
- An increase in triglycerides and LDL (bad) cholesterol levels
- Liver disease

Name virtually any disease, and you will find elevated insulin levels is a primary risk factor. This is why, if you want to be healthy, let alone optimally healthy, you simply MUST restrict your fructose consumption.

And if you're currently eating a diet full of processed foods, sodas and sweetened drinks, that restriction will need to be quite severe, because you're ingesting *massive amounts* of fructose in the form of HFCS and other forms of corn syrup, such as crystalline fructose.

Please understand that if you eat processed foods, there's fructose in practically every single bite of food you put in your mouth.

Ironically, diet foods are clear culprits here as well.

Yes, the very products that most people rely on to lose weight—low-fat diet foods—are often those that contain the most fructose!

The downside of this is that fructose does not stimulate your insulin secretion, nor enhance leptin production. (Leptin is a hormone thought to be involved in appetite regulation.) Because insulin and leptin act as key signals in regulating how much food you eat, as well as your body weight, this suggests that dietary fructose may contribute to increased food intake and weight gain.

So, any "diet" food containing fructose will not help you lose any weight. And neither will diet foods containing artificial sweeteners for that matter. . . .

Another significant health concern of HFCS is that the majority of it is made from genetically modified corn, which is fraught with its own well documented side effects. And, adding insult to injury, last year nearly 50 percent of tested HFCS-containing foods and beverages were found to be contaminated with mercury.

What about Fructose from Fruit?

Fresh fruits also contain fructose, although an ameliorating factor is that whole fruits also contain fiber, vitamins, and antioxidants that reduce the hazardous effects of the fructose.

Nearly every canned or bottled commercial juice, on the other hand, are actually worse than soda, because a glass of juice is loaded with fructose, and a lot of the antioxidants are lost. Additionally the processed juice has methanol which has its own toxicities.

It is important to remember that fructose in and of itself isn't evil as fruits are certainly beneficial. (HFCS, however, is far from natural. It's a highly processed product that does not exist anywhere in nature. Changing the name to 'corn sugar' will not change this fact.)

But when you consume high amounts of fructose—regardless of its source—it will absolutely devastate your biochemistry and physiology.

Remember the AVERAGE fructose dose is 70 grams per day which exceeds the recommended limit by 300 percent.

So, I urge you to be careful with your fruit consumption as well—especially if you eat processed foods of any kind.

I recommend limiting your total fructose consumption to 25 grams per day, and your fructose from fruit to below 15 grams, since you are virtually guaranteed to consume plenty of "hidden" fructose in other foods.

Keep in mind, 15 grams of fructose is not much—it represents two bananas, one-third cup of raisins, or just two Medjool dates! (For comparison, however, the average 12-ounce can of soda contains 40 grams.)

If you're a raw food advocate, have a pristine diet, and exercise very well, then perhaps you could be the exception that could exceed this limit and stay healthy. Dr. Johnson has a handy chart, included below, which you can use to estimate how much fructose you're getting in your diet.

Fruit	Serving Size	Grams of Fructose
Limes	1 medium	0
Lemons	1 medium	0.6
Cranberries	1 cup	0.7
Passion fruit	1 medium	0.9
Prune	1 medium	1.2
Apricot	1 medium	1.3
Guava	2 medium	2.2
Date (Deglet Noor style)	1 medium	2.6
Cantaloupe	1/8 of med. melon	2.8

(Continued)

Fruit	Serving Size	Grams of Fructose
Raspberries	1 cup	3.0
Clementine	1 medium	3.4
Kiwifruit	1 medium	3.4
Blackberries	1 cup	3.5
Star fruit	1 medium	3.6
Cherries, sweet	10	3.8
Strawberries	1 cup	3.8
Cherries, sour	1 cup	4.0
Pineapple	1 slice (3.5" x .75")	4.0
Grapefruit, pink or red	1/2 medium	4.3
Boysenberries	1 cup	4.6
Tangerine/mandarin orange	1 medium	4.8
Nectarine	1 medium	5.4
Peach	1 medium	5.9
Orange (navel)	1 medium	6.1
Papaya	1/2 medium	6.3
Honeydew	1/8 of med. melon	6.7
Banana	1 medium	7.1
Blueberries	1 cup	7.4
Date (Medjool)	1 medium	7.7
Apple (composite)	1 medium	9.5
Persimmon	1 medium	10.6
Watermelon	1/16 med. melon	11.3
Pear	1 medium	11.8
Raisins	1/4 cup	12.3
Grapes, seedless (green or red)	1 cup	12.4
Mango	1/2 medium	16.2
Apricots, dried	1 cup	16.4
Figs, dried	1 cup	23.0

In his book, *The Sugar Fix*, Dr. Johnson includes detailed tables showing the content of fructose in different foods—an information base that isn't readily available when you're trying to find out exactly how much fructose is in various foods. I encourage you to pick up a copy of this excellent resource. It is important to note however, that Dr. Johnson does promote the use of artificial sweeteners in this book—which I do not recommend, under any circumstances.

One of the Simplest Ways to Improve Your Health NOW!

I recommend that you avoid sugar as much as possible, particularly fructose in all its forms.

This is especially important if you are overweight or have diabetes, high cholesterol, or high blood pressure as fructose will clearly worsen all of these conditions.

However, I also realize we don't live in a perfect world, and following rigid dietary guidelines is not always practical or even possible.

If you want to use a sweetener occasionally, this is what I recommend:

1. Use the herb stevia. My favorites are the flavored liquid bottles.
2. Use organic cane sugar in moderation.
3. Use organic raw honey in moderation, but remember, honey is also very high in fructose so it is not an ideal replacement.
4. Avoid ALL artificial sweeteners, which can damage your health even more quickly than fructose.
5. Avoid agave syrup since it is a highly processed sap that is *almost all fructose*. Your blood sugar will spike just as it would if you were consuming regular sugar or HFCS. Agave's meteoric rise in popularity is due to another great marketing campaign, but any health benefits present in the original agave plant are eliminated during processing.
6. Avoid so-called energy drinks, sports drinks, and vitamin-enriched waters because they are loaded with sugar, sodium and chemical additives. Rehydrating with pure, fresh water is your best choice.

    If you or your child is involved in athletics, I recommend you read my article Energy Rules for some great tips on how to optimize your child's energy levels and physical performance through optimal nutrition.

As a last precaution, if you have high fasting insulin levels (anything above 3), high blood pressure, high cholesterol, diabetes, or if you're overweight, I strongly recommend avoiding ALL sweeteners, including stevia, until you've normalized your condition.

This is because any sweetener can decrease your insulin sensitivity, which as I've mentioned before, which drives up your risk of nearly every disease there is, from diabetes to cancer.

Questions & Answers About High Fructose Corn Syrup

*S*ince its introduction in the 1970s, high fructose corn syrup has become a widely accepted American sweetener made from corn. This brochure offers answers to some frequently asked questions about this highly versatile sweetener.

What Is High Fructose Corn Syrup?

High fructose corn syrup (HFCS) is a sweetener made from corn and can be found in numerous foods and beverages on grocery store shelves in the United States. HFCS is composed of either 42 percent or 55 percent fructose, with the remaining sugars being primarily glucose and higher sugars. In terms of composition, HFCS is nearly identical to table sugar (sucrose), which is composed of 50 percent fructose and 50 percent glucose. Glucose is one of the simplest forms of sugar that serves as a building block for most carbohydrates. Fructose is a simple sugar commonly found in fruits and honey.

HFCS is used in foods and beverages because of the many benefits it offers. In addition to providing sweetness at a level equivalent to sugar, HFCS enhances fruit and spice flavors in foods such as yogurt and spaghetti sauces, gives chewy breakfast bars their soft texture and also protects freshness. HFCS keeps products fresh by maintaining consistent moisture. For more details, see *Facts About Caloric Sweeteners* on the back cover.

What Is the Difference Between HFCS and Sugar?

Sugar and HFCS have the same number of calories as most carbohydrates; both contribute 4 calories per gram. They are also equal in sweetness.

Sugar and HFCS contain nearly the same one-to-one ratio of two sugars—fructose and glucose:

- *Sugar is 50 percent fructose and 50 percent glucose.*
- *HFCS is sold principally in two formulations—42 percent and 55 percent fructose—with the balance made up of primarily glucose and higher sugars.*

HIGH FRUCTOSE CORN SYRUP QUICK FACTS

- Research confirms that high fructose corn syrup is safe and no different from other common sweeteners like table sugar and honey. All three sweeteners contain nearly the same one-to-one ratio of two sugars—fructose and glucose.
- High fructose corn syrup has the same number of calories as table sugar and is equal in sweetness. It contains no artificial or synthetic ingredients.
- The U.S. Food and Drug Administration granted high fructose corn syrup "Generally Recognized as Safe" status for use in food, and reaffirmed that ruling in 1996 after thorough review.
- High fructose corn syrup offers numerous benefits. It keeps food fresh, enhances fruit and spice flavors, retains moisture in bran cereals, helps keep breakfast and energy bars moist, maintains consistent flavors in beverages and keeps ingredients evenly dispersed in condiments.

Comparison of Caloric Sweetener Compositions

Component Percentage	HFCS-42	HFCS-55	Table Sugar	Invert Sugar*	Honey**
Fructose	42	55	50	45	49
Glucose	53	42	50	45	43
Other Sugars	5	3	0	10	5

* Hydrolyzed sugar comprised equally of free fructose and glucose.
** Does not sum to 100 because honey also contains some proteins, amino acids, vitamins and minerals.
For more information on different types of sweeteners, see www.SweetSurprise.com.

Once the combination of glucose and fructose found in HFCS and sugar are absorbed into the blood stream, the two sweeteners appear to be metabolized similarly in the body.

In terms of chemical structure, table sugar and HFCS differ by the bonding of their sugars. Table sugar is a disaccharide, in which fructose and glucose are linked by a chemical bond. Fructose and glucose are not bonded in HFCS, and so are sometimes referred to as "free" sugars.

Is HFCS a "Natural" Sweetener?

HFCS is made from corn, a natural grain product. HFCS contains no artificial or synthetic ingredients or color additives and meets the U.S. Food and Drug Administration's (FDA) requirements for use of the term "natural."

Is HFCS Sweeter Than Sugar?

No. When HFCS was developed, it was specifically formulated to provide sweetness equivalent to sugar. In order for food and beverage makers to use HFCS in place of sugar, it was important that it provide the same level of sweetness as sugar so that consumers would not perceive a difference in product sweetness and taste.

HFCS-55 has sweetness equivalent to sugar and is used in many carbonated soft drinks in the United States. HFCS-42 is somewhat less sweet and is used in many fruit-flavored noncarbonated beverages, baked goods and other products in which its special characteristics such as fermentability, lower freezing point, surface browning and flavor enhancement add value to the product. See *Facts About Caloric Sweeteners* on the back cover.

Is there a Correlation Between the Introduction of HFCS and the Rise of Obesity in the Past 30 Years?

Many factors contribute to the development of obesity, yet nutritionists, health experts and researchers generally agree that the chief cause is an imbalance between calories consumed and calories burned. Excessive calories can be consumed as fats, proteins, alcohol or carbohydrates. The American Dietetic Association notes, "Excess body fat [obesity] arises from the energy imbalance caused by taking in too much energy and expending too little energy. . . . Obesity is a complex problem and its cause cannot be simply attributed to any one component of the food supply such as sweeteners."

Further, the prevalence of obesity is increasing around the world, according to the International Obesity Task Force—even though use of HFCS outside of the United States is limited or nonexistent. In fact, sugar accounts for about 92 percent of caloric sweeteners consumed worldwide.

Scientific studies continue to find that HFCS does not contribute to obesity any differently than sugar.

An expert panel, led by Richard Forshee, Ph.D. of the University of Maryland Center for Food, Nutrition and Agriculture Policy, concluded that "the currently available evidence is insufficient to implicate HFCS per se as a causal factor in the overweight and obesity problem in the United States." The panel's report was published in the August 2007 issue of *Critical Reviews in Food Science and Nutrition*.

The report found that there are many other "plausible explanations for rising overweight and obesity rates" in the United States, listing such factors as "a decrease in smoking; an increase in sedentary occupations; an increase in two-income households and single-parent households; transportation and infrastructure changes that discourage physical activity; a decrease in PE classes and extracurricular sports programs in schools; an increase in sedentary forms of entertainment (i.e. TV/movie viewing, video games, etc.);

demographic changes (i.e. aging population, immigration, etc.); a decrease in food costs with increase in food availability; and changes in food consumption patterns."

Another peer-reviewed study summized that those who frequently consume sweetened soft drinks do not have a higher obesity rate than those who rarely drink them. The study found higher obesity rates correlated with several other factors, such as the amount of time in front of the computer or TV, or the consumption of high amounts of dietary fat.

Further, the November/December 2005 issue of *Nutrition Today* includes a report from the Center for Food, Nutrition and Agriculture Policy and its Ceres Workshop, which was compiled by scientists who reviewed a number of critical commentaries about HFCS. Their analysis found that HFCS is not a unique contributor to obesity, concluding "there is currently no convincing evidence to support a link between HFCS consumption and overweight/obesity."

Is HFCS Known to Cause Diabetes?

No. Many parts of the world, including Australia, Mexico and Europe, have rising rates of obesity and diabetes despite having little or no HFCS in their foods and beverages, which supports findings by the U.S. Centers for Disease Control and the American Diabetes Association that the primary causes of diabetes are obesity, advancing age and heredity.

U.S. Department of Agriculture (USDA) data show that per capita consumption of HFCS has been declining in recent years, yet the incidence of obesity and diabetes in the United States remains on the rise.

Has the Use of HFCS in the Food Supply Increased the Amount of Fructose in the Diet?

No. Many press reports note the dramatic increase of HFCS in the food supply since it's introduction in the 1970s. However, it is important to note that as HFCS consumption increased, sugar consumption decreased. USDA data show that the per capita use of HFCS in the U.S. food supply was matched with an almost equal decline, on a one-to-one basis, in the per capita use of sugar. In fact, consumption of HFCS has declined since its peak in 1999. The USDA estimates per capita sugar consumption in 2007 was 44.2 lbs per year and 40.1 lbs per year for HFCS.

As HFCS use increased in the United States, it replaced sugar in various foods and beverages on a nearly one-for-one basis, as the chart (lower right) illustrates. Yet because sugar and HFCS share a common composition, the ratio of fructose-to-glucose in the diet has remained relatively unchanged over time. This confirms that the approximate overall sugars mixture in the foods and beverages we consume—principally glucose and fructose—is nearly the same today as it was 30 years ago, before HFCS was introduced.

Is HFCS Considered a Safe Food Ingredient?

Yes. In 1983, the FDA listed HFCS as "Generally Recognized as Safe" (known as GRAS status) for use in food and reaffirmed that ruling in 1996. In its 1996 GRAS ruling, the FDA noted that "the saccharide composition (glucose to fructose ratio) of HFCS is approximately the same as that of honey, invert sugar and the disaccharide sucrose [table sugar]." GRAS recognition by FDA is important because it is only assigned to food ingredients that are recognized by experts as having a long history of safe use or as having their safety shown through adequate scientific studies.

According to the American Dietetic Association, "Consumers can safely enjoy a range of nutritive and nonnutritive sweeteners when consumed in a diet that is guided by current federal nutrition recommendations . . . as well as individual health goals."

Does Consumption of HFCS, as Compared to Sugar, Reduce the Ability of the Body to Produce Insulin?

No. Both have largely the same effect on insulin production. Insulin is essentially responsible for the uptake of glucose into cells and the lowering of blood sugar. All caloric sweeteners trigger an insulin response to a greater or lesser extent. Among common sweeteners, pure glucose triggers the greatest insulin release, while pure fructose triggers the least. Both table sugar and HFCS trigger about the same intermediate insulin release because they contain nearly equal amounts of glucose and fructose.

It is extremely rare for pure fructose to be consumed alone in the diet. Fructose is usually consumed together with glucose, as it is in HFCS, table sugar and honey. It is important to remember that no matter the source of the ingredients—whether from sugar or HFCS—the human body produces insulin in response to the whole meal consumed.

Kathleen J. Melanson, *et al.,* at the University of Rhode Island reviewed the effects of HFCS and sugar on circulating levels of glucose, leptin, insulin and ghrelin in a study group of lean women. All four tested substances have been hypothesized to play a role in metabolism and obesity. The study found "no differences in the metabolic effects" of HFCS and sugar in this short-term study, and called for additional studies of obese individuals and males.

Does the Body Process HFCS Differently Than Other Sugars?

No. HFCS contains approximately equal ratios of fructose and glucose, as does table sugar, honey and many fruits.

Once the combination of glucose and fructose found in HFCS and sugar are absorbed into the blood stream, the two sweeteners appear to be metabolized similarly in the body.

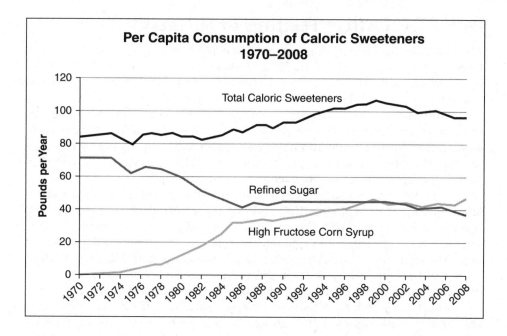

Per Capita Consumption of Caloric Sweeteners 1970–2008

Leptin and Ghrelin

Kathleen J. Melanson, *et al.*, at the University of Rhode Island reviewed the effects of HFCS and sugar on circulating levels of glucose, leptin, insulin and ghrelin in a study group of lean women. The study found "no differences in the metabolic effects" of HFCS and sugar.

Triglycerides

A study by Linda M. Zukley, *et al.*, at the Rippe Lifestyle Institute reviewed the effects of HFCS and sugar on triglycerides in a study group of lean women. This short-term study found "no differences in the metabolic effects in lean women [of HFCS] compared to sucrose," and called for additional studies of obese individuals or individuals at risk for the metabolic syndrome.

The metabolic syndrome is a collection of metabolic risk factors including abdominal obesity, atherogenic dyslipidemia, raised blood pressure, insulin resistance, prothrombotic state and proinflammatory state, which increase the chance of developing vascular disease.

Uric Acid

Joshua Lowndes, *et al.*, at the Rippe Lifestyle Institute reviewed the effects of HFCS and sugar on circulating levels of uric acid in a study group of lean women. Uric acid is believed to play a role in the development of the metabolic syndrome. This short-term study found "no differences in the metabolic effects in lean women [of HFCS] compared to sucrose," and called for additional studies of obese individuals and males.

Does HFCS Affect Feelings of Fullness?

No credible research has demonstrated that HFCS affects calorie control differently than sugar. A study by Pablo Monsivais, *et al.*, at the University of Washington found that beverages sweetened with sugar and HFCS, as well as 1% milk, all have similar effects on feelings of fullness.

Stijn Soenen and Margriet S. Westerterp-Plantenga, researchers at the Department of Human Biology at Maastricht University in The Netherlands, studied the effects of milk and beverages sweetened with sugar and HFCS on feelings of fullness. The researchers found "no differences in satiety, compensation or overconsumption" between the three beverages.

Tina Akhavan and G. Harvey Anderson at the Department of Nutritional Sciences, Faculty of Medicine, University of Toronto studied the effect of solutions containing sugar, HFCS and various ratios of glucose to fructose on food intake, average appetite, blood glucose, plasma insulin, ghrelin and uric acid in men. The researchers found that sugar, HFCS, and 1:1 glucose/fructose solutions do not differ significantly in their short-term effects on subjective and physiologic measures of satiety, uric acid and food intake at a subsequent meal.

Further, research by Almiron-Roig and co-workers in 2003 showed that a regular soft drink, orange juice and low-fat milk were not significantly different in their effects on hunger or satiety ratings, or in calories consumed at a subsequent meal.

Does HFCS Have a High Glycemic Index?

The Glycemic Index (GI) is a ranking of foods, beverages and ingredients based on their immediate effect on blood glucose levels. The GI measures how much blood sugar increases over a period of two or three hours after a meal. Some scientists believe that selecting foods with a low GI helps in diabetes management.

Carbohydrate foods that break down quickly during digestion have the highest GI. The benchmark in many indexes is glucose, with a GI of 100. Compared with glucose, the GI of fructose is very low with a value of 20. Sugar and honey, both with similar compositions to HFCS, have moderate GI values that range from 55 to 60. Although it has not yet been specifically measured, HFCS would be expected to have a moderate GI because of its similarity in composition to honey and sugar.

It must be kept in mind that the body does not respond to the GI of individual ingredients, but rather to the GI of the entire meal. Since *added sugars* (principally sugar and HFCS) typically contribute less than 20 percent of calories, it is clear that HFCS is a minor contributor to the overall GI in a normal diet.

Is HFCS Allergemic?

A number of cereal grains are known to cause allergic reactions (e.g., wheat, rye, barley), but corn is not among them. In fact, the prevalence of corn allergy in the U.S. is extremely low—estimated to affect no more than 0.016 percent of the general population. Food allergies are caused by certain proteins in foods. Nearly all of the corn protein is removed during the production of HFCS. Moreover, the trace protein remaining in HFCS likely bears little immunological resemblance to allergens in the original kernel.

How Is HFCS Made?

The corn wet milling industry makes HFCS from corn starch using a series of unit processes that include steeping corn to soften the hard kernel; physical separation of the kernel into its separate components—starch, corn hull, protein and oil; breakdown of the starch to glucose; use of enzymes to invert glucose to fructose; removal of impurities; and blending of glucose and fructose to make HFCS-42 and HFCS-55. . . .

Facts About Caloric Sweeteners

Sweeteners that contribute calories to the diet are called caloric or nutritive sweeteners. All common caloric sweeteners have the same composition: they contain fructose and glucose in essentially equal proportions. All caloric sweeteners require processing to produce a food-grade product.

Fructose	a simple sugar commonly found in fruits and honey
Glucose	a simple sugar that serves as a building block for most carbohydrates
High fructose corn syrup (HFCS)	free (unbonded) fructose and glucose in liquid (syrup) form; produced from corn
Sucrose	crystalline white table sugar; produced from sugar cane or sugar beets; fructose and glucose bonded together
Invert sugar	free fructose and glucose in liquid (syrup) form; produced from the breakdown of sugar
Hydrolyzed cane juice	free fructose and glucose in liquid (syrup) form; produced from the breakdown of cane juice
Honey	liquid (syrup) product; principally free fructose and glucose with minor levels of other sugars and some trace minerals
Fruit juice concentrate	concentrated, filtered, clarified fruit juice; fructose-to-glucose ratio varies by fruit source, but generally equivalent to other nutritive sweeteners (orange juice and grape juice have a fructose to glucose ratio of 1 to 1, while apple juice has a ratio of 2 to 1)

For more information on different types of sweeteners, see www.SweetSurprise.com.

(Continued)

Nutritional Characteristics

Common caloric sweeteners share the same general nutritional characteristics:

- each has roughly the same composition—equal proportions of the simple sugars fructose and glucose;
- each offers approximately the same sweetness on a per-gram basis;
- one gram (dry basis) of each adds 4 calories to foods and beverages;
- each is absorbed from the gut at about the same rate;
- similar ratios of fructose and glucose arrive in the bloodstream after a meal, which are indistinguishable in the body.

Since caloric sweeteners are nutritionally equivalent, they are interchangeable in foods and beverages with no measurable change in metabolism.

What if caloric sweeteners are removed from foods?

To replace one caloric sweetener with another provides no change in nutritional value. To remove sweeteners entirely from their commonly used applications and replace them with high intensity sweeteners would drastically alter product flavor and sweetness, require the use of chemical preservatives to ensure product quality and freshness, result in a reduction in perceived food quality (bran cereal with the caloric sweeteners removed would have the consistency of sawdust), and would likely require the addition of bulking agents to provide the expected texture, mouth feel or volume for most baked goods.

Why is HFCS used in specific applications?

If consumers are sometimes surprised to find HFCS in particular foods or beverages, it may be because they do not have a full appreciation of its versatility and value. HFCS often plays a key role in the integrity of food and beverage products that has little to do with sweetening. Here are some examples in popular products:

Baked goods	HFCS gives a pleasing brown crust to breads and cakes; contributes fermentable sugars to yeast-raised products; reduces sugar crystallization during baking for soft-moist textures; enhances flavors of fruit fillings
Yogurt	HFCS provides fermentable sugars; enhances fruit and spice flavors; controls moisture to prevent separation; regulates tartness
Spaghetti sauces, ketchup and condiments	HFCS enhances flavor and balance – replaces the "pinch of table sugar grandma added" to enhance spice flavors; balances the variable tartness of tomatoes
Beverages	HFCS provides greater stability in acidic carbonated sodas than sucrose; flavors remain consistent and stable over the entire shelf-life of the product
Granola, breakfast and energy bars	HFCS enhances moisture control, retards spoilage and extends product freshness; provides soft texture; enhances spice and fruit flavors

WWW.HFCSfacts.com

Corn Refiners Association, 1701 Pennsylvania Ave, NW, Suite 950, Washington, DC 20006-5806, phone: (202) 331-1634 fax: (202) 331-2054

CHALLENGE QUESTIONS

Does a Diet High in Fructose Increase Body Fat?

1. List foods that contain HFCS and the type HFCS (42 percent or 55 percent) they contain.
2. Based on the Mercola article, explain how fructose increases lipid levels in the body.
3. Compare the health effects of HFCS outlined by Mercola to the claims made by the Corn Refiners Association.
4. Obesity, type 2 diabetes, and the metabolic syndrome have increased since HFCS was introduced 30 years ago. Do you feel that HFCS has caused these problems? Justify your answer.
5. Select 10 processed foods from your kitchen cabinets. Determine which foods contain HFCS. Go to the grocery store and identify HFCS-free foods you could use in place of the items with HFCS and compare the prices of the two.
6. Consider the definition of "government subsidy." Do you think it is prudent for the U.S. government to subsidize corn in the United States? Explain your answer.

Additional Internet Resources

Corn Refiners Association

The national trade association representing the U.S. corn refining industry. Web site features educational material on corn products for people working in schools, government, journalism, and the agriculture sector.

http://www.corn.org/

The Sugar Association, Inc. (Sugar—Sweet by Name)

An association of U.S. sugar producers and growers. The Web site contains information on consumption trends by Americans and educational materials for "health professionals, media, government officials, and the public about sugar's goodness."

http://www.sugar.org

ISSUE 6

Does Eating Soy Improve Health?

YES: Silk Soy Nutrition Center, from "Health Benefits of Soy," *Soy Nutrition* (2009)

NO: Cornucopia Institute, from "Behind the Bean: The Heroes and Charlatans of the Natural and Organic Soy Foods Industry, the Social, Environmental, and Health Impacts of Soy," *Cornucopia Institute* (2009)

As you read the issue, focus on the following points:

1. Health claims about soy related to heart disease and menopause.
2. Controversies surrounding the FDA-approved claim that soy improves heart health.
3. Differences in soy foods eaten in Asian countries compared to soy foods consumed in the United States.
4. Accusations made by Cornucopia about the negative impact of hexane and isoflavones found in soy proteins.

ISSUE SUMMARY

YES: The Silk Soy Nutrition Center claims that scientific studies show that soy lowers cholesterol and reduces the risk of heart disease. They also claim that "populations eating diets high in soy-based foods have a lower incidence of breast cancer, prostate cancer and menopausal problems."

NO: Representing Cornucopia, Charlotte Vallayes and colleagues consider isolated soy proteins to be highly overrated, and possibly hazardous to the health of women and infants. They say that the heart health claim "is a direct product of corporate boardrooms searching for ways to sell more soy products—and to turn the soy 'waste' soy-products of soybean oil extraction into profits."

U se of soybeans originated in China around 1,100 BC and spread to Japan and Korea by the first century AD. In the United States, soybean seeds from China were planted in Georgia in 1765 and used by Americans to make soy sauce, which had been popular in Europe and China for many years. In the late 1870s, a few farmers began to plant soybeans to feed their livestock. By the turn of the century, the United States Department of Agriculture (USDA) began to encourage farmers to plant soybeans as an animal feed.

In 1904, George Washington Carver discovered that soybeans are a valuable source of protein and oil. A few years later, the American Soybean Association was established, which began to explore other varieties of soybeans and uses of them. Eventually, in the 1940s soybean farming really took off in America. Prior to this time, soybeans from China, which had been the major supplier of the world, were devastated by World War II. The U.S. farmers began to produce more soybeans.

Soybeans are the United States' second largest crop in cash sales and the number one export crop. About 40 percent of soybeans in the world come from the United States. The majority of the soybean crop is processed into oil and meal. Oil extracted from soybeans is made into margarine, shortening, and cooking oil. About 80 percent of the fats and oils in the average American diet are from soybeans.

Oil is extracted from soy (and other grains) using hexane. Cornucopia says that in conventional processing of oil from soybeans, the beans "are immersed in what the industry calls a 'hexane bath' before they are further processed into ingredients such as oil, soy protein isolate, or texturized soy protein (TVP)." And the soy protein in most nonorganic foods, such as vegetarian burgers and nutrition bars, is processed with the use of hexane. The concern of this extraction process is linked to the fact that hexane is a neurotoxin. And a small amount of hexane remains in the oil or protein after processing. Cornucopia points out that

> FDA does not set a maximum residue level in soy foods for hexane, and does not require that food manufacturers test for hexane residues. Very little research has been conducted concerning the potential effects of consuming hexane residues in edible oils and other processed foods that contain soy protein, such as infant formula, energy bars, protein powders, and meat analogs. Food processors that use hexane tend to assume that nearly all hexane residues evaporate before reaching the consumer, but this may not be the case. Studies on hexane-extracted oils show that not all hexane evaporates before consumption—residues can appear in foods.

Soy proteins are added to a variety of American foods. Recall the "mystery meat" in the school cafeteria. School lunch programs are allowed up to 30 percent of soy protein in ground meat products and still call it "ground meat." They are called "meat extenders" since they add weight and bulk to the food at a much lower cost than real meat. If schools have more than 30 percent soy, the burger must be called a "veggie-burger."

In 1999, the FDA approved the claim that soy protein is "heart-healthy." The claim states that *"25 grams of soy protein a day, as part of a diet low in saturated fat and cholesterol, may reduce the risk of heart disease. A serving of (name of food) provides _____ grams of soy protein."* After this claim, soy protein products have increased in popularity. (Recently, the American Heart Association has asked the FDA to remove this claim.)

In the "Dark Side of Soy," Mary Vance points out that "Asian diets include small amounts—about 9 grams a day—of primarily fermented soy products, such as miso, natto, and tempeh, and some tofu. Fermenting soy creates health-promoting probiotics, the good bacteria our bodies need to maintain digestive and overall wellness." But Vance says that in the United States, many processed snacks may have "over 20 grams of nonfermented soy protein in one serving." And with that comes possible traces of hexane.

So what is your opinion about soy proteins? After you read the selections, decide if you agree with the Silk Soy Nutrition Center that soy proteins are heart-healthy and isoflavones decrease hot flashes. Or do you agree with Cornucopia's accusations?

TIMELINE

1100 BC First soybeans are grown in China.

1765 Soybeans are grown in Georgia.

1860 A few farmers grow soybeans as animal feed.

1904 George Washington Carver isolates protein and oil from soybeans.

1940s Soybean production in the United States increases.

1960s Soybeans become more popular for oil and protein isolates.

1999 FDA allows "Heart-Healthy" claim on soy protein products.

DEFINITIONS

Isoflavone A phytoestrogen (plant based) found in soy products that mimics estrogen in the body.

Hexane Solvent used to extract oil from soybeans; it is a known neurotoxin.

Neurotoxin Chemical that damages the nerve cells.

Soy Protein Concentrates Produced by removing the oil and most of the soluble sugars from defatted soybean; contains 65–90 percent protein.

Soy Protein Isolates Also called isolated soy proteins, are essentially soy protein concentrates minus almost all their dietary fiber; contains at least 90 percent protein.

Textured Soy Protein Products Made by texturizing concentrates, isolates, or defatted soy flour.

YES

Health Benefits of Soy

Americans began adding more soy to their diets in recent years because scientific studies suggest that various soy products offer possible health benefits, such as lowering cholesterol and reducing the risk of heart disease.

Studies on the health benefits of soy are promising. Some studies suggest that populations eating diets high in soy-based foods have a lower incidence of breast cancer, prostate cancer and menopausal problems. More studies are needed, but in the meantime, soy foods are readily available in North America and can be easily added to a meal plan.

However, soy health claims are not necessarily applicable to all soy foods—just foods containing soy protein. Therefore, only foods identified as containing "whole soy," or foods that specify soy protein, are likely to offer these health benefits. Research is continuing on the health effects of isoflavones, one of the naturally occurring chemicals found in soy beans. It's important to note that some people may be allergic to soy bean products.

Soy Foods, Blood Cholesterol and Heart Health

Coronary heart disease (CHD) looms large over the United States, with almost 17 million Americans diagnosed. Approximately one-half of men and one-third of women in America will develop CHD after age 40.

While individual genetics play a role, four decades of rigorous investigation have proven the relationship between CHD and high blood cholesterol, high blood pressure, a sedentary lifestyle, smoking and obesity. In fact, research has shown that proper diet along with other heart-healthy lifestyle changes can actually reverse severe coronary atherosclerosis.

Soy foods can play an important role in a healthy diet designed to decrease dietary intake of cholesterol and saturated fat and reduce blood cholesterol levels. . . .

Elevated cholesterol is just one CHD risk factor. Evidence suggests that proper diet and soy foods may favorably affect several other factors as well, including elevated blood pressure and damaged arteries.

Soy Protein and Cholesterol

The first human study to show that soy protein lowered blood cholesterol was published in 1967. But it was not for another 30 years that the hypocholesterolemic effects of soy protein came to the attention of the medical community. In 1995, a comprehensive statistical analysis that included 34 studies showed conclusively that soy protein lowered LDLC. The decrease was a direct effect of the protein, and not because soy foods are low in saturated fat.

In 1999, the Food and Drug Administration issued the following health claim in recognition of the cholesterol-lowering effects of soy protein: 25 grams of soy protein per day, as part of a diet low in saturated fat and cholesterol, may reduce the risk of heart disease.

Since the health claim was issued, many more clinical trials have been conducted. Recent analyses confirm that soy protein lowers LDLC, but suggest that the magnitude of the effect is less than initially reported. Current estimates suggest that soy protein lowers LDLC by 3 to 5 percent. Although this impact appears modest, it is important to note that each 1 percent drop in LDLC is associated with as much as a 2 to 4 percent decrease in heart disease risk. As a result, soy protein could be associated with a CHD risk decrease of 10 to 15% over time.

Fatty Acid Content of Soy Foods

Many soy foods have relatively high polyunsaturated and low saturated fat content. In addition to offering the direct cholesterol-lowering effect of soy protein, these foods can help lower serum cholesterol by displacing higher-saturated fats from the diet.

In their recent review of the scientific literature, the American Heart Association (AHA) emphasized the important role that polyunsaturated fat can play in reducing risk of CHD. Not surprisingly therefore, the AHA recently stated that using soy protein as a replacement for animal protein products that are high in saturated fat may provide cholesterol-lowering benefits. Given the many heart-healthy attributes of soy foods, it is also not surprising that they have played a key role in research diets that have been shown to lower cholesterol by as much as 30 percent.

Furthermore, the soybean is one of the few good plant sources of the essential fatty acid, α-linolenic acid (ALA), an omega-3 fatty acid. Although the omega-3 fatty acid in soy differs from those found in certain types of fish, ALA is thought to have independent coronary benefits. A recent analysis found that subjects who consumed the most ALA were approximately 20 percent less likely to die from CHD than those who ate the least α-linolenic acid. Importantly, the difference between the high- and low-consumers was only 1.2 g/day, the amount found in about 3 cups of full-fat soy milk.

Interestingly, one recent study found that soy oil was almost as effective as fish oil in increasing heart rate variability, which decreases risk of cardiac arrhythmia. This is likely due to the ALA content of the soy.

Substantially reducing the risk of heart disease through lifestyle changes requires commitment and effort in many areas. But it is clear that soy foods play an important lead role in a heart-healthy diet.

Beyond Cholesterol Reduction

As noted previously, elevated cholesterol is one just one CHD risk factor. Happily, evidence suggests that the coronary benefits [of] soy foods extend beyond the effects of cholesterol reduction alone.

Several recently conducted Asian epidemiologic studies provide indirect support for the multiple coronary benefits of soy foods. For example, in a study involving nearly 65,000 women in Shanghai, China, even after controlling for a wide variety of risk factors, soy protein intake was associated with a reduction of more than 80% in the risk of having a heart attack. Similar benefits were noted in a study of Japanese women. A study in southern China found that higher soy food intake was associated with a 44 to 82% reduction in the risk of stroke among both men and women. Generally, the high-soy consumers in these studies were eating about two servings of soy each day. Such protective effects can't be attributed solely to a reduction in cholesterol.

These observations are intriguing, but only the results from strict clinical studies can be used as a basis for firm conclusions. Many such studies, although not all, have shown that soy foods may lower blood pressure, directly improve the health of the arteries, and make LDLC less harmful. Research into these effects continues.

Take Home Message

Soy foods have a lot to offer toward the goal of substantially reducing the risk of CHD. They provide high-quality protein but are low in saturated and high in polyunsaturated fat. They are also one of the few plant sources of omega-3 fatty acids. Furthermore, soy protein directly lowers blood cholesterol. There is also suggestive evidence that soy foods exert coronary benefits independent of their effects on blood cholesterol levels. For all of these reasons, soy foods can play an important role in a heart-healthy diet.

Soy & Menopausal Symptom Relief

. . . Menopause refers to the permanent ending of menstruation—a natural part of a woman's life cycle. As a result of the marked decline in estrogen levels that occurs at this time many women, as much as two-thirds of the menopausal population in Western countries, report having hot flashes. The decline in estrogen levels also leads to a loss in bone density as bone breakdown exceeds bone formation. Consequently, risk of developing osteoporosis and having a fracture increases. Although heart disease risk increases with age, the extent to which the lower estrogen levels contribute to this increase is a matter of debate.

For multiple reasons, many women object to the medicalization of menopauses and would prefer to avoid conventional medical treatments for menopause symptoms. Interest in identifying alternatives to medication increased markedly after the Women's Health Initiative Trial showed that the harmful effects of conventional hormone therapy—long the first choice for menopause symptom relief—outweighed the benefits. One of the most popular alternatives is soy, which is of interest to the medical community because it contains a group of compounds called isoflavones.

Isoflavones

Soy foods are a rich, and essentially unique, dietary source of isoflavones. Isoflavones are often referred to as phytoestrogens because they have a similar chemical structure to the hormone estrogen and exert estrogen-like effects under certain conditions. However, although isoflavones do share some common properties with estrogen, they are also different in many ways. In fact, in some tissues isoflavones have no effects, whereas estrogen does and in others, isoflavones have effects opposite to those of estrogen.

It is well recognized that Japanese women report having fewer hot flashes than European and North American women. Furthermore, some studies show that among Japanese women, those who consume the most soy have fewer hot flashes. There is also clinical evidence indicating that isoflavone supplements may offer an effective treatment for hot flashes.

Hot Flashes

For many women, hot flashes are a classic sign of menopause, and the most common reason for seeking treatment. A hot flash produces a sudden sensation of warmth or even intense heat that spreads over various parts of the body, especially the chest, face and head. In about 10 to 15 percent of women with hot flashes, the symptoms are frequent and severe.

More than 50 hot flash trials evaluating the efficacy of isoflavone-containing products have been conducted. To simplify the experimental design, many of the more recently conducted trials have used soy extracts (isoflavone supplements) rather than soy foods. Generally, most trials used the amount of isoflavones found in about two servings of soy foods. Over the past few years, several reviews and analyses of the study results have been published, but with mixed conclusions. Several explanations for the mixed data have been proposed.

In an attempt to provide some clarity about the effects of isoflavones on the alleviation of hot flashes, a team of investigators including those from the National Institutes of Health in Japan and the University of Minnesota conducted a comprehensive analysis of the literature, although only studies evaluating the effects of isoflavone supplements—not whole soy foods—were considered. Isoflavone supplements were found to reduce the frequency and severity of hot flashes by approximately 50 percent. For women suffering from hot flashes, this degree of relief represents a significant improvement in the quality of life.

Summary and Conclusion

For many women hot flashes can greatly impact quality of life. Although the hormone estrogen is known to alleviate hot flashes, for many reasons a large portion of menopausal women prefer to seek relief with a more natural, non-pharmaceutical approach. Clinical evidence suggests that soy foods may offer one such approach.

Soy Infant Formula & Safety

Controversy about soy exposure early in life focuses primarily on soy infant formula. Approximately 20 million infants have consumed this formula since the early 1960s without apparent adverse effects. In fact, there is essentially no human evidence that soy infant formula is harmful. Certainly, it is well established that soy formula produces normal short-term growth and development.

A retrospective study of health outcomes among adults 25–34 years old who were fed soy infant formula as infants concluded that it is safe.

More recently, Italian researchers found no hormonal abnormalities in children ages 7 months to 8 years who had consumed soy infant formula as infants for at least six months. Korean researchers also found no differences in anthropometric assessments and development tests among infants breast-fed, or fed soy or cow's milk formula.

It is important to distinguish soy infant formula from other soy foods. Soy infant formula is made from isolated soy protein, making it nutritionally different from soy milk, which is made from the whole soy bean and *is not designed and fortified to provide adequate nutrition for infants.*

Soy infant formula does provide high isoflavone exposure (approximately tenfold higher on a bodyweight basis) and serum isoflavone levels. However, it is not proven that isoflavones produce biological effects in infants. Huggett et al. noted that, in infants, isoflavones in serum are essentially completely conjugated and likely biologically inactive.

A recent report indicated that children in Taiwan consume as much as 35 to 40 mg/day of isoflavones (the amount found in about 2 cups of soy milk). No adverse effects have been reported in the study population either anecdotally or in scientific literature.

As infants progress into childhood and begin to incorporate different foods into their diet, isoflavone exposure on a body weight basis deceases dramatically.

Furthermore, the first few months of life represent an extremely sensitive period during which tissues may be more likely to respond to minor hormonal inputs compared to childhood. Early childhood represents a different physiological state than infancy.

Myths About Soy

Recent research has proven the health benefits of soy, but misconceptions remain among many health professionals and the public. Learn the truth behind some common soy myths.

Myth: Large Amounts of Soy Food Must Be Consumed to Get Health Benefits.

The U.S. Food and Drug Administration (FDA) recommends 25 g/day of soy protein as the threshold intake required for cholesterol reduction. This amounts to about three to four servings of soy foods since, on average, each serving of traditional soy foods (e.g., 1 cup of soy milk or 3 oz of tofu) contains roughly 6 to 8 grams of protein.

However, the soy protein recommendation applies only to reduction of heart disease risk and not other possible benefits of soy or isoflavones.

Using Asian diets for guidelines, particularly those in Japan and China, mean soy food consumption ranges dramatically, from as little as one to two servings of soy food per day to eight or more.

While the mean intake serves as a guideline, Asian epidemiologic studies still show that individuals eatrng above average amounts of soy have lower disease rates than those consuming the average or less.

In fact, clinical data suggests that 50 mg to 100 mg of isoflavones per day is necessary to derive health benefits. Two large, long-term osteoporosis trials funded by the U.S. government are studying the use of 80 and 120 mg/day of isoflavones. . . .

Myth: Soy Foods Contain Estrogen Compounds That May Cause Hormonal Disturbances

The isoflavones found in soy foods are sometimes called phytoestrogens (plant-estrogens) because they have a chemical structure similar to the hormone estrogen. Also, isoflavones can bind to estrogen receptors and exert some estrogen-like effects in cells.

That said, isoflavones are actually quite different from estrogen. Estrogen-like effects are rarely observed in clinical studies measuring the ingestion of soy foods or isoflavones.

This is not surprising since receptor binding—a common *in vitro* measure of estrogenicity—is a poor predictor of *in vivo* activity.

Compounds that bind to estrogen receptors often have different, and sometimes opposite, physiological effects depending upon how the isoflavone and receptor interact within different cells.

Clinical studies do show that neither soy foods nor isoflavones affect serum levels of testosterone or estrogen. In fact, several studies have found no effects on testosterone despite ingestion of isoflavones at levels that were 20 to 30 times higher than the typical Japanese intake.

No hormone-related abnormalities, such as thelarche or precocious puberty, have been ascribed to soy formula use in infants.

Myth: Fermented Soy Foods Are Better For You Than Nonfermented Soy Foods Since Traditional Asian Cuisine Uses Fermented Soy Products

It's true that many traditional Asian soy foods (miso, natto and tempeh) undergo fermentation while tofu and soy milk do not. It's also true that fermented and non-fermented soy foods have some nutritional differences.

In fermented soy foods, microbial hydrolysis causes a greater proportion of the isoflavones to occur as aglycones (without an attached sugar molecule), while the isoflavones of unprocessed soy beans appear as glycosides (with the sugar molecule attached). However, due to in vivo hydrolysis there is little difference in overall bioavailability between isoflavone aglycones and glycosides.

Fermentation reduces the phytate content of soy foods and, therefore improves mineral absorption somewhat, but the extent of this effect in unclear. Some research suggests that the allergenicity of soy protein may be reduced by fermentation.

Behind the Bean: The Heros and Charlatans of the Natural and Organic Soy Foods Industry, the Social, Environmental, and Health Impacts of Soy

Isolating Nutrients: Soy Protein

The Politics Behind the "Heart-Healthy" Claim

Food companies routinely place the needs of stockholders over considerations of public health, and the purpose of the soy 'heart-healthy' claim was to increase market share.

—Marion Nestle, Professor of Nutrition at New York University
and author of *Food Politics*

As best-selling author and [*The*] *New York Times Magazine* contributor Michael Pollan points out in his latest book, *In Defense of Food*, we should trust foods that are "real" and whole. When a food is part of a traditional diet throughout human history, chances are that it can be a safe and healthy part of a balanced and varied diet. He suggests that new, inventive, novel, genetically engineered, and highly processed foods be met with a healthy dose of skepticism. He refers to them as "food-like substances."

Scientists agree; Dr. William Helferich, who studies the effects of soy on cancer, found in one study that isolated soy ingredients stimulated the growth of tumors. He notes, however, that some studies have shown that more wholesome soy foods such as soy flour did not have this effect. Such scientific studies support the idea that wholesome foods, minimally processed, are preferable to highly processed foods including isolated ingredients.

Soy foods such as tofu, tempeh, and miso have been part of the diet in Asian countries for centuries. William Shurtleff, co-author of *The Book of Tofu* and director of the SoyInfo Center, points out that Okinawa, Japan, has the highest consumption of tofu in that country, and its people have the longest life span compared to other regions. Soy foods such as tofu and soymilk from many companies that are rated highly in our scorecard are only minimally processed—soaked, heated, ground, strained, curdled, and pressed—and are not processed more than other traditional foods such as cheese and yogurt produced from cow's milk.

The SoyInfo Center, which promotes soy foods as a healthy, environmentally friendly, and humane alternative to meat products, has a database of approximately 1,000 scientific, peer-reviewed, published studies showing health benefits of eating soy foods.

However, not all researchers and advocacy groups agree about the benefits of soy in the human diet. The Weston A. Price Foundation's (WAPF) president, Sally Fallon, objects to the widespread promotion of soy foods as a miracle health food. WAPF's web site lists scientific studies indicating that soy consumption, especially excessive consumption of isolated soy ingredients, may be harmful to one's health. Fallon says, "The propaganda that has created the soy sales miracle is all the more remarkable because only a few centuries ago the soybean was considered unfit to eat—even in Asia."

Today, many Americans are familiar with the health benefits of soy foods through the FDA-approved "heart-healthy" claim on food packages containing soy protein ingredients. It is important for American consumers to understand that this health claim is a direct product of corporate boardrooms searching for ways to sell more soy products—and to turn the soy "waste" by-products of soybean oil extraction into profits. In 1999, the FDA approved a health claim for soy foods: "Diets low in saturated fat and cholesterol that include 25 grams of soy protein a day may reduce the risk of heart disease."

This health claim was first proposed in 1998 not by doctors or public interest groups, but by Protein Technologies International, a company that stood to profit tremendously if it could convince the American public to buy more soy protein (Protein Technologies International is now known as Solae). The key to selling more soy protein was convincing the American public that soy protein was a desirable product, and a health claim would go a long way to establish this reputation. Health claims on foods have long been recognized as an effective marketing tool. Even on the FDA web site, the value of health claims to corporate profits is acknowledged: Brian Sansoni, senior manager for public policy at the Grocery Manufacturers of America is quoted as saying that "[a health claim] brings attention to products; there are newspaper and TV stories and information on the Internet." So what better way to convince the American public to spend money on soy protein than to widely spread the message that it could reduce heart disease? With corporate funding, scientists published articles making this connection. In a cloud of controversy and doubt in the scientific community, the FDA allowed the health claim in 1999, opening the door to a new world of opportunity and profits for soy processors.

In her book *Food Politics,* which explores the influences of the food industry on nutrition policy, New York University Professor of Nutrition Marion Nestle explains that "under the various laws and court decisions governing FDA's actions in this area, the agency must approve claims backed up by well-conducted studies, no matter how out of context they may be or how quickly contradicted by further research."

When the U.S. Agency for Healthcare Research and Quality reviewed the scientific evidence related to soy protein and cardiovascular health in 2005, it found few credible studies to support the heart health claim. Based on its review of more than 50 scientific studies, the committee found that soy consumption had "no effect on HDL cholesterol levels," "neither isoflavone or soy protein dose was associated with net effect on triglycerides," and "soy consumption does not appear to affect blood pressure level."

The American Heart Association (AHA) has also strongly recommended that the heart-healthy claim be removed. The AHA initially supported the heart-healthy claim for soy protein, but after their expert committee reviewed the scientific research, the organization rescinded its support. In February 2008, the president of the AHA wrote to the FDA that the organization "strongly recommends that FDA revoke the soy protein and CHD health claim." He stated, "There are no evident benefits of soy protein consumption on HDL cholesterol, triglycerides, lipoprotein (a), or blood pressure. Thus, the direct cardiovascular health benefit of soy protein or isoflavone supplements is minimal at best."

Many of the studies showing benefits to eating highly processed soy foods, as well as the health claim on these highly processed foods, are funded either by corporations or soybean grower associations. These foods contain novel and highly processed isolated nutrients, and organic consumers looking for wholesome nutrition should be skeptical of "heart-healthy" claims found on these food packages.

Whole foods, minimally processed, are preferable. Soy foods such as tofu, and especially fermented soy foods such as miso and tempeh, have long been part of traditional Asian diets and are viewed by many as a much more wholesome and healthful choice than foods with soy protein isolates or concentrates.

Soy Isoflavones as Estrogen Mimicks

When the whole food is consumed you get a very different effect than if you consume the concentrated constituents individually.

—Dr. William Helferich, Professor of Nutrition, University of Illinois

The debate surrounding the benefits or risks of soy consumption is not confined to heart health. The effects of isoflavones in soy, substances that are structurally similar to the hormone estrogen, are worth noting. Soy isoflavones are phytoestrogens; they bind to estrogen receptors in the human body and exhibit weak estrogen-like effects. Due to these estrogen-mimicking qualities, isoflavones have been touted as a foodbased way of reducing symptoms, such as hot flashes, in menopausal women. However, a review of scientific studies on this topic concludes that "the available evidence suggests that phytoestrogens available as soy foods, soy extracts, and red clover extracts do not improve hot flushes or other menopausal symptoms."

When it comes to cancer risk, soy isoflavones have made contradictory headlines as both dangerous and beneficial. Some studies suggest that these phytoestrogens reduce the risk of cancer, while others suggest that isoflavones stimulate the growth of estrogen-sensitive breast cancer cells in rodents.

Some scientists are also concerned with the effects of phytoestrogens on infants given soy-based infant formula. Researchers found that the daily exposure of infants to isoflavones in soy infant formulas is 6- to 11-fold higher on a bodyweight basis than the dose that has hormonal effects in adults consuming soy foods. Researchers have also reported that soy-formulafed infants had isoflavone concentrations that were 13,000- to 22,000-fold higher than normal estradiol concentrations in infants. Breast milk, which is the gold standard for infant nutrition, contributes negligible amounts of isoflavones, which is why some scientists are very concerned that these high rates of isoflavones in soy formula may disrupt the normal course of development in infants.

Others argue that there is little evidence that infants raised on soy-based formula experience adverse effects as adults. One retrospective study of 811 men and women found no differences in height, weight, time of puberty, general health, or pregnancy outcomes between those fed soy-based formula as infants and those fed cow's-milk-based formula. The only difference was that women fed soy-based formula as infants reported significantly greater use of asthma or allergy drugs than women fed cow's-milk formula as infants. While isoflavone concentrations in soy-formula-fed infants are much higher than in human-milk-fed infants, a recent study found that the levels of certain hormones did not differ. These researchers did, however, point out that whether phytoestrogens in soy formula are biologically active in infants is still an open question. Additional research in this critical area certainly seems to be justified.

Infants on soy-based formula consume the same foods at every single feeding for the first months of crucial development. The only nutritionally "normal" food for human infants is human milk, which is why the fact that soy-based infant formula contains more than 10,000 times of a hormone-mimicking substance is disturbing. For this reason, the French government will require manufacturers to remove isoflavones from all soy-based infant formula, as well as require manufacturers to put a warning label on soy foods. When Dr. Mariette Gerber, M.D., Ph.D., who is a professor at the University of Montpelier in France, presented the potential health hazards of isoflavones in infant formula while explaining the new French regulations to industry representatives in the United States, the corporate officials scoffed that even onions have possible health hazards. Quite aptly, Dr. Gerber replied: "Do you feed infants [an exclusive diet of] only onions?"

CHALLENGE QUESTIONS

Does Eating Soy Improve Health?

1. Define isoflavone and soy protein isolate.
2. List the health benefits of soy foods outlined by Silk Soy Nutrition Center.
3. Describe the health concerns that Cornucopia has about soy.
4. Your best friend's infant is allergic to regular infant formula. Her pediatrician recommends switching to a soy protein–based formula. Your friend asks for your opinion on soy formula. What would you tell her and why?
5. You work for the Silk Soy Nutrition Center and have been asked to write a written response to the accusations that soy is not heart-healthy and the isoflavones and hexane residue may be damaging to health. Write a two- to three-paragraph response defending your company.

Additional Internet Resources

Silk Soy Nutrition Center

An education and research initiative promoting a better understanding of soy nutrition among health care professionals and the general population. Provides information and resources on a variety of health topics related to soy products.

http://soynutrition.com/SoyHealth.html

Cornucopia Institute

Wisconsin-based Cornucopia Institute will engage in educational activities supporting the ecological principles and economic wisdom underlying sustainable and organic agriculture. Provides research-based information on investigations on agricultural issues to consumers, family farmers, and the media.

http://www.cornucopia.org

Internet References . . .

Overweight and Obesity Information

Overweight and obesity information from the Centers for Disease Control and Prevention (CDC) is provided on this Web site. The CDC is a federal agency that provides statistical information and dietary advice about obesity prevention and control. Maps on this site document dramatic increases in statewide levels of obesity from the late 1980s to the present. Click on the "Obesity Trends" button to see these maps.

http://www.cdc.gov/nccdphp/dnpa/obesity/index.htm

National Association to Advance Fat Acceptance

The Fat Acceptance Movement on the Web site lists organizations and resources devoted to promoting the human and civil rights of "people of size."

http://www.naafaonline.com/dev2/

The National Academies Press: Dietary Reference Intakes

The Food and Nutrition Board of the Institute of Medicine (IOM) is responsible for developing the national standards for intake of essential nutrients, the Dietary Reference Intakes. This site provides the entire report, which includes sections on energy intake and expenditure.

http://www.nap.edu/books/0309085373/html/

President's Council on Physical Fitness and Sports

The President's Council on Physical Fitness and Sports promotes research and education about the benefits of physical activity. This Web site provides information and reports, but also offers links to physical activity resources of federal agencies and private health organizations.

http://www.fitness.gov

UNIT 3

Diet, Physical Activity, and Weight Maintenance

*I*ssues in this unit focus on obesity, which is the most publicized nutrition-related problem in the world. Debate begins with issues surrounding the definition of desirable and undesirable body size. Body mass index (BMI) has been used to classify the degree of underweight or overweight for the last two decades. The ease of calculating BMI has made it so popular. Both the authors for Issue 7 agree that BMI is not accurate in determining the level of body fat, but they debate on whether physicians should use it to diagnose obesity.

- Should Physicians Use BMI to Assess Overall Health?

- Do Americans Need Vitamin D Supplements?

- Does Obesity Cause a Decline in Life Expectancy?

ISSUE 7

Should Physicians Use BMI to Assess Overall Health?

YES: Jeremy Singer-Vine, from "Beyond BMI: Why Doctors Won't Stop Using an Outdated Measure for Obesity," *Slate* (July 20, 2009)

NO: Keith Devlin, from "Do You Believe in Fairies, Unicorns, or the BMI?" *Mathematical Association of America,* http://www.maa.org/devli/devlin_05_09.html (May 2009)

As you read the issue, focus on the following points:

1. How and when the BMI formula was developed.
2. Mathematical and health-related criticisms of using BMI as an indicator of health status.
3. Why BMI is currently used by physicians and the medical community to assess weight status.

ISSUE SUMMARY

YES: Journalist Jeremy Singer-Vine points out that "the circumference around a person's waist provides a much more accurate reading of his or her abdominal fat and risk for disease than BMI." But "waist measurements require slightly more time and training than it takes to record a BMI." Since BMI is cheap and easy to use, physicians and the medical community will continue using it.

NO: Mathematician Keith Devlin, who is classified as "overweight" by his physician, since Keith's BMI is 25.1, despite his 32-inch waist, considers that BMI is "numerological nonsense." While he applauds the knowledge that physicians have about the human body and health issues, he feels that the mathematics behind the BMI calculations are used irresponsibly and says BMI should not be used in medical practice. He calls for mathematicians to demand responsible use of math.

Although the mathematical formula to determine BMI was developed almost 200 years ago, it was not widely used to define weight status until the 1980s. Its popularity is credited to Ancel Keys who wrote the "Indices of

Relative Weight and Obesity" that was published in the July 1972 issue of *Journal of Chronic Disease*. The results of his landmark study have become one of the most debated topics related to obesity. Based on data from more than 7,400 men in five countries, Keys examined which of the height–weight formulas matched up best with each subject's body-fat percentage. It turned out that the best predictor came from the Quetelet Index, developed in 1832. Keys renamed it the "body mass index," and the rest is history.

Before BMI, doctors generally used weight-for-height tables, one for men and one for women, which included ranges of body weights for each inch of height. The tables were originally developed by the Association of Life Insurance Medical Directors of America in 1897 and refined by the Metropolitan Life Insurance Company in 1943. They provide a weight range based on frame size, with desirable weight higher as frame size increases. One of the criticisms with the tables was that a decision had to be made to determine if the person had a small, medium, or large frame. The larger the frame, the more weight a person could weigh, and many people would classify themselves as "large" framed to prevent being in the overweight category.

BMI became an international standard for obesity measurement in the 1980s. The public learned about BMI in the late 1990s, when the government launched an initiative to encourage healthy eating and exercise.

Originally, men with a BMI of 27.8 and above were defined as "overweight," whereas women with a BMI of 27.3 or higher were classified as overweight. In 1998, the National Institutes of Health (NIH) lowered the overweight threshold to 25 to match international guidelines. The move added 30 million Americans who were previously in the "healthy weight" category to the "overweight" category. Today, the NIH advises doctors to include BMI in a complete assessment of a person's overall health. The 2000 NIH report *The Practical Guide: Identification, Evaluation, and Treatment of Overweight and Obesity in Adults* includes the following recommendation for physicians:

> Assessment of a patient should include the evaluation of body mass index (BMI), waist circumference, and overall medical risk. . . . There is evidence to support the use of BMI in risk assessment since it provides a more accurate measure of total body fat compared with the assessment of body weight alone. Neither bioelectric impedance nor height–weight tables provide an advantage over BMI in the clinical management of all adult patients, regardless of gender. Clinical judgment must be employed when evaluating very muscular patients because BMI may overestimate the degree of fatness in these patients. The recommended classifications for BMI [were] adopted by the Expert Panel on the Identification, Evaluation, and Treatment of Overweight and Obesity in Adults and endorsed by leading organizations of health professionals.

Is BMI valuable in assessing health and should it be part of routine health assessments? As you read the following articles, decide why BMI has become the "standard measure" to determine weight status, the pitfalls associated with it, and why physicians continue to use it.

TIMELINE:

1832 Belgian's Adolphe Quetelet devises Quetelet Index

1897 A standard height and weight table is adopted by the Association of Life Insurance Medical Directors of America.

1942 The Metropolitan Life Insurance Company introduces their standard height-weight tables for men and women.

1972 Ancel Keys publishes "Indices of Relative Weight and Obesity" in the July issue of *Journal of Chronic Disease* and coins the term "body mass index" (BMI) which use Quetelet's Index to assess weight status.

1985 CDC adopts BMI to describe weight status using BMI over 27.8 for men and 27.3 for women to define overweight.

1998 NIH lowers "overweight" BMI threshold from 27.8 to 25 to match international (WHO) guidelines.

DEFINITION

Polymath A person whose expertise spans a significant number of different subject areas.

YES

Jeremy Singer-Vine

Beyond BMI: Why Doctors Won't Stop Using an Outdated Measure for Obesity

A few extra pounds can extend your life. Or so chirped the press, reporting on a recent study from the journal *Obesity*. The new research, which supports earlier findings that being slightly overweight is associated with living longer, has added to an ongoing controversy over how we measure obesity. At the center of this debate is the body mass index, a simple equation (your weight in kilograms divided by the square of your height in meters) that has in the last decade claimed a near-monopoly on obesity statistics. Some researchers now argue that this flawed and overly reductive measure is skewing the results of research in public health.

For years, critics of the body mass index have griped that it fails to distinguish between lean and fatty mass. (Muscular people are often misclassifed as overweight or obese.) The measure is mum, too, about the distribution of body fat, which makes a big difference when it comes to health risks. And the BMI cutoffs for "underweight," "normal," "overweight," and "obese" have an undeserved air of mathematical authority. So how did we end up with such a lousy statistic?

Belgian polymath Adolphe Quetelet devised the equation in 1832 in his quest to define the "normal man" in terms of everything from his average arm strength to the age at which he marries. This project had nothing to do with obesity-related diseases, nor even with obesity itself. Rather, Quetelet used the equation to describe the standard proportions of the human build—the ratio of weight to height in the average adult. Using data collected from several hundred countrymen, he found that weight varied not in direct proportion to height (such that, say, people 10 percent taller than average were 10 percent heavier, too) but in proportion to the square of height. (People 10 percent taller than average tended to be about 21 percent heavier.)

The new equation had little impact among the medical community until long after Quetelet's death. While doctors had suspected the ill effects of obesity since at least as far back as the 18th century, their evidence was anecdotal. The first large-scale studies of obesity and health were conducted in the early 20th century, when insurance companies began using comparisons of height and weight among their policyholders to show that "overweight" people died earlier than those of "ideal" weight. Subsequent actuarial and medical studies found that obese people were also were more likely to get diabetes, hypertension, and heart disease.

By the early 1900s, it was well-established that these ailments were the result of having too much adipose tissue—so the studies used functions of height and weight as little more than a proxy for determining how much excess body fat people had. It would have been more accurate for the actuaries to compare longevity data with more direct assessments of body fat—such as caliper-measured skinfold thickness or hydrostatic weighing. But these data were much harder for them to obtain than standard information on height, weight, and sex.

The insurance tables gave us correlations between these physical characteristics and expected lifespan. But medical researchers needed a standard measure of fatness, so they could look at the health outcomes of varying degrees of obesity across an entire population. For decades doctors couldn't agree on the best formula for combining height and weight into a single number—some used weight divided by height; others used weight divided by height cubed. Then, in 1972, physiology professor and obesity researcher Ancel Keys published his "Indices of Relative Weight and Obesity," a landmark study of more than 7,400 men in five countries. Keys examined which of the height-weight formulas matched up best with each subject's body-fat percentage, as measured more directly. It turned out that the best predictor came from Quetelet: weight divided by height squared. Keys renamed this number the *body mass index.*

The new measure caught on among researchers who had previously relied on slower and more expensive measures of body fat or on the broad categories (underweight, ideal weight, and overweight) identified by the insurance companies. The cheap and easy BMI test allowed them to plan and execute ambitious new studies involving hundreds of thousands of participants and to go back through troves of historical height and weight data and estimate levels of obesity in previous decades.

Gradually, though, the popularity of BMI spread from epidemiologists who used it for studies of population health to doctors who wanted a quick way to measure body fat in individual patients. By 1985, the NIH started defining obesity according to body mass index, on the theory that official cutoffs could be used by doctors to warn patients who were at especially high risk for obesity-related illness. At first, the thresholds were established at the 85th percentile of BMI for each sex: 27.8 for men and 27.3 for women. (Those numbers now represent something more like the 50th percentile for Americans.) Then, in 1998, the NIH changed the rules: They consolidated the threshold for men and women, even though the relationship between BMI and body fat is different for each sex, and added another category, "overweight." The new cutoffs—25 for overweight, 30 for obesity—were nice, round numbers that could be easily remembered by doctors and patients.

Keys had never intended for the BMI to be used in this way. His original paper warned against using the body mass index for individual diagnoses, since the equation ignores variables like a patient's gender or age, which affect how BMI relates to health. It's one thing to estimate the average percent body fat for large groups with diverse builds, Keys argued, but quite another to slap a number and label on someone without regard for these factors.

Now Keys' misgivings are gaining traction across the world of medicine: BMI simply doesn't work when it comes to individual measurements. Whether that's a problem worth worrying about is another question. Some researchers say BMI's inaccuracies in individual measurements result in little actual harm, since an attentive doctor can spot outliers and adjust her diagnosis accordingly. But this begs the question: If a doctor's eye is better than BMI at determining a patient's healthy weight, then why use BMI for individuals at all?

No matter how attentive they might be, health professionals have increasingly used body mass index to justify lifestyle recommendations for their patients. And online BMI calculators—there's even one hosted by the NIH—invite people to diagnose themselves without any medical supervision whatsoever. Faulty readings could promote a negative self-image among healthy people and lead them to pursue unnecessary diets. Or the opposite problem: People with a little too much body fat might be lulled into a false sense of complacency by a misleading BMI.

A recent critique (PDF) of the body mass index in the journal *Circulation* suggests that BMI's imprecision and publicity-friendly cutoffs may distort even the large epidemiological studies. (There's no definitive count of how many people are misclassified by BMI, but several studies have suggested that the error rate is significant for people of certain ages and ethnicities.) It's impossible to know which studies have been affected and in what direction they might have been skewed.

Our continuing reliance on BMI is especially grating given there's a very reasonable alternative. It turns out that the circumference around a person's waist provides a much more accurate reading of his or her abdominal fat and risk for disease than BMI. And wrapping a tape measure around your gut is no more expensive than hopping on a scale and standing in front of a ruler. That's why the American Society for Nutrition, the American Diabetes Association, and other prominent medical groups have lately promoted waist circumference measurements as a supplement to, or replacement for, the body mass index.

Yet few doctors have made the switch. The waist measurements require slightly more time and training than it takes to record a BMI reading, and they don't come with any official cutoffs that can be used to make easy assessments. The sensitivity of doctors to these slight inconveniences signals just how difficult it will be to unseat Quetelet's equation. The body mass index is cheap and easy, and it has the incumbent advantage. In short, BMI is here to stay—despite, but also because of, its flaws.

Do You Believe in Fairies, Unicorns, or the BMI?

. . . [T]he Centers for Disease Control and Prevention classify people as overweight on a number called the body mass index, or BMI]. Overweight, according to this CDC endorsed metric, are athletes and movie stars Kobe Bryant, George Clooney, Matt Damon, Johnny Depp, Brad Pitt, Will Smith, and Denzel Washington. Tom Cruise scored even worse, being classified as downright obese, as was Arnold Shwarzenegger when he was a world champion body-builder. With definitions like that, no wonder Americans think of themselves as having an overweightness epidemic. (Using the CDC's BMI measure, 66 percent of adults in the United States are considered overweight or obese.)

Yes, it's that time of year again, when I go for my annual physical. I know the routine. My body mass index regularly comes out at around 25.1, putting me just into the "overweight category," and the doctor sends me a fact sheet telling me I need to lose weight, exercise more, and watch my diet. Notwithstanding that fact that the person *he has just examined* has a waist of 32 inches, rides a bicycle in the California mountains between 120 and 160 miles a week, competes regularly in competitive bicycle events up to 120 miles, does regular upper-body work, has a resting pulse of 59 beats per minute, blood pressure generally below 120/80, healthy cholesterol levels, and eats so much broccoli I would not be surprised to wake up one morning to find it sprouting out of my ears. . . . No, I'm not a "fitness junkie." And I am certainly not a professional athlete. I'm just a fairly ordinary guy who was lucky to be born with good genes and who likes being outdoors on my bike when the weather is nice, and I have a competitive streak that makes me want to race every now and then. A not atypical Californian academic, in fact.)

Why do we have this annual BMI charade? Why would otherwise well-educated medical professionals ignore the evidence of their own eyes? Because the BMI is one of those all-powerful magic entities: a *number*. And not just any number, but one that is generated by a *mathematical formula*. So it has to be taken seriously, right?

Sadly, despite that fact that completion of a calculus course is a necessary prerequisite for entry into medical school, the medical profession often seems no less susceptible than the general population to a misplaced faith in anything that looks mathematical, and at times displays unbelievable naivety when it comes to numbers.

(Actually, my own physician is smarter than that. I chose him because he is every bit as compulsive an outdoorsy, activities person as I am, and he seems to know that the BMI routine we go through is meaningless, though the system apparently requires that he play along and send me the "You need to lose weight and exercise more" letter, despite our having spent a substantial part of the consultation discussing our respective outdoors activities.)

So what is the BMI? A quick web search on "BMI" or "body mass index" will return hundreds of sites, many of which offer calculators to determine your BMI. All you do is feed in your height and your weight, and out comes that magic number. Many of the sites also give you a helpful guide so you can interpret the results. For instance, the CDC website gives these ranges:

below 18.5 = Underweight

18.5 to 24.9 = Ideal

25.0 to 29.9 = Overweight

30.0 and above = Obese

(Tom Cruise, with a height of 5'7" and weight of 201 lbs, has a body mass index of 31.5, while the younger Schwarzenegger, at just over six feet tall and about 235 pounds, had a BMI over 31. The figures I quote for athletes and movie stars are from data available on the web, and I believe they are accurate, or were when the information was entered.)

Some sites even tell you how this mystical number is calculated:

BMI = weight in pounds/(height in inches × height in inches) × 703

Hmmm. No mention of waist-size here? Or rump? That's odd. Isn't the amount of body fat you carry related to the size belt you need to wear or how baggy is the seat of the jeans the belt holds up?

And what about the stuff inside the body? One thing all those "overweight" and "obese" athletes and movie stars have in common is that they have very little fat and a lot of muscle, and possibly also stronger, healthier bones. Now, a quick web-search reveals that mean density figures for these three body component materials are: fat 0.9 gm/ml, muscle 1.06 gm/ml, and bone 1.85. In other words, the less fat you have, and the more your body weight is made up of muscle and bone, the greater the numerator in that formula, and the higher your BMI. In other words, if you are a fit, healthy individual with little body fat but strong bones and lots of muscle, the CDC (and other medical authorities) will classify you as overweight. Note the absurdity of the whole approach. If I actually did take my physician's BMI-triggered, form-letter advice and exercise more, I would put on even more muscle and lose even more of what little body fat I have, and my BMI would increase! With a medical profession like that, who needs high cholesterol as an enemy?

Admittedly, those same authorities also say that a male waistline of 40 inches and a female waistline of 35 inches are where "overweight" begins. But this of course is totally inconsistent with their claim that the BMI is a reliable indicator of excess body fat. In contrast, it is consistent with my observation that it is the density of the stuff inside the body that is key, not the body weight. If you ignore that wide variation in densities, then of course you will end up classifying people with 32 inch waists as overweight. Yet this blatant inconsistency does not seem to cause anyone to pause and ask if there is not something just a little odd going on here. Isn't it time to inject some science into this part of medical practice?

Time to take a look at that BMI formula and ask where it came from. I've already noted that it ignores waistline, rump-size, and the different densities of fat, muscle, and bone. Next question: Why does it mysteriously *square* the height? What possible *scientific* reason could there be to square someone's height for heaven's sake? (Multiplying height by girth at least has some rationale, as it would give an indication of total body volume, but it would put girth into the denominator in the formula, which is not what you want.) But height squared? Beats me.

Then there is that mysterious number 703. Most websites simply state it as if it were some physical constant. A few make the helpful remark that it is a "conversion factor." But I could not find a single source that explains what exactly it is converting. It did not take long to figure it out, however. The origins of the BMI, of which more later, goes back to a Belgian mathematician. The original formula would thus have been in metric units, say

BMI = weight in kilograms/(height in meters × height in meters)

To give an equivalent formula in lbs and inches, you need to solve the following equation for C

$$1lb/(1in \times 1in) \times C = 0.4536kg/(0.0254m \times 0.0254m)$$

which gives C = 703 (to the nearest whole number).

Well that at least explains the 703. Sort of. But given that the formula is self-evidently just a kludge, why not round it to 700. Stating it as 703 gives an air of accuracy the formula cannot possibly merit, and suggests that the folks who promote this piece of numerological nonsense either have no real understanding of numbers or they want to blind us by what they think we will accept as science.

Another question: Why is the original metric formula expressed in terms of kilograms and meters? Why not grams and centimeters? Or some other units? Well, given the scientific absurdity of dividing someone's weight by the square of their height it really doesn't matter what the units are. I suspect the ones chosen were so that the resulting number comes out between 1 and 100, and thus looks reassuringly like a percentage. I'm beginning to suspect my "blind-us-with-science" conspiracy theory may be right after all.

So which clown first dreamt up this formula and why? Well, it was actually no clown at all, but one of the smartest mathematicians in history: the Belgian polymath Lambert Adolphe Jacques Quetelet (1796–1874). Quetelet received a doctorate in mathematics from the University of Ghent in 1819, and went on to do world class work in mathematics, astronomy, statistics, and sociology. Indeed, he was one of the founders of both these last two disciplines, being arguably the first person to use statistical methods to draw conclusions about societies.

It is to Quetelet that we can trace back that important figure in twentieth century society, the "average man." (You know, the one with 2.4 children.) He (Quetelet, not the average man) realized that the most efficient way to organize society, allocate resources, etc. was to count and measure the population, using statistical methods to determine the (appropriate) "averages." He looked for mathematical formulas that would correlate, *numerically,* with those "average citizens."

(Elementary) statistics being the highly simplistic (but extremely powerful) tool[,] it is generally not difficult to find simple formulas that correlate pretty well with society's averages. You just play around with a few variables until you find a formula that fits. If you can provide a scientific rationale for the formula, so much the better, and you are justified in having more confidence in your ability to use the formula predictively. But it is generally enough that your formula is empirically representative. *Provided* that all you are doing is trying to draw conclusions about society as a whole . . . Quetelet knew what he was doing. Many since then, including, it appears, the CDC, do not.

The absurdity of using statistical formulas to make *any* claim about a single individual is made clear by the old joke about the man who had his head in the refrigerator and his feet in the fire: on average he felt fine!

Yet the CDC says, on its website,

"BMI is a reliable indicator of body fatness for people."

Nonsense. It is off-the-charts unreliable for me and for millions of people like me. True, a few sentences later, the CDC—doubtless at the insistence of their lawyers—says

"However, BMI is not a diagnostic tool."

You're telling me! Come on guys, either the BMI is, as you claim, "a reliable indicator of body fatness," in which case you can so use it or, as you also admit, it cannot be used to diagnose excess body fat. Which is it to be?

The CDC's answer becomes clear as we read on. Lest we note the disclaimer that the BMI cannot be used to diagnose excess body fat and demand a more reliable procedure, they immediately go on to mask their legal get-out by claiming,

> Calculating BMI is one of the best methods for population assessment of overweight and obesity. Because calculation requires only height and weight, it is inexpensive and easy to use for clinicians and for the general public. The use of BMI allows people to compare their own weight status to that of the general population.

I'll say it again. This statement is completely false; there are several *much* better methods—some of which the CDC actually lists on its website! The only part of this second statement that I see as having any validity is the very telling admission that the BMI method is inexpensive and easy to use.

There is another problem with the manner in which the CDC and other medical authorities explain the BMI. Notice that the interpretive ranges into the categories underweight, ideal, etc. are given to one decimal place, with equal signs. This suggests a level of precision in the formula that cannot possibly be warranted. (Some sites give two decimal places.) It would at least be more honest to give the ranges like this:

below 19 you are likely to be underweight

between 19 and 25 is the range generally viewed as ideal

between 25 and 30 suggests you may be overweight

if you are above 30 you are likely to be obese

This would not make the formula any less a piece of numerological junk, but at least would indicate that the ranges are just rough guidelines. The only possible reason for giving the ranges in the precise way the CDC does is to try to mislead patients that there is something scientific going on here. It's a classic example of "lying with numbers."

So here is the beef (lean, of course). The BMI was formulated, *by a mathematician, not a medical physician,* to provide a simple, easy-to-apply mathematical formula to give a broad, society-level measure of weight issues. It has absolutely no scientific or medical basis. It is based purely on a crude statistical analysis. It measures a general society trend, it does not predict. Since the majority of people today (and in Quetelet's time) lead fairly sedentary lives, and are not particularly active, the formula tacitly assumes low muscle mass and high relative fat content. It applies moderately well when applied to such people because it was formulated by focusing on them! Duh!

But this is not science—it's not even good statistics—and as a result it should not be accepted medical practice, to be regularly flouted as some magical mumbo jumbo and used as a basis for giving advice to patients. (For heavens sake, even seven times Tour de France winner Lance Armstrong's own Livestrong website provides a BMI calculator, despite the fact that the boss himself, when he first became a world champion cyclist—before chemotherapy for cancer took 20 lbs off him—found himself classified as "overweight" by the wretched formula.)

As you might expect, once a piece of numerological nonsense is held up for proper scrutiny, it doesn't take long before the whole house of cards comes tumbling down. The surprising thing about the BMI is that it has survived for so long (as a diagnostic for individual patients). As I indicated earlier, I suspect that much of the appeal is that it is a single number, easy to calculate, given an air of scientific authority by a *mathematical formula,* and (just as my earlier quote from the CDC makes clear) it is easier and quicker to base a diagnosis on a number than on properly examining a patient. But at that point you have stopped doing medicine and are just doing kindergarten arithmetic.

The good news is, at last there is hope of some sanity entering the story. The science (the real science) is finally coming. For instance, a study of 33,000

American adults, published recently in the *American Journal of Public Health* (Vol 96, No. 1, January 2006, 173–178), showed that male life expectancy is greatest for BMIs of about 26—overweight under the CDC's rule, and equivalent to 24 lb extra for the typical man. For women, the study found an optimum BMI of about 23.5, about 7 lbs heavier than the CDC's standard.

The paper's author, Dr Jerome Gronniger, a government scientist, concluded that, "I found that the current definitions of obesity and overweight are imprecise predictors of mortality risk."

"Imprecise predictors"? Gronniger was clearly using "scientific understatement." It was, after all, a scientific publication. Dr David Haslam, the clinical director of Britain's National Obesity Forum was more blatant in a statement he made to the Daily Telegraph newspaper: "It's now widely accepted that the BMI is *useless* for assessing the healthy weight of individuals." (My italics.) [In the UK, it's almost impossible to be sued, and there is no massive lobby of medical insurance companies looking for ways to avoid paying for your medical treatment, so commentators tend to be more forthcoming.]

Of course, any mathematician surely knew what Haslam now confirms the moment he or she took their first look at Quetelet's formula. It screams "junk math."

Numbers are one of the most powerful tools we have to understand our world and to improve our lives. But like all powerful tools, when used irresponsibly, they can do more harm than good. Medical professionals have enormous knowledge and experience that we all benefit from. I do regularly go for my annual physical, and for the most part I listen to my physician's advice. He knows a lot more than I do about the human body and health issues. I trust him—for the most part. But when the BMI comes up, we are definitely into territory where my expertise trumps his, and I can recognize a piece of numerological nonsense when I see it, and as a result I ignore that part of the proceedings. But if trained medical practitioners, backed up by august professional organizations such as a the CDC, are still so over-awed by such rubbish (mathematics does that to people, I see it all the time) that they continue to preach it as if it were gospel, then how can a patient with less mathematical sophistication hope to resist this annual incantation.

Since the entire sorry saga of the BMI was started by a mathematician—one of us—I think the onus is on us, as the world's experts on the formulation and application of mathematical formulas, to start to eradicate this nonsense and demand the responsible use of our product.

Heavens, next thing we know, some authority will be claiming that the golden ratio is the aspect ratio of the rectangle most pleasing to the human eye. Where will it all end?

After all that, I think I need a good long bike ride over the mountains to bring my blood pressure down.

CHALLENGE QUESTIONS

Should Physicians Use BMI to Assess Overall Health?

1. Describe how the BMI formula was developed.
2. List the strengths and weaknesses of using BMI to assess health status of an adult.
3. You have been asked to conduct a study to determine the prevalence of overweight and obesity of students at your university. Ideally, you need to include at least 1000 students in your study. Outline the steps you would take to gather and assess the weight status and the methods you would use.
4. Compare the probable health status of a man whose BMI is 31 and has a waist circumference of 35.5 inches to a nonpregnant woman whose BMI is 27 and waist circumference is 36 inches.
5. What is your opinion on use of BMI for weight assessment by physicians and in other health care practices. Write a letter to NIH explaining your position on the topic; include specific suggestions to either change the method or strengthen the existing one.

Additional Internet Resources

National Heart, Lung, and Blood Institute, National Institutes of Health

Contains guidelines related to health and body weight. Includes a BMI calculator and other interactive tools and resources helpful to physicians and other health care professionals.

http://www.nhlbi.nih.gov/

ISSUE 8

Do Americans Need Vitamin D Supplements?

YES: Jane Brody, from "What Do You Lack? Probably Vitamin D," *The New York Times* (July 26, 2010)

NO: Institute of Medicine, from "Dietary Reference Intakes for Calcium and Vitamin D," The National Academies Press (November 30, 2010)

As you read the issue, focus on the following points:

1. Possible health problems associated with vitamin D deficiency.
2. Differences in blood levels of vitamin D considered to be deficient by the nutrition experts mentioned by Brody compared to the level proposed by the Institute of Medicine (IOM).
3. The amount of vitamin D recommended in the Brody selection compared to the EAR and RDA established by the IOM.
4. Possible problems associated with excessive vitamin D intake.

ISSUE SUMMARY

YES: Best-selling author Jane Brody says that a huge part of the population is deficient in vitamin D and that studies indicate deficiency increases risk of cancer, heart disease, arthritis, and a host of other conditions. She also reports that the "experts" recommend a supplement of 1,000–2,000 IU each day.

NO: The 14-member committee appointed by the Institute of Medicine (IOM) of the National Academy of Sciences to set the Recommended Dietary Allowance (RDA) disagrees. After reviewing over 1,000 studies and listening to testimonies from scientists and other stakeholders, the committee set the RDA for people up to age 70 years at 600 IU and at 800 IU for those over age 70. They conclude that few people are deficient in vitamin D and the only health benefit is the vitamin's role in bone health.

J ane Brody is on target when she writes that vitamin D is "the most talked-about and written-about supplement of the decade." From the 1930s until the late 1990s, it was generally agreed that most healthy people had ample vitamin D. Because we synthesize the vitamin when our skin is exposed to sun, the vitamin is commonly known as "the sunshine vitamin." During warm months, if our arms and legs are exposed to sun, we make plenty of vitamin D. According to the Vitamin D Council, "Caucasian skin produces approximately 10,000 IU vitamin D in response to 20–30 minutes summer sun exposure." However, during colder months, when our skin is covered in warm clothing, additional vitamin D may be needed. People with dark skin and those who just don't go outside may also need additional vitamin D.

In the early 1920s, scientists found that rickets could be corrected by giving a fat-soluble substance that was found in cod liver oil. It was originally called the "antirachitic factor" and later named vitamin D. In those days, a daily dose of cod liver oil was given to ward off rickets. The first recommendation about the amount of vitamin D needed was published with the initial edition of the RDA in 1941. It was set at 400 IU because it was the approximate amount found in one teaspoon of cod liver oil. The RDA remained at this level until 1997, when the IOM expanded the RDA to the Dietary Reference Intakes (DRIs). The DRIs are composed of four different nutrient recommendation levels:

- **Estimated Average Requirements (EARs)** The amount expected to satisfy the needs of 50 percent of people.
- **Recommended Dietary Allowances (RDAs)** The daily intake level of a nutrient considered sufficient to meet the requirements of nearly all (97–98 percent) healthy individuals.
- **Adequate Intake (AI)** Used when no RDA has been established; the amount believed to be adequate for all healthy people.
- **Tolerable Upper Intake Levels (ULs)** The highest amount that should be consumed; higher intakes may be harmful.

The 1997 IOM committee that developed the new guidelines did not find adequate scientific studies to base an actual RDA on so they established an AI. The AI for people up to age 50 years was 200 IU, from ages 51 to 70 the AI was 400 IU, and for those over age 70 it increased to 600 IU.

For most of the 20th century, vitamin D was thought to only be involved in bone formation. In the 1980s, a few researchers began looking at other functions of the vitamin and the fact that many cells contain vitamin D receptors. Since that time, reports of new research have exploded. In fact, the IOM reviewed over 1,000 studies to base their 2010 recommendations. Even though many of the studies conclude that we need 1,000–2,000 IU each day and supplements are the only way to achieve the level of vitamin D needed for optimal health, the IOM report disagrees. They report that the majority of Americans and Canadians are receiving adequate vitamin D. Although the IOM did increase the RDA to 600 IU for people up to age 70 years and to 800 IU for those over age 70, the amount is still lower than what most scientists recommend.

You may be wondering what foods provide vitamin D. Actually, hardly any foods contain it naturally. A few oily fishes are the main sources. Recently, the mushroom industry has developed a portabella mushroom that contains about 400 IU of the vitamin. They found that exposing the mushrooms to UV light stimulates vitamin D synthesis, similar to the way our bodies produce it. Studies are still being conducted to see the bioavailability of the UV-produced vitamin D in mushrooms to humans. Most milk processors fortify fluid milk with 100 IU per 8 ounces. This, combined with the small amount of natural vitamin D in milk, translates into about 120 IU per 8 ounces. Notice in the table below that fluid milk is the only significant dairy source of the vitamin. Also, look at the amount found in various types of mushrooms—only those exposed to UV light are significant sources. With recent interest on the vitamin, more cereal and juice manufacturers fortify their products.

Vitamin D Content of Selected Foods

Food	Serving Size	IU Vitamin D
Salmon, sockeye canned with bones	3 oz	667
Salmon, pink canned with bones	3 oz	466
Cod liver oil	1 tsp	450
Mushroom, portabella exposed to UV light	1 cup	384
Tuna, light canned in oil	3 oz	229
Sardines, canned in oil	3 oz	164
Tuna, canned in water	3 oz	154
Orange juice, fortified with vitamin D	8 oz	137
Milk, low fat	8 oz	120
Flounder	3 oz	103
Total Raisin Bran cereal	1 cup	100
Froot Loops cereal	1 cup	41
Mushrooms, shitake	1 cup	41
Cod, Atlantic	3 oz	40
Egg, medium	1	36
Mushrooms, canned	1 cup	12
Mushrooms, portabella not exposed to UV light	1 cup	9
Butter	1 tbsp	9
Cheddar cheese	1 oz	7
Mushrooms, white button	1 cup	7
Ice cream, vanilla	½ cup	5

Source: USDA Nutrient Database (retrieved January 8, 2011).

The debate of this issue focuses on how much vitamin D is needed and whether supplements are required to get this amount. The new RDA is higher than it was in previous years, but it's still much lower than the amount many researchers recommend. Even Harvard's Nutrition Faculty recommends a supplement of vitamin D for most people in their Health Eating Pyramid.

A criticism of the new IOM RDA was posted on Harvard's *The Nutrition Source*. They consider that the new guidelines are

> . . . overly conservative about the recommended intake, and they do not give enough weight to some of the latest science on vitamin D and health. For bone health and chronic disease prevention, many people are likely to need more vitamin D than even these new government guidelines recommend.

The Vitamin D Council, which is sponsored by four companies that market vitamin D supplements or sell tanning beds, considers that adults may need 5,000 IU per day and that blood levels should be between 50 and 80 ng/ml. Both of these levels are much higher than that of the IOM recommendations. (The IOM considers blood levels of 20 ng/ml to be adequate.) The Council also recommends 20–30 minutes of midday sun exposure from spring to fall and to use a tanning bed during the winter months.

What do you think? Do you agree with the IOM that few people are deficient in vitamin D and intakes of 600 IU are adequate? Or do you think we need to take supplements of vitamin D for optimal health?

YES

Jane Brody

What Do You Lack? Probably Vitamin D

Vitamin D promises to be the most talked-about and written-about supplement of the decade. While studies continue to refine optimal blood levels and recommended dietary amounts, the fact remains that a huge part of the population—from robust newborns to the frail elderly, and many others in between—are deficient in this essential nutrient.

If the findings of existing clinical trials hold up in future research, the potential consequences of this deficiency are likely to go far beyond inadequate bone development and excessive bone loss that can result in falls and fractures. Every tissue in the body, including the brain, heart, muscles and immune system, has receptors for vitamin D, meaning that this nutrient is needed at proper levels for these tissues to function well.

Studies indicate that the effects of a vitamin D deficiency include an elevated risk of developing (and dying from) cancers of the colon, breast and prostate; high blood pressure and cardiovascular disease; osteoarthritis; and immune-system abnormalities that can result in infections and autoimmune disorders like multiple sclerosis, Type 1 diabetes and rheumatoid arthritis.

Most people in the modern world have lifestyles that prevent them from acquiring the levels of vitamin D that evolution intended us to have. The sun's ultraviolet-B rays absorbed through the skin are the body's main source of this nutrient. Early humans evolved near the equator, where sun exposure is intense year round, and minimally clothed people spent most of the day outdoors.

"As a species, we do not get as much sun exposure as we used to, and dietary sources of vitamin D are minimal," Dr. Edward Giovannucci, nutrition researcher at the Harvard School of Public Health, wrote in *The Archives of Internal Medicine*. Previtamin D forms in sun-exposed skin, and 10 to 15 percent of the previtamin is immediately converted to vitamin D, the form found in supplements. Vitamin D, in turn, is changed in the liver to 25-hydroxyvitamin D, the main circulating form. Finally, the kidneys convert 25-hydroxyvitamin D into the nutrient's biologically active form, 1,25-dihydroxyvitamin D, also known as vitamin D hormone.

A person's vitamin D level is measured in the blood as 25-hydroxyvitamin D, considered the best indicator of sufficiency. A recent study showed that maximum bone density is achieved when the blood serum level of 25-hydroxyvitamin D reaches 40 nanograms per milliliter or more.

"Throughout most of human evolution," Dr. Giovannucci wrote, "when the vitamin D system was developing, the 'natural' level of 25-hydroxyvitamin D was probably around 50 nanograms per milliliter or higher. In modern societies, few people attain such high levels."

A Common Deficiency

Although more foods today are supplemented with vitamin D, experts say it is rarely possible to consume adequate amounts through foods. The main dietary sources are wild-caught oily fish (salmon, mackerel, bluefish, and canned tuna) and fortified milk and baby formula, cereal and orange juice.

People in colder regions form their year's supply of natural vitamin D in summer, when ultraviolet-B rays are most direct. But the less sun exposure, the darker a person's skin and the more sunscreen used, the less previtamin D is formed and the lower the serum levels of the vitamin. People who are sun-phobic, babies who are exclusively breast-fed, the elderly and those living in nursing homes are particularly at risk of a serious vitamin D deficiency.

Dr. Michael Holick of Boston University, a leading expert on vitamin D and author of *The Vitamin D Solution* (Hudson Street Press, 2010), said in an interview, "We want everyone to be above 30 nanograms per milliliter, but currently in the United States, Caucasians average 18 to 22 nanograms and African-Americans average 13 to 15 nanograms." African-American women are 10 times as likely to have levels at or below 15 nanograms as white women, the third National Health and Nutrition Examination Survey [NHANES III] found.

Such low levels could account for the high incidence of several chronic diseases in this country, Dr. Holick maintains. For example, he said, in the Northeast, where sun exposure is reduced and vitamin D levels consequently are lower, cancer rates are higher than in the South. Likewise, rates of high blood pressure, heart disease, and prostate cancer are higher among dark-skinned Americans than among whites.

The rising incidence of Type 1 diabetes may be due, in part, to the current practice of protecting the young from sun exposure. When newborn infants in Finland were given 2,000 international units a day, Type 1 diabetes fell by 88 percent, Dr. Holick said.

The current recommended intake of vitamin D, established by the Institute of Medicine, is 200 I.U. a day from birth to age 50 (including pregnant women); 400 for adults aged 50 to 70; and 600 for those older than 70. While a revision upward of these amounts is in the works, most experts expect it will err on the low side. Dr. Holick, among others, recommends a daily supplement of 1,000 to 2,000 units for all sun-deprived individuals, pregnant and lactating women, and adults older than 50. The American Academy of Pediatrics recommends that breast-fed infants receive a daily supplement of 400 units until they are weaned and consuming a quart or more each day of fortified milk or formula.

Given appropriate sun exposure in summer, it is possible to meet the body's yearlong need for vitamin D. But so many factors influence the rate of vitamin D formation in skin that it is difficult to establish a universal public health recommendation. Asked for a general recommendation, Dr. Holick suggests going outside in summer unprotected by sunscreen (except for the face, which should always be protected) wearing minimal clothing from 10 a.m. to 3 p.m. two or three times a week for 5 to 10 minutes.

Slathering skin with sunscreen with an SPF of 30 will reduce exposure to ultraviolet-B rays by 95 to 98 percent. But if you make enough vitamin D in your skin in summer, it can meet the body's needs for the rest of the year, Dr. Holick said.

Can You Get Too Much?

If acquired naturally through skin, the body's supply of vitamin D has a built-in cutoff. When enough is made, further exposure to sunlight will destroy any excess. Not so when the source is an ingested supplement, which goes directly to the liver.

Symptoms of vitamin D toxicity include nausea, vomiting, poor appetite, constipation, weakness and weight loss, as well as dangerous amounts of calcium that can result in kidney stones, confusion and abnormal heart rhythms.

But both Dr. Giovannucci and Dr. Holick say it is very hard to reach such toxic levels. Healthy adults have taken 10,000 I.U. a day for six months or longer with no adverse effects. People with a serious vitamin D deficiency are often prescribed weekly doses of 50,000 units until the problem is corrected. To minimize the risk of any long-term toxicity, these experts recommend that adults take a daily supplement of 1,000 to 2,000 units.

Dietary Reference Intakes for Calcium and Vitamin D

Calcium and vitamin D are two essential nutrients long known for their role in bone health. Over the last ten years, the public has heard conflicting messages about other benefits of these nutrients—especially vitamin D—and also about how much calcium and vitamin D they need to be healthy.

To help clarify this issue, the U.S. and Canadian governments asked the Institute of Medicine (IOM) to assess the current data on health outcomes associated with calcium and vitamin D. The IOM tasked a committee of experts with reviewing the evidence, as well as updating the nutrient reference values, known as Dietary Reference Intakes (DRIs). These values are used widely by government agencies, for example, in setting standards for school meals or specifying the nutrition label on foods. Over time, they have come to be used by health professionals to counsel individuals about dietary intake.

The committee provided an exhaustive review of studies on potential health outcomes and found that the evidence supported a role for these nutrients in bone health but not in other health conditions. Overall, the committee concludes that the majority of Americans and Canadians are receiving adequate amounts of both calcium and vitamin D. Further, there is emerging evidence that too much of these nutrients may be harmful.

Health Effects of Vitamin D and Calcium Intake

The new reference values are based on much more information and higher-quality studies than were available when the values for these nutrients were first set in 1997. The committee assessed more than one thousand studies and reports and listened to testimony from scientists and stakeholders before making its conclusions. It reviewed a range of health outcomes, including but not limited to cancer, cardiovascular disease and hypertension, diabetes and metabolic syndrome, falls, immune response, neuropsychological functioning, physical performance, preeclampsia, and reproductive outcomes. This thorough review found that information about the health benefits beyond bone health—benefits often reported in the media—were from studies that provided often mixed and inconclusive results and could not be considered reliable. However, a strong body of evidence from rigorous testing substantiates the importance of vitamin D and calcium in promoting bone growth and maintenance.

Dietary Reference Intakes

The DRIs are intended to serve as a guide for good nutrition and provide the basis for the development of nutrient guidelines in both the United States and Canada. The science indicates that on average 500 milligrams of calcium per day meets the requirements of children ages 1 through 3, and on average 800 milligrams daily is appropriate for those ages 4 through 8 (see table for the Recommended Dietary Allowance—a value that meets the needs of most people). Adolescents need higher levels to support bone growth: 1,300 milligrams per day meets the needs of practically all adolescents. Women ages 19 through 50 and men up to 71 require on average 800 milligrams daily. Women over 50 and both men and women 71 and older should take in 1,000 milligrams per day on average to ensure they are meeting their daily needs for strong, healthy bones.

Determining intake levels for vitamin D is somewhat more complicated. Vitamin D levels in the body may come from not only vitamin D in the diet but also from synthesis in the skin through sunlight exposure. The amount of sun exposure one receives varies greatly from person to person, and people are advised against sun exposure to reduce the risk of skin cancer. Therefore, the committee assumed minimal sun exposure when establishing the DRIs for vitamin D, and it determined that North Americans need on average 400 International Units (IUs) of vitamin D per day (see table for the Recommended Dietary Allowances—values sufficient to meet the needs of virtually all persons). People age 71 and older may require as much as 800 IUs per day because of potential changes in people's bodies as they age.

Dietary Reference Intakes for Vitamin D

Life Stage Group	Estimated Average Requirement (IU/day)	Recommended Dietary Allowance (IU/day)	Upper Level Intake (IU/day)
Infants 0 to 6 months	*	*	1,000
Infants 6 to 12 months	*	*	1,500
1–3 years old	400	600	2,500
4–8 years old	400	600	3,000
9–13 years old	400	600	4,000
14–18 years old	400	600	4,000
19–30 years old	400	600	4,000
31–50 years old	400	600	4,000
51–70 years old males	400	600	4,000
51–70 years old females	400	600	4,000
>70 years old	400	800	4,000
14–18 years old, pregnant/lactating	400	600	4,000
19–50 years old, pregnant/lactating	400	600	4,000

*For infants, adequate intake is 400 IU/day for 0 to 6 months of age and 400 IU/day for 6 to 12 months of age.

Questions About Current Intake

National surveys in both the United States and Canada indicate that most people receive enough calcium, with the exception of girls ages 9–18, who often do not take in enough calcium. In contrast, postmenopausal women taking supplements may be getting too much calcium, thereby increasing their risk for kidney stones.

Information from national surveys shows vitamin D presents a complicated picture. While the average total intake of vitamin D is below the median requirement, national surveys show that average blood levels of vitamin D are above the 20 nanograms per milliliter that the IOM committee found to be the level that is needed for good bone health for practically all individuals. These seemingly inconsistent data suggest that sun exposure currently contributes meaningful amounts of vitamin D to North Americans and indicates that a majority of the population is meeting its needs for vitamin D. Nonetheless, some subgroups—particularly those who are older and living in institutions or who have dark skin pigmentation—may be at increased risk for getting too little vitamin D.

Before a few years ago, tests for vitamin D were conducted infrequently. In recent years, these tests have become more widely used, and confusion has grown among the public about how much vitamin D is necessary. Further, the measurements, or cut-points, of sufficiency and deficiency used by laboratories to report results have not been set based on rigorous scientific studies, and no central authority has determined which cut-points to use. A single individual might be deemed deficient or sufficient, depending on the laboratory where the blood is tested. The number of people with vitamin D deficiency in North America may be overestimated because many laboratories appear to be using cut-points that are much higher than the committee suggests is appropriate.

Tolerable Upper Levels of Intake

The upper level intakes set by the committee for both calcium and vitamin D represent the safe boundary at the high end of the scale and should not be misunderstood as amounts people need or should strive to consume. While these values vary somewhat by age, as shown in the table, the committee concludes that once intakes of vitamin D surpass 4,000 IUs per day, the risk for harm begins to increase. Once intakes surpass 2,000 milligrams per day for calcium, the risk for harm also increases.

As North Americans take more supplements and eat more of foods that have been fortified with vitamin D and calcium, it becomes more likely that people consume high amounts of these nutrients. Kidney stones have been associated with taking too much calcium from dietary supplements. Very high levels of vitamin D (above 10,000 IUs per day) are known to cause kidney and tissue damage. Strong evidence about possible risks for daily vitamin D at lower levels of intake is limited, but some preliminary studies offer tentative signals about adverse health effects.

Conclusion

Scientific evidence indicates that calcium and vitamin D play key roles in bone health. The current evidence, however, does not support other benefits for vitamin D or calcium intake. More targeted research should continue. However, the committee emphasizes that, with a few exceptions, all North Americans are receiving enough calcium and vitamin D. Higher levels have not been shown to confer greater benefits, and in fact, they have been linked to other health problems, challenging the concept that "more is better."

CHALLENGE QUESTIONS

Do Americans Need Vitamin D Supplements?

1. List the health problems associated with low levels of vitamin D.
2. State the blood levels of vitamin D that Brody considers are desirable compared to the levels considered adequate by the IOM.
3. Explain the controversies related to blood levels of vitamin D used to determine vitamin D status.
4. Plan a one-day menu that provides the RDA for vitamin D for an 80-year-old female. Use either MyPyramid (http://www.mypyramid.gov) or the USDA Nutrient Database (http://www.nal.usda.gov/fnic/foodcomp/search/) to determine vitamin D content of the foods.
5. Select 20 types of fish or other seafood. Using the USDA Nutrient Database, compile a table with the amount of vitamin D in a 3-ounce serving of each.

Additional Internet Resources on Vitamin D

The Institute of Medicine (IOM)

A nonprofit, nongovernmental organization that is part of the National Academy of Sciences. The IOM recruits experts to examine policies and make recommendations pertaining to public health and nutrition.

http://www.iom.edu/Reports/2010/Dietary-Reference-Intakes-for-Calcium-and-Vitamin-D.aspx

The Office of Dietary Supplements of the National Institutes of Health

The federal office whose mission is to expand knowledge and understanding of dietary supplements by evaluating scientific information, supporting and disseminating research results, and educating the public about supplements. The site provides resources for health professionals and consumers and "Quick-Fact" sheets on various vitamins, minerals, and other dietary supplements.

http://ods.od.nih.gov/factsheets/list-all/VitaminD/

The Vitamin D Council

A nonprofit group whose goal is to educate the public and professionals about vitamin D deficiency. They sponsor a free newsletter with a circulation of over 40,000. Their Web site contains an extensive list of the research on vitamin D divided by various health aspects.

http://www.vitamindcouncil.org/

The Vitamin D Society

A Canadian nonprofit group organized to increase awareness of health conditions linked to vitamin D deficiency. They encourage all Canadians to have their vitamin D blood levels tested annually. The group also funds vitamin D research.

http://www.vitamindsociety.org/

ISSUE 9

Does Obesity Cause a Decline in Life Expectancy?

YES: Samuel H. Preston, from "Deadweight?—The Influence of Obesity on Longevity," *The New England Journal of Medicine* (March 17, 2007)

NO: Paul Campos, from "The Weighting Game: Why Being Fat Isn't Bad for You," *The New Republic* (January 13, 2003)

As you read the issue, focus on the following points:

1. Factors that have impacted the increases in life expectancy over the last 100 years and the impact that excessive body fat has on longevity.
2. How the lifestyles and health and wellness practices of people influence longevity.
3. The influence that the weight-loss product industry has had on promoting the concept that weight loss improves health and increases longevity.

ISSUE SUMMARY

YES: Demographics professor Samuel Preston maintains that obesity is a major health problem in America and the problems associated with it cause obese people to die earlier than those who are thinner.

NO: Law professor Paul Campos disagrees and points out that the health consequences of obesity are not as dire as governmental health officials claim.

The increasing rate of overweight and obesity among Americans has made the headlines for the last 30 years, but it appears that it may be leveling off. The "Prevalence and Trends in Obesity among US Adults, 1999–2008" was outlined in the January 20, 2010, issue of the *Journal of the American Medical Association*. The report concludes:

> "In 2007–2008, the prevalence of obesity was 32.2% among adult men and 35.5% among adult women. The increases in the prevalence of

obesity previously observed do not appear to be continuing at the same rate over the past 10 years."

So, the good news is that sharp increase in obesity is not continuing like it was a few years back, but it doesn't mean it's still not a problem.

Definitions of overweight and obesity are pretty standard around the world. The Centers for Disease Control and Prevention (CDC) and most other health agencies and organizations define "overweight" as having a body mass index (BMI) between 25 and 29.9 and obese as having a BMI 30 and above. The most severe form of obesity, classified as "Class III," is sometimes referred to as "extreme" or "morbid" obesity. It begins at a BMI of 40, which translates into about 100 pounds above desirable weight. About 6 percent of the U.S. adult population meets these criteria.

For years, we have been told to keep our weight in the healthy range to improve overall health. According to the CDC, overweight and obesity increase the risks for the following health conditions:

- Coronary heart disease
- Type 2 diabetes
- Cancers (endometrial, breast, and colon) Hypertension
- Dyslipidemia (high levels of cholesterol or triglycerides)
- Stroke
- Liver and gallbladder disease
- Sleep apnea and respiratory problems
- Osteoarthritis (a degeneration of cartilage and its underlying bone within a joint)

Many of these conditions, especially heart disease, cancer, and stroke, are the leading causes of death. But, is a person's actual body weight the problem? Many studies show conflicting results. Recent studies of football players show that linemen, who are typically encouraged to be the biggest on the team with weights often topping 300 pounds, die earlier than players whose weights are closer to 200–250 pounds. In contrast, other studies are finding that obese people with chronic diseases have a better chance of survival than thinner individuals do. This finding has been called the "obesity paradox."

At what weight are people most likely to be healthiest and at what weight do people live the longest? Samuel Preston says that obesity is a major health problem in America and the problems associated with it cause obese people to die earlier than those who are thinner.

Paul Campos disagrees and points out that the health consequences of obesity are not as dire as governmental health officials' claim. After reading both articles, decide for yourself what impact body weight has on longevity.

Life expectancy Predicted years of life; typically from birth to death or a particular age to death

Body Mass Index classifications

BMI	Classification
<18.5	Underweight
18.5–24.9	Normal weight
25.0–29.9	Overweight
30.0–34.9	Class I obesity
35.0–39.9	Class II obesity
≥0.0	Class III obesity

YES

Samuel H. Preston

Deadweight?—The Influence of Obesity on Longevity

Obesity has clearly become a major personal and public health problem for Americans; it affects many aspects of our society. In this issue of the *Journal*, Olshansky et al.[1] make an important contribution to national discussions of the future of longevity by calling attention to the very substantial increase in the prevalence and severity of obesity since 1980 and its consequences on health and mortality. They estimate that the current life expectancy at birth in the United States would be one third to three quarters of a year higher if all overweight adults were to attain their ideal weight.

Although Olshansky et al. put obesity in the foreground of their vision of the future, the background for their vision is at least as bleak. They argue that past gains in life expectancy were largely a product of saving the young, which is unrepeatable. They claim that advances in life expectancy at older ages will be much smaller than in previous decades and that demographers and actuaries fail to recognize the disjunction and blindly continue to extrapolate the past into the future. They add to this concern that AIDS, antibiotic-resistant pathogens, and influenza pandemics represent additional threats to health. In their scenario, our children may have lives shorter than our own.

I believe that these background elements are excessively gloomy. Decreases in the rate of death at older ages have been the principal force driving American longevity for at least half a century, and they show no signs of abating. Sixty percent of the 9.23-year increase in life expectancy at birth between 1950 and 2002 is attributable to decreases in mortality among persons above 50 years of age.[2] Although improvements in life expectancy among women have slowed in the past decade, improvements among men have accelerated. The mean of male and female life expectancies at 65 years of age grew by 0.081 year per calendar year between 1950 and 1990, and by an identical 0.081 year per year between 1990 and 2002, the last year for which official U.S. life tables have been prepared.[3]

Demographers and actuaries use extrapolation to project the future of life expectancy because it seems to work better than any alternatives.[4-6] The biggest mistake, which has been made repeatedly in projections of mortality in the past, is to assume that life expectancy is close to a biologic maximum.[7] Confidence in the use of extrapolation is increased by the very steady behavior

From *The New England Journal of Medicine*, March 17, 2005, pp. 1135–1137. Copyright © 2005 by Massachusetts Medical Society. All rights reserved. Reprinted by permission.

of mortality trends themselves. The mean of life expectancies at birth in 21 high-income countries shows a nearly perfect fit (a coefficient of determination, R^2, of 0.994) to a linear time trend during the period from 1955 to 1996.[8]

The effect of an increase in the prevalence and severity of obesity on the longevity of U.S. citizens is already embedded in extrapolated forecasts made in recent periods. In fact, these forecasts implicitly assume that the severity of obesity will continue to worsen, and the prevalence will rise, since it is the rate of change in the determinants of mortality, rather than the level, that drives projected changes in life expectancy. Hundreds of factors affect a population's rate of death in any particular period, and it is their combined effect that establishes the trend.

Although Olshansky et al. cite threats to future improvements in life expectancy, it is important to recognize that many factors are at work to maintain a steady pace of advance. These include medical research organizations whose products have, for example, been responsible for much of the massive decrease in the rates of death from cardiovascular causes during the past four decades.[9] Public support for the National Institutes of Health remains very strong, and private companies will continue to have incentives to develop new products that enhance health and longevity. Longevity seems to have a strong genetic component,[10] which holds out the possibility that genetic engineering may, sometime within the 75-year projection of the Social Security Administration, begin to enhance longevity.

Other positive influences on longevity are embodied in cohorts of young persons who are approaching the ages at which death occurs most commonly and who will presumably enjoy greater protection from many diseases than will the people who have already reached those ages. Younger cohorts are better educated than older cohorts, and mortality is profoundly influenced by education. In 1998, life expectancy at age 25 was 7.1 years higher for men with some college education than for men with only a high-school education. For women, the discrepancy was 4.2 years.[11]

Younger cohorts have had lives less scarred by infectious diseases, which influence the development of many chronic diseases of adulthood.[12,13] Younger cohorts have consumed fewer cigarettes at a given age than older cohorts, and the effect of smoking is clearly manifested in the rates of death of the general population. In fact, a large fraction of the decrease in the rate of the decline in mortality among older women in recent years is a result of the rising rate of death from lung cancer in this group, which is a reflection of the delayed uptake of smoking among women in comparison with men.[14,15] Significant "cohort effects" have been demonstrated in the prevalence of cardiovascular disease, emphysema, and arthritis, suggesting that younger cohorts will have lower morbidity from these conditions as they age.[16]

Another reason to expect the longevity of U.S. citizens to continue to increase is that some populations have achieved life spans far longer than those of people in the United States, thus demonstrating what is possible even with no further technological advances. Japan has achieved a life expectancy of nearly 82 years, 4.5 years higher than that achieved by the United States and higher than that projected by the Social Security Administration for the

United States for 2055.[17,18] Some researchers have used a wide variety of data to suggest that within the United States, subgroups with the healthiest lifestyles may have already achieved life expectancies of 90 years or more.[19]

But let me be clear. The rising prevalence and severity of obesity are capable of offsetting the array of positive influences on longevity. How likely is that to happen? One promising observation is that the recent increase in the levels of obesity was produced by relatively few excess calories in the typical daily diet. The consumption of a median of 30 excess calories a day produced the observed increase in weight during an eight-year period for Americans 20 to 40 years of age.[20] At the 90th percentile of weight gain, the excess consumed was about 100 calories a day. Reversing the increase in body mass might be accomplished through small behavioral changes that fit relatively easily into most people's life-styles. The food and restaurant industries would be valuable allies in this effort, and there are recent indications of their willingness to cooperate.[21]

The fact that the U.S. population has already shown the ability to shift to healthier lifestyles is encouraging. Forty-two percent of U.S. adults were smokers in 1965, as compared with 23 percent in 2001.[14] The percentage of Americans 20 to 74 years of age with high levels of serum cholesterol fell from 33 percent in 1961 to 18 percent in 1999 and 2000.[14] Primarily because of behavioral changes, the incidence of AIDS has fallen by nearly 50 percent since 1992.[22] The percentage of fatal crashes involving drunk drivers declined from 30 percent in 1982 to 17 percent in 1999.[23] Each of these improvements in risk factors was facilitated by national campaigns that warned of the hazards of particular behaviors.[23]

The time has come to consider another major campaign. Even though the requisite behavioral changes may be small, they may be difficult to accomplish. The fact that most health-related behaviors have improved while obesity has worsened may be an indication of just how daunting the prospect of reducing levels of obesity may be. The rising prevalence and severity of obesity are already reducing life expectancy among the U.S. population. A failure to address the problem could impede the improvements in longevity that are otherwise in store.

Notes

I am indebted to John Wilmoth and Mitch Lazar for suggestions and assistance.
From the Population Studies Center, University of Pennsylvania, Philadelphia.

1. Olshansky SJ, Passaro D, Hershow R, et al. A potential decline in life expectancy in the United States in the 21st century. N Engl J Med 2005;352:1138–45.

2. Arias E. United States life tables, 2002. National vital statistics reports. Vol. 53. No. 6. Hyattsville, Md.: National Center for Health Statistics, 2002:25, 29. (DHHS publication no. (PHS) 2005–1120 PRS 04-0554.)

3. *Idem.* United States life tables, 2002. Vol. 53. No. 6. Hyattsville, Md.: National Center for Health Statistics, 2002:29. (PHS) 2005-1120 PRS 04–0554.

4. Lee R, Miller T. Evaluating the performance of the Lee-Carter method for forecasting mortality. Demography 2001;38:537–49.

5. Rosenberg M, Luckner W. Summary of results of survey of seminar attendees. North Am Actuarial J 1998;2:64–82.

6. Tuljaparkar S, Boe C. Mortality change and forecasting: how much and how little do we know? North Am Actuarial J 1998;2:13–47.

7. Oeppen J, Vaupel JW. Broken limits to life expectancy. Science 2002;296: 1029–31.

8. White K. Longevity advances in high income countries, 1955–96. Popul Dev Rev 2002;28:59–76.

9. Cutler D. Your money or your life: strong medicine for America's health care system. New York: Oxford University Press, 2004.

10. Perls TT, Wilmoth J, Levenson R, et al. Life-long sustained mortality advantage of siblings of centenarians. Proc Natl Acad Sci U S A 2002;99:8442–7.

11. Molla MT, Madans JH, Wagener DK. Differentials in adult mortality and activity limitation by education in the United States at the end of the 1990s. Popul Dev Rev 2004;30:625–46.

12. Costa DL. Understanding the twentieth-century decline in chronic conditions among older men. Demography 2000;37:53–72.

13. Zimmer C. Do chronic diseases have an infectious root? Science 2001; 293:1974–7.

14. Freid VM, Prager K, MacKay AP, Xia H. Health, United States, 2003: with chartbook on trends in the health of Americans. Washington, D.C.: Government Printing Office, 2003:169, 212, 228. (DHHS publication no. 2003–1232.)

15. Pampel FC. Declining sex differences in mortality from lung cancer in high-income nations. Demography 2003;40:45–66.

16. Reynolds SL, Crimmins EM, Saito Y. Cohort differences in disability and disease presence. Gerontologist 1998;38:578–90.

17. OECD health data 2004. Paris: Organisation for Economic Co-operation and Development, 2004.

18. Board of Trustees. Federal old-age and survivors insurance and disability insurance trust funds: 2004 annual report. Baltimore, Md.: U.S. Social Security Administration, 2004.

19. Manton KG, Stallard E, Tolley DH. Limits to human life expectancy: evidence, prospects, and implications. Popul Dev Rev 1991;17:603–37.

20. Hill JO, Wyatt HR, Reed GW, Peters JC. Obesity and the environment: where do we go from here? Science 2003;299:853–8.

21. Carpenter D. Food industry push: cater to health needs. Press release of the Associated Press, New York, January 18, 2005.

22. Jaffe H. Whatever happened to the U.S. AIDS epidemic? Science 2004;305: 1243–4.

23. Cutler DM. Behavioral health interventions: what works and why? In: Anderson NB, Bulatao RA, Cohen B, eds. Critical perspectives on racial and ethnic differences in health in late life. Washington, D.C.: National Academies Press, 2004:643–74.

Paul Campos  **NO**

The Weighting Game

Perhaps America's most common New Year's resolution is to lose weight. This week, as we push ourselves away from the increasingly guilty pleasures of the holiday table, we will be bombarded with ads imploring us to slim down with the help of health club memberships, exercise equipment, or the latest miracle diet. Yet, however common it may be, the resolution to lose weight appears to be a particularly ineffective one: The latest figures indicate that 65 percent of the adult population—more than 135 million Americans—is either "overweight" or "obese." And government officials are increasingly eager to declare America's burgeoning waistline the nation's number-one public health problem. The Surgeon General's recent Call to Action to Prevent and Decrease Overweight and Obesity labels being fat an "epidemic" that kills upward of 300,000 Americans per year. Such declarations lend our obsession with being thin a respectable medical justification. But are they accurate? A careful survey of medical literature reveals that the conventional wisdom about the health risks of fat is a grotesque distortion of a far more complicated story. Indeed, subject to exceptions for the most extreme cases, it's not at all clear that being overweight is an independent health risk of any kind, let alone something that kills hundreds of thousands of Americans every year. While having a sedentary lifestyle or a lousy diet—both factors, of course, that can contribute to being overweight—do pose health risks, there's virtually no evidence that being fat, in and of itself, is at all bad for you. In other words, while lifestyle is a good predictor of health, weight isn't: A moderately active fat person is likely to be far healthier than someone who is svelte but sedentary. What's worse, Americans' (largely unsuccessful) efforts to make themselves thin through dieting and supplements are themselves a major cause of the ill health associated with being overweight—meaning that America's war on fat is actually helping cause the very disease it is supposed to cure.

The most common way researchers determine whether someone is overweight is by using the "body mass index" (BMI), a simple and rather arbitrary mathematical formula that puts people of varying heights and weights on a single integrated scale. According to the government, you're "overweight" (that is, your weight becomes a significant health risk) if you have a BMI figure of 25 and "obese" (your weight becomes a major health risk) if your BMI is 30 or higher. A five-foot-four-inch woman is thus labeled "overweight" and "obese" at weights of 146 pounds and 175 pounds, respectively; a five-foot-ten-inch man crosses those thresholds at weights of 174 pounds and 210 pounds. Such claims have been given enormous publicity by, among other government officials, former Surgeons General C. Everett Koop—whose Shape Up America foundation has been a leading source for the claim that fat kills 300,000 Americans per year—and David Satcher, who in 1998 declared that America's young people are "seriously at risk of starting out obese and dooming themselves to the difficult task of overcoming a tough illness." And the federal government is beginning to put its money where its mouth is: Last April, the Internal Revenue Service announced that diet-related costs could henceforth be deducted as medical expenses, as long as such expenses were incurred in the course of treating the "disease" of being fat—a ruling that will create a multibillion dollar per year public subsidy for the weight-loss industry.

Yet, despite the intense campaign to place fat in the same category of public health hazards as smoking and drug abuse, there is in fact no medical basis for the government's BMI recommendations or the public health policies based on them. The most obvious flaw lies with the BMI itself, which is simply based on height and weight. The arbitrariness of these charts becomes clear as soon as one starts applying them to actual human beings. As *The Wall Street Journal* pointed out last July, taking the BMI charts seriously requires concluding that Brad Pitt, George Clooney, and Michael Jordan are all "overweight," and that Sylvester Stallone and baseball star Sammy Sosa are "obese." According to my calculations, fully three-quarters of National Football League running backs—speedy, chiseled athletes, all of whom, it's safe to say, could beat the world's fastest obesity researcher by a wide margin in a 100-yard dash—are "obese."

To be sure, even if the BMI categories can be spectacularly wrong in cases such as those involving professional athletes, they're often a pretty good indicator of how "fat" most people are in everyday life. The real question is whether being fat—as determined by the BMI or by any other measure—is actually a health risk. To answer this question, it's necessary to examine the epidemiological evidence. Since the measurable factors that affect whether someone contracts any particular disease or condition can easily number in the hundreds or thousands, it's often difficult to distinguish meaningful data from random statistical noise. And, even where there are clear correlations, establishing cause and effect can be a complicated matter. If researchers observe that fat people are more prone to contract, say, heart disease than thin people, this fact by itself doesn't tell them whether being fat contributes to acquiring heart disease. It could easily be the case that some other factor or set of factors—i.e., being sedentary or eating junk food or dieting aggressively—contributes both to being fat and to contracting heart disease.

Unfortunately, in the world of obesity research these sorts of theoretical and practical complications are often dealt with by simply ignoring them. The most cited studies purporting to demonstrate that fat is a major health risk almost invariably make little or no attempt to control for what medical researchers refer to as "confounding variables." For example, the research providing the basis for the claim that fat contributes to the deaths of 300,000 Americans per year—a 1999 study published in the *Journal of the American Medical Association* (*JAMA*)—did not attempt to control for any confounding variables other than age, gender, and smoking.

And, even among studies—such as the *JAMA* one—that ignore variables such as diet or activity levels, there is tremendous disagreement: For every study that indicates some sort of increased health risk for people with BMI figures between 25 and 30 (a category that currently includes more than one out of every three adult Americans), another study indicates such people enjoy lower overall health risks than those whom the government and the medical establishment have labeled "ideal-weight" individuals (i.e., people with BMI figures between 18.5 and 24.9). Perhaps the most comprehensive survey of the literature regarding the health risks of different weight levels is a 1996 study by scientists at the National Center for Health Statistics and Cornell University. This survey analyzed data from dozens of previous studies involving more than 600,000 subjects. It concluded that, for nonsmoking men, the lowest mortality rate was found among those with BMI figures between 23 and 29, meaning that a large majority of the healthiest men in the survey would be considered "overweight" by current government standards. For nonsmoking women, the results were even more striking: The authors concluded that, for such women, the BMI range correlating with the lowest mortality rate is extremely broad, from about 18 to 32, meaning that a woman of average height can weigh anywhere within an 80-pound range without seeing any statistically meaningful change in her risk of premature death.

What accounts for the conflict between studies that claim being "overweight" is a significant health risk and those that suggest such weight levels might actually be optimal? The biggest factor is that researchers fail to point out that, in practical terms, the differences in risk they are measuring are usually so small as to be trivial. For example, suppose that Group A consists of 2,500 subjects and that over the course of a decade five of these people die from heart attacks. Now suppose that Group B consists of 4,000 subjects and that five members of this group also die from heart attacks over the same ten-year span. One way of characterizing these figures is to say that people in Group A are subject to a (implicitly terrifying) 60 percent greater risk of a fatal heart attack than those in Group B. But the practical reality is that the relevant risk for members of both groups is miniscule. Indeed, upon closer examination, almost all studies that claim "overweight" people run significantly increased health risks involve this sort of interpretation (or, less generously, distortion) of their data.

This phenomenon is in part a product of the fact that studies that purport to find significant elevations of mortality risk associated with different weight levels usually focus on mortality rates among relatively young adults. Since these studies typically involve very small numbers of deaths among very large numbers of subjects, it isn't surprising to see what appear to be large oscillations in relative risk across different studies. Indeed, one often observes large, apparently random oscillations in risk even within studies. Lost in the uproar over the *JAMA* study's 300,000 deaths figure is the peculiar fact that the report actually found that supposedly "ideal-weight" individuals with a BMI of 20 had essentially the same mortality risk as "obese" persons with BMI figures of 30 and that both groups had a slightly higher mortality risk than "overweight" people with BMI figures of 25.

In short, the Cornell survey of the existing literature merely confirmed what anyone who actually examines the data will discover: In a decided majority of studies, groups of people labeled "overweight" by current standards are found to have equal or lower mortality rates than groups of supposedly "ideal-weight" individuals. University of Virginia professor Glenn Gaesser has estimated that three-quarters of all medical studies on the effects of weight on health between 1945 and 1995 concluded either that "excess" weight had no effect on health or that it was actually beneficial. And again, this remains the case even before one begins to take into account complicating factors such as sedentary lifestyle, poor nutrition, dieting and diet drugs, etc. "As of 2002," Gaesser points out in his book *Big Fat Lies*, "there has not been a single study that has truly evaluated the effects of weight alone on health, which means that 'thinner is healthier' is not a fact but an unsubstantiated hypothesis for which there is a wealth of evidence that suggests the reverse."

As we have seen, most of the people the government and the health establishment claim are too fat—those categorized as "overweight" or "mildly obese"—do not in fact suffer from worse health than supposedly "ideal-weight" individuals. It is true that some groups of fat people—generally those with BMI figures well above 30—are less healthy than average, although not nearly to the extent the anti-fat warriors would have you believe. (Large-scale mortality studies indicate that women who are 50 or even 75 pounds "overweight" will on average still have longer life expectancies than those who are 10 to 15 pounds "underweight," a.k.a. fashionably thin.) Yet there is considerable evidence that even substantially "obese" people are not less healthy because they're fat. Rather, other factors are causing them to be both fat and unhealthy. Chief among these factors are sedentary lifestyle and diet-driven weight fluctuation.

The most comprehensive work regarding the dangers of sedentary lifestyle has been done at the Cooper Institute in Dallas. The institute's director of research, Steven Blair, is probably the world's leading expert on the relationship between activity levels and overall health. For the past 20 years, the Cooper Institute has maintained a database that has tracked the health, weight, and basic fitness levels of tens of thousands of individuals. What Blair and his colleagues have discovered turns the conventional wisdom about the relationship between fat and fitness on its head. Quite simply, when researchers factor in the activity levels of the people being studied, body mass appears to have no relevance to health whatsoever—even among people who are substantially "obese." It turns out that "obese" people who engage in moderate levels of physical activity have radically lower rates of premature death than sedentary people who maintain supposedly "ideal-weight" levels.

For example, a 1999 Cooper Institute study found the highest death rate to be among sedentary men with waist measurements under 34 inches and the lowest death rate to be among physically fit men with waist measurements of 40 inches or more. And these results do not change when the researchers control for body-fat percentage, thus dispensing with the claim that such percentages, rather than body mass itself, are the crucial variables when measuring the health effects of weight. Fat people might be less healthy if they're fat because of a sedentary lifestyle. But, if they're fat and active, they have nothing to worry about.

Still, even if it's clear that it's better to be fat and active than fat and sedentary—or even thin and sedentary—isn't it the case that being thin and active is the best combination of all? Not according to Blair's research: His numerous studies of the question have found no difference in mortality rates between fit people who are fat and those who are thin.

Of course, in a culture as anti-fat as ours, the whole notion of people who are both fat and fit seems contradictory. Yet the research done by Blair and others indicates that our belief that fatness and fitness are in fundamental tension is based on myths, not science. "Fitness" in Blair's work isn't defined by weight or body-fat percentage but rather by cardiovascular and aerobic endurance, as measured by treadmill stress tests. And he has found that people don't need to be marathon runners to garner the immense health benefits that follow from maintaining good fitness levels. Blair's research shows that to move into the fitness category that offers most of the health benefits of being active, people need merely to engage in some combination of daily activities equivalent to going for a brisk half-hour walk. To move into the top fitness category requires a bit more—the daily equivalent of jogging for perhaps 25 minutes or walking briskly for close to an hour. (Our true public health scandal has nothing to do with fat and everything to do with the fact that 80 percent of the population is so inactive that it doesn't even achieve the former modest fitness standard.)

Other researchers have reached similar conclusions. For instance, the Harvard Alumni Study, which has tracked the health of Harvard graduates for many decades, has found the lowest mortality rates among those graduates who have gained the most weight since college while also expending at least 2,000 calories per week in physical activities. Such work suggests strongly that when obesity researchers have described the supposed health risks of fat, what they have actually been doing is using fat as a proxy—and a poor one at that—for a factor that actually does have a significant effect on health and mortality: cardiovascular and metabolic fitness. As Blair himself has put it, Americans have a "misdirected obsession with weight and weight loss. The focus is all wrong. It's fitness that is the key."

If fat is ultimately irrelevant to health, our fear of fat, unfortunately, is not. Americans' obsession with thinness feeds an institution that actually is a danger to Americans' health: the diet industry.

Tens of millions of Americans are trying more or less constantly to lose 20 or 30 pounds. (Recent estimates are that, on any particular day, close to half the adult population is on some sort of diet.) Most say they are doing so for their health, often on the advice of their doctors. Yet numerous studies—two dozen in the last 20 years alone—have shown that weight loss of this magnitude (and indeed even of as little as ten pounds) leads to an increased risk of premature death, sometimes by an order of several hundred percent. By contrast, over this same time frame, only a handful of studies have indicated that weight loss leads to lower mortality rates—and one of these found an eleven-hour increase in life expectancy per pound lost (i.e., less than an extra month of life in return for a 50-pound weight loss). This pattern holds true even when studies take into account "occult wasting," the weight loss that sometimes accompanies a serious but unrelated illness. For example, a major American Cancer Society study published in 1995 concluded in no uncertain terms that healthy "overweight" and "obese" women were better off if they didn't lose weight. In this study, healthy women who intentionally lost weight over a period of a year or longer suffered an all-cause increased risk of prema- ture mortality that was up to 70 percent higher than that of healthy women who didn't intentionally lose weight. Meanwhile, unintentional weight gain had no effect on mortality rates. (A 1999 report based on the same data pool found similar results for men.) The only other large study that has examined the health effects of intentional weight loss, the Iowa Women's Health Study, also failed to find an association between weight loss and significantly lower mortality rates. In fact, in this 42,000-person study, "overweight" women had an all-cause mortality rate 5 to 10 percent lower than that of "ideal-weight" women.

One explanation for the ill effects of intentional weight loss is diet drugs (others include the binge eating to which chronic dieters are especially prone). The havoc wrought by drugs such as Redux and fen-phen is well-known and has resulted in billions of dollars' worth of legal liability for their manufactur- ers. What has been less publicized is that other diet drugs are being discov- ered to have similarly devastating effects: For example, a recent Yale University study indicates that women between the ages of 18 and 49 who use appetite suppressants containing phenylpropanolamine increase their risk of hem- orrhagic stroke by 1,558 percent. (This over-the-counter drug was used by approximately nine million Americans at any given time during the late '90s. The Food and Drug Administration, which is in the process of formally ban- ning the drug, has requested that in the interim manufacturers remove it from the market voluntarily.)

The grim irony lurking behind these statistics is that, as numerous stud- ies have demonstrated, people who lose weight via dieting and diet drugs often end up weighing a good deal more than people of similar initial weight who never diet. The explanation for this perverse result can be found in the well-documented "set-point" phenomenon—that is, the body's tendency to fight the threat of starvation by slowing its metabolism in response to a caloric reduction. For example, obesity researcher Paul Ernsberger has done several studies in which rats are placed on very low-calorie diets. Invariably, when the rats are returned to their previous level of caloric intake, they get fat by eating exactly the same number of calories that had merely maintained their weight before they were put on diets. The same is true of human beings. "Put people on crash diets, and they'll gain back more weight than they lost," Ernsberger has said.

The literature on the health effects of dieting and diet drugs suggests that, as Gaesser pointed out, what most studies that find a correlation between higher mortality and higher body mass really demonstrate is a correlation between higher mortality and higher rates of dieting and diet-drug use. Under these circumstances, advising fat people to diet for the sake of their health is tantamount to prescribing a drug that causes the disease it's supposed to cure.

What is it about fat that renders so many otherwise sensible Americans more than a little bit crazy? The war on fat is based on many things: the deeply neurotic relationship so many Americans have developed toward food and their bodies, the identification of thinness with social privilege and of fat with lower-class status, the financial interests of the diet industry, and many other factors as well. Ultimately, the fundamental forces driving our national obsession with fat fall into two broad and interrelated categories: economic interest and psychological motivation.

Obesity research in the United States is almost wholly funded by the weight-loss industry. For all the government's apparent interest in the fat "epidemic," in recent years less than 1 percent of the federal health research budget has gone toward obesity-related research. (For example, in 1995, the National Institutes of Health spent $87 million on obesity research out of a total budget of $11.3 billion.) And, while it's virtually impossible to determine just how much the dieting industry spends on such research, it is safe to say that it is many, many times more. Indeed, many of the nation's most prominent obesity researchers have direct financial stakes in companies that produce weight-loss products. (When they are quoted in the media, such researchers routinely fail to disclose their financial interests in the matters on which they are commenting, in part because journalists fail to ask them about potential conflicts.) And the contamination of supposedly disinterested research goes well beyond the effects of such direct financial interests. As Laura Fraser points out in her book *Losing It: False Hopes and Fat Profits in the Diet Industry*, "Diet and pharmaceutical companies influence every step along the way of the scientific process. They pay for the ads that keep obesity journals publishing. They underwrite medical conferences, flying physicians around the country expense-free and paying them large lecture fees to attend."

This situation creates a kind of structural distortion, analogous to that which takes place in the stock market when analysts employed by brokerage houses make recommendations to clients intended to inflate the price of stock issued by companies that in return send their business to the brokerages' investment-banking divisions. In such circumstances, it's easy for all the players to convince themselves of the purity of their motives. "It isn't diabolical," eating-disorders specialist David Garner told Fraser. "Some people are very committed to the belief that weight loss is a national health problem. It's just that, if their livelihood is based in large part on the diet industry, they can't be impartial." Fraser writes that when she asked one obesity researcher, who has criticized dieting as ineffective and psychologically damaging, to comment on the policies of one commercial weight-loss program, he replied, "What can I say? I'm a consultant for them."

What makes this structural distortion particularly insidious is that, just as Americans wanted desperately to believe that the IPO bubble of the '90s would never burst—and were therefore eager to accept whatever the experts at Merrill Lynch and on *The Wall Street Journal's* editorial page had to say about the "New Economy"—they also long to believe that medical experts can solve the problem of their expanding waistlines. The reason for this can be summed up in six words: Americans think being fat is disgusting. That psychological truth creates an enormous incentive to give our disgust a respectable motivation. In other words, being fat must be terrible for one's health, because if it isn't that means our increasing hatred of fat represents a social, psychological, and moral problem rather than a medical one.

The convergence of economic interest and psychological motivation helps ensure that, for example, when former Surgeon General Koop raised more than $2 million from diet-industry heavyweights Weight Watchers and Jenny Craig for his Shape Up America foundation, he remained largely immune to the charge that he was exploiting a national neurosis for financial gain. After all, "everyone knows" that fat is a major health risk, so why should we find it disturbing to discover such close links between prominent former public health officials and the dietary-pharmaceutical complex?

None of this is to suggest that the war against fat is the product of some sort of conscious conspiracy on the part of those whose interests are served by it. The relationship between economic motives, cultural trends, social psychology, and the many other factors that fuel the war on fat is surely far more complex than that. But it does suggest that the conventional wisdom about fat in the United States is based on factors that have very little to do with a disinterested evaluation of the medical and scientific evidence, and therefore this conventional wisdom needs to be taken for what it is: a pervasive social myth rather than a rational judgment about risk.

So what should we do about fat in the United States? The short answer is: nothing. The longer answer is that we should refocus our attention from people's waistlines to their levels of activity. Americans have become far too sedentary. It sometimes seems that much of American life is organized around the principle that people should be able to go through an average day without ever actually using their legs. We do eat too much junk that isn't good for us because it's quick and cheap and easier than taking the time and money to prepare food that is both nutritious and satisfies our cravings.

A rational public health policy would emphasize that the keys to good health (at least those that anyone can do anything about—genetic factors remain far more important than anything else) are, in roughly descending order of importance: not to smoke, not to be an alcoholic or drug addict, not to be sedentary, and not to eat a diet packed with junk food. It's true that a more active populace that ate a healthier diet would be somewhat thinner, as would a nation that wasn't dieting obsessively. Even so, there is no reason why there shouldn't be millions of healthy, happy fat people in the United States, as there no doubt would be in a culture that maintained a rational attitude toward the fact that people will always come in all shapes and sizes, whether they live healthy lives or not. In the end, nothing could be easier than to win the war on fat: All we need to do is stop fighting it.

CHALLENGE QUESTIONS

Does Obesity Cause a Decline in Life Expectancy?

1. Define life expectancy.
2. Describe the changes in life expectancy since 1950 and explain why these changes have occurred.
3. Consider a woman who is currently age 65 years with a BMI of 19.5. What information would you need about her to be able to discuss/predict her life expectancy?
4. Consider a man who is currently age 50 years with a BMI of 29. What lifestyle factors would put him at risk for a reduced life expectancy and what lifestyle factors would put him at risk for an extended life expectancy?
5. Preston points out how antismoking campaigns were successful in reducing cigarette use among adults from 42 percent in 1965 to 23 percent in 2001. Some of the campaigns included slogans such as "Be smart, don't start," "Smoking? You must be joking," and "Kissing a smoker is like licking an ashtray." Design an antiobesity campaign with a slogan to promote healthy weights among U.S. adults. Include how the campaign would be funded, the people who would promote the campaign, and the method that would be used to disseminate it to the public.

Internet References . . .

Food and Drug Administration (FDA)

The Food and Drug Administration (FDA) Web site provides information about specific supplements as well as about rules and regulations affecting their use. Also see the section that explains the rules for health claims on the labels of foods and supplements. This site includes a link to the current list of authorized claims.

http://vm.cfsan.fda.gov/~dms/supplmnt.html

Office of Dietary Supplements at the National Institutes of Health

The Office of Dietary Supplements at the National Institutes of Health site provides ready access to the latest studies on the health effects of dietary supplements of all types, nutritional and herbal. Click on the "Health Information" and "Fact Sheets" buttons to obtain the latest information on the safety and efficacy of specific supplements of interest. This site also provides useful links to government agencies involved in supplement regulation.

http://dietary-supplements.info.nih.gov

National Center for Complementary and Alternative Medicine

The National Center for Complementary and Alternative Medicine is also part of the National Institutes of Health, and it is the government's principal agency for scientific research on complementary and alternative medicine, including herbal and nutritional therapies. This site provides information on the mission and history of the center, funding opportunities for research and training, and the results of clinical trials that test treatments or therapies, such as those involving vitamin or herbal supplements.

http://nccam.nih.gov

Our Food Supply

What we eat depends largely on foods that are available. Therefore, the food industry has a tremendous influence on the nation's nutritional status. Debate begins with the way foods are grown, starting with farming practices. Advances in agriculture allow farmers to use seeds that are genetically modified, soil enhanced with fertilizer, and industrial-strength pesticides. Debate focuses on the unknown, since these practices are relatively new. Many ask "what impact will they have in the long term?" And the concern is not only over the health status of humans, but for animals, other plants, and the environment. Other apprehension centers around new food products—new food products hit the market every week. The leading food manufacturers employ food and nutrition experts to formulate new products and recipes—and most have a marketing team to persuade the public to eat their company's products. Are these new products beneficial or detrimental to health?

- Are Organic Foods Better Than Conventional Foods?
- Does the World Need Genetically Modified Foods?
- Are Probiotics and Prebiotics Beneficial in Promoting Health?
- Should Energy Drinks Be Banned?

ISSUE 10

Are Organic Foods Better Than Conventional Foods?

YES: Ed Hamer and Mark Anslow, from "10 Reasons Why Organic Can Feed the World" *The Ecologist* (March 2008)

NO: Mark Bittman, from "Eating Food That's Better for You, Organic or Not?" *The New York Times* (March 22, 2009)

As you read the issue, focus on the following points:

1. Factors that make organic foods superior to conventionally grown foods and the benefits they provide to the environment and our bodies.
2. Benefits that eating an organic, locally grown plant-based diet will have for the environment and our health.
3. Trends in organic food consumption by Americans and people of the United Kingdom.

ISSUE SUMMARY

YES: Ed Hamer and Mark Anslow indicate that organically produced foods use less energy, water, and pesticides and produce less pollution while producing foods that taste better and contain more nutrients.

NO: Mark Bittman disagrees and insists that eating "organic" offers no guarantee of eating well, healthfully, sanely, even ethically. He points out that many people may feel better about eating an organic Oreo than a conventional Oreo, and sides with Marion Nestle who says, "Organic junk food is still junk food."

For centuries, organic farming was all that existed. During the first few decades of the 1900s, farmers began to use fertilizers, pesticides, and herbicides to increase crop production. Then, use of antibiotics, vaccinations, and hormones to improve the quality of livestock and other farm animals became widespread throughout the world. And handpicking was replaced with large machines.

The organic movement, as we know it today, began when a few environmentally conscious people objected to this "industrialized agriculture."

One of the first people to speak out against the new way of farming was British botanist Sir Albert Howard, who is often thought of as the father of organic farming. He wrote several books about farming practices in India where he used compost as a natural fertilizer and promoted that compost is superior to modern fertilizers. In the United States, Jerome Irving Rodale published the magazine *Organic Farming and Gardening* that focuses on how to grow food without using chemicals. The magazine, which began publication in 1942, is one of the most highly read gardening magazines.

In 1962, environmentalist Rachel Carson's book *Silent Spring* was published. Her book is credited with further increasing awareness of organics. She describes how the insecticide dichlorodiphenyltrichloroethane (DDT) destroys not only malaria-spreading mosquitoes, but also birds and other wildlife. She was concerned that chemicals were being used with "little or no advance investigation of their effect on soil, water, wildlife, and man himself." Her book was instrumental in the formation of the Environmental Protection Agency (EPA) and the ban of DDT in 1972.

Another factor that stimulated awareness of organics was the hippy movement of the 1960s. Hippies rebelled against the established ways of life, opting for a more natural lifestyle. Females burned their bras, stopped wearing makeup, and were among the first to return to breast-feeding. Men let their hair grow long and quit shaving. They formed communes where they lived off the land. Part of their return to nature included organic gardening. By the early 1970s, people who preached "organic and natural" were considered by most of mainstream America to be hippies.

Farmers of California led the nation in organic agriculture and founded the California Certified Organic Farmers (CCOF) association in 1973. The organization is still considered a leader in organic certification in North America. California was first to pass its "Organic Food Act" in 1979. Members of CCOF were instrumental with the passage of the Federal Organic Foods Production Act of 1990.

Even after the federal act was passed, there was still no way that a person could look at food in a local grocery store and know the product was organic or not. Therefore, in 2004, the United States Department of Agriculture (USDA) and the Food and Drug Administration (FDA) developed the USDA-certified labeling. Organic-related definitions allowed on food labels are listed below.

- **100 percent organic.** Products that are completely organic or made of all organic ingredients.
- **Organic.** Products that are at least 95 percent organic.
- **Made with organic ingredients.** These are products that contain at least 70 percent organic ingredients. The organic seal can't be used on these packages.
- **All-natural, free-range, or hormone-free.** These descriptions *do not* mean the food is organic.

More and more of us are grabbing organic foods. According to Ed Hamer and Mark Anslow, organic foods can feed the world, if we farm and eat differently. They say organically produced foods are more nutritious than conventionally grown foods and are earth friendly. Mark Bittman disagrees and insists that eating organically offers "no guarantee of eating well, healthfully, sanely, even ethically." After you read their articles, decide if organic foods are better than conventionally grown ones.

Distinctions Between Conventional and Organic Farming

Conventional Farming	Organic Farming
Apply chemical fertilizers to promote plant growth.	Apply natural fertilizers, such as manure or compost, to feed soil and plants.
Spray insecticides to reduce pests and disease.	Use beneficial insects and birds, mating disruption or traps to reduce pests and disease.
Use chemical herbicides to manage weeds.	Rotate crops, till, hand weed, or mulch to manage weeds.
Give animals antibiotics, growth hormones, and medications to prevent disease and spur growth.	Give animals organic feed and allow them access to the outdoors. Use preventive measures—such as rotational grazing, a balanced diet, and clean housing—to help minimize disease.

Source: http://usda-fda.com/Articles/Organic.htm.

TIMELINE

Early 1900s Industrialized agriculture begins.
1942 J.I. Rodale publishes *Organic Farming and Gardening*.
1962 Rachel Carson's book *Silent Spring* is published.
1972 DDT banned in the United States.
1973 California Certified Organic Farmers (CCOF) is formed.
1979 California Organic Food Act is passed.
1990 Federal Organic Foods Production Act is passed.
2002 USDA and FDA begin organic foods labeling.

10 Reasons Why Organic Can Feed the World

Can organic farming feed the world? Ed Hamer and Mark Anslow say yes, but we must eat and farm differently.

1. Yield

Switching to organic farming would have different effects according to where in the world you live and how you currently farm.

Studies show that the less industrialised world stands to benefit the most. In southern Brazil, maize and wheat yields doubled on farms that changed to green manures and nitrogen-fixing leguminous vegetables instead of chemical fertilisers. In Mexico, coffee-growers who chose to move to fully organic production methods saw increases of 50 per cent in the weight of beans they harvested. In fact, in an analysis of more than 286 organic conversions in 57 countries, the average yield increase was found to be an impressive 64 per cent.

The situation is more complex in the industrialised world, where farms are large, intensive facilities, and opinions are divided on how organic yields would compare.

Research by the University of Essex in 1999 found that, although yields on US farms that converted to organic initially dropped by between 10 and 15 per cent, they soon recovered, and the farms became more productive than their all-chemical counterparts. In the UK, however, a study by the Elm Farm Research Centre predicted that a national transition to all-organic farming would see cereal, rapeseed and sugar beet yields fall by between 30 and 60 percent. Even the Soil Association admits that, on average in the UK, organic yields are 30 per cent lower than non-organic.

So can we hope to feed ourselves organically in the British Isles and Northern Europe? An analysis by former *Ecologist* editor Simon Fairlie in *The Land* journal suggests that we can, but only if we are prepared to rethink our diet and farming practices.

In Fairlie's scenario, each of the UK's 60 million citizens could have organic cereals, potatoes, sugar, vegetables and fruit, fish, pork, chicken and beef, as well as wool and flax for clothes and biomass crops for heating. To achieve this we'd each have to cut down to around 230 g of beef (½ lb), compared to an average of 630 g (1½ lb) today, 252 g of pork/bacon, 210 g of chicken and just under 4 kg (9 lb) of dairy produce each week—considerably more than the country enjoyed in 1945. We would probably need to supplement our diet with home-grown vegetables, save our food scraps as livestock feed and reform the sewage system to use our waste as an organic fertiliser.

2. Energy

Currently, we use around 10 calories of fossil energy to produce one calorie of food energy. In a fuel-scarce future, which experts think could arrive as early as 2012, such numbers simply won't stack up.

Studies by the Department for Environment, Food and Rural affairs over the past three years have shown that, on average, organically grown crops use 25 per cent less energy than their chemical cousins. Certain crops achieve even better reductions, including organic leeks (58 per cent less energy) and broccoli (49 per cent less energy).

When these savings are combined with stringent energy conservation and local distribution and consumption (such as organic box schemes), energy-use dwindles to a fraction of that needed for an intensive, centralised food system. A study by the University of Surrey shows that food from Tolhurst Organic Produce, a smallholding in Berkshire, which supplies 400 households with vegetable boxes, uses 90 per cent less energy than if non-organic produce had been delivered and bought in a supermarket.

Far from being simply 'energy-lite', however, organic farms have the potential to become self-sufficient in energy—or even to become energy exporters. The 'Dream Farm' model, first proposed by Mauritius-born agroscientist George Chan, sees farms feeding manure and waste from livestock and crops into biodigesters, which convert it into a methane-rich gas to be used for creating heat and electricity. The residue from these biodigesters is a crumbly, nutrient-rich fertiliser, which can be spread on soil to increase crop yields or further digested by algae and used as a fish or animal feed.

3. Greenhouse Gas Emission and Climate Change

Despite organic farming's low-energy methods, it is not in reducing demand for power that the techniques stand to make the biggest savings in greenhouse gas emissions.

The production of ammonium nitrate fertiliser, which is indispensable to conventional farming, produces vast quantities of nitrous oxide—a greenhouse gas with a global warming potential some 320 times greater than that of CO_2. In fact, the production of one tonne of ammonium nitrate creates 6.7 tonnes of greenhouse gases (CO_2^e), and was responsible for around 10 percent of all industrial greenhouse gas emissions in Europe in 2003.

The techniques used in organic agriculture to enhance soil fertility in turn encourage crops to develop deeper roots, which increase the amount of organic matter in the soil, locking up carbon underground and keeping it out of the atmosphere.

The opposite happens in conventional farming: high quantities of artificially supplied nutrients encourage quick growth and shallow roots. A study published in 1995 in the journal *Ecological Applications* found that levels of carbon in the soils of organic farms in California were as much as 28 per cent higher as a result. And research by the Rodale Institute shows that if the US were to convert all its corn and soybean fields to organic methods, the amount of carbon that could be stored in the soil would equal 73 per cent of the country's Kyoto targets for CO_2 reduction.

Organic farming might also go some way towards salvaging the reputation of the cow, demonised in 2007 as a major source of methane at both ends of its digestive tract. There's no doubt that this is a problem: estimates put global methane emissions from ruminant livestock at around 80 million tonnes a year, equivalent to around two billion tonnes of CO_2, or close to the annual CO_2 output of Russia and the UK combined. But by changing the pasturage on which animals graze to legumes such as clover or birdsfoot trefoil (often grown anyway by organic farmers to improve soil nitrogen content), scientists at the Institute of Grassland and Environmental Research believe that methane emissions could be cut dramatically. Because the leguminous foliage is more digestible, bacteria in the cow's gut are less able to turn the fodder into methane. Cows also seem naturally to prefer eating birdsfoot trefoil to ordinary grass.

4. Water Use

Agriculture is officially the most thirsty industry on the planet, consuming a staggering 72 per cent of all global freshwater at a time when the UN says 80 per cent of our water supplies are being overexploited.

This hasn't always been the case. Traditionally, agricultural crops were restricted to those areas best suited to their physiology, with drought-tolerant species grown in the tropics and water-demanding crops in temperate regions.

Global trade throughout the second half of the last century led to a worldwide production of grains dominated by a handful of high-yielding cereal crops, notably wheat, maize and rice. These thirsty cereals—the 'big three'—now account for more than half of the world's plant-based calories and 85 per cent of total grain production.

Organic agriculture is different. Due to its emphasis on healthy soil structure, organic farming avoids many of the problems associated with compaction, erosion, salinisation and soil degradation, which are prevalent in intensive systems. Organic manures and green mulches are applied even before the crop is sown, leading to a process known as 'mineralisation'—literally the fixing of minerals in the soil. Mineralised organic matter, conspicuously absent from synthetic fertilisers, is one of the essential ingredients required physically and chemically to hold water on the land.

Organic management also uses crop rotations, undersowing and mixed cropping to provide the soil with near-continuous cover. By contrast, conventional farm soils may be left uncovered for extended periods prior to sowing, and again following the harvest, leaving essential organic matter fully exposed to erosion by rain, wind and sunlight.

In the US, a 25-year Rodale Institute experiment on climatic extremes found that, due to improved soil structure, organic systems consistently achieve higher yields during periods both of drought and flooding.

5. Localisation

The globalisation of our food supply, which gives us Peruvian apples in June and Spanish lettuces in February, has seen our food reduced to a commodity in an increasingly volatile global marketplace.

Although year-round availability makes for good marketing in the eyes of the biggest retailers, the costs to the environment are immense.

Friends of the Earth estimates that the average meal in the UK travels 1,000 miles from plot to plate. In 2005, Defra released a comprehensive report on food miles in the UK, which valued the direct environmental, social and economic costs of food transport in Britain at £9 billion each year. In addition, food transport accounted for more than 30 billion vehicle kilometres, 25 percent of all HGV journeys and 19 million tonnes of carbon dioxide emissions in 2002 alone.

The organic movement was born out of a commitment to provide local food for local people, and so it is logical that organic marketing encourages localisation through veg boxes, farm shops and stalls. Between 2005 and 2006, organic sales made through direct marketing outlets such as these increased by 53 per cent, from £95 to £146 million, more than double the sales growth experienced by the major supermarkets. As we enter an age of unprecedented food insecurity, it is essential that our consumption reflects not only what is desirable, but also what is ultimately sustainable. While the 'organic' label itself may inevitably be hijacked, 'organic and local' represents a solution with which the global players can simply never compete.

6. Pesticides

It is a shocking testimony to the power of the agrochemical industry that in the 45 years since Rachel Carson published her pesticide warning *Silent Spring*, the number of commercially available synthetic pesticides has risen from 22 to more than 450.

According to the World Health Organization there are an estimated 20,000 accidental deaths worldwide each year from pesticide exposure and poisoning. More than 31 million kilograms of pesticide were applied to UK crops alone in 2005, 0.5 kilograms for every person in the country. A spiralling dependence on pesticides throughout recent decades has resulted in a catalogue of repercussions, including pest resistance, disease susceptibility, loss of natural biological controls and reduced nutrient-cycling.

Organic farmers, on the other hand, believe that a healthy plant grown in a healthy soil will ultimately be more resistant to pest damage. Organic systems encourage a variety of natural methods to enhance soil and plant health, in turn reducing incidences of pests, weeds and disease.

First and foremost, because organic plants grow comparatively slower than conventional varieties they have thicker cell walls, which provide a tougher natural barrier to pests. Rotations or 'break-crops', which are central to organic production, also provide a physical obstacle to pest and disease lifecycles by removing crops from a given plot for extended periods. Organic systems also rely heavily on a rich agro-ecosystem in which many agricultural pests can be controlled by their natural predators.

Inevitably, however, there are times when pestilence attacks are especially prolonged or virulent, and here permitted pesticides may be used. The use of organic pesticides is heavily regulated and the International Federation of Organic Agriculture Movements (IFOAM) requires specific criteria to be met before pesticide applications can be justified.

There are in fact only four active ingredients permitted for use on organic crops: copper fungicides, restricted largely to potatoes and occasionally orchards; sulphur, used to control additional elements of fungal diseases; Rotenone, a naturally occurring plant extract; and soft soap, derived from potassium soap and used to control aphids. Herbicides are entirely prohibited.

7. Ecosystem Impact

Farmland accounts for 70 per cent of UK land mass, making it the single most influential enterprise affecting our wildlife. Incentives offered for intensification under the Common Agricultural Policy are largely responsible for negative ecosystem impacts over recent years. Since 1962, farmland bird numbers have declined by an average of 30 per cent. During the same period more than 192,000 kilometres of hedgerows have been removed, while 45 per cent of our ancient woodland has been converted to cropland.

By contrast, organic farms actively encourage biodiversity in order to maintain soil fertility and aid natural pest control. Mixed farming systems ensure that a diversity of food and nesting sites [is] available throughout the year, compared with conventional farms where autumn sow crops leave little winter vegetation available.

Organic production systems are designed to respect the balance observed in our natural ecosystems. It is widely accepted that controlling or suppressing one element of wildlife, even if it is a pest, will have unpredictable impacts on the rest of the food chain. Instead, organic producers regard a healthy ecosystem as essential to a healthy farm, rather than a barrier to production.

In 2005, a report by English Nature and the RSPB on the impacts of organic farming on biodiversity reviewed more than 70 independent studies of flora, invertebrates, birds and mammals within organic and conventional farming systems. It concluded that biodiversity is enhanced at every level of the food chain under organic management practices, from soil micro-biota right through to farmland birds and the largest mammals.

8. Nutritional Benefits

While an all-organic farming system might mean we'd have to make do with slightly less food than we're used to, research shows that we can rest assured it would be better for us. In 2001, a study in the *Journal of Complementary*

Medicine found that organic crops contained higher levels of 21 essential nutrients than their conventionally grown counterparts, including iron, magnesium, phosphorus and vitamin C. The organic crops also contained lower levels of nitrates, which can be toxic to the body.

Other studies have found significantly higher levels of vitamins—as well as polyphenols and antioxidants—in organic fruit and veg, both of which are thought to play a role in cancer-prevention within the body.

Scientists have also been able to work out why organic farming produces more nutritious food. Avoiding chemical fertilizer reduces nitrates levels in the food; better quality soil increases the availability of trace minerals, and reduced levels of pesticides mean that the plants' own immune systems grow stronger, producing higher levels of antioxidants. Slower rates of growth also mean that organic food frequently contains higher levels of dry mass, meaning that fruit and vegetables are less pumped up with water and so contain more nutrients by weight than intensively grown crops do.

Milk from organically fed cows has been found to contain higher levels of nutrients in six separate studies, including omega-3 fatty acids, vitamin E, and beta-carotene, all of which can help prevent cancer. One experiment discovered that levels of omega-3 in organic milk were on average 68 per cent higher than in non-organic alternatives.

But as well as giving us more of what we do need, organic food can help to give us less of what we don't. In 2000, the UN Food and Agriculture Organization (FAO) found that organically produced food had 'lower levels of pesticide and veterinary drug residues' than non-organic did. Although organic farmers are allowed to use antibiotics when absolutely necessary to treat disease, the routine use of the drugs in animal feed—common on intensive livestock farms—is forbidden. This means a shift to organic livestock farming could help tackle problems such as the emergence of antibiotic-resistant bacteria.

9. Seed-Saving

Seeds are not simply a source of food; they are living testimony to more than 10,000 years of agricultural domestication. Tragically, however, they are a resource that has suffered unprecedented neglect. The UN FAO estimates that 75 per cent of the genetic diversity of agricultural crops has been lost over the past 100 years.

Traditionally, farming communities have saved seeds year on year, both in order to save costs and to trade with their neighbours. As a result, seed varieties evolved in response to local climatic and seasonal conditions, leading to a wide variety of fruiting times, seed size, appearance and flavour. More importantly, this meant a constant updating process for the seed's genetic resistance to changing climatic conditions, new pests and diseases.

By contrast, modern intensive agriculture depends on relatively few crops—only about 150 species are cultivated on any significant scale worldwide. This is the inheritance of the Green Revolution, which in the late 1950s perfected varieties Filial 1, or F1 seed technology, which produced hybrid seeds with specifically desirable genetic qualities. These new high-yield seeds were widely adopted, but because the genetic makeup of hybrid F1 seeds becomes diluted following the first harvest, the manufacturers ensured that farmers return for more seed year on year.

With its emphasis on diversity, organic farming is somewhat cushioned from exploitation on this scale, but even Syngenta, the world's third-largest biotech company, now offers organic seed lines. Although seed-saving is not a prerequisite for organic production, the holistic nature of organics lends itself well to conserving seed.

In support of this, the Heritage Seed Library, in Warwickshire, is a collection of more than 800 open-pollinated organic varieties, which have been carefully preserved by gardeners across the country.

Although their seeds are not yet commercially available, the Library is at the forefront of addressing the alarming erosion of our agricultural diversity.

Seed-saving and the development of local varieties must become a key component of organic farming, giving crops the potential to evolve in response to what could be rapidly changing climatic conditions. This will help agriculture keeps pace with climate change in the field, rather than in the laboratory.

10. Job Creation

There is no doubt British farming is currently in crisis. With an average of 37 farmers leaving the land every day, there are now more prisoners behind bars in the UK than there are farmers in the fields.

Although it has been slow, the decline in the rural labour force is a predictable consequence of the industrialisation of agriculture. A mere one per cent of the UK workforce is now employed in land-related enterprises, compared with 35 per cent at the turn of the last century.

The implications of this decline are serious. A skilled agricultural workforce will be essential in order to maintain food security in the coming transition towards a new model of post-fossil fuel farming. Many of these skills have already been eroded through mechanisation and a move towards more specialised and intensive production systems.

Organic farming is an exception to these trends. By its nature, organic production relies on labour-intensive management practices. Smaller, more diverse farming systems require a level of husbandry that is simply uneconomical at any other scale. Organic crops and livestock also demand specialist knowledge and regular monitoring in the absence of agrochemical controls.

According to a 2006 report by the University of Essex, organic farming in the UK provides 32 per cent more jobs per farm than comparable non-organic farms. Interestingly, the report also concluded that the higher employment observed could not be replicated in non-organic farming through initiatives such as local marketing. Instead, the majority (81 per cent) of total employment on organic farms was created by the organic production system itself. The report estimates that 93,000 new jobs would be created if all farming in the UK were to convert to organic.

Organic farming also accounts for more younger employees than any other sector in the industry. The average age of conventional UK farmers is now 56, yet organic farms increasingly attract a younger more enthusiastic workforce, people who view organics as the future of food production. It is for this next generation of farmers that Organic Futures, a campaign group set up by the Soil Association in 2007, is striving to provide a platform.

Mark Bittman    **NO**

Eating Food That's Better for You, Organic or Not

In the six-and-one-half years since the federal government began certifying food as "organic," Americans have taken to the idea with considerable enthusiasm. Sales have at least doubled, and three-quarters of the nation's grocery stores now carry at least some organic food. A Harris poll in October 2007 found that about 30 percent of Americans buy organic food at least on occasion, and most think it is safer, better for the environment and healthier.

"People believe it must be better for you if it's organic," says Phil Howard, an assistant professor of community, food and agriculture at Michigan State University.

So I discovered on a recent book tour around the United States and Canada.

No matter how carefully I avoided using the word "organic" when I spoke to groups of food enthusiasts about how to eat better, someone in the audience would inevitably ask, "What if I can't afford to buy organic food?" It seems to have become the magic cure-all, synonymous with eating well, healthfully, sanely, even ethically.

But eating "organic" offers no guarantee of any of that. And the truth is that most Americans eat so badly—we get 7 percent of our calories from soft drinks, more than we do from vegetables; the top food group by caloric intake is "sweets"; and one-third of nation's adults are now obese—that the organic question is a secondary one. It's not unimportant, but it's not the primary issue in the way Americans eat.

To eat well, says Michael Pollan, the author of "In Defense of Food," means avoiding "edible food-like substances" and sticking to real ingredients, increasingly from the plant kingdom. (Americans each consume an average of nearly two pounds a day of animal products.) There's plenty of evidence that both a person's health—as well as the environment's—will improve with a simple shift in eating habits away from animal products and highly processed foods to plant products and what might be called "real food." (With all due respect to people in the "food movement," the food need not be "slow," either.)

From these changes, Americans would reduce the amount of land, water and chemicals used to produce the food we eat, as well as the incidence of lifestyle diseases linked to unhealthy diets, and greenhouse gases from industrial meat production. All without legislation.

And the food would not necessarily have to be organic, which, under the United States Department of Agriculture's definition, means it is generally free of synthetic substances; contains no antibiotics and hormones; has not been irradiated or fertilized with sewage sludge; was raised without the use of most conventional pesticides; and contains no genetically modified ingredients.

Those requirements, which must be met in order for food to be labeled "U.S.D.A. Organic," are fine, of course. But they still fall short of the lofty dreams of early organic farmers and consumers who gave the word "organic" its allure—of returning natural nutrients and substance to the soil in the same proportion used by the growing process (there is no requirement that this be done); of raising animals humanely in accordance with nature (animals must be given access to the outdoors, but for how long and under what conditions is not spelled out); and of producing the most nutritious food possible (the evidence is mixed on whether organic food is more nutritious) in the most ecologically conscious way.

The government's organic program, says Joan Shaffer, a spokeswoman for the Agriculture Department, "is a marketing program that sets standards for what can be certified as organic. Neither the enabling legislation nor the regulations address food safety or nutrition."

People don't understand that, nor do they realize "organic" doesn't mean "local." "It doesn't matter if it's from the farm down the road or from Chile," Ms. Shaffer said. "As long as it meets the standards it's organic."

Hence, the organic status of salmon flown in from Chile, or of frozen vegetables grown in China and sold in the United States—no matter the size of the carbon footprint left behind by getting from there to here.

Today, most farmers who practice truly sustainable farming, or what you might call "organic in spirit," operate on small scale, some so small they can't afford the requirements to be certified organic by the government. Others say that certification isn't meaningful enough to bother. These farmers argue that, "When you buy organic you don't just buy a product, you buy a way of life that is committed to not exploiting the planet," says Ed Maltby, executive director of the Northeast Organic Dairy Producers Alliance.

But the organic food business is now big business, and getting bigger. Professor Howard estimates that major corporations now are responsible for at least 25 percent of all organic manufacturing and marketing (40 percent if you count only processed organic foods). Much of the nation's organic food is as much a part of industrial food production as midwinter grapes, and becoming more so. In 2006, sales of organic foods and beverages totaled about $16.7 billion, according to the most recent figures from Organic Trade Association.

Still, those sales amounted to slightly less than 3 percent of overall food and beverage sales. For all the hoo-ha, organic food is not making much of an impact on the way Americans eat, though, as Mark Kastel, co-founder of The Cornucopia Institute, puts it: "There are generic benefits from doing organics. It protects the land from the ravages of conventional agriculture," and safeguards farm workers from being exposed to pesticides.

But the questions remain over how we eat in general. It may feel better to eat an organic Oreo than a conventional Oreo, but, says Marion Nestle, a professor at New York University's department of nutrition, food studies and public health, "Organic junk food is still junk food."

Last [year], Michelle Obama began digging up a patch of the South Lawn of the White House to plant an organic vegetable garden to provide food for the first family and, more important, to educate children about healthy, locally grown fruits and vegetables at a time when obesity and diabetes have become national concerns.

But Mrs. Obama also emphasized that there were many changes Americans can make if they don't have the time or space for an organic garden.

"You can begin in your own cupboard," she said, "by eliminating processed food, trying to cook a meal a little more often, trying to incorporate more fruits and vegetables."

Popularizing such choices may not be as marketable as creating a logo that says "organic." But when Americans have had their fill of "value-added" and overprocessed food, perhaps they can begin producing and consuming more food that treats animals and the land as if they mattered. Some of that food will be organic, and hooray for that. Meanwhile, they should remember that the word itself is not synonymous with "safe," "healthy," "fair" or even necessarily "good."

CHALLENGE QUESTIONS

Are Organic Foods Better Than Conventional Foods?

1. Define what is meant by "organic and local."
2. Describe how both the articles compare the way organic foods are grown today to the way the early organic farmers originally intended them to be grown.
3. List the benefits that organic foods provide to people, the environment, and society.
4. Ed Hamer and Mark Anslow say that organic farming can feed the world if we "farm and eat differently." Explain what they mean by this.
5. Design a program that will ensure all people in your city have access to affordable organic foods.

ISSUE 11

Does the World Need Genetically Modified Foods?

YES: Henry I. Miller and Gregory Conko, from "Scary Food," *Policy Review* (June/July 2006)

NO: Ed Hamer and Mark Anslow, from "10 Reasons Genetically Modified Foods Cannot [Feed the World]," *The Ecologist* (March 2008)

As you read the issue, focus on the following points:

1. How genetic modification makes certain plants disease resistant.
2. The two types of genetic modifications that are currently used.
3. The benefits that GM provides to our food supply and the possible hazards that could occur if we continue to use GM seeds.

ISSUE SUMMARY

YES: Henry Miller and Gregory Conko defend biotechnology used in genetically modifying (GM) crops and foods and believe they bring many advantages and help ensure a safe food supply.

NO: Ed Hamer and Mark Anslow argue that GM foods cost farmers and governments more money than they are worth, that they are ruining the environment, and point to the health risks associated with GM foods.

If you eat any processed foods, chances are you have eaten genetically modified (GM) ones without even knowing it. Most people have heard of the term, but may not know exactly what "genetically modified" means. The World Health Organization (WHO) defines it as "organisms in which the genetic material (DNA) has been altered in a way that does not occur naturally." Other names for GM are "genetic engineering," "modern biotechnology," "gene technology," "gene splicing," and "bioengineered."

Scientists have been working on GM techniques for many years in an effort to improve and extend the world's food supply. Some GM involves improving the vitamin, omega-3 fatty acid, or other nutrient content of crops or animals. Others try to speed up the growth or improve the taste or appearance of a food.

Some GM that are commonly used focus on making crops resistant to infestation from pests while others make the product tolerant to herbicides. The most common herbicide used in developed countries is Roundup, which contains the potentially toxic glyphosate. (EPA currently considers it safe, but environmentalists are concerned about long-term exposure.) Many farmers use it to kill the weeds and grasses around their crops. (This keeps them from having to pull weeds out of the garden.) The only problem is that Roundup is so strong that it kills the plant.

A seed that is modified to become "Roundup Ready" means a farmer can plant the GM seeds and spray Roundup in the field, on both weeds and plants. Since the plants are tolerant of Roundup, they do not die but the weeds do. To date, "Roundup Ready" is the most common GM procedure used. It is used in soy, corn, sorghum, canola, alfalfa, and cotton. According to the Cornucopia Institute, in 2008, 92 percent of soybeans grown in the US were GM. This is a tremendous increase since 2000, when GM accounted for only 54 percent of soybeans.

As related to Roundup Ready crops, people are concerned about two things. First, what impact does the Roundup residue that remains on the plant—and the food we eat—have on our bodies? The second is related to the actual genetic changes in the DNA. Is it safe for humans? GM foods have only been around since 1996, so their long-term impact is not known. Some laboratory studies have reported problems with fertility, abnormalities in offspring, and kidney problems in laboratory studies using GM foods.

After you read the two articles, decide if you believe we need GM foods to help feed the world. Or better yet, do you want to eat these foods that some call "Frankenfoods." Henry Miller and Gregory Conko defend biotechnology used in GM crops and believe they bring many advantages to the world's food supply. Ed Hamer and Mark Anslow argue that GM foods cost farmers and governments more money than they are worth, that they are the ruining environment, and point out the health risks associated with them.

TIMELINE

1996 GM foods are introduced in the United States.
2002 54% of U.S. soybeans are GM.
2008 92% of U.S. soybeans are GM.

DEFINITIONS

Bt gene The gene from *Bacillus thuringiensis* that produces a protein, which destroys insects that infect corn; GM makes it possible for the Bt gene to be spliced into corn.

Ergot A fungus that infects various cereals such as rye and wheat is called the "cereal killer" because it is often deadly.

Fumonisin Deadly toxin produced from the mold *Fusarium*, an example of a mycotoxin.

Glyphosate Chemical in herbicides like Roundup that is suspected to be toxic to humans.

Mycotoxin A poisonous substance produced by a fungus such as mold.

Parathion A highly poisonous insecticide that is banned in most countries.

Methamidophos Insecticide use to control insects on potatoes, cotton, and tomatoes.

YES  Henry I. Miller and Gregory Conko

Scary Food

Like a scene from some Hollywood thriller, a team of U.S. Marshals stormed a warehouse in Irvington, New Jersey, last summer to intercept a shipment of evildoers from Pakistan. The reason you probably haven't heard about the raid is that the objective was not to seize Al Qaeda operatives or white slavers, but $80,000 worth of basmati rice contaminated with weevils, beetles, and insect larvae, making it unfit for human consumption. In regulation-speak, the food was "adulterated," because "it consists in whole or in part of any filthy, putrid, or decomposed substance, or if it is otherwise unfit for food."

Americans take food safety very seriously. Still, many consumers tend to ignore Mother Nature's contaminants while they worry unduly about high technology, such as the advanced technologies that farmers, plant breeders, and food processors use to make our food supply the most affordable, nutritious, varied, and safe in history.

For example, recombinant DNA technology—also known as food biotechnology, gene-splicing, or genetic modification (GM)—is often singled out by critics as posing a risk that new allergens, toxins, or other nasty substances will be introduced into the food supply. And, because of the mainstream media's "if it bleeds, it leads" approach, news coverage of food biotech is dominated by the outlandish claims and speculations of anti-technology activists. This has caused some food companies—including fast-food giant McDonald's and baby-food manufacturers Gerber and Heinz—to forgo superior (and even cost-saving) gene-spliced ingredients in favor of ones the public will find less threatening.

Scientists agree, however, that gene-spliced crops and foods are not only better for the natural environment than conventionally produced food crops, but also safer for consumers. Several varieties now on the market have been modified to resist insect predation and plant diseases, which makes the harvested crop much cleaner and safer. Ironically (and also surprisingly in these litigious times), in their eagerness to avoid biotechnology, some major food companies may knowingly be making their products less safe and wholesome for consumers. This places them in richly deserved legal jeopardy.

From *Policy Review,* June/July 2006, pp. 61–69. Copyright © 2006 by Henry I. Miller and Gregory Conko. Reprinted by permission of Policy Review/Hoover Institution/Stanford University and Henry I. Miller and Gregory Conko.

Don't Trust Mother Nature

Every year, scores of packaged food products are recalled from the American market due to the presence of all-natural contaminants like insect parts, toxic molds, bacteria, and viruses. Because farming takes place out-of-doors and in dirt, such contamination is a fact of life. Fortunately, modern technology has enabled farmers and food processors to minimize the threat from these contaminants.

The historical record of mass food poisoning in Europe offers a cautionary tale. From the ninth to the nineteenth centuries, Europe suffered a succession of epidemics caused by the contamination of rye with ergot, a poisonous fungus. Ergot contains the potent toxin ergotamine, the consumption of which induces hallucinations, bizarre behavior, and violent muscle twitching. These symptoms gave rise at various times to the belief that victims were possessed by evil spirits. Witch-hunting and persecution were commonplace—and the New World was not immune. One leading explanation for the notorious 1691–92 Salem witch trials also relates to ergot contamination. Three young girls suffered violent convulsions, incomprehensible speech, trance-like states, odd skin sensations, and delirious visions in which they supposedly saw the mark of the devil on certain women in the village. The girls lived in a swampy meadow area around Salem; rye was a major staple of their diet; and records indicate that the rye harvest at the time was complicated by rainy and humid conditions, exactly the situation in which ergot would thrive.

Worried villagers feared the girls were under a spell cast by demons, and the girls eventually named three women as witches. The subsequent panic led to the execution of as many as 20 innocent people. Until a University of California graduate student discovered this link, a reasonable explanation had defied historians. But the girls' symptoms are typical of ergot poisoning, and when the supply of infected grain ran out, the delusions and persecution likewise disappeared.

In the twenty-first century, modern technology, aggressive regulations, and a vigorous legal liability system in industrialized countries such as the United States are able to mitigate much of this sort of contamination. Occasionally, though, Americans will succumb to tainted food picked from the woods or a backyard garden. However, elsewhere in the world, particularly in less-developed countries, people are poisoned every day by fungal toxins that contaminate grain. The result is birth defects, cancer, organ failure, and premature death.

About a decade ago, Hispanic women in the Rio Grande Valley of Texas were found to be giving birth to an unusually large number of babies with crippling and lethal neural tube defects (NTDS) such as spina bifida, hydrocephalus, and anencephaly—at a rate approximately six times higher than the national average for non-Hispanic women. The cause remained a mystery until recent research revealed a link between NTDS and consumption of large amounts of unprocessed corn like that found in tortillas and other staples of the Latino diet.

The connection is obscure but fascinating. The culprit is fumonisin, a deadly mycotoxin, or fungal toxin, produced by the mold *Fusarium* and sometimes found in unprocessed corn. When insects attack corn, they open wounds in the plant that provide a perfect breeding ground for *Fusarium*. Once molds get a foothold, poor storage conditions also promote their post-harvest growth on grain.

Fumonisin and some other mycotoxins are highly toxic, causing fatal diseases in livestock that eat infected corn and esophageal cancer in humans. Fumonisin also interferes with the cellular uptake of folic acid, a vitamin that is known to reduce the risk of NTDS in developing fetuses. Because fumonisin prevents the folic acid from being absorbed by cells, the toxin can, in effect, induce functional folic acid deficiency—and thereby cause NTDS—even when the diet contains what otherwise would be sufficient amounts of folic acid.

The epidemiological evidence was compelling. At the time that the babies of Hispanic women in the Rio Grande Valley experienced the high rate of neural tube defects, the fumonisin level in corn in that locale was two to three times higher than normal, and the affected women reported much higher dietary consumption of homemade tortillas than in women who were unaffected.

Acutely aware of the danger of mycotoxins, regulatory agencies such as the U.S. Food and Drug Administration and Britain's Food Safety Agency have established recommended maximum fumonisin levels in food and feed products made from corn. Although highly processed cornstarch and corn oil are unlikely to be contaminated with fumonisin, unprocessed corn or lightly processed corn (e.g., cornmeal) can have fumonisin levels that exceed recommended levels.

In 2003, the Food Safety Agency tested six organic cornmeal products and twenty conventional corn meal products for fumonisin contamination. All six organic cornmeals had elevated levels—from nine to 40 times greater than the recommended levels for human health—and they were voluntarily withdrawn from grocery stores.

A Technical Fix

The conventional way to combat mycotoxins is simply to test unprocessed and processed grains and throw out those found to be contaminated—an approach that is both wasteful and dubious. But modern technology—specifically in the form of gene-splicing—is already attacking the fungal problem at its source. An excellent example is "Bt corn," crafted by splicing into commercial corn varieties a gene from the bacterium *Bacillus thuringiensis*. The "Bt" gene expresses a protein that is toxic to corn-boring insects but is perfectly harmless to birds, fish, and mammals, including humans.

As the Bt corn fends off insect pests, it also reduces the levels of the mold *Fusarium,* thereby reducing the levels of fumonisin. Thus, switching to the gene-spliced, insect-resistant corn for food processing lowers the levels of fumonisin—as well as the concentration of insect parts—likely to be found in the final product. Researchers at Iowa State University and the U.S. Department of Agriculture found that Bt corn reduces the level of fumonisin by as much as 80 percent compared to conventional corn.

Thus, on the basis of both theory and empirical knowledge, there should be potent incentives—legal, commercial, and ethical—to use such gene-spliced grains more widely. One would expect public and private sector advocates of public health to demand that such improved varieties be cultivated and used for food—not unlike requirements for drinking water to be chlorinated and fluoridated. Food producers who wish to offer the safest and best products to their customers—to say nothing of being offered the opportunity to advertise "New and Improved!"—should be competing to get gene-spliced products into the marketplace.

Alas, none of this has come to pass. Activists have mounted intractable opposition to food biotechnology in spite of demonstrated, significant benefits, including reduced use of chemical pesticides, less runoff of chemicals into waterways, greater use of farming practices that prevent soil erosion, higher profits for farmers, and less fungal contamination. Inexplicably, government oversight has also been an obstacle, by subjecting the testing and commercialization of gene-spliced crops to unscientific and draconian regulations that have vastly increased testing and development costs and limited the use and diffusion of food biotechnology.

The result is jeopardy for everyone involved in food production and consumption: Consumers are subjected to avoidable and often undetected health risks, and food producers have placed themselves in legal jeopardy. The first point is obvious, the latter less so, but as described first by Drew Kershen, professor of law at the University of Oklahoma, it makes a fascinating story: Agricultural processors and food companies may face at least two kinds of civil liability for their refusal to purchase and use fungus-resistant, gene-spliced plant varieties, as well as other superior products.

Food for Thought

In 1999 the Gerber foods company succumbed to activist pressure, announcing that its baby food products would no longer contain any gene-spliced ingredients. Indeed, Gerber went farther and promised it would attempt to shift to organic ingredients that are grown without synthetic pesticides or fertilizers. Because corn starch and corn sweeteners are often used in a range of foods, this could mean changing Gerber's entire product line.

But in its attempt to head off a potential public relations problem concerning the use of gene-spliced ingredients, Gerber has actually increased the health risk for its baby consumers—and, thereby, its legal liability. As noted above, not only is gene-spliced corn likely to have lower levels of fumonisin than conventional corn; organic corn is likely to have the highest levels, because it suffers greater insect predation due to less effective pest controls.

If a mother some day discovers that her "Gerber baby" has developed liver or esophageal cancer, she might have a legal case against Gerber. On the child's behalf, a plaintiff's lawyer can allege liability based on mycotoxin contamination in the baby food as the causal agent of the cancer. The contamination would be considered a *manufacturing defect* under product liability law because the baby food did not meet its intended product specifications or level of safety. According to Kershen, Gerber could be found liable "even though all possible care was exercised in the preparation and marketing of the product," simply because the contamination occurred.

The plaintiff's lawyer could also allege a *design defect* in the baby food, because Gerber knew of the existence of a less risky design—namely, the use of gene-spliced varieties that are less prone to *Fusarium* and fumonisin contamination—but deliberately chose not to use it. Instead, Gerber chose to use non-gene-spliced, organic food ingredients, knowing that the foreseeable risks of harm posed by them could have been reduced or avoided by adopting a reasonable alternative design—that is, by using gene-spliced Bt corn, which is known to have a lower risk of mycotoxin contamination.

Gerber might answer this design defect claim by contending that it was only responding to consumer demand, but that alone would not be persuasive. Product liability law subjects defenses in design defect cases to a risk-utility balancing in which consumer expectations are only one of several factors used to determine whether the product design (e.g., the use of only non-gene-spliced ingredients) is reasonably safe. A jury might conclude that whatever consumer demand there may be for non-biotech ingredients does not outweigh Gerber's failure to use a technology that is known to lower the health risks to consumers.

Even if Gerber was able to defend itself from the design defect claim, the company might still be liable because it failed to provide adequate instructions or warnings about the potential risks of non-gene-spliced ingredients. For example, Gerber could label its non-gene-spliced baby food with a statement such as: "This product does not contain gene-spliced ingredients. Consequently, this product has a very slight additional risk of mycotoxin contamination. Mycotoxins can cause serious diseases such as liver and esophageal cancer and birth defects."

Whatever the risk of toxic or carcinogenic fumonisin levels in non-biotech corn may be (probably low in industrialized countries, where food producers generally are cautious about such contamination), a more likely scenario is potential liability for an allergic reaction.

Six percent to 8 percent of children and 1 to 2 percent of adults are allergic to one or another food ingredient, and an estimated 150 Americans die each year from exposure to food allergens. Allergies to peanuts, soybeans, and wheat proteins, for example, are quite common and can be severe. Although only about 1 percent of the population is allergic to peanuts, some individuals are so highly sensitive that exposure causes anaphylactic shock, killing dozens of people every year in North America.

Protecting those with true food allergies is a daunting task. Farmers, food shippers and processors, wholesalers and retailers, and even restaurants must maintain meticulous records and labels and ensure against cross-contamination. Still, in a country where about a billion meals are eaten every day, missteps are inevitable. Dozens of processed food items must be recalled every year due to accidental contamination or inaccurate labeling.

Fortunately, biotechnology researchers are well along in the development of peanuts, soybeans, wheat, and other crops in which the genes coding for allergenic proteins have been silenced or removed. According to University of California, Berkeley, biochemist Bob Buchanan, hypoallergenic varieties of wheat could be ready for commercialization within the decade, and nuts soon thereafter. Once these products are commercially available, agricultural processors and food companies that refuse to use these safer food sources will open themselves to products-liability, design-defect lawsuits.

Property Damage and Personal Injury

Potato farming is a growth industry, primarily due to the vast consumption of french fries at fast-food restaurants. However, growing potatoes is not easy, because they are preyed upon by a wide range of voracious and difficult-to-control pests, such as the Colorado potato beetle, virus-spreading aphids, nematodes, potato blight, and others.

To combat these pests and diseases, potato growers use an assortment of fungicides (to control blight), insecticides (to kill aphids and the Colorado potato beetle), and fumigants (to control soil nematodes). Although some of these chemicals are quite hazardous to farm workers, forgoing them could jeopardize the sustainability and profitability of the entire potato industry. Standard application of synthetic pesticides enhances yields more than 50 percent over organic potato production, which prohibits most synthetic inputs.

Consider a specific example. Many growers use methamidophos, a toxic organophosphate nerve poison, for aphid control. Although methamidophos is an EPA-approved pesticide, the agency is currently reevaluating the use of organophosphates and could ultimately prohibit or greatly restrict the use of this entire class of pesticides. As an alternative to these chemicals, the Monsanto Company developed a potato that contains a gene from the bacterium *Bacillus thuringiensis* (Bt) to control the Colorado potato beetle and another gene to control the potato leaf roll virus spread by the aphids. Monsanto's NewLeaf potato is resistant to these two scourges of potato plants, which allowed growers who adopted it to reduce their use of chemical controls and increase yields.

Farmers who planted NewLeaf became convinced that it was the most environmentally sound and economically efficient way to grow potatoes. But after five years of excellent results it encountered an unexpected snag. Under pressure from anti-biotechnology organizations, McDonald's, Burger King, and other restaurant chains informed their potato suppliers that they would no longer accept gene-spliced potato varieties for their french fries. As a result, potato processors such as J.R. Simplot inserted a nonbiotech-potato clause into their farmer-processor contracts and informed farmers that they would no longer buy gene-spliced potatoes. In spite of its substantial environmental, occupational safety, and economic benefits, NewLeaf became a sort of contractual poison pill and is no longer grown commercially. Talk about market distortions.

Now, let us assume that a farmer who is required by contractual arrangement to plant nonbiotech potatoes sprays his potato crop with methamidophos (the organophosphate nerve poison) and that the pesticide drifts into a nearby stream and onto nearby farm laborers. Thousands of fish die in the stream, and the laborers report to hospital emergency rooms complaining of neurological symptoms.

This hypothetical scenario is, in fact, not at all far-fetched. Fish-kills attributed to pesticide runoff from potato fields are commonplace. In the potato-growing region of Prince Edward Island, Canada, for example, a dozen such incidents occurred in one 13-month period alone, between July 1999 and August 2000. According to the UN's Food and Agriculture Organization, "normal" use of the pesticides parathion and methamidophos is responsible for some 7,500 pesticide poisoning cases in China each year.

In our hypothetical scenario, the state environmental agency might bring an administrative action for civil damages to recover the cost of the fish-kill, and a plaintiff's lawyer could file a class-action suit on behalf of the farm laborers for personal injury damages.

Who's legally responsible? Several possible circumstances could enable the farmer's defense lawyer to shift culpability for the alleged damages to the contracting food processor and to the fast-food restaurants that are the ultimate purchasers of the potatoes. These circumstances include the farmer's having planted Bt potatoes in the recent past; his contractual obligation to the potato processor and its fast-food retail buyers to provide only nonbiotech varieties; and his demonstrated preference for planting gene-spliced, Bt potatoes, were it not for the contractual proscription. If these conditions could be proved, the lawyer defending the farmer could name the contracting processor and the fast-food restaurants as cross-defendants, claiming either contribution in tort law or indemnification in contract law for any damages legally imposed upon the farmer client.

The farmer's defense could be that those companies bear the ultimate responsibility for the damages because they compelled the farmer to engage in higher-risk production practices than he would otherwise have chosen. The companies chose to impose cultivation of a non-gene-spliced variety upon the farmer although they knew that in order to avoid severe losses in yield, he would need to use organophosphate pesticides. Thus, the defense could argue that the farmer should have a legal right to pass any damages (arising from contractually imposed production practices) back to the processor and the fast-food chains.

Why Biotech?

Companies that insist upon farmers' using production techniques that involve foreseeable harms to the environment and humans may be—we would argue, *should* be—legally accountable for that decision. If agricultural processors and food companies manage to avoid legal liability for their insistence on nonbiotech crops, they will be "guilty" at least of externalizing their environmental costs onto the farmers, the environment, and society at large.

Food biotechnology provides an effective—and cost-effective—way to prevent many of these injurious scenarios, but instead of being widely encouraged, it is being resisted by self-styled environmental activists and even government officials.

It should not fall to the courts to resolve and reconcile what are essentially scientific and moral issues. However, other components of society—industry, government, and "consumer advocacy" groups—have failed abjectly to fully exploit a superior, life-enhancing, and life-saving technology. Even the biotechnology trade associations have been unhelpful. All are guilty, in varying measures, of sacrificing the public interest to self-interest and of helping to perpetuate a gross public misconception—that food biotechnology is unproven, untested, and unregulated.

If consumers genuinely want a safer, more nutritious, and more varied food supply at a reasonable cost, they need to know where the real threats lie. They must also become better informed, demand public policy that makes sense, and deny fringe anti-technology activists permission to speak for consumers.

Ed Hamer and Mark Anslow  **NO**

10 Reasons Genetically Modified Foods Cannot [Feed the World]

Failure to Deliver

Despite the hype, genetic modification consistently fails to live up to industry claims. Only two GM traits have ever made it to market: herbicide resistance and BT toxin expression (see below). Other promises of genetic modification have failed to materialise. The much vaunted GM 'golden rice'—hailed as a cure to vitamin A deficiency—has never made it out of the laboratory, partly because in order to meet recommended levels of vitamin A intake, consumers would need to eat 12 bowls of the rice every day. In 2004, the Kenyan government admitted that Monsanto's GM sweet potatoes were no more resistant to feathery mottle virus than ordinary strains, and in fact produced lower yields. And in January 2008, news that scientists had modified a carrot to cure osteoporosis by providing calcium had to be weighed against the fact that you would need to eat 1.6 kilograms of these vegetables each day to meet your recommended calcium intake.

Costing the Earth

GM crops are costing farmers and governments more money than they are making. In 2003, a report by the Soil Association estimated the cost to the US economy of GM crops at around $12 billion (£6 billion) since 1999, on account of inflated farm subsidies, loss of export orders and various seed recalls. A study in Iowa found that GM soyabeans required all the same costs as conventional farming but, because they produced lower yields (see below), the farmers ended up making no profit at all. In India, an independent study found that BT cotton crops were costing farmers 10 per cent more than non-BT variants and bringing in 40 per cent lower profits. Between 2001 and 2005, more than 32,000 Indian farmers committed suicide, most as a result of mounting debts caused by inadequate crops.

Contamination and Gene Escape

No matter how hard you try, you can never be sure that what you are eating is GM-free. In a recent article, the *New Scientist* admitted that contamination and cross-fertilisation between GM and non-GM crops 'has happened on many occasions already'. In late 2007, US company Scotts Miracle-Gro was fined $500,000 by the US Department of Agriculture when genetic material from a new golf-course grass Scotts had been testing was found in native grasses as far as 13 miles away from the test sites, apparently released when freshly cut grass was caught and blown by the wind. In 2006, an analysis of 40 Spanish conventional and organic farms found that eight were contaminated with GM corn varieties, including one farmer whose crop contained 12.6 per cent GM plants.

Reliance on Pesticides

Far from reducing dependency on pesticides and fertilisers, GM crops frequently increase farmers' reliance on these products. Herbicide-resistant crops can be sprayed indiscriminately with weedkillers such as Monsanto's 'Roundup' because they are engineered to withstand the effect of the chemical. This means that significantly higher levels of herbicide are found in the final food product, however, and often a second herbicide is used in the late stages of the crop to promote 'dessication' or drying, meaning these crops receive a double dose of harmful chemicals. BT maize, engineered to produce an insecticidal toxin, has never eliminated the use of pesticides, and because the BT gene cannot be 'switched off' the crops continue to produce the toxin right up until harvest, reaching the consumer at its highest possible concentrations.

'Frankenfoods'

Despite the best efforts of the biotech industry, consumers remain staunchly opposed to GM food. In 2007, the vast majority of 11,700 responses to the Government's consultation on whether contamination of organic food with traces of GM crops should be allowed were strongly negative.

The Government's own 'GM Nation' debate in 2003 discovered that half of its participants 'never want to see GM crops grown in the United Kingdom under any circumstances', and 96 per cent thought that society knew too little about the health impacts of genetic modification. In India, farmers' experience of BT cotton has been so disastrous that the Maharashtra government now advises that farmers grow soybeans instead. And in Australia, over 250 food companies lodged appeals with the state governments of New South Wales and Victoria over the lifting of bans against growing GM canola crops.

Breeding Resistance

Nature is smart, and there are already reports of species resistant to GM crops emerging. This is seen in the emergence of new 'superweeds' on farms in North America-plants that have evolved the ability to withstand the industry's chemicals. A report by then UK conservation body English Nature (now Natural England), in 2002, revealed that oilseed rape plants that had developed resistance to three or more herbicides were 'not uncommon' in Canada. The superweeds had been created through random crosses between neighbouring

GM crops. In order to tackle these superweeds, Canadian farmers were forced to resort to even stronger, more toxic herbicides. Similarly, pests (notably the diamondback moth) have been quick to develop resistance to BT toxin, and in 2007 swarms of mealy bugs began attacking supposedly pest-resistant Indian cotton.

Creating Problems for Solutions

Many of the so-called 'problems' for which the biotechnology industry develops 'solutions' seem to be notions of PR rather than science. Herbicide resistance was sold under the claim that because crops could be doused in chemicals, there would be much less need to weed mechanically or plough the soil, keeping more carbon and nitrates under the surface. But a new long-term study by the US Agricultural Research Service has shown that organic farming, even with ploughing, stores more carbon than the GM crops save. BT cotton was claimed to increase resistance to pests, but farmers in East Africa discovered that by planting a local weed amid their com crop, they could lure pests to lay their eggs on the weed and not the crop.

Health Risks

The results of tests on animals exposed to GM crops give serious cause for concern over their safety. In 1998, Scottish scientists found damage to every single internal organ in rats fed blight-resistant GM potatoes. In a 2006 experiment, female rats fed on herbicide-resistant soybeans gave birth to severely stunted pups, of which half died within three weeks. The survivors were sterile. In the same year, Indian news agencies reported that thousands of sheep allowed to graze on BT cotton crop residues had died suddenly. Further cases of livestock deaths followed in 2007. There have also been reports of allergy-like symptoms among Indian labourers in BT cotton fields. In 2002, the only trial ever to involve human beings appeared to show that altered genetic material from GM soybeans not only survives in the human gut, but may even pass its genetic material to bacteria within the digestive system.

Left Hungry

GM crops have always come with promises of increased yields for farmers, but this has rarely been the case. A three-year study of 87 villages in India found that non-BT cotton consistently produced 30 per cent higher yields than the (more expensive) GM alternative. It is now widely accepted that GM soybeans produce consistently lower yields than conventional varieties. In 1992, Monsanto's own trials showed that the company's Roundup Ready soybeans yield 11.5 per cent less on harvest. Later Monsanto studies went on to reveal that some trials of GM canola crops in Australia actually produced yields 16 per cent below the non-GM national average.

Wedded to Fertilisers and Fossil Fuels

No genetically modified crop has yet eliminated the need for chemical fertilisers in order to achieve expected yields. Although the industry has made much of the possibility of splicing nitrogen-fixing genes into commercial food crops in order to boost yields, there has so far been little success. This means that GM crops are just as dependent on fossil fuels to make fertilisers as conventional agriculture. In addition to this, GM traits are often specifically designed to fit with large-scale industrial agriculture. Herbicide resistance is of no real benefit unless your farm is too vast to weed mechanically, and it presumes that the farmers already farm in a way that involves the chemical spraying of their crops. Similarly, BT toxin expression is designed to counteract the problem of pest control in vast monocultures, which encourage infestations. In a world that will soon have to change its view of farming—facing as it does the twin challenges of climate change and peak oil—GM crops will soon come to look like a relic of bygone practices.

CHALLENGE QUESTIONS

Does the World Need Genetically Modified Foods?

1. Explain why foods in the US are genetically modified and which foods may contain them.
2. Explain what the Bt gene is. How could this gene benefit farmers? How could it become detrimental?
3. List and discuss the two strongest reasons that Miller and Conko have in favor of GM foods.
4. List and discuss the two strongest reasons that Hamer and Anslow have against GM foods.
5. Currently, the FDA does not require food manufacturers to print on the food label if a food contains GM products. (The UK does require labeling.) Write a 1-page letter to your congressman requesting that GM become a part of the requirements on food labels.

ISSUE 12

Are Probiotics and Prebiotics Beneficial in Promoting Health?

YES: **Anneli Rufus**, from "Poop Is the Most Important Indicator of Your Health," *AlterNet* (March 27, 2010)

NO: **Peta Bee**, from "Probiotics, Not So Friendly After All?" *The Times* (London) (November 10, 2008)

As you read the issue, focus on the following points:

1. What prebiotics and probiotics are and sources of each.
2. How prebiotics and probiotics function in the body.
3. The therapy that allows doctors to recolonize patients' bowels with beneficial bacteria.
4. How to tell if a food contains adequate amounts of beneficial bacteria.
5. The type people, because of certain health conditions, who should avoid foods still containing live bacteria. They type people who will benefit from foods containing live bacteria.

ISSUE SUMMARY

YES: Journalist Anneli Rufus describes how chemicals added to today's food supply destroy the good bacteria (probiotics) and various ways to restore the bacteria to the body. She also encourages us to start looking for prebiotic-fortified foods, since it is hard to get an adequate amount from foods.

NO: Health and fitness journalist Peta Bee is skeptical of probiotics and counters that some products that claim to contain probiotics may not actually have bacteria that are still "live and active" by the time we eat it. She points out that some bacteria added to foods may even be harmful.

Even though the terms are relatively new, the concept of probiotics and prebiotics has been around for centuries. German researchers Jürgen Schrezenmeir and Michael de Vrese provide a brief history of the two in the February 2001 supplement to the *Journal of Clinical Nutrition*. In the article "Probiotics, Prebiotics, and Synbiotics—Approaching a Definition," they trace the history back to the *Old Testament*.

> There is a long history of health claims concerning living microorganisms in food, particularly lactic acid bacteria. In a Persian version of the *Old Testament* (Genesis 18:8) it states that "Abraham owed his longevity to the consumption of sour milk." In 76 BC the Roman historian Plinius recommended the administration of fermented milk products for treating gastroenteritis. . . . Metchnikoff [1907] claimed that the intake of yogurt containing *lactobacilli* results in a reduction of toxin-producing bacteria in the gut and that this increases the longevity of the host. Tissier [1905] recommended the administration of bifidobacteria to infants suffering from diarrhea, claiming that bifidobacteria supersede the putrefactive bacteria that cause the disease. He showed that bifidobacteria were predominant in the gut flora of breast-fed infants.

Schrezenmeir and de Vrese write that the actual term "probiotic" was first used by "Lilly and Stillwell in 1965 to describe 'substances secreted by one microorganism which stimulates the growth of another' and thus was contrasted with the term "antibiotic." They report that "prebiotic" was introduced in 1995 by Gibson and Roberfroid who define it as "a non-digestible food ingredient that beneficially affects the host by selectively stimulating the growth and/or activity of one or a limited number of bacteria in the colon."

And, to complicate things, they define "synbiotic" as a product that contains probiotics and prebiotics. (Synergism is when two things work together.)

Before the media and food industry began to capitalize on the term "probiotic," we called the bacteria that live in our gastrointestinal (GI) tract "friendly bacteria" or "gut microflora." The bacteria are beneficial since they synthesize certain vitamins, reduce GI problems, and control the level of pathogenic bacteria. A tremendous amount of research is being conducted on other aspects of these bacteria related to health. Some even think they may have a role in treating obesity. The main sources of probiotics are fermented products like yogurt, buttermilk, sweet acidophilus milk, sauerkraut, kefir, and tempeh.

The only thing new about prebiotics is the name. They are naturally occurring and have been in our diets from the beginning of time. Many people think that the "non-digestible food ingredient" is anything that contains fiber. But not all fibers have prebiotic activity. To be considered a prebiotic, the substance must resist digestion and make it to the colon where the bacteria reside. Then, it must be a food that the bacteria will eat. So far, the only two that are classified as prebiotics are inulin and oligofructose. Traditional American foods are low in these two prebiotics. Keep in mind that 100 g is almost a half cup. And eating a half cup of *dried* garlic or onions would be pretty potent.

The average American gets about 5 g of prebiotics per day, whereas people in other parts of the world average twice as much. The *2010 Dietary Guidelines* Advisory Committee believes that "the gut microbiota do play a role in health, although the research in this area is still developing." Therefore, they have not established a recommendation for intake of inulin and oligofructose.

Food manufactures have been adding it to foods for a few years, mainly in the form of chicory root.

Do we need to increase our probiotic and prebiotic intake? Will they make us healthier, happier, and thinner? David Williams says yes. He describes studies that showcase health benefits of both probiotics and prebiotics and concludes that we should all be on probiotics to avoid trouble. Peta Bee is skeptical of probiotics and counters that some products that contain bacteria may not be "alive and active" by the time we eat it. She points out that some added bacteria may even be harmful to people with certain health conditions.

DEFINITIONS

Antibiotic A substance produced by various microorganisms that are used to destroy disease-causing bacteria.

Ferment The process by which bacteria or yeast convert sugar (from milk, fruits, or vegetables) to an acid, typically lactic acid.

Probiotic A live microorganism, which when administered in adequate amounts, confers a health benefit.

Prebiotic A nondigestible food ingredient that bacteria in the colon feed on.

Synbiotic A food that contains a probiotic and prebiotic.

TIMELINE

76 B.C. Plinus recommends fermented milk to treat GI problems.

1907 Russian scientist Elie Metchnikoff proposes that yogurt increases longevity.

1965 Lilly and Stillwell coin the term "probiotics."

1995 Gibson and Roberfroid introduce the term "prebiotic."

YES

Anneli Rufus

Poop Is the Most Important Indicator of Your Health

*L*ike it or not, our bowels are the ID cards of our bodies, charting our recent histories with terrifying accuracy. So, how do we ensure a healthy gut?

According to a lawsuit filed this month, Ron and Sarah Bowers bought their son a Subway sandwich in Lombard, Illinois on February 27. After eating it, he had agonizing cramps and diarrhea. According to the suit, what the couple really bought was a shit sandwich.

It had been contaminated with *Shigella sonnei,* a bacteria transmitted via the fecal-oral route and can cause vomiting, dysentery and death. Over 100 people claim to have been sickened at Lombard's Subway, according to attorney Drew Falkenstein, whose firm has filed suit on behalf of Ron and Sarah Bowers and two other customers.

We don't want to think about excrement. We don't want to see it, smell it or touch it. We definitely don't want to eat it with chicken teriyaki, on toast. Yet intestinal goings-on are in our faces everywhere these days, whether the news is about probiotics and prebiotics appearing in new food products or yet another outbreak of norovirus—the painful gastroenteritis that is spread via fecally contaminated food, water and surfaces and has sickened thousands of cruise-ship passengers in eight unprecedentedly massive outbreaks so far this year.

And "poopular culture" is upon us: Witness *Slumdog Millionaire's* outhouse-plunge scene. Witness Oprah's "Everybody Poops" episode, in which Dr. Mehmet Oz avows that excrement should enter the toilet with not a plop but a swoosh "like a diver from Acapulco." In a scene from the forthcoming film *Life As We Know It*, a young mom portrayed by Katherine Heigl is interrupted by visitors while changing a diaper. "Sweetie," one of the visitors tells her, "you have shit on your face."

In a dirty, crowded world where germs are outsmarting drugs by leaps and bounds and our health care options may or may not be mired in red tape for years, we're being forced to face feces. Which is kind of a good thing. They're the ID cards our bodies issue, charting with terrifying accuracy where we've been and what we've done. *The bowel knows.*

Good Bugs vs. Bad Bugs

"A gram of feces can contain 10 million viruses, one million bacteria, 1,000 parasite cysts and 100 worm eggs," asserts Rose George, author of *The Big Necessity: The Unmentionable World of Human Waste and Why It Matters* (Metropolitan, 2008). She despairs over the fact that 2.6 billion people "have no access to any latrine, toilet bucket or box. . . . They do it in plastic bags and fling them through the air in narrow slum alleyways." Four out of every 10 human beings, George laments, "live in situations where they are surrounded by human excrement."

In the developed world, our relationship with our bowels mostly entails controlling the flora that live in them. *Lactobacillus. Peptococcus. Streptococcus.* A hundred trillion microbes belonging to as many as 1,000 different species coexist at any given time in a single gut, which measures over three yards. What are they doing down there? Battling it out, rendering us well or ill.

Over 70 percent of the human body's immune cells are found in the gut's mucosal lining. A healthy gut means more immunity, and a healthy gut is a gut in which good bacteria outnumber bad. And they're all hitchhikers that rushed in from outside, mounting an invasion that began the instant our placentas broke. "We're all bacteria-free until then," says Emory University School of Medicine associate professor Andrew Gewirtz, the senior author of a study released this month on the effects of imbalanced gut flora. Once the placenta breaks, Gewirtz says, "the colonization begins."

Garnering such headlines in the mainstream media as "You can blame bacteria in your stomach for those unwanted pounds" and "Germs are making you fat," his study found that mice whose guts contained too many of the class of bacteria known as *Firmicutes* ate much more than other mice, experienced metabolic changes and became obese.

This finding undermines the assumption that obesity is driven by laziness and easy access to cheap fattening foods.

"You can't ask the mice" why they ate more, "but how much they ate was clearly not affected by price or marketing schemes," Gewirtz says. Instead, bad bugs can promote excessive appetite and fat storage. They can also make us sick in a million other ways.

The Business of the Gut

"Good bugs form an invisible barrier preventing pathogenic bugs to take root and multiply," says Ann Louise Gittleman, a doctor of holistic nutrition who has appeared on "Dr. Phil" and authored over 30 books including *Fat Flush for Life* (Da Capo, 2009).

She urges us to wage "the new germ warfare" that optimizes "the balance of power in what amounts to a huge fungi kingdom. We have to, because in our bodies we have more bacteria than we have cells."

Because of their crucial role in immune function, the bad ones "can turn into a source of bad health that can affect us from head to toe," creating not just irritable bowel syndrome, colitis and Crohn's disease but conditions such as nasal congestion, itchy skin, bleeding gums, acne and depression that we might not think had anything to do with our bowels, Gittleman says. Online, she sells stool-sample testing kits that come with vials and a discreet white box printed with the address of the lab that does the analysis.

"The intestine is an unappreciated organ. It's a beautiful membrane," asserts vegan physician Michael Klaper, who appeared in the PBS documentaries *Diet for a New America and Food for Thought* and has served as an adviser to NASA. "Think of all the intestine does while supporting a population of alien organisms. Miraculous things happen on our gut linings."

At True North Health Education and Fasting Center in Santa Rosa, California, Klaper and his fellow doctors supervise patients undergoing water-only fasts that can last up to 40 days. "Like other organs, the gut could use a rest. We're talking about 22 feet of small intestine. Its lining is a very active membrane and it needs a holiday sometimes, too.

"The body is perfectly capable of going for weeks without food as you burn off your fat stores. Of course, it's no picnic. In the first few days, people are very energetic, as all the energy that would have been used to digest food is put to other purposes. At the end of the second week, they get very quiet, meditative. They're in a different space," said Klaper.

When it's over, "they're very light and clean, and we very gently re-feed them on highly diluted fruit juices and steamed vegetables." However long the fast lasted, refeeding takes half that long. "There's an art to it, of course," Klaper says.

How did we get so messed-up?

"In the old days, our ancestors drank water out of streams and wells. They ate fruit and vegetables harvested in gardens. They lived in close connection with the natural world, and part of the natural world would set up housekeeping in their intestines," he said.

Traditional diets lacking chemical additives kept their gut bugs in balance, "but modern life is an assault on our normal bacterial flora. We put five or six majorly disruptive substances down there every day."

The first of these is chlorine, found in tap water. "Okay, so we don't get cholera or typhoid. That's great. But every time you drink this water, you're drinking a chlorine-dilute solution," he said. That kills good bugs along with bad. Ditto phosphoric acid, a key soft-drink ingredient. "We're a nation of tea and coffee drinkers. What happens in your gut when you're constantly sloshing down a known bactericide?"

Sugar is yet another villain, as are antibiotics, which wipe out nearly every bug in sight—which saves lives but leaves guts thinking *What the hell*?

And they do think, insists Chicago colon therapist Alyce Sorokie, the author of *Gut Wisdom: Understanding and Improving Your Digestive Health* (Career, 2004). "The gut is always speaking to us. It has more emotional receptor sites than anywhere else in the body. The gut is filled with neurons and neuropeptides, the same things that are in our brains, so it can take in information. It can learn. It can respond to events even more rapidly that our brain does," says Sorokie.

"You feel something in the gut, and the vagus nerve brings that 'gut feeling' up the spinal cord to the brain, and the brain makes up a story about it.

The brain can always rationalize, but when we feel something in the gut, it's unedited. It's very primal. That's the gut's voice, and the more we don't listen, the louder it gets."

And that is why Sorokie says her clients get emotional during colonics, as filtered water flowing through a hose inserted into the anus bathes the colon, bringing out with it accumulated fecal matter that can be viewed through a clear portion of the mechanism, foot by wiggly, rubbery, slippery, corn-kernel-studded foot.

Releasing stored material from digestive tracts releases stored material from hearts and minds as well, Sorokie says.

"It lets everything come out. These clients say they wish they could bring the hose along with them to their psychotherapy appointments. Nobody wants to think, 'I harbor toxic thoughts and toxic waste within me,' but then there's a liberation: Here it is and there it goes. This was part of me, and now it's not," she said.

Short of anal hoses and doctor-supervised starvation, we can give our bowels a break by eating prebiotics. Found in dandelion greens, Jerusalem artichokes, chicory, milk and a few other natural sources, these are soluble fibers that we can't digest, but our beneficial flora *can*. In other words, prebiotics (which aren't alive) fuel probiotics (which are), making them more active and fighting-fit. So, eating prebiotics is like sprinkling fish-food into a tank full of hungry fish.

"Most people are already comfortable with the idea of fiber in their diets," says microbiologist Mary Ellen Sanders, who belongs to the International Scientific Association of Probiotics and Prebiotics.

"Now you can start to think of eating fiber not just for the traditional fiber effects, but to feed beneficial members of your bacterial community," she explained.

These communities, which are unique to each of us, remained almost a total mystery until recently. Only in the last few years has DNA research brought the identities and functions of much of this flora to light. Up to 80 percent of the various types of human bacterial microbes have still never been grown outside the body under laboratory conditions, Sanders says. "It will be very interesting to see how all this develops in the next five years."

In the meantime, she says eating probiotics and prebiotics "lets us feed the right microbes in the right way." As it would be difficult to eat enough chicory and dandelion greens to get the recommended five to eight daily grams of prebiotics, we can start looking for prebiotic-fortified food products and supplements, often identified by the presence of oligofructose and/or inulin on their labels.

We'll be seeing those words more and more, as products containing prebiotics are among the food industry's fastest-growing sectors. New ones keep popping up, such as the Jamba Juice frozen sorbet and yogurt bars that hit stores this month. The bars' marketing material promises that Coconut-Pineapple Passion Smashin' and its fellow treats-on-sticks "contain prebiotic fiber, allowing customers to satisfy their sweet tooth without feeling guilty."

One hundred trillion microbes are too many to kill, so we're never out of bugs. But when they go way out of balance, a new kind of therapy lets doctors recolonize patients' bowels with what Emory University's Andrew Gewirtz calls "cocktails of good bacteria."

As seen on "Grey's Anatomy" and in real life, the treatment is an extreme measure for people suffering from *Clostridium difficile*, a bad bacteria whose overpopulation causes debilitating intestinal infections when antibiotics wipe out the good bacteria that would normally quell it. (*Clostridium difficile* rates are skyrocketing in American hospitals these days.) Known as fecal bacteriotherapy, fecal transfusion or fecal transplant, the treatment entails inserting a healthy person's feces into the sick person.

Rich in good bacteria, these feces enter the patient's intestine from either end: via enemas or orally, through a tube. "These patients are at the ends of their ropes," says Gewirtz. "They're willing to try something that isn't very pleasant."

So: Bad gut bacteria stay bad when Subway workers don't wash their hands after doing you-know-what. Good gut bacteria stay good even after they exit one body in feces and are more or less fed to another. And in this brave new world, eating shit might save lives.

Peta Bee  **NO**

Probiotics, Not So Friendly After All?

New research indicates that many probiotics are ineffective and some may even cause harm. Now scientists say we should switch to prebiotics.

Over the past two decades, it seemed that our guts had never had it so good. Probiotic products claiming to rid the body of the bad bacteria that causes illness burst on to the market and two million of us now swallow their promise of improved digestive health, provided by [the] so-called "friendly bacteria." We spend almost £350 million a year on drinks, yoghurts, powders and capsules, in the hope of improving our gut health. But is it money well spent? A growing number of experts think not. While they do not dispute that a balance of gut flora is beneficial, many believe that probiotics are not as helpful as was once thought.

Studies supporting the use of probiotics for general well-being, and as an additional support for people with specific illnesses, have been plentiful in recent years. [F]or instance, Swedish researchers revealed that a course of probiotics can offer protection for those with pneumonia. But critics are now doubting their usefulness. "In some areas, there is evidence that taking a probiotic supplement can be helpful," says Anna Denny, a nutrition scientist at the British Nutrition Foundation. "But it is not clear-cut and not all probiotics are helpful to all people."

The Russian Nobel prize winner, Élie Metchnikoff, is credited with having discovered probiotics at the beginning of the 20th century when he discovered that Bulgarian peasants who consumed milk containing fermenting bacteria appeared to enjoy extraordinarily good health.

It is now accepted among nutrition scientists that [the] so-called friendly bacteria account for 10–15 per cent of bacteria in a healthy adult gut and that levels become depleted through a poor, low-fibre diet, or other factors such as stress, courses of antibiotics or illness. Proponents claim that probiotic supplements, which provide a regular shot of live, beneficial bacteria, help to top-up a body's natural supplies. But even those who were once self-confessed fanatics are questioning their place and proposing alternatives.

"Only highly resistant forms of bacteria, such as lactobacillus and bifidobacteria, have been shown to survive transit to the gut—others are likely to be destroyed by the highly acidic environment in the stomach," says Professor

Glenn Gibson, a food microbiologist at the University of Reading's school of life biosciences who is widely regarded as the UK's leading expert. "Unless capsules have a special enteric coating, they won't survive the transit. Heat also destroys probiotic bacteria, so if someone drinks a cup of coffee just before or after consuming them, the bacteria will be killed off." In some tests, even if certain probiotics did survive, Professor Gibson found that they did not necessarily enhance gut flora, rendering them useless.

Lax labeling laws also mean that it is difficult for people to know which products are effective. [Four] years ago, Professor Gibson and Professor Christine Edwards, the head of human nutrition at Glasgow University, cautioned that 50 per cent of probiotic products do not have the healthy bacteria claimed on the label. Shoppers should be suspicious unless manufacturers stipulate that a capsule or drink provides a minimum of ten million bacteria per dose. Although the leading brands such as Yakult, Activia, Danone and Multibionta contain these amounts, many others "either have the wrong bacteria or the wrong numbers," Professor Gibson says. One powder was withdrawn a couple of years ago as it contained clostridium, a bacteria that causes diarrhoea and colitis.

Probiotics have also been widely used for childhood allergies. Eczema is believed to be a disorder of the immune system and, since probiotics can enhance immunity, they have been considered effective. Yet two new studies question their use. [In October 2008,] Dr Robert Boyle, a senior lecturer in paediatric allergy at Imperial College, London, found that use of probiotics in the treatment of childhood eczema was ineffective, even risky. In a review of 12 studies involving 781 children for the Cochrane Database of Systematic Reviews, Boyle found no evidence that probiotics reduced symptoms or altered the severity. He does not recommend that even healthy children take probiotics and he would not advise them for anyone with eczema.

Another . . . trial, conducted at the University of Western Australia, showed that giving children a type of "good bacteria" early in life did nothing to reduce allergies as they grew up. Indeed, in one of their trials, Dr Susan Prescott and her colleagues gave 178 children either a probiotic or a placebo for the first six months of their life, those given the good bacteria were more, not less, likely to develop a sensitivity to allergens.

There are concerns, too, that in people with compromised immune systems friendly bacteria could be treated as hostile invaders by the body. Indeed, in their recent trial, the Cochrane researchers found probiotics to carry a risk of bowel damage and infection in children who were given them to treat their eczema. "A wide trawl of literature showed that, although probiotics are recognised as a safe treatment in otherwise healthy people, in those who are severely unwell, there is a significant risk in using them," Dr Boyle says.

[Earlier in 2008], a controversial study at the University Medical Centre in Utrecht, Netherlands, reported that 24 out of 296 patients died during a study to find out whether probiotics affected inflammation of the pancreas. The Dutch food and consumer product safety authority ruled that the supplements should not be given to patients in intensive care.

Some NHS hospitals employ wide use of probiotics, often considered beneficial in the fight against MRSA, but others are becoming more cautious.

At St George's Hospital in London, the chief dietitian, Catherine Collins, says that the risks for some patients are high. "A growing number of hospitals don't embrace probiotics as they used to, simply because we now know they can cause infections in vulnerable people," Collins says. "They can lead to a potentially fatal illness called lactobacillus septicaemia and we have treated a few cases at St George's."

According to some experts, the new bugs on the block—prebiotics, naturally present in food and easily obtained in the diet—are what we should have been taking all along. "Whereas probiotics provide new doses of bacteria, prebiotics nourish and feed the friendly bacteria already present," Denny explains. Found naturally in breast milk, prebiotics are also present in foods that contain non-digestive carbohydrate. . . . "Substances such as inulin, a non-digestible part of carbohydrate, and oligosaccharides sail through the digestive system and are fermented to boost the immune system."

Emerging trials on prebiotics, which are also available in supplement form and added to foods as diverse as breakfast cereals and desserts, show promise. [In November 2008], Professor Gibson has published a trial in the *American Journal of Clinical Nutrition* showing how the prebiotic powder Bimuno helped to prevent the natural decline in immunity for people aged 65 and older. "Typically, there is a natural decline in gut bacteria with age," Professor Gibson says. "But in the study on volunteers aged 64 to 79, the prebiotic had a direct effect on immune defence cells and boosted immune function compared with a placebo."

Another small study conducted by Dr Gemma Walton, a colleague of Professor Gibson's, compared the effects of prebiotics and probiotics in eight subjects. "We examined the faeces of the subjects daily to see whether the good bacteria had multiplied in number," she says. "In the prebiotic group, there was an increase in good bacteria by 133 million, small in bacteria terms but an encouraging effect." However, the probiotic group showed little change. "It seems that the best thing you can do is to treat your good bacteria to a prebiotic meal," Dr Walton says.

Professor Gibson says: "Research on prebiotics is in its infancy, but is very encouraging. Not all probiotics are unhelpful. Some people can benefit. But if I was asked to choose, then I'd take prebiotic every time."

Prebiotics: The New Bugs on the Block

Research at the Institute of Food Research in Norwich identified that finely ground almonds increased beneficial gut bacteria, although the effect was not seen when the fat content of the nuts was removed, suggesting that the gut bacteria used the almond lipids to grow.

A prebiotic-rich diet should contain 7g a day of inulin, found in oats, chicory, bananas, garlic and onions.

Commercially produced prebiotics, including cheese and dairy products, as well as supplements such as Bimuno, sprinkled on to cereals, can be helpful.

Breakfast cereals and cereal bars have a naturally occurring prebiotic. Eating cereals, including Shredded Wheat, Shreddies and Cheerios, was shown to increase two types of friendly bacteria in a test and in trials of 38 people who ate cereal daily for three weeks.

Some honey has prebiotic properties, says the University of Reading and the Instituto de Fermentaciones Industriales in Madrid. Manuka honey from New Zealand has been shown in trials to encourage the growth of healthy bacteria.

CHALLENGE QUESTIONS

Are Probiotics and Prebiotics Beneficial in Promoting Health?

1. Define the following: probiotic, prebiotic, and synbiotic, and list three foods that are considered to be a good source of each.
2. Probiotics are often called "friendly bacteria." Explain what this means and why Peta Bee warns us that they may "not be so friendly after all."
3. Record all the foods you eat for a day. Determine which foods provide probiotics and which provide prebiotics. Were any of the foods synbiotic?
4. Go to the grocery store and find five products whose labels claim they "contain live active cultures." What types of bacteria are in the products and what other health claims are on the label? How do you tell if the bacteria will actually survive the journey from the food manufacturer to your large intestine?
5. Refer to the definition of symbiotic. Describe three things that meet the criteria of synbiotic and state which component of the food provides probiotic activity and which provides prebiotic components.

Additional Internet Resources

International Scientific Association for Probiotics and Prebiotics (ISAPP)

Web site for ISAPP, which is the international association of academic and industrial scientists involved in research on fundamental and applied aspects of probiotics and prebiotics. The site provides the latest news and research about probiotics and prebiotics for consumers and professionals.

http://www.isapp.net/default.asp

ISSUE 13

Should Energy Drinks Be Banned?

YES: Chad J. Reissig, Eric C. Strain, and Roland R. Griffiths, from "Caffeinated Energy Drinks—A Growing Problem," *Drug and Alcohol Dependence* (January 2009)

NO: Ellen Coleman, from "Back to the Grind: The Return of Caffeine as an Ergogenic Aid," *Today's Dietitian* (March 2009)

As you read the issue, focus on the following points:

1. FDA regulations for the caffeine content of beverages and the World Anti-Doping Association (WADA) and the National Collegiate Athletic Association (NCAA) rules regarding caffeine.
2. Adverse health effects associated with energy drinks linked to caffeine.
3. Benefits of caffeine for athletes and the general population.

ISSUE SUMMARY

YES: Chad Reissig, Eric Strain, and Roland Griffiths, medical researchers at Johns Hopkins, say there are increasing reports of caffeine intoxication from energy drinks and predict that problems with caffeine intoxication may be on the rise.

NO: California sports nutritionist and exercise physiologist Ellen Coleman is not concerned about the potential side effects of caffeine in energy drinks and bars. She writes that "substantial research suggests that caffeine enhances endurance performance."

T he first energy drink was introduced in 1962 by the Japan-based company Taisho Pharmaceuticals. The drink was called Lipovitan and advertised to help employees "work hard well into the night." Still sold today throughout the world, the drink contains the amino acid taurine, sugar, caffeine, and B-complex vitamins.

Intrigued by the Asian energy drinks, entrepreneur Dietrich Mateschitz developed and began selling the energy drink Red Bull in Austria during 1987. Red Bull hit the U.S. market in 1997 and is currently the leading energy drink sold in the world. Currently, there are more than 100 types of energy drinks made worldwide.

Many people wonder how energy drinks differ from soft drinks and sports drinks. Soft drinks are mainly carbonated water, sugar, and artificial flavorings. Other than adding calories, they don't do anything for your body—they just taste good. (Colas, Mountain Dew, and Sundrop do contain about half as much caffeine as Red Bull.) Sports drinks, like Gatorade and Powerade, are designed to replenish fluids lost during activity and contain electrolytes and about half the sugar as soft drinks; they typically are caffeine-free. Standard energy drinks do have caffeine, sugar, and other ingredients such as guarana (a natural source of caffeine) and taurine, claimed to "improve exercise and energy performance."

Much controversy has developed worldwide about energy drinks, due mainly to their caffeine content. Caffeine content found in energy drinks varies from 80 mg per can of Red Bull to 505 mg for Wired X505. Caffeine is well recognized as a stimulant, even though in 2004, the World Anti-Doping Agency (WADA), the group that sets standards for the Olympic Games, lifted the ban on caffeine. They do not consider caffeine to meet their definition of "stimulant," which they describe as follows:

> They [stimulants] work directly on the central nervous system. They increase heart rate and blood flow. They improve alertness and reduce fatigue. They also may increase competiveness and hostility. The banned drugs in this category include: amphetamines, beta2 agonists, ephedrine, pseudoephedrine, fencamfamine, cocaine, methamphetamine, mesocarb, and other substances with a similar chemical structure and similar biological effect. Side effects of these drugs include: high blood pressure, increased and irregular heartbeat, anxiety, loss of appetite, loss of judgment and tremor. These drugs are potentially lethal.

In contrast, the National Collegiate Athletic Association (NCAA) does consider caffeine to be a stimulant and banned excessive caffeine in 2006 and defines the upper limit as "concentration [of caffeine] in urine exceeds 15 µg/ml." This translates into the average person being able to consume up to 6 mg caffeine per kg body weight. In 2010, WADA reported they may put caffeine back on the banned list.

Should high caffeinated energy drinks be banned? Advertisements for the drinks target young people. Many children, eager to be better ball players, convince their parents to buy energy drinks. Do energy drinks harm these children? Toronto dietitian Jennifer Sygo has a very logical opinion on the topic. In an article in the *Edmonton Post* (August 23, 2010) she concludes:

> "While adults certainly have the right to choose what they eat or drink, the thought of a child or teen guzzling back the equivalent of two cups of coffee in a single energy shot is alarming. When you add in the massive sugar content, you have a recipe for a nutritional disaster that's best avoided by almost anyone."

What about the impact of energy drinks on adolescents and adults? Should they be banned for the general public or for athletes? Johns Hopkins' medical researchers Chad Reissig, Eric Strain, and Roland Griffiths say there are increasing reports of caffeine intoxication from energy drinks and predict problems with caffeine abuse. Nutritionist Ellen Coleman concludes that caffeine can be a helpful training aid by allowing the athlete to engage in harder, more consistent workouts.

TIMELINE

1962 Japan introduces the first energy drink, Lipovitan.

1980 FDA proposes to eliminate caffeine from beverages.

1985 Jolt Cola is introduced in the United States.

1987 Red Bull is introduced in Austria.

1994 Dietary Supplement and Health Education Act is passed.

1997 Red Bull is introduced in the United States.

2002–2004 Forty-one cases of caffeine abuse are reported to U.S. Poison Control.

2004 WADA removes caffeine from banned list.

2006 NCAA bans excessive caffeine.

2009 Red Bull from Austria is found to contain trace amounts of cocaine.
Jolt Cola files bankruptcy.

DEFINITIONS

Taurine An amino acid that occurs naturally in the human body and some foods, and added to some beverages.

Caffeine A stimulant found naturally in some plants and added to certain beverages.

Guarana Extract from a South American plant that may be used to provide flavor. In its natural form, guarana contains a high level of caffeine, ranging from 3 to 5 percent by dry weight.

YES

Chad J. Reissig, Eric C. Strain, and
Roland R. Griffiths

Caffeinated Energy Drinks—A Growing Problem

1. Introduction

In 2006, annual worldwide energy drink consumption increased 17% from the previous year to 906 million gallons, with Thailand leading the world in energy drink consumption per person, but the U.S. leading the world in total volume sales. Although "energy drinks" first appeared in Europe and Asia in the 1960s, the introduction of "Red Bull" in Austria in 1987 and in the U.S. in 1997 sparked the more recent trend toward aggressive marketing of high caffeine content "energy drinks." Since its inception, the energy drink market has grown exponentially, with nearly 500 new brands launched worldwide in 2006, and 200 new brands launched in the U.S. in the 12-month period ending July 2007. From 2002 to 2006, the average annual growth rate in energy drink sales was 55% (Fig. 1). The

Figure 1

Energy drink sales in millions of dollars in the United States from 2002 to 2006.

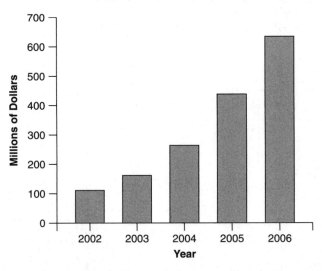

From *Drug and Alcohol Dependence*, vol. 99, 2009, pp. 1–10. Copyright © 2009 by Elsevier Health Sciences. Reprinted by permission.

total U.S. retail market value for energy drinks (from all sources) was estimated to be \$5.4 billion in 2006 and has shown a similar annual growth rate over this same period (47%). These drinks vary widely in both caffeine content (ranging from 50 to 505 mg per can or bottle) and caffeine concentration (ranging from 2.5 to 171 mg per fluid ounce) (Table 1). For comparison, the caffeine content of a 6 oz cup of brewed coffee varies from 77 to 150 mg. The main active ingredient in energy drinks is caffeine, although other substances such as taurine, riboflavin, pyridoxine, nicotinamide, other B vitamins, and various herbal derivatives are also present. The acute and long-term effects resulting from excessive and chronic consumption of these additives alone and in combination with caffeine are not fully known. Although the full impact of the rise in popularity of energy drinks has yet to be realized, the potential for adverse health consequences should be considered and may be cause for preemptive regulatory action.

Table 1

Energy drinks in the United States

	Ounces per bottle or can	Caffeine concentration (mg/oz)	Total caffeine (mg)
Top selling energy drinks[a]			
Red Bull	8.3	9.6	80
Monster	16	10	160
Rockstar	16	10	160
Full Throttle	16	9	144
No Fear	16	10.9	174
Amp	8.4	8.9	75
SoBe Adrenaline Rush	8.3	9.5	79
Tab Energy	10.5	9.1	95
Higher caffeine energy drinks[b]			
Wired X505	24	21	505
Fixx	20	25	500
BooKoo Energy	24	15	360
Wired X344	16	21.5	344
SPIKE Shooter	8.4	35.7	300
Viso Energy Vigor	20	15	300

Continued

Cocaine Energy Drink	8.4	33.3	280
Jolt Cola	23.5	11.9	280
NOS	16	16.3	250
Redline RTD	8	31.3	250
Blow (Energy Drink Mix)	8	30	240
Lower caffeine energy drinks[b]			
Bomba Energy	8.4	8.9	75
HiBall Energy	10	7.5	75
Airforce Nutrisoda Energize	8.5	5.9	50
Whoop Ass	8.5	5.9	50
Vitamin Water (Energy Citrus)	20	2.5	50
High concentration energy drinks[b]			
RedLine Power Rush	2.5	140	350
Ammo	1	171	171
Powershot	1	100	100
Fuel Cell	2	90	180
Classic soft drinks			
Coca-Cola Classic	12	2.9	34.5
Pepsi Cola	12	3.2	38
Dr Pepper	12	3.4	41
Mountain Dew	12	4.5	54

Data on drink volume and caffeine content were obtained from the manufacturer via product label, website, or personal communication with manufacturer representatives. The one exception was that the caffeine content for BooKoo Energy was obtained from the energyfiend website which indicates the information was obtained from a BooKoo representative. When the authors contacted the BooKoo company directly, a BooKoo representative refused to disclose the drink's caffeine content but did indicate that accurate information for the caffeine content of BooKoo Energy was available online.

[a]Top selling energy drinks in the U.S. 2006, listed sequentially as a percentage of market share.
[b]Examples of energy drinks drawn from the hundreds of energy drink products currently marketed in the U.S., listed sequentially on total caffeine content.

2. Regulatory Aspects

The regulation of beverages to which caffeine is added has been challenging, partly because of the widespread and long-term use of beverages such as coffee and tea in which caffeine is a natural constituent. Nonetheless, several countries have enacted measures to regulate the labeling, distribution, and sale of energy drinks that contain significant quantities of caffeine. The European Union requires that energy drinks have a "high caffeine content" label and Canada requires labels indicating that Red Bull should not be mixed with alcohol and that maximum daily consumption not exceed two 8.3 oz cans. Norway restricts the sale of Red Bull to pharmacies, while France (until recently) and Denmark have prohibited the sale of Red Bull altogether.

The history of the regulation of caffeine containing beverages in the U.S. serves as an illustrative example of the complexity of the regulatory issues involved in their sale, use, and promotion. Historically, the U.S. Food and Drug Administration (FDA) has regulated caffeine-containing soft drinks as foods. In 1980, citing health concerns about caffeine, the FDA proposed to eliminate caffeine from soft drinks. In response, soft drink manufacturers justified adding caffeine to soft drinks on the basis that caffeine was a flavor enhancer, although the scientific basis for that claim has since been challenged. If caffeine had not been accepted as a flavor enhancer, but had been regarded as a psychoactive ingredient, soft drinks might have been regulated by the FDA as drugs. However, the FDA approved caffeine and limited the maximum caffeine content of cola-type soft drinks to 0.02% caffeine, or 71 mg/12 fluid oz.

Although drink manufacturers initially complied with the FDA caffeine limits, the marketplace has changed dramatically since the introduction of energy drinks. At least 130 energy drinks now exceed 0.02% caffeine, including one that contains 505 mg in a 24 oz can (the equivalent of 14 cans of a typical cola or several cups of coffee. Many manufacturers are not subject to the prior caffeine limits by claiming that their new products fall under the 1994 Dietary Supplement Health and Education Act, which classifies products deriving from herbs and natural sources as dietary supplements rather than drugs. Other manufacturers appear to be ignoring the FDA caffeine limits and FDA has not enforced the limits. The FDA has been lax in regulating the caffeine content of energy drinks and does not require warning labels advising proper use or the amount of caffeine in the product, as it does for over-the-counter (OTC) caffeinecontaining stimulants. According to the FDA, over-the-counter stimulant drug products must contain the following warnings and directions on the product label:

- The recommended dose of this product contains about as much caffeine as a cup of coffee. Limit the use of caffeinecontaining medications, foods, or beverages while taking this product because too much caffeine may cause nervousness, irritability, sleeplessness, and, occasionally, rapid heart beat.
- For occasional use only. Not intended for use as a substitute for sleep. If fatigue or drowsiness persists or continues to recur, consult a (select one of the following: "physician" or "doctor").

- Directions: Adults and children 12 years of age and over: oral dosage is 100–200 mg not more often than every 3–4 h.

It is a striking inconsistency that, in the U.S. an OTC stimulant medication containing 100 mg of caffeine per tablet (e.g., NoDoz) must include all the above warnings, whereas a 500 mg energy drink can be marketed with no such warnings and no information on caffeine dose amount in the product.

3. Advertising

Energy drinks are promoted for their stimulant effects and claim to offer a variety of benefits including increased attention, endurance and performance, weight loss, and "having fun, kicking butt and making a difference." The majority of these claims however, remain to be substantiated. The most consistent result to emerge is that caffeine reduces performance decrements due to reduced alertness (e.g., conditions of fatigue, or sleep deprivation). Other studies have shown that, relative to placebo, caffeine can increase long-term exercise endurance, and improve speed and/or power output. However, because many of the studies claiming to demonstrate performance enhancement by caffeine have been confounded by caffeine withdrawal, there is debate over whether caffeine has net positive or performance enhancing effects (e.g., improved mood, alertness or mental function) or whether these effects are due to the reversal of caffeine withdrawal symptoms. Based on preclinical literature that clearly documents the behavioral stimulant effects of caffeine, it seems quite likely that caffeine enhances human performance on some types of tasks (e.g., vigilance), especially among nontolerant individuals. Among high-dose habitual consumers, performance enhancements above and beyond withdrawal reversal effects are likely to be modest at best.

Advertising of energy drinks is targeted primarily towards young males, with alluring product names such as "Full Throttle," "AMP Energy," and "Cocaine." These advertising campaigns promote the psychoactive, performance-enhancing, and stimulant effects of energy drinks and appear to glorify drug use. In a survey of 795 undergraduate students, self-reported measures of masculinity and risk taking behaviors were positively associated with frequency of energy drink consumption.

One of the more blatant examples of such advertising tactics is found in the drink additive "Blow." This "energy drink additive" is packaged in glass vials and shipped with a mirror and plastic credit cards in an apparent attempt to model cocaine use. Blow founder Logan Gola describes the product as "sexy, edgy and fun." The energy drink "Cocaine" was initially marketed as "The Legal Alternative" with its product name displayed as a white granular substance which resembled cocaine powder, and with video clips on the company website showing consumers "snorting" its liquid product. Recently, the FDA claimed jurisdiction over both "Cocaine" and "Blow," informing the companies that their products were marketed as an alternative to an illicit street drug, not a dietary supplement, and subject to regulation as a drug. In early 2008, the manufacturer re-released "Cocaine," with revised product claims, yet retaining the drink's characteristic moniker, "Cocaine" still prominently displayed as a white powdery substance resembling cocaine powder. The product "Blow" currently remains on the market.

The marketing of energy drinks as products to be used for their stimulant and recreational effects stands in marked contrast to the marketing of soft drinks. For decades, advertising for soft drinks has been restricted to rather innocuous and somewhat ambiguous claims such as those used to promote CocaCola: "The pause that refreshes." As mentioned previously, in response to an FDA proposal to eliminate caffeine from soft drinks, soft drink manufacturers justified adding caffeine by calling it a flavor enhancer. After claiming that caffeine was added just for its flavor, manufacturers were likely reluctant to publicly promote their products as stimulants for fear of jeopardizing their regulatory rationale for adding caffeine. No such restraint is exercised on promotion of energy drinks, many of which are regulated under the 1994 dietary supplement act.

4. Caffeine Toxicity/Overdose

Concern regarding the caffeine content of energy drinks is prompted by the potential adverse consequences of caffeine use. One such adverse effect is caffeine intoxication. . . . Caffeine toxicity is defined by specific symptoms that emerge as a direct result of caffeine consumption. Common features of caffeine intoxication include nervousness, anxiety, restlessness, insomnia, gastrointestinal upset, tremors, tachycardia, psychomotor agitation and in rare cases, death. The symptoms of caffeine intoxication can mimic those of anxiety and other mood disorders.

The consumption of energy drinks may increase the risk for caffeine overdose in caffeine abstainers as well as habitual consumers of caffeine from coffee, soft drinks, and tea. The potential for acute caffeine toxicity due to consumption of energy drinks may be greater than other dietary sources of caffeine for several reasons:

(1) Lack of adequate labeling: As mentioned earlier, many energy drinks do not label their product with the amount of caffeine, and are not required to display warning labels advising proper use. Consumers may be completely unaware of the amount of caffeine they are ingesting.
(2) Advertising: Many energy drinks are marketed with claims of performance enhancing effects although, as discussed previously, the existence and extent of such effects is subject to debate. Red Bull, for example, advertises several benefits of consumption including improved performance, endurance, concentration and reaction speed, and increased metabolism. Consumers may falsely believe that "more is better" and ingest multiple servings of these products. As an added risk, some energy drinks encourage rapid consumption of their products. For instance, "Spike Shooter" claims "the flavor's so good, you'll want to slam the whole can."

(3) Consumer demographics: Since there are no restrictions on the sale of energy drinks, adolescents and children (who may be inexperienced and less tolerant to the effects of caffeine) may be at an increased risk for caffeine intoxication.

Forty-one cases of caffeine abuse from caffeine-enhanced beverages were reported to a U.S. poison control center from 2002 to 2004. Another U.S. poison control center reported nine cases of adverse reactions to the energy drink Redline from January 2004 to March 2006. Eight of the nine patients were male, the youngest being 13 years of age. The symptoms were: nausea/vomiting (56%), tachycardia (44%), hypertension (100%) (for patients evaluated in a health care facility), jittery/agitated/tremors (67%), dizziness (44%), chest pain (11%), and bilateral numbness (11%). In a survey of 496 college students, 51% reported consuming at least one energy drink during the last month. Of these energy drink users, 29% reported "weekly jolt and crash episodes," 22% reported headaches, and 19% reported heart palpitations from drinking energy drinks.

Media reports have also highlighted several cases of caffeine intoxication resulting from energy drink consumption. A 28-year-old motorcycle (motocross) athlete nearly died when his heart stopped during a competition. He had consumed eight cans of Red Bull over a 5 h period. "Spike Shooter" has been removed from several U.S. convenience stores, and banned from local high schools when students became sick after consuming cans of the product that were purported to have been given away at a promotional event. Similar action has been taken at another U.S. high school after two student athletes fainted after drinking "Speed Stack." Local store owners have also banned the selling of energy drinks to minors, after three teenage boys displayed signs of caffeine intoxication after rapidly ingesting "BooKoo" energy drink.

In addition to caffeine intoxication, the consumption of energy drinks has been linked to seizures, acute mania, and stroke. Deaths attributed to energy drink consumption have been reported in Australia, Ireland, and Sweden. Considerable debate has ensued as to whether these fatalities were a direct result of energy drink consumption.

5. Caffeine Dependence

The [*Diagnostic and Statistical Manual of Mental Disorders (DSM-IV-TR)*] defines substance dependence using a generic set of cognitive, physiological, and behavioral symptoms, including the inability to quit, use despite harm, using more than intended, withdrawal, and tolerance. Although DSM-IV-TR specifically excludes caffeine from its diagnostic schema for substance dependence, the World Health Organization's International Classification of Diseases (ICD-10) includes this diagnosis. While there is debate regarding the extent of reinforcing effects and abuse potential of caffeine, there is compelling evidence that caffeine can produce a substance dependence syndrome in some people. For example, studies in adults and adolescents have shown high rates of endorsement of inability to quit, use despite harm, and withdrawal. A population-based survey showed that 30% of a sample of 162 caffeine users fulfilled diagnostic criteria for substance dependence when applied to caffeine. The prevalence of caffeine dependence may increase as a result of marketing campaigns promoting the use of energy drinks among adolescents. By analogy with tobacco and alcohol use, the earlier the onset of smoking or drinking, the greater the risk for later dependence.

6. Caffeine Withdrawal

Symptoms of caffeine withdrawal have been described in the medical literature for more than a century. There have been at least 66 studies of caffeine withdrawal in the medical literature, the majority of which have been published within the last 10 years. The symptoms of caffeine withdrawal, the most common of which is headache, begin 12–24 h after the last dose of caffeine. In double-blind studies, about 50% of individuals report headache which may be severe in intensity. In addition to headache, other caffeine withdrawal symptoms include tiredness/fatigue, sleepiness/drowsiness, dysphoric mood (e.g., miserable, decreased well-being/contentedness), difficulty concentrating/decreased cognitive performance, depression, irritability, nausea/vomiting, and muscle aches/stiffness. These withdrawal symptoms may be severe in intensity, and the incidence of clinically significant distress and impairment in daily functioning due to caffeine withdrawal is 13% in experimental studies. Caffeine withdrawal is recognized as an official diagnosis in ICD-10 and a research diagnosis in DSM-IV-TR. Studies have also documented caffeine withdrawal in teenagers, and children the incidence of which may increase substantially with the aggressive marketing of energy drinks to these age groups.

7. Combined Use of Caffeine and Alcohol May Be Problematic

There is an association between the heavy use of caffeine and the heavy use of alcohol, and the ingestion of energy drinks in combination with alcohol is becoming increasingly popular, with 24% of a large stratified sample of college students reporting such consumption within the past 30 days. In the previously mentioned survey of 496 college students, 27% reported mixing alcohol and energy drinks in the past month. Of those that mixed energy drinks and alcohol, 49% used more than three energy drinks per occasion when doing so. In a survey of 1253 college students, energy drink users were disproportionately male and consumed alcohol more frequently than non-energy drink users.

One study showed that ingestion of a caffeinated energy drink (Red Bull) with vodka reduced participants perception of impairment of motor coordination in comparison to vodka alone, but did not significantly reduce objective measures of alcohol-induced impairment of motor coordination, reaction time, or breath alcohol concentration. These results are consistent with other studies investigating caffeine–alcohol interactions. Thus, when mixing energy drinks and alcohol, users may not feel the symptoms of alcohol intoxication. This may increase the potential for alcohol-related injury. Indeed, a recent survey of college students found that in comparison to those who consumed alcohol alone, students who consumed alcohol mixed with energy drinks had a significantly higher prevalence of alcohol-related consequences including: being taken advantage of, or taking advantage of another student sexually, riding in an automobile with a driver under the influence of alcohol, or being hurt or injured. In addition, mixing energy drinks with alcohol was associated with increased heavy episodic drinking and episodes of weekly drunkenness. The recent introduction of pre-mixed caffeine–alcohol combination drinks may exacerbate these problems and has prompted regulatory action. Accordingly, as part of a legal settlement reached in 2008 with State Attorneys in 11 states in the U.S., Anheuser-Busch has agreed to stop the manufacture and sale of caffeinated alcoholic beverages.

8. Relationship of Caffeine to Dependence on Other Substances

Studies in adult twins show that lifetime caffeine intake, caffeine toxicity and caffeine dependence are significantly and positively associated with various psychiatric disorders including major depression, generalized anxiety disorder, panic disorder, antisocial personality disorder, alcohol dependence, and cannabis and cocaine abuse/dependence. Studies in adult twins examining caffeine use, alcohol use, and cigarette smoking concluded that a common genetic factor (polysubstance use) underlies the use of these three substances, although another twin study suggested that caffeine and nicotine were associated with genetic factors unique to these substances. A study examining the co-occurrence of substance use among drug abusers concluded that dependence on caffeine, nicotine, and alcohol were governed by the same factors. In a study of caffeine dependent adults, . . . a clustering of histories of caffeine, nicotine, and alcohol dependence [was reported]. In a study of pregnant women, those who fulfilled criteria for a diagnosis of caffeine dependence and who had a family history of alcoholism were six times more likely to have a lifetime history of alcohol abuse or dependence.

More specifically, with regard to cigarette smoking, human and animal studies show that caffeine increases the reinforcing effects of nicotine. Epidemiology studies show that cigarette smokers consume more caffeine than non-smokers, an effect that may be partially due to increased caffeine metabolism among cigarette smokers. Self-administration studies show that cigarette smoking and coffee drinking covary temporally within individuals, although acute caffeine administration does not always increase cigarette smoking. As described above, twin and co-occurrence studies suggest links between caffeine use and smoking. A study of pregnant women showed that those who met criteria for caffeine dependence were nine times more likely to report a history of daily cigarette smoking compared to those who did not meet dependence criteria.

Whether caffeine serves as a gateway to other forms of drug dependence as suggested by some studies bears further investigation. With regard to energy drinks in particular, one study of 1253 college students found that energy drink consumption significantly predicted subsequent nonmedical prescription stimulant use. It is plausible that the use of energy drinks that are promoted as alternatives to illicit drugs (e.g., "Blow" and "Cocaine") may, in fact, increase interest in the use of such drugs.

9. Vulnerability to Caffeine Affected by Tolerance and Genetic Factors

Vulnerability to caffeine intoxication after bolus caffeine doses, such as those delivered in energy drinks, is markedly affected by pharmacological tolerance. Tolerance refers to a decrease in responsiveness to a drug as a result of drug exposure. Daily administration of very high doses of caffeine (e.g., 750–1200 mg/day) can produce complete or partial tolerance to caffeine's subjective, pressor, and neuroendocrine effects. Thus, individuals such as children and adolescents who do not use caffeine daily, are at greater risk for caffeine intoxication due to energy drink consumption than habitual caffeine consumers.

Genetic factors are relevant to vulnerability to both caffeine intoxication as well as caffeine dependence and withdrawal. Studies comparing monozygotic versus dizygotic twins have shown higher concordance rates for monozygotic twins for caffeine intoxication, total caffeine consumption, heavy use, caffeine tolerance, and caffeine withdrawal, with heritabilities ranging between 35% and 77%. . . .

10. Conclusions and Implications

The consumption of high caffeine content energy drinks has increased markedly in recent years. Regulation of energy drinks, including content labeling and health warnings has differed across countries, with among the most lax regulatory requirements in the U.S., which is also the largest market for these products. The absence of regulatory oversight has resulted in aggressive marketing of energy drinks, targeted primarily toward young males, for psychoactive, performance-enhancing and stimulant drug effects. There are increasing reports of caffeine intoxication from energy drinks, and it seems likely that problems with caffeine dependence and withdrawal will also increase. The combined use of caffeine and alcohol is increasing sharply, which studies suggest may increase the rate of alcohol-related injury. Given that clinical pharmacology and epidemiological studies demonstrate an association of caffeine use with dependence on alcohol, nicotine, and other drugs, and one study showed that energy drink use predicts subsequent nonmedical use of prescription stimulants, further study of whether energy drink use serves as a gateway to other forms of drug dependence is warranted.

One limitation of the present review is that the great majority of the knowledge about caffeine intoxication, withdrawal, and dependence is derived from studies of coffee consumption. However, studies that have examined these phenomena in the context of caffeine delivered via soft drinks or capsules have shown similar results. Thus, there is no reason to suppose that delivery of caffeine via energy drinks would appreciably alter these processes.

These observations have several regulatory and clinical implications. Considering the variable and sometimes very high caffeine content of energy drinks, in combination with the aggressive marketing to youthful and inexperienced consumers, it would be prudent to require full disclosure of the amount of caffeine and other ingredients in energy drinks on the product labeling. Product label warnings about risks when used alone and in combination with alcohol would also be appropriate. Restrictions on advertising and the aggressive marketing of energy drinks to youthful and inexperienced users should also be considered. The promotion of the use of drugs for their recreational and stimulant properties sends a potentially harmful message to adolescents that glamorizes and encourages drug use. Ingesting an energy drink to enhance athletic performance may not be far removed from the nonmedical use of anabolic steroids or pharmaceutical stimulants such as methylphenidate or amphetamine to gain a competitive advantage. Along the same lines, the rapid onset of stimulant effects provided by energy drinks may encourage users to seek out the more intense effects of prescription and illicit stimulants. Finally, it is important for clinicians to be familiar with energy drinks and the potential health consequences associated with their use. Recognizing the features of caffeine intoxication, withdrawal, and dependence may be especially relevant when treating younger persons who may be more likely to consume energy drinks.

Back to the Grind: The Return of Caffeine as an Ergogenic Aid

Caffeine is a socially acceptable stimulant that is used in various forms worldwide. In addition to helping people get started each day, caffeine has been an integral part of many athletes' diets. Most believe it helps their performance, and research now supports this belief.

Caffeine is a naturally occurring methylxanthine that stimulates the release and activity of the catecholamine epinephrine. The major dietary sources of caffeine (e.g., tea, coffee, chocolate, cola drinks) typically provide 30 to 100 milligrams of caffeine per serving. Some over-the-counter medications (e.g., NoDoz, Vivarin) contain 100 to 200 milligrams of caffeine per tablet. Caffeine is also found in the herbs guarana, yerba mate, and kola nut.

Substantial research suggests that caffeine enhances endurance performance. It also provides a small but worthwhile improvement during short-term, intense aerobic exercise lasting four to eight minutes and prolonged, high-intensity aerobic exercise lasting 20 to 60 minutes. The stimulant's effect on strength/power and sprints lasting less than 90 seconds is unclear. Caffeine will not turn a couch potato into a triathlete, as it does not improve exercise capacity in untrained subjects, regardless of dose.

The World Anti-Doping Agency (WADA) removed caffeine from its list of prohibited substances in January 2004. Athletes who compete in sports compliant with the WADA code can consume caffeine as part of their everyday diet or specifically as an ergogenic aid without fear of sanctions. A moderate amount of caffeine (up to 6 milligrams of caffeine per kilogram of body weight) does not raise urinary caffeine levels above the National Collegiate Athletic Association's [NCAA] doping threshold of 15 micrograms per milliliter.

Recent research has challenged two widely held beliefs about the use of caffeine as an ergogenic aid: first, that caffeine enhances endurance performance by increasing the utilization of fat and sparing muscle glycogen, and second, that caffeine has a diuretic effect and increases the risk of dehydration. The latter belief has caused concern among athletes, since proper hydration is essential.

Mechanism of Action

Caffeine has several effects on skeletal muscle, involving calcium handling, sodium-potassium pump activity, elevation of cyclic adenosine monophosphate (AMP), and direct action on enzymes such as glycogen phosphorylase. Caffeine's effects on epinephrine and cyclic AMP may increase lipolysis in adipose and muscle tissue, thereby raising plasma free fatty acid concentrations and increasing the availability of intramuscular triglyceride.

Three potential mechanisms have been proposed for the performance-enhancing effects of caffeine. In the classic, or "metabolic," theory, caffeine may increase fat utilization and decrease glycogen utilization. Caffeine mobilizes free fatty acids from adipose and/or intramuscular triglyceride by increasing circulating epinephrine levels. The increased availability of free fatty acids increases fat oxidation and spares muscle glycogen, thereby enhancing endurance performance.

At the lowest dose, caffeine improved performance without an increase in plasma epinephrine or free fatty acids.

Caffeine Dose and Timing

Caffeine is rapidly absorbed, reaching peak concentrations in the blood within one hour of ingestion. A commonly recommended dose to improve performance is 3 to 6 milligrams of caffeine per kilogram, consumed one hour before exercise. However, recent evidence suggests that the beneficial effects of caffeine occur at low levels of intake—1 to 3 milligrams of caffeine per kilogram—when caffeine is consumed before and/or during exercise. There is also little evidence of a dose-response relationship to caffeine, as the benefits in exercise performance do not increase with higher doses of caffeine.

Cox and colleagues [*Journal of Applied Physiology*, 2002] found a similar 3% improvement in time trial performance with the following:

- six doses of 1 milligram of caffeine per kilogram spread throughout two hours of submaximal cycling prior to the time trial;
- 6 milligrams of caffeine per kilogram consumed one hour prior to the cycling bout; or
- 1.5 milligrams of caffeine per kilogram (from Coca-Cola) consumed over the last one third of the exercise protocol.

This study found that consuming 6 milligrams per kilogram of caffeine improved performance independent of the timing of intake. Also, an intake of only 1.5 milligrams of caffeine per kilogram consumed toward the end of exercise enhanced time trial performance to the same degree as an intake of 6 milligrams per kilogram consumed before or during exercise. Although it is impossible to prove, it is thought that the subjects may have become more sensitive to small amounts of caffeine as they became fatigued.

Kovacs and associates [*Journal of Applied Physiology, 1998*] evaluated the effect on performance during a one-hour cycling time trial of different dosages of caffeine (2.1, 3.2, and 4.5 milligrams per kilogram) added to a 7% carbohydrate-electrolyte drink. All three caffeine doses improved performance compared with the carbohydrate-electrolyte drink alone. The improvement in performance was the same with caffeine doses of 3.2 milligrams per kilogram and 4.5 milligrams per kilogram and greater than with 2.1 milligrams per kilogram. This study suggests that once the threshold dose of caffeine was reached, there was no further performance benefit from a higher amount of caffeine.

Jenkins and associates [*International Journal of Sports Nutrition and Exercise Metabolism, 2008*] found that low doses of caffeine improved high-intensity aerobic cycling performance. The subjects consumed 1, 2, or 3 milligrams of caffeine per kilogram one hour prior to a 15-minute performance ride. Compared with placebo, the caffeine dose of 2 milligrams per kilogram improved performance by 4%, and the 3-milligrams-per-kilogram dose improved performance by 3%. The ergogenic effects of caffeine varied considerably in magnitude among individual cyclists. The authors recommended further research to explain the considerable variability of caffeine's ergogenic properties between individuals.

Ideally, the optimal caffeine dose is the amount that elicits the greatest performance benefit for the minimum level of risk or side effect. Further research is necessary to help identify the smallest caffeine dose that produces a meaningful improvement in performance. Additional study is also needed to investigate the potential for strategically timing caffeine intake.

Caffeine and Dehydration

Athletes and active people are commonly advised to avoid caffeinated beverages before, during, and after exercise. The rationale is that the diuretic effect of caffeine increases urinary water losses and contributes to dehydration, thereby harming athletic performance and/or health. This has become so firmly entrenched in the common wisdom that many athletes believe it must be based on substantial research. But recent research and literature reviews (Armstrong LE. Caffeine, body fluid-electrolyte balance, and exercise performance. *Int J Sport Nutr Exerc Metab*. 2002) refute this notion. There is also virtually no evidence in the scientific literature that caffeine intake impairs fluid status.

Armstrong and colleagues [*Int J Sport Nutr Exerc Metab*. 2005] evaluated hydration status and urine losses in subjects who were first habituated to a daily caffeine intake of 3 milligrams per kilogram for six days. The subjects then consumed either 0 milligrams per kilogram, 3 milligrams per kilogram (average dose was 226 milligrams), or 6 milligrams per kilogram (average dose was 452 milligrams) of caffeine for five days. There were no differences in body weight, urine losses, or serum osmolality. These findings counter the widely held belief that caffeine acts chronically as a diuretic.

Caffeine is unlikely to elevate urine output or cause dehydration if consumed in moderation. The effect of caffeine on diuresis is overstated and may be minimal in those who regularly consume caffeine. Furthermore, caffeine-containing drinks such as tea, coffee, and cola provide a significant source of fluid in many athletes' everyday diets.

Burke and associates [*Clinical Sports Nutrition, 2006*] noted that any small fluid loss due to caffeine-containing beverages can be easily offset by an athlete's fluid intake during meals and social gatherings. Furthermore, if the athlete is abruptly advised to remove caffeinated beverages from the diet or postexercise meal and does not replace these beverages with an equal volume of other fluids, he or she could become dehydrated.

Caffeine and Carbohydrate

Consuming carbohydrate alone and caffeine alone during endurance exercise have both been shown to delay the onset of fatigue and increase exercise capacity. The benefits of carbohydrate ingestion are attributed to the maintenance of blood glucose levels and high rates of carbohydrate oxidation in the latter stages of exercise, when muscle and liver glycogen stores are low. Kovacs and associates found that the addition of moderate amounts of caffeine (3.2 and 4.5 milligrams per kilogram) to a 7% carbohydrate-electrolyte drink (0.5 grams of carbohydrate per minute) significantly improved one-hour cycling time trial performance compared with a lower dose of caffeine (2.1 milligrams per kilogram) and the carbohydrate-electrolyte drink.

The addition of caffeine to carbohydrate may enhance performance by increasing intestinal carbohydrate absorption and exogenous carbohydrate oxidation. Increasing exogenous carbohydrate oxidation reduces the reliance on endogenous carbohydrate sources (muscle and liver glycogen). It appears that exogenous carbohydrate oxidation is primarily limited by intestinal carbohydrate absorption.

In a 2000 *Journal of Applied Physiology* article, Van Nieuwenhoven and colleagues found that adding a small amount of caffeine (1.4 milligrams of caffeine per kilogram) to a carbohydrate-electrolyte drink (0.5 grams glucose per minute) produced 23% greater intestinal glucose absorption compared with the carbohydrate-electrolyte drink during 90 minutes of cycling at 70% of maximum power output.

Yeo and colleagues [*Journal of Applied Physiology, 2005*] from the University of Birmingham in the United Kingdom evaluated the effect of caffeine on exogenous carbohydrate oxidation. The subjects consumed either a 5.8% glucose solution (0.8 grams glucose per minute), glucose with caffeine (0.8 grams glucose per minute and 10 milligrams of caffeine per kilogram), or water during two hours of cycling at 64% of VO2max. The average exogenous carbohydrate oxidation during the final 30 minutes of exercise was 26% higher for glucose with caffeine compared with glucose. The combination of caffeine and glucose produced a significantly higher total rate of carbohydrate oxidation (2.47 grams per minute) compared with glucose (1.84) and water (1.12), possibly due to an enhanced intestinal absorption of glucose.

Hulstin and Jeukendrup [*Medicine and Science in Sports and Exercise, 2008*], also from the University of Birmingham, conducted a follow-up study to evaluate the effect of caffeine on exogenous carbohydrate oxidation and determine whether the combined ingestion of caffeine and carbohydrate enhanced cycling performance compared with carbohydrate alone. The subjects consumed either a 6.4% glucose solution (0.71 grams per minute), glucose with caffeine (0.71 grams per minute and 5.3 milligrams of caffeine per kilogram), or a placebo during 105 minutes of steady-state cycling at 62% of VO2max. This was followed by a time trial lasting about 45 minutes, during which the subjects drank water. The combination of glucose and caffeine enhanced time trial performance by 4.6% compared with glucose and by 9% compared with placebo. However, caffeine did not influence exogenous carbohydrate oxidation during exercise.

Hulstin and Jeukendrup noted that the disparate findings from Yeo and colleagues may be explained by the use of a lower caffeine dose and/or individual differences between subjects in the two studies. It is also difficult to determine the most effective caffeine dose given the variability of experimental protocols used in research studies. Nevertheless, the findings of Hulstin and Jeukendrup and other studies demonstrate that the combined ingestion of caffeine and carbohydrate enhances endurance performance compared with carbohydrate alone. Further research is required to elucidate the mechanism for the additional performance effect of caffeine.

Source of Caffeine

Studies utilizing coffee as the source of caffeine have found that it can either enhance performance or fail to have a noticeable effect. Coffee is not an ideal source of caffeine due to the large variability in caffeine content depending on brand, variety, method of preparation, and serving size. Furthermore, other chemicals within coffee (e.g., derivates of the chlogogenic acids) may counteract the ergogenic effect of caffeine.

Cox and colleagues investigated the effect of a cola drink on endurance cycling performance to replicate athletes' common practice of replacing carbohydrate-electrolyte drinks with "de-fizzed" cola drinks during the latter stages of an endurance race. The authors found that consuming Coca-Cola (1.5 milligrams of caffeine per kilogram) toward the end of the protocol improved time trial performance by 3% and that most of this effect could be explained by Coke's modest caffeine content.

Hogervorst and associates [*Medical and Science in Sports and Exercise,* 2008] examined the effects of ingesting a caffeinated sports bar (PowerBar with Acti-Caf, which contains 100 milligrams of caffeine and 45 grams of carbohydrate) before and during cycling exercise on physical and cognitive performance. The subjects cycled for 2.5 hours at 60% of VO2max, followed by a time-to-exhaustion trial at 75% of VO2max. They consumed the caffeinated sports bar, a noncaffeinated sports bar (PowerBar, with 45 grams of carbohydrate), or placebo before exercise and after 55 and 115 minutes of exercise. The caffeinated sports bar improved time to exhaustion by 27% compared with the noncaffeinated sports bar and by 84% compared with the placebo. Caffeine also improved complex cognitive ability during and after exercise.

The majority of research studies have used pure caffeine rather than caffeinated drinks (e.g., colas, energy drinks) or products such as caffeinated gels and sports bars. Further research is required on the effectiveness of caffeinated products (energy drinks, caffeinated beverages, and caffeinated gels and sports bars) that athletes commonly use. Athletes who wish to try caffeine should experiment with pure caffeine during training.

Other Considerations

Most studies of caffeine and performance have been conducted in laboratories. Studies investigating performance in elite athletes during real-life sporting events should be undertaken to help provide specific recommendations for caffeine supplementation protocols. In addition to enhancing competitive performance, caffeine is also likely to be a helpful training aid by allowing the athlete to engage in harder, more consistent workouts.

The effects of caffeine vary between individuals. Some athletes do not respond and others experience adverse effects such as tremors, increased heart rate, headaches, and disrupted sleep. These side effects may both directly and indirectly impair performance.

For example, excessive caffeine intake can cause disrupted sleep and therefore interfere with the ability to recover between training sessions and multiday competitions. This side effect is more common at caffeine doses exceeding 6 to 9 milligrams per kilogram. Often, athletes will increase their intake of caffeine to offset the fatigue they experience due to disrupted sleep patterns, thus perpetuating and worsening the problem. The potential for adverse effects at high caffeine doses emphasizes the importance of finding the lowest effective dose of caffeine that can be used to achieve a performance enhancement.

Athletes' caffeine supplementation practices are often improvised and haphazard. Many athletes are unaware of current research demonstrating that beneficial effects of caffeine occur at low intake levels. They're also uninformed about the potential for side effects or negative outcomes from excess caffeine use. Dietitians who counsel athletes should inquire about their supplement use and educate them about the potential benefits and risks of popular sports supplements, including caffeine. Athletes who wish to use caffeine should experiment with pure caffeine in training before and during exercise to determine the dose that elicits the greatest benefits and least adverse effects.

Summary

Caffeine enhances endurance performance and provides a small but worthwhile improvement during short-term, intense aerobic exercise lasting four to eight minutes and prolonged, high-intensity aerobic exercise lasting 20 to 60 minutes. Although caffeine's mechanism of action is unknown, it is highly unlikely that caffeine improves endurance by increasing fat oxidation and sparing muscle glycogen utilization.

Recent evidence suggests that the beneficial effects of caffeine occur at low intake levels—1 to 3 milligrams of caffeine per kilogram—when caffeine is consumed before and/or during exercise. There is also little evidence of a dose-response relationship to caffeine. Caffeine is unlikely to elevate urine output or cause dehydration if consumed in moderation.

Coffee is not an ideal vehicle for caffeine supplementation for athletes due to the variability of caffeine content and the possible presence of chemicals that may impair exercise performance. Athletes who want to use caffeine should experiment with pure caffeine in training before and during exercise to determine the dose that elicits the greatest benefits and least adverse effects.

CHALLENGE QUESTIONS

Should Energy Drinks Be Banned?

1. Explain why many energy drinks have more than the FDA-allowed 0.02 percent caffeine, or 71 mg/12 oz can.
2. Compare how the WADA and the NCAA differ in their sanctions regarding caffeine.
3. Outline the health problems of caffeine discussed in both the articles.
4. The mother of a boy who weighs 75 lbs asks you about her son drinking two cans of Red Bull before going to soccer practice each day. What advice would you give and why?
5. You are aware that some of the girls on the cross-country team drink a can of Wired X505 about 30 minutes before the race. Why do you think they do this and what advice would you give them about it?
6. No mention is made of the effect of taurine found in energy drinks. While taurine is naturally found in breast milk and added to infant formulas, studies on the effect on humans are limited. Find a peer-reviewed study on the impact of taurine in sports drinks and describe the results of the study.

Finding the Common Ground

In response to the article "Caffeinated Energy Drinks—A Growing Problem," the American Beverage Association (ABA) wrote: "Quite simply, energy drinks can be part of a balanced lifestyle when consumed sensibly" (ABA Web site, September 28, 2008). Do you agree or disagree with their statement? Should energy drinks be totally banned for all populations? Do you think there is a level of caffeine (and taurine) that would be more appropriate or that caffeine content should be more clearly labeled to allow people to make informed decisions? Discuss your opinions.

Additional Internet Resources

American Beverage Association

National organization for the nonalcoholic beverage industry. Web site contains information on all ingredients in typical sports drinks.

http://www.ameribev.org/

World Anti-Doping Agency

Promotes, sets rules, and monitors the fight against doping in sport in all its forms.

http://www.wada-ama.org/

Internet References . . .

Center for Nutrition Policy and Promotion (CNPP)

This Center for Nutrition Policy and Promotion (CNPP) Web site provides recent United States Department of Agriculture (USDA) publications on diet and health, including the USDA Pyramid graphic, brochure, and the history of its development; the Food Guide Pyramid for Children; the Dietary Guidelines for Americans; the Healthy Eating Index (a 10-component index of foods and nutrients designed to measure overall dietary quality); and data on the dietary intake of Americans. Click on the *Nutrition Insights* button to see especially, Insight 2, Escobar A., "Are All Food Pyramids Created Equal?" (April 1997).

http://www.usda.gov/cnpp/

Economic Research Service (ERS)

This Economic Research Service (ERS) research reports site offers the complete text of *America's Eating Habits: Changes & Consequences*. The site also offers a large range of USDA publications on food and nutrition policy.

http://www.ers.usda.gov/Publications/

The American Dietetic Association

The American Dietetic Association Web site is primarily designed for members, but it also offers information for the public about dozens of issues in nutrition, resources for studying those issues, legislation affecting food and nutrition, and nutrition careers.

http://www.eatright.org/Public/

Food and Nutrition Policy

*T**he government is heavily involved in food and nutrition laws and policies that affect matters as diverse as foods allowed in school cafeterias to the amount we pay for foods. Because food is such a big business, the food industry reacts to almost any action taken by local, state, and federal governments that might impact their profits. In this unit, debates center around policies that relate to sugary foods and the impact these foods have on health, such as the issue over the possibility of initiating a national "fat tax." Proponents of a tax claim that sugar-sweetened beverages result in an obese population laden with obesity-induced diseases. They claim a tax on these foods might reduce calories in the nation and reduce health-care costs that result from these conditions. Opponents feel a tax would take away basic liberties of Americans and result in too much government control. The final issue focuses on "Let's Move," a new government initiative spearheaded by the First Lady. Michelle Obama feels that if families, schools, business, and communities all work together, childhood obesity can be a thing of the past. Critics say that the program is no different than antiobesity programs of the past and are skeptical of the program's success.*

- Is Hunger in America a Real Problem?
- Should Government Levy a Fat Tax?
- Can Michelle Obama's "Let's Move" Initiative Halt Childhood Obesity?

ISSUE 14

Is Hunger in America a Real Problem?

YES: Joel Berg, from "Hunger in the U.S.: A Problem as American as Apple Pie," *AlterNet* (February 4, 2009)

NO: Sam Dolnick, from "The Obesity-Hunger Paradox," *The New York Times* (March 12, 2010)

As you read the issue, focus on the following points:

1. Differences between food insecurity and hunger.
2. Causes of the increasing number of Americans who are food insecure or hungry, including the political impact.
3. The relationship between food insecurity and obesity.
4. Strategies that the Bronx is taking to reduce food insecurity.

ISSUE SUMMARY

YES: Hunger advocate Joel Berg says that 35.5 million Americans either suffer from hunger or struggle at the brink of hunger, which results in stunted growth in millions of American children. As the executive director of New York City Coalition Against Hunger, he points out that hunger is becoming a significant problem in the suburbs and is no longer only seen in poor inner city and isolated rural areas.

NO: New York journalist Sam Dolnick says that few Americans are hungry, if you picture hunger as a rail-thin child with nothing to eat. But he points out that Americans are "food insecure," which he describes as people "unable to get to the grocery or unable to find fresh produce among the pizza shops, doughnut stores and fried-everything restaurants." In fact, obesity often results from this type of food insecurity, where there is little access to affordable fresh produce and other lower calorie foods.

For years people have asked, "how can there be hunger in the land of plenty?" The amount of food grown in the America far exceeds the needs of our population. And we are an extremely wealthy nation; theoretically, no one should be without food. Now, a new question is surfacing, "how can an obese person suffer from hunger?" Most people think a person who is hungry suffers from lack of food and calories that results in a frail, emaciated person, but this is no longer true in America. We have now seen obesity in a person who lacks food, or at least quality food. The phenomenon is called the "Obesity–Hunger Paradox."

Before we go any further, let's define hunger. In 2006, the federal government decided to stop using the term "hunger" to describe people who simply lacked food. They felt the concept of "food security" or "food insecurity" gives a better idea of the problem. Based on the USDA's definitions, food insecurity is a "household-level economic and social condition of limited or uncertain access to adequate food." They go one step further and divide it into two categories:

- *Low food security*: Reports of reduced quality, variety, or desirability of the diet; little or no indication of reduced food intake.
- *Very low food security*: Reports of multiple indications of disrupted eating patterns and reduced food intake.

They suggest that hunger "should refer to a potential consequence of food insecurity that, because of prolonged, involuntary lack of food, results in discomfort, illness, weakness, or pain that goes beyond the usual uneasy sensation."

Based on these definitions, people whose diets consist of ample refined white bread, peanut butter, macaroni and cheese, and canned pork and beans, but lack a variety of high-quality fresh fruits and vegetables, are in the low food security category. A steady diet of these foods is all very calorie dense, which can easily lead to obesity. In contrast, very low food security is when there's virtually nothing at all in the kitchen; hunger is when the very low food insecurity causes weakness, illness, and pain from hunger.

Income impacts the ability to purchase food. To resolve this problem, the federal government began the Food Stamp Program to help feed the poor. When the program began in 1964, recipients were given paper food stamps that could be used like money to buy any food or nonalcoholic beverage. Today, recipients use Electronic Benefit Transfer (EBT) cards to purchase items. The name of the program has also been changed to the Supplemental Nutrition Assistance Program (SNAP). In 2009, 39 million Americans were on SNAP.

Only people with virtually no assets and very little income qualify for SNAP. That is where food banks step in.

The first food bank was founded in 1967 by retired Arizona businessman John Van Hengel. He had volunteered in a local soup kitchen and soon realized that many grocery stores threw out processed food that had been damaged during packaging or were near expiration. He began collecting these items to serve in the soup kitchen. When he received more food than the kitchen could handle, he would store them in a warehouse and distribute the canned and boxed foods to the needy. The warehouse was soon called the "food bank" based on the idea that individuals and companies who had the resources could make a "deposit" of food (and funds) through donations and agencies who serve the needy could make "withdrawals."

Today, about 80 percent of all food banks in the United States are networked through Feeding America, formerly called Second Harvest. It is the largest domestic hunger relief organization with over 200 food banks, at least one located in each of the 50 states. In 2009, Feeding America served 37 million Americans, almost as many served by SNAP. According to their 2010 report, 41 percent of Feeding America recipients are also on SNAP.

So what type of foods are distributed from food banks? Because the food must be stored in large warehouses, most items are canned or boxed. If a food bank gave fresh produce or dairy products, they would need large refrigerated storage areas and the recipients would need to come several times each month. Most food banks shelf stable foods such as peanut butter, boxed pasta, and canned beans—all very high calorie and with loads of sodium. While this type of food does provide needed calories to prevent true "hunger," they also contribute to obesity. Some people speculate that it may precipitate the hunger–obesity link.

In 2004, the Food Research and Action Center hosted the "Roundtable on Understanding the Paradox of Hunger and Obesity." During their discussions, it became apparent that obesity is prevalent in poverty, especially among women. They point out that no one knows exactly why obesity is seen in low-income women, but do theorize that it may be linked to the fact that "mothers go without food when food and money for food are limited in order to ensure that their children have something to eat, and that there is an association between food insecurity and a binge-like pattern of eating, a feast/famine eating pattern." So basically, women eat very meagerly when funds are low, then binge on very high-calorie foods at the beginning of the month when their paychecks (or EBT allotments) are available—or when they receive their box from the food bank.

A second theory is that they eat less fruits and vegetables because of the cost. The report explains that obese lower income women consume more "less expensive, energy-dense foods, rather than more expensive per calorie, less energy-dense fruits and vegetables," and this could contribute to a higher risk of obesity.

Food activist Michael Pollan agrees with this. In an interview with *Sierra Magazine* (September 23, 2004) he said, "High-quality food is better for your health. When you go to the grocery store, you find that the cheapest calories are the ones that are going to make you the fattest . . . the added sugars and fats in processed foods." Next time you are in the grocery store, look at the prices of apples, oranges, and asparagus. It is much cheaper to pick up a bag of store brand chips or cookies than to buy quality fresh produce. And pork and beans are cheaper than fresh salmon or turkey.

Do we have people in America who are truly hungry resulting in stunted growth? Joel Berg says "yes" that hunger is so prevalent that it causes stunted growth in millions of children. Sam Dolnick disagrees and says that few Americans are truly hungry, but does concede that many Americans are "food insecure" using the definition of not having access to *quality* food. He describes how food insecurity is causing obesity, especially in metropolitan areas. After reading the selections, decide if true *hunger* is a problem. Also, think about the foods that are available to lower income people and how they may contribute to obesity.

TIMELINE

1960 Some U.S. children die of malnutrition.

1964 Food Stamp Program begins.

1967 First U.S. food bank opens.

1969 George McGovern brings hunger to the national limelight.

1970s Nixon and McGovern form nutrition "safety net."

1980s Programs formed under the safety net result in hunger almost eliminated in the United States.

2004 Roundtable on "Understanding the Paradox of Hunger and Obesity" is held.

2005 Hurricane Katrina draws attention to hunger problems in America.

2008 Second Harvest changes its name to Feeding America. Approximately 35.5 million Americans request assistance from food banks, which is a 15–20 percent increase over previous years; 84 percent of food banks are unable to serve all who request food. The Food Stamp Program changes its name to Supplemental Nutrition Assistance Program (SNAP).

2009 39 million Americans are on SNAP.

DEFINITIONS

Food Insecurity Lack of access, at times, to enough food for an active, healthy life for all household members; limited or uncertain availability of nutritionally adequate foods.

Hunger A potential consequence of food insecurity that, because of prolonged, involuntary lack of food, results in discomfort, illness, weakness, or pain that goes beyond the usual uneasy sensation.

YES

Hunger in the U.S.: A Problem as American as Apple Pie

The following is an excerpt from *All You Can Eat: How Hungry Is America,* by Joel Berg.

> *We have long thought of America as the most bounteous of nations . . . [t]hat hunger and malnutrition should persist in a land such as ours is embarrassing and intolerable. More is at stake here than the health and well-being of [millions of] American children. . . . Something like the very honor of American democracy is involved*

—President Richard Nixon, May 6, 1969, Special Message to Congress Recommending a Program to End Hunger in America

Try explaining to an African that there is hunger in America. I've tried, and it's not easy.

In 1990, while on vacation, I was wandering alone through the dusty streets of Bamako, the small capital of the West African nation Mali, when a young man started walking alongside me and struck up a conversation. At first, I thought he wanted to sell me something or ask me for money, but it turned out he just wanted to talk, improve his English and learn a little about America. (He had quickly determined by my skin color that I was non-African and by my sneakers that I was American.)

When he asked me whether it was true that everyone in America was rich, I knew I was in trouble. How could I explain to him that a country as wealthy as mine still has tens of millions suffering from poverty and hunger? How could I explain to him that America—the nation of Bill Gates, "streets paved with gold," Shaquille O'Neal and all-you-can-eat-buffets—actually has a serious hunger problem? That in a country without drought or famine and with enough food and money to feed the world twice over 1-in-8 of our own people struggles to put food on their tables?

In Mali, such a statement was a hard sell. While that nation has one of the planet's most vibrant cultures, it also has one of the least-developed economies. The country has a per capita annual income of $470, meaning the average person makes $1.28 per day—and many earn far less than that, eking out subsistence livings through small-scale farming or other backbreaking manual

From *All You Can Eat: How Hungry is America?* by Joel Berg (Seven Stories Press, 2009). Copyright © 2009 by Seven Stories Press. Reprinted by permission.

labor. With the Sahara desert growing and enveloping ever-increasing swaths of Mali, the nation frequently suffers from widespread drought and famine. According to the United Nations, 28 percent of Mali's population is seriously undernourished.

I tried to tell him that not all Americans were as rich as he thought, and that much of the wealth he saw was concentrated among a small number of people while the majority toiled to make a basic living. I explained that living in a cash economy such as America's presents a different set of challenges than living in a subsistence and barter-based economy, which exists in much of Mali. That in America, you have to pay a company for oil, gas, and all other basic necessities. You must pay a landlord large sums of money to live virtually anywhere. That while many workers in America earn a minimum wage equaling less than $11,000 a year for full-time work (the U.S. federal minimum wage was then $5.15 per hour), they often pay more than $1,500 per month in rent, which equals $18,000 per year. So, many actually pay more in rent than they earn. Then they have to figure out a way to pay for health care, child care, transportation, and yes, food. When Americans have expenses that are greater than their income, they must go without basic necessities.

I thought I was very persuasive, but I still don't think I convinced him. Given that English was likely his third or fourth language, perhaps he didn't precisely understand what I was saying. Perhaps concepts such as paying for child care didn't resonate with him since few Malians pay others to care for their children. Moreover, I bet that—all my caveats aside—$11,000 a year sounded like a great deal of money to him.

Standing there in Africa, for the first time in my life I briefly had a hard time convincing even myself that hunger in the United States was something that I should seriously worry about given that things were obviously so much worse elsewhere. After all, I was forced to consider that, as bad as hunger is in America, US children rarely starve to death anymore, while they still do in parts of the developing world.

But then I recalled all the people I had met throughout America who couldn't afford to feed their families—who had to ration food for their children, choose between food and rent, or go without medicine to be able to buy dinner—and I reminded myself that, just because they weren't quite dropping dead in the streets didn't mean that their suffering wasn't significant indeed. And then I further reminded myself that America was the nation of Bill Gates—and more than 400 other billionaires, not to mention more than 7 million millionaires—so it was particularly egregious that my homeland allowed millions of children to suffer from stunted growth due to poor nutrition. I thus came back to the same conclusion I reach every day: while hunger anywhere on the planet is horrid and preventable, having it in America is truly unforgivable.

It is not surprising that it is often difficult to convince average Americans that there is a serious hunger problem in the United States. Our nation tends to think of hunger as a distant, overseas, Third World problem. Our collective mental images of hunger are usually of African children with protruding ribs and bloated bellies—surrounded by flies and Angelina Jolie—sitting in parched, cracked dirt. When I try to explain U.S. hunger to Americans, some automatically assume I am inflating the extent of the problem. They simply don't see it in their daily living. They know that America is the richest and most agriculturally abundant nation in the history of the world. They can't believe that a place with so much obesity can have hunger. And besides, they assume that I am exaggerating because I am an advocate, and it is my job to exaggerate.

35.5 Million . . . and Counting

When people look at the facts for themselves, they discover the shocking reality: hunger amidst a sea of plenty is a phenomenon as American as baseball, jazz, and apple pie. Today in the United States—because tens of millions of people live below the meager federal poverty line and because tens of millions of others hover just above it—35.5 million Americans, including 12.6 million children, live in a condition described by the government as "food insecurity." Which means their households either suffer from hunger or struggle at the brink of hunger.

Primarily because federal antihunger safety net programs have worked, American children are no longer dying in significant numbers as an immediate result of famine-like conditions—although children did die of malnutrition here as recently as the late 1960s. Still, despite living in a nation with so many luxury homes that the term "McMansion" has come into popular usage, millions of American adults and children have such little ability to afford food that they do go hungry at different points throughout the year—and are otherwise forced to spend money on food that should have been spent on other necessities like heat, health care, or proper child care.

Most alarmingly, the problem has only gotten worse in recent years. The 35.5 million food-insecure Americans encompass a number roughly equal to the population of California. That figure represents a more than 4 million-person increase since 1999. The number of children who live in such households also increased during that time, rising by more than half a million children. The number of adults and children who suffered from the most severe lack of food—what the Bush administration now calls "very low food security" and what used to be called "hunger"—also increased in that period from 7.7 million to 11.1 million people—a 44 percent increase in just seven years.

While once confined to our poor inner cities (such as Watts, Harlem, Southeast D.C., the Chicago South Side, and the Lower Ninth Ward of New Orleans) and isolated rural areas (such as Appalachia, the Mississippi Delta, Indian reservations, and the Texas/Mexico border region), hunger—and the poverty that causes it—has now spread so broadly that it is a significant and increasing problem in suburbs throughout the nation.

Meanwhile, just as more people need more food from pantries and kitchens, these charities have less to give. Since the government and private funding that they receive is usually fixed, when food prices increase, charities are forced to buy less. When those fixed amounts from government actually decrease (as they have in recent years), the situation goes from bad to worse.

In May 2008, America's Second Harvest Food Bank Network—the nation's dominant food bank network (which, in late 2008, changed its name to Feeding America)—reported that 100 percent of their member agencies served more clients than in the previous year, with the overall increases estimated to be 15 to 20 percent. Fully 84 percent of food banks were unable to meet the growing demand due to a combination of three factors: increasing number of clients; decreasing government aid; and soaring food prices.

The number of "emergency feeding programs" in America—consisting mostly of food pantries (which generally provide free bags of canned and boxed groceries for people to take home) and soup kitchens (which usually provide hot, prepared food for people to eat on site)—has soared past 40,000. As of 2005, a minimum of 24 million Americans depended on food from such agencies. Yet, given that more than 35 million Americans were food insecure, this statistic meant that about 11 million—roughly a third of those without enough food—didn't receive any help from charities.

We live in a new [G]ilded [A]ge. Inequality of wealth is spiraling to record heights, and the wealthiest are routinely paying as much as $1,500 for a case of champagne—equal to five weeks of full-time work for someone earning the minimum wage. While welfare reform is still moving some families to economic self-sufficiency, families being kicked off the rolls are increasingly ending up on the street. Homelessness is spiking. Poverty is skyrocketing. And the middle class is disappearing.

Meanwhile, soaring food prices have made it even more difficult for families to manage. Food costs rose 4 percent in 2007, compared with an average 2.5 percent annual rise for the 1990–2006 period, according to the U.S. Department of Agriculture. For key staples, the hikes were even worse: milk prices rose 7 percent in 2007, and egg prices rose by a whopping 29 percent.

It was even tougher for folks who wanted to eat nutritiously. A study in the Seattle area found that the most nutritious types of foods (fresh vegetables, whole grains, fish and lean meats) experienced a 20 percent price hike, compared to 5 percent for food in general. The USDA predicted that 2008 would be worse still, with an overall food price rise that could reach 5 percent, and with prices for cereal and bakery products projected to increase as much as 8.5 percent.

As author Loretta Schwartz-Nobel has chronicled in her 2002 book, *Growing Up Empty: The Hunger Epidemic in America*, the nation's hunger problem manifests itself in some truly startling ways. Even our armed forces often don't pay enough to support the food needs of military families. Schwartz-Nobel describes a charitable food distribution agency aimed solely at the people who live on a Marine base in Virginia and includes this quote from a Marine: "The way the Marine Corps made it sound, they were going to help take care of us, they made me think we'd have everything we needed. . . . They never said you'll get no food allowance for your family. They never said you'll need food stamps . . . and you still won't have enough." Schwatz-Nobel also quoted a Cambodian refugee in the Midwest: "My children are hungry. Often we are as hungry in America as I was in the (refugee) camps."

America's Dirty Secret Comes Out of Hiding

From 1970 to 2005, the mass media ignored hunger. But due to the surge of intense (albeit brief) media coverage of poverty in the aftermath of Hurricane Katrina, and subsequent reporting of food bank shortages and the impact of increasing food prices on the poor, the American public has been slowly waking to the fact that hunger and poverty are serious, growing problems domestically. Plus, more and more Americans suffer from hunger, have friends or relatives struggling with the problem, or volunteer at feeding charities where they see the problem for themselves.

Harmful myths about poverty are also starting to be discredited. While Americans have often envisioned people in poverty as lazy, healthy adults who just don't want to work, 72 percent of the nation's able-bodied adults living in poverty reported to the Census Bureau in 2006 that they had at least one job, and 88 percent of the households on food stamps contained either a child, an elderly person, or a disabled person. It is harder and harder to make the case that the trouble is laziness and irresponsibility. The real trouble is the inability of many working people to support their families on meager salaries and the inability of others to find steady, full-time work.

Fundamentally a Political Problem

As far as domestic issues go, hunger is a no-brainer. Every human being needs to eat. Hunger is an issue that is universally understandable. And everyone is against hunger in America. Actually, you'd be hard-pressed to find anyone in America who says they're for hunger.

Unlike other major issues such as abortion, gun control, and gay marriage—over which the country is bitterly divided based on deeply held values—Americans of all ideologies and religions are remarkably united in their core belief that, in a nation as prosperous as America, it is unacceptable to have people going hungry.

Even ultraconservative President Ronald Reagan, after being embarrassed when his top aide Edwin Meese suggested that there was not really hunger in America and that people were going to soup kitchens just so they could get a "free lunch," was quickly forced to issue a memo stating his abhorrence of domestic hunger and his intention to end it. Since then, Presidents George H.W. Bush, Bill Clinton, and George W. Bush—and high-profile members of the Senate and the House—have all given speeches laced with ringing denunciations of domestic hunger. Even right-wing think tanks—[who] often minimize the extent of hunger or say that hunger is the fault of hungry people—claim they want to end any hunger that may exist.

So why haven't we ended this simple problem? One word: politics.

If we were to put the American political system on trial for its failures, hunger would be "Exhibit A." Domestic hunger is not a unique problem; it is actually emblematic of our society's broader problems. The most characteristic features of modern American politics—entrenched ideological divisions, the deceptive use of statistics, the dominance of big money, the passivity and vacuity of the media, the undue influence of interest groups, and empty partisan posturing— all work in tandem to prevent us from ending domestic hunger.

If we can't solve a problem as basic as domestic hunger—over which there is so much theoretical consensus—no wonder we can't solve any of our more complicated issues such as immigration and the lack of affordable health care. In 1969, reaching a similar conclusion, Sen. George McGovern, D-S.D., chairman of the Senate Select Committee on Nutrition and Human Needs, put it this way:

> Hunger is unique as a public issue because it exerts a special claim on the conscience of the American people. . . . Somehow, we Americans are able to look past slum housing . . . and the chronic unemployment of our poor. But the knowledge that human beings, especially little children, are suffering from hunger profoundly disturbs the American conscience. . . . To admit the existence of hunger in America is to confess that we have failed in meeting the most sensitive and painful of human needs. To admit the existence of widespread hunger is to cast doubt on the efficacy of our whole system. If we can't solve the problem of hunger in our society, one wonders if we can resolve any of the great social issues before the nation.

It is not surprising that liberal McGovern would make such a statement, but it is a bit shocking that Republican Nixon—McGovern's opponent in the 1972 presidential election—made similar statements during his presidency, after having denied that hunger was a serious problem. The reason Nixon finally acknowledge[d] domestic hunger—and ultimately took serious action to rescue it—was that he was forced to do so by a combination of grassroots citizen agitation and concentrated national media attention on the issue.

In more recent decades, we've gone backward, and our modern elected officials deserve most of the blame. While, in the 1970s, the newly instituted federal nutrition safety net that Nixon and McGovern helped create ended starvation conditions and almost eliminated food insecurity altogether, in the early 1980s, Reagan and a compliant Democratic Congress slashed federal nutrition assistance and other antipoverty programs. Reagan also began the multi-decade process of selling the nation on the false notion that the voluntary and uncoordinated private charity could somehow make up for a large-scale downsizing in previously mandatory government assistance. Predictably, hunger again rose.

Both Bush administrations and the Newt Gingrich Congress enacted policies that worsened America's hunger problem. But when a somewhat more aggressive Democratic [C]ongress took over in 2007, Congress slightly raised the minimum wage and added a bit more money for the Special Supplemental Nutrition Program for Women, Infants, and Children—better known as the WIC food program—and, in 2008, they somewhat increased food stamp benefits. Certainly, small advances under Democratic leadership were much better than the consistent setbacks under the Republicans. But even liberal

Democratic leaders have proved unlikely to propose bolder efforts because they worry that such a focus might turn off middle-class "swing voters," and because big-money donors—who now control the Democratic Party nearly as much as they control the Republican Party—have different priorities.

Even when elected officials of both parties do want to substantively address hunger and poverty, they usually get bogged down in all-but-meaningless ideological debates, rhetorical excesses, and score-settling partisan antics. Certainly, it's not just elected officials who are to blame. Many religious denominations that denounce hunger also teach their congregations (consciously or unconsciously) that hunger is an inevitable part of both human history and God's will. While it should be ameliorated with charitable acts, they sadly teach, it can't really be eliminated. Businesses that donate food to charities often oppose increases in the minimum wage and other government policies that would decrease people's need for such donated food. The news media, funded by ads from businesses and politicians, rarely point out these discrepancies and focus instead on cheerleading for superficial, holiday-time charitable efforts.

But most harmfully, Americans all over the country have been tricked into thinking that these problems can't be solved and that the best we can hope for is for private charities to make the suffering marginally less severe. America can end hunger. By implementing a bold new political and policy agenda to empower low-income Americans and achieve fundamental change based upon mainstream values, America can end hunger quickly and cost-effectively. That achievement would concretely improve tens of millions of lives, and, in the process, provide a blueprint for fixing the broader problems of our entire, bilge-ridden political system.

Outside the Taylor Grocery and Restaurant (which serves the world's best grilled catfish) in Taylor, Miss., is a sign that says, "Eat or We Both Starve." Not only is that slogan a good way to sell catfish, it is a great way to sum up why our collective self-interest should compel us to end domestic hunger.

No society in the history of the world has sustained itself in the long run with as much inequality of wealth as exists in America. Growing hunger and poverty, if left unchecked, will eventually threaten the long-term food security, finances, and social stability of all Americans, even the ones who are currently middle class or wealthy. At the dawn of a new presidency, as the nation clamors for change and a new direction, hunger is a problem too simple and too devastating to ignore.

The Obesity–Hunger Paradox

When most people think of hunger in America, the images that leap to mind are of ragged toddlers in Appalachia or rail-thin children in dingy apartments reaching for empty bottles of milk.

Once, maybe.

But a recent survey found that the most severe hunger-related problems in the nation are in the South Bronx, long one of the country's capitals of obesity. Experts say these are not parallel problems persisting in side-by-side neighborhoods, but plagues often seen in the same households, even the same person: the hungriest people in America today, statistically speaking, may well be not sickly skinny, but excessively fat.

Call it the Bronx Paradox.

"Hunger and obesity are often flip sides to the same malnutrition coin," said Joel Berg, executive director of the New York City Coalition Against Hunger. "Hunger is certainly almost an exclusive symptom of poverty. And extra obesity is one of the symptoms of poverty."

The Bronx has the city's highest rate of obesity, with residents facing an estimated 85 percent higher risk of being obese than people in Manhattan, according to Andrew G. Rundle, an epidemiologist at the Mailman School of Public Health at Columbia University.

But the Bronx also faces stubborn hunger problems. According to a survey released in January by the Food Research and Action Center, an antihunger group, nearly 37 percent of residents in the 16th [c]ongressional [d]istrict, which encompasses the South Bronx, said they lacked money to buy food at some point in the past 12 months. That is more than any other [c]ongressional district in the country and twice the national average, 18.5 percent, in the fourth quarter of 2009.

Such studies present a different way to look at hunger: not starving, but "food insecure," as the researchers call it (the Department of Agriculture in 2006 stopped using the word "hunger" in its reports). This might mean simply being unable to afford the basics, unable to get to the grocery, or unable to find fresh produce among the pizza shops, doughnut stores, and fried-everything restaurants of East Fordham Road.

Precious, the character at the center of the Academy Award-winning movie by the same name, would probably count as food insecure even though she is severely obese (her home, Harlem, ranks 49th on the survey's list, with

24.1 percent of residents saying they lacked money for food in the previous year). There she is stealing a family-size bucket of fried chicken from a fast-food restaurant. For breakfast.

That it is greasy chicken, and that she vomits it up in a subsequent scene, points to the problem that experts call a key bridge between hunger and obesity: the scarcity of healthful options in low-income neighborhoods and the unlikelihood that poor, food-insecure people like Precious would choose them.

Full-service, reasonably priced supermarkets are rare in impoverished neighborhoods, and the ones that are there tend to carry more processed foods than seasonal fruits and vegetables. A 2008 study by the city government showed that 9 of the Bronx's 12 community districts had too few supermarkets, forcing huge swaths of the borough to rely largely on unhealthful, but cheap, food.

"When you're just trying to get your calorie intake, you're going to get what fills your belly," said Mr. Berg, the author of "All You Can Eat: How Hungry Is America?" "And that may make you heavier even as you're really struggling to secure enough food."

For the center's survey, Gallup asked more than 530,000 people across the nation a single question: "Have there been times in the past 12 months when you did not have enough money to buy food that you or your family needed?"

The unusually large sample size allowed researchers to zero in on trouble spots like the South Bronx.

New York's 10th [c]ongressional [d]istrict, which zigzags across Brooklyn and includes neighborhoods like East New York and Bedford-Stuyvesant, ranked sixth in the survey, and Newark ranked ninth, both with about 31 percent of residents showing food hardship. (At the state level, the South is the hungriest: Mississippi tops the list at 26 percent, followed by Arkansas, Alabama, Tennessee, Kentucky, Louisiana, the Carolinas, and Oklahoma. New York ranks 27th, with 17.4 percent; New Jersey is 41st, with 15.5 percent; and Connecticut is 47th, with 14.6 percent.)

The survey, conducted over the past two years, showed that food hardship peaked at 19.5 percent nationwide in the fourth quarter of 2008, as the economic crisis gripped the nation. It dropped to 17.9 percent by the summer of 2009, then rose to 18.5 percent.

Though this was the first year that the center did such a survey, it used a question similar to one the Department of Agriculture has been asking for years. The most recent survey by the agency, from 2008, found that 14.6 percent of Americans had low to very low food security.

Bloomberg administration officials see hunger and obesity as linked problems that can be addressed, in part, by making healthful food more affordable.

"It's a subtle, complicated link, but they're very much linked, so the strategic response needs to be linked in various ways," said Linda I. Gibbs, the deputy mayor for health and human services. "We tackle the challenge on three fronts—providing income supports, increasing healthy options and encouraging nutritious behavior."

To that end, the city offers a Health Bucks program that encourages people to spend their food stamps at farmers' markets by giving them an extra $2 coupon for every $5 spent there.

The city has also created initiatives to send carts selling fresh fruits and vegetables to poor neighborhoods, and to draw grocery stores carrying fresh fruit and produce to low-income areas by offering them tax credits and other incentives. The city last month announced the first recipients of those incentives: a Foodtown store that burned down last year will be rebuilt and expanded in the Norwood section of the Bronx, and a Western Beef store near the Tremont subway station will be expanded.

But the Bronx's hunger and obesity problems are not simply related to the lack of fresh food. Experts point to a swirling combination of factors that are tied to, and exacerbated by, poverty.

Poor people "often work longer hours and work multiple jobs, so they tend to eat on the run," said Dr. Rundle of Columbia. "They have less time to work out or exercise, so the deck is really stacked against them."

Indeed, the food insecurity study is hardly the first statistical measure in which the Bronx lands on the top—or, in reality, the bottom. The borough's 14.1 percent unemployment rate is the highest in the state. It is one of the poorest counties in the nation. And it was recently ranked the unhealthiest of New York's 62 counties.

"If you look at rates of obesity, diabetes, poor access to grocery stores, poverty rates, unemployment and hunger measures, the Bronx lights up on all of those," said Triada Stampas of the Food Bank for New York City. "They're all very much interconnected."

CHALLENGE QUESTIONS

Is Hunger in America a Real Problem?

1. Compare the definitions of "hunger" to "food insecurity."
2. Prepare a table contrasting Berg's description of food insecurity/ hunger in America to Dolnick's description.
3. Describe the causes of hunger in America as discussed by Berg. Include the political ramifications.
4. Consider the ways that the Bronx is working to help reduce obesity among its poor. Describe things currently being done in your community to reduce hunger and new things that could be done. List steps you would take to implement the new ideas.
5. Berg points out that "hunger anywhere on the planet is horrid and preventable; having it in America is truly unforgivable." Describe how we, as a global community, can prevent hunger in our home country and around the world.

ISSUE 15

Should Government Levy a Fat Tax?

YES: **Kelly D. Brownell, et al.,** from "The Public Health and Economic Benefits of Taxing Sugar-Sweetened Beverages" *The New England Journal of Medicine* (October 15, 2009)

NO: **Daniel Engber,** from "Let Them Drink Water! What a Fat Tax Really Means for America" *Slate* (September 21, 2009)

As you read the issue, focus on the following points:

1. Why sugar-sweetened beverages are targeted for a "fat tax."
2. The different methods used to calculate a "sugar tax," as suggested by Brownell and colleagues.
3. The properties of junk foods that make them addictive.
4. The impact that a "fat tax" will have on poor, nonwhite people.

ISSUE SUMMARY

YES: Kelly Brownell and colleagues propose a "fat tax" targeting sugar-sweetened beverages. They feel a tax will decrease the amount of sugary drinks people consume and ultimately help reduce obesity. They also suggest that the tax has the "potential to generate substantial revenue" to help fund health-related initiatives.

NO: Daniel Engber disagrees with a fat tax on sugary beverages since it will impact poor, nonwhite people most severely and they would be deprived of the pleasures of drinking palatable beverages. He says that the poor would be forced to "drink from the faucet" while the more affluent will sip exotic beverages such as POM Wonderful, at about $5 a pop.

Throughout history, governments have levied taxes on people and businesses. Revenues generated are used to support the government and various programs. We typically pay taxes on income, property, and purchases. Businesses pay an excise tax on the products they produce, and some of the taxes are pretty hefty. Tobacco manufacturers pay $1.01 per pack for cigarettes in federal taxes. On top of that, states and cities add sales tax on tobacco products. As of 2010, anyone who buys cigarettes in New York City pays a whopping $10 per pack. [Tax breakdown: $1.01 to the Feds, $2.75 to the state, and $1.60 to the city.] These taxes are often called "sin taxes" since the products being taxed are not necessities of life and are considered to be "sinful" by many.

Sin taxes have a twofold purpose. First is to discourage use of the products, and at $10 pack, fewer New Yorkers are smoking. The second is to generate revenue; some of it may be used to cover health care costs related to tobacco- or alcohol-induced conditions and the other use is to help balance the government's budget.

Many health and economic experts have proposed various forms of "fat taxes" to help pay for obesity-related health problems. Some actually have proposed to tax fat people based on their body weight. Daniel Engber, author of the YES article, describes a fat tax proposed by A.J. Carlson during World War II. Carlson's idea was to charge the nation's largest citizens a fee for every pound of overweight. He thought proceeds from the taxes could have been used to help feed soldiers who were overseas, while helping to reduce obesity at home. His proposal did not become a reality.

More recently, economist Adam Creighton designed a similar "fat-*person* tax," which was published in *The American,* August 8, 2007. His tongue-in-check proposal calls for a "fat-*person* tax" to be administered by the Internal Revenue Service (IRS). He suggests that everyone would submit a self-reported body mass index (BMI) with their annual tax returns. Creighton describes that it would be

> a progressive tax: the fatter the taxpayer, the higher the tax. The top of the "normal" range for BMI is 24. A BMI above 25 would pay a small surtax, say 5 percent, BMI 30s would pay 10 percent, etc. The brilliance of Art Laffer's flat income tax notwithstanding, a flat *fat* tax simply would not work, since it would not encourage weight-control once the taxpayer's BMI was well above the taxation threshold.

To deter falsified BMIs, IRS doctors could offer a second opinion. BMI audits might be required at 3 or 6-month intervals to get an accurate reading of each taxpayer's average BMI during the year, and to prevent unhealthy fasting during the tax season. And given the latest research showing obesity spreads socially, the IRS could even demand friendship data (cross-checked) to ensure individual friendship networks don't exceed a particular fat-friends quota.

We as Americans may find Creighton's satire about taxation humorous, but Japan does impose a penalty based on the girth of its citizens. They are among the thinnest nations in the world with only 5 percent of Japanese people obese, but this is double what it was 30 years ago. To put the brakes on this increasing trend, in 2008, the government passed a law requiring businesses and local governments to measure the waist circumferences of all employees over age 40. The upper limit for men is 33.5 inches while women are allowed a waist of 35.4 inches. (In the United States, we like women a tad smaller and encourage waists to be less than 35 inches, but don't consider a man fat until his waist reaches 40.) If the overweight employee does not reduce his/her girth, the Japanese government recommends dieting advice. To encourage compliance, the business or local government is fined if their employees do not lose weight.

Most Americans feel that this type of tax would infringe upon our freedom and right to privacy. Therefore, taxing fattening foods is more realistic. In this issue's NO article, Daniel Engber points out that about 40 states already have a tax on junk foods or soda, but there is no federal tax. Kelly Brownell, lead author of the YES article, began his crusade for a "Twinkie tax" in the 1990s. He wrote an article for *The New York Times* (December 15, 1994) proposing that Americans can "Get Slim with Higher Taxes." He called for a "sin tax" on unhealthy foods similar to what had been done for years on cigarettes and alcohol. However, a challenge with taxing "junk foods" is how do you define what should be taxed? Surely high calorie foods would be the target, but how does one decide if a bag of Reece's Pieces, with 230 kcal and 11 g of fat, should be taxed while a bag of "natural and healthy" peanuts, with their 280 kcal and 25 g of fat, be exempted? Due to the complexity of such labeling, most proponents of taxing calorie-laden foods are targeting sugar-sweetened beverages.

In 2006, Barry Popkin (one of the authors of the YES article) led a team who developed a guidance system for beverages. The system divides beverages into six levels with plain water rated the best choice (Level 1) to drink since it provides no calories. The least preferred choice is any sugar-sweetened beverage (Level 6), with no nutritional value such soft drinks are the least preferred choice. Levels 2 through 5 are progressively less desirable because of their calorie to nutrient ratios.

Kelly Brownell and colleagues propose a "fat tax" targeting beverages rated at Level 6, the sugar-sweetened ones. They feel a tax will decrease the amount of sugary drinks people consume and ultimately help reduce obesity. Daniel Engber disagrees since he believes the tax will impact poor, nonwhite people most severely and they would be deprived of the pleasures of drinking palatable beverages. What are your thoughts on the topic? Do you think a "fat tax" on sugar-sweetened beverages will decrease our consumption, while raising dollars to spend on obesity-related conditions? After reading both selections, decide for yourself if a fat tax is fair and will help reduce obesity.

DEFINITIONS

Brioche A sweat French bread made with eggs and butter.

Pain au levain A dense French bread.

Hedonic A learned preference for a flavor.

YES

Kelly D. Brownell, et al.

The Public Health and Economic Benefits of Taxing Sugar-Sweetened Beverages

The consumption of sugar-sweetened beverages has been linked to risks for obesity, diabetes, and heart disease[1-3]; therefore, a compelling case can be made for the need for reduced consumption of these beverages. Sugar-sweetened beverages are beverages that contain added, naturally derived caloric sweeteners such as sucrose (table sugar), high-fructose corn syrup, or fruit-juice concentrates, all of which have similar metabolic effects.

Taxation has been proposed as a means of reducing the intake of these beverages and thereby lowering health care costs, as well as a means of generating revenue that governments can use for health programs.[4-7] Currently, 33 states have sales taxes on soft drinks (mean tax rate, 5.2%), but the taxes are too small to affect consumption and the revenues are not earmarked for programs related to health. This article examines trends in the consumption of sugar-sweetened beverages, evidence linking these beverages to adverse health outcomes, and approaches to designing a tax system that could promote good nutrition and help the nation recover health care costs associated with the consumption of sugar-sweetened beverages.

Consumption Trends and Health Outcomes

In recent decades, intake of sugar-sweetened beverages has increased around the globe; for example, intake in Mexico doubled between 1999 and 2006 across all age groups.[8] Between 1977 and 2002, the per capita intake of caloric beverages doubled in the United States across all age groups[9] (Fig. 1). The most recent data (2005–2006) show that children and adults in the United States consume about 172 and 175 kcal daily, respectively, per capita from sugar-sweetened beverages.

The relationship between the consumption of sugar-sweetened beverages and body weight has been examined in many cross-sectional and longitudinal studies and has been summarized in systematic reviews.[1,2] A meta-analysis showed positive associations between the intake of sugar-sweetened beverages and body weight—associations that were stronger in longitudinal studies than in cross-sectional studies and in studies that were not funded by the

From *The New England Journal of Medicine*, October 15, 2009, pp. 1599–1605. Copyright © 2009 by Massachusetts Medical Society. All rights reserved. Reprinted by permission.

Figure 1

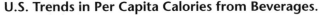

U.S. Trends in Per Capita Calories from Beverages.

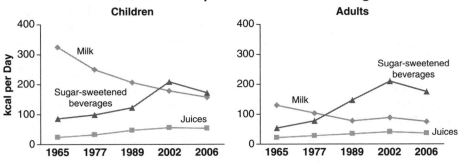

Data are for U.S. children 2 to 18 years of age and adults 19 years of age or older. Data have been weighted to be nationally representative, with the use of methods that generate measures of each beverage that are comparable over time. Data for 1965–2002 are from Duffey and Popkin[9]; data for 2005–2006 have not been published previously.

beverage industry than in those that were.[2] A meta-analysis of studies involving children[10]—a meta-analysis that was supported by the beverage industry—was interpreted as showing that there was no evidence of an association between consumption of sugar-sweetened beverages and body weight, but it erroneously gave large weight to several small negative studies; when a more realistic weighting was used, the meta-analysis summary supported a positive association.[11] A prospective study involving middle-school students over the course of 2 academic years showed that the risk of becoming obese increased by 60% for every additional serving of sugar-sweetened beverages per day.[12] In an 8-year prospective study involving women, those who increased their consumption of sugar-sweetened beverages at year 4 and maintained this increase gained 8 kg, whereas those who decreased their intake of sugar-sweetened beverages at year 4 and maintained this decrease gained only 2.8 kg.[13]

Short-term clinical trials provide an experimental basis for understanding the way in which sugar-sweetened beverages may affect adiposity. Tordoff and Alleva[14] found that as compared with total energy intake and weight during a 3-week period in which no beverages were provided, total energy intake and body weight increased when subjects were given 530 kcal of sugar-sweetened beverages per day for 3 weeks but decreased when subjects were given noncaloric sweetened beverages for the same length of time. Raben et al.[15] reported that obese subjects gained weight when they were given sucrose, primarily in the form of sugar-sweetened beverages, for 10 weeks, whereas they lost weight when they were given noncaloric sweeteners for the same length of time.

Four long-term, randomized, controlled trials examining the relationship between the consumption of sugar-sweetened beverages and body weight have been reported; the results showed the strongest effects among overweight persons. A school-based intervention to reduce the consumption of carbonated beverages was assessed among 644 students, 7 to 11 years of age, in the United Kingdom with the use of a cluster design.[16] After 1 year, the intervention group, as compared with the control group, had a nonsignificantly lower mean body-mass index (the weight in kilograms divided by the square of the height in meters) and a significant 7.7% lower incidence of obesity. In a study involving 1140 Brazilian schoolchildren, 9 to 12 years of age, that was designed to discourage the consumption of sugar-sweetened beverages, no overall effect on body-mass index was observed during the 9-month academic year.[17] Among students who were overweight at baseline, the body-mass index was nonsignificantly decreased in the intervention group as compared with the control group; the difference was significant among overweight girls. In another clinical trial, 103 high-school students in Boston were assigned to a control group or to an intervention group that received home delivery of noncaloric beverages for 25 weeks. The body-mass index was nonsignificantly reduced in the overall intervention group, but among students in the upper third of body-mass index at baseline, there was a significant decrease in the body-mass index in the intervention group, as compared with the control group (a decrease of 0.63 vs. an increase of 0.12).[18] The effects of replacing sugar-sweetened beverages with milk products were examined among 98 overweight Chilean children.[19] After 16 weeks, there was a nonsignificantly lower increase in the percentage of body fat in the intervention group than in the control group (0.36% and 0.78% increase, respectively), whereas there was a significantly greater increase in lean mass in the intervention group (0.92 vs. 0.62 kg).

Three prospective, observational studies—one involving nurses in the United States, one involving Finnish men and women, and one involving black women—each showed positive associations between the consumption of sugar-sweetened beverages and the risk of type 2 diabetes.[13,20,21] Among the 91,249 women in the Nurses' Health Study II who were followed for 8 years, the risk of diabetes among women who consumed one or more servings of sugar-sweetened beverages per day was nearly double the risk among women who consumed less than one serving of sugar-sweetened beverages per month[13]; about half the excess risk was accounted for by greater body weight. Among black women, excess weight accounted for most of the excess risk.

Among 88,520 women in the Nurses' Health Study, the risk of coronary heart disease among women who consumed one serving of sugar-sweetened beverages per day, as compared with women who consumed less than one serving per month, was increased by 23%, and among those who consumed two servings or more per day, the risk was increased by 35%.[3] Increased body weight explained some, but not all, of this association.

Mechanisms Linking Sugar-Sweetened Beverages with Poor Health

A variety of behavioral and biologic mechanisms may be responsible for the associations between the consumption of sugar-sweetened beverages and adverse health outcomes, with some links (e.g., the link between intake of sugar-sweetened beverages and weight gain) better established than others. The well-documented adverse physiological and metabolic consequences of a high intake of refined carbohydrates such as sugar include the elevation of triglyceride levels and of blood pressure and the lowering of high-density lipoprotein cholesterol levels, which would be expected to increase the risk of coronary heart disease.[22] Because of the high glycemic load of sugar-sweetened beverages, consumption of these beverages would be expected to increase the risk of diabetes by causing insulin resistance and also through direct effects on pancreatic islet cells.[23] Observational research has shown that consumption of sugar-sweetened beverages, but not of noncalorically sweetened beverages, is associated with markers of insulin resistance.[24]

Intake of sugar-sweetened beverages may cause excessive weight gain owing in part to the apparently poor satiating properties of sugar in liquid form. Indeed, adjustment of caloric intake at subsequent meals for energy that had been consumed as a beverage is less complete than adjustment of intake for energy that had been consumed as a solid food.[25] For example, in a study involving 323 adults, in which 7-day food diaries were used, energy from beverages added to total energy intake instead of displacing other sources of calories.[26] The results of a study of school-age children were consistent with the data from adults and showed that children who drank 9 oz or more of sugar-sweetened beverages per day consumed nearly 200 kcal per day more than those who did not drink sugar-sweetened beverages.[27]

Short-term studies of the effect of beverage consumption on energy intake support this mechanism. Among 33 adults who were given identical test lunches on six occasions but were given beverages of different types (sugar-sweetened cola, noncaloric cola, or water) and amounts (12 oz [355 ml] or 18 oz [532 ml]),[28] the intake of solid food did not differ across conditions; the result was that there was significantly greater total energy consumption when the sugar-sweetened beverages were served.

Sugar-sweetened beverages may also affect body weight through other behavioral mechanisms. Whereas the intake of solid food is characteristically coupled to hunger, people may consume sugar-sweetened beverages in the absence of hunger, to satisfy thirst or for social reasons. Sugar-sweetened beverages may also have chronic adverse effects on taste preferences and food acceptance. Persons—especially children—who habitually consume sugar-sweetened beverages rather than water may find more satiating but less sweet foods (e.g., vegetables, legumes, and fruits) unappealing or unpalatable, with the result that their diet may be of poor quality.

Economic Rationale

Economists agree that government intervention in a market is warranted when there are "market failures" that result in less-than-optimal production and consumption.[29,30] Several market failures exist with respect to sugar-sweetened beverages. First, because many persons do not fully appreciate the links between consumption of these beverages and health consequences, they make consumption decisions with imperfect information. These decisions are likely to be further distorted by the extensive marketing campaigns that advertise the benefits of consumption. A second failure results from time-inconsistent preferences (i.e., decisions that provide short-term gratification but long-term harm). This problem is exacerbated in the case of children and adolescents, who place a higher value on present satisfaction while more heavily discounting future consequences. Finally, financial "externalities" exist in the market for sugar-sweetened beverages in that consumers do not bear the full costs of their consumption decisions. Because of the contribution of the consumption of sugar-sweetened beverages to obesity, as well as the health consequences that are independent of weight, the consumption of sugar-sweetened beverages generates excess health care costs. Medical costs for overweight and obesity alone are estimated to be $147 billion—or 9.1% of U.S. health care expenditures—with half these costs paid for publicly through the Medicare and Medicaid programs.[31]

An Effective Tax Policy and Projected Effects

Key factors to consider in developing an effective policy include the definition of taxable beverages, the type of tax (sales tax or excise tax), and the tax rate. We propose an excise tax of 1 cent per ounce for beverages that have any added caloric sweetener. An alternative would be to tax beverages that exceed a threshold of grams of added caloric sweetener or of kilocalories per ounce. If this approach were used, we would recommend that the threshold be set at 1 g of sugar per ounce (30 ml) (32 kcal per 8 oz [237 ml]). Another option would be a tax assessed per gram of added sugar, but such an approach would be difficult to administer. The advantage of taxing beverages that have any added sugar is that this kind of tax is simpler to administer and it may promote the consumption of no-calorie beverages, most notably water; however, a threshold approach would also promote calorie reductions and would encourage manufacturers to reformulate products. A consumer who drinks a conventional soft drink (20 oz [591 ml]) every day and switches to a beverage below this threshold would consume approximately 174 fewer calories each day.

A specific excise tax (a tax levied on units such as volume or weight) per ounce or per gram of added sugar would be preferable to a sales tax or an ad valorem excise tax (a tax levied as a percentage of price) and would provide an incentive to reduce the amount of sugar per ounce of a sugar-sweetened beverage. Sales taxes added as a percentage of retail cost would have three disadvantages: they could simply encourage the purchase of lower-priced brands (thus resulting in no calorie reduction) or of large containers that cost less per ounce; consumers would become aware of the added tax only after making the decision to purchase the beverage; and the syrups that are used in fountain drinks, which are often served with multiple refills, would remain untaxed. A number of states currently exempt sugar-sweetened beverages from sales taxes along with food, presumably because food is a necessity. This practice should be eliminated, whether or not an excise tax is enacted.

Excise taxes could be levied on producers and wholesalers, and the cost would almost certainly be passed along to retailers, who would then incorporate it into the retail price; thus, consumers would become aware of the cost at the point of making a purchase decision. Taxes levied on producers and wholesalers would be much easier to collect and enforce than taxes levied on retailers because of the smaller number of businesses that would have to comply with the tax; in addition, the sugar used in syrups could be taxed—a major advantage because of the heavy sales of fountain drinks. Experience with tobacco and alcohol taxes suggests that specific excise taxes have a greater effect on consumption than do ad valorem excise taxes and can also generate more stable revenues because they are less dependent on industry pricing strategies.[32] In addition, tax laws should be written with provisions for the regular adjustment of specific excise taxes to keep pace with inflation, in order to prevent the effect of the taxes on both prices and revenues from eroding over time.

A tax of 1 cent per ounce of beverage would increase the cost of a 20-oz soft drink by 15 to 20%. The effect on consumption can be estimated through research on price elasticity (i.e., consumption shifts produced by price). The price elasticity for all soft drinks is in the range of –0.8 to –1.0.[33] (Elasticity of –0.8 suggests that for every 10% increase in price, there would be a decrease in consumption of 8%, whereas elasticity of –1.0 suggests that for every 10% increase in price, there would be a decrease in consumption of 10%.) Even greater price effects are expected from taxing only sugar-sweetened beverages, since some consumers will switch to diet beverages. With the use of a conservative estimate that consumers would substitute calories in other forms for 25% of the reduced calorie consumption, an excise tax of 1 cent per ounce would lead to a minimum reduction of 10% in calorie consumption from sweetened beverages, or 20 kcal per person per day, a reduction that is sufficient for weight loss and reduction in risk (unpublished data). The benefit would be larger among consumers who consume higher volumes, since these consumers are more likely to be overweight and appear to be more responsive to prices.[7] Higher taxes would have greater benefits.

A controversial issue is whether to tax beverages that are sweetened with noncaloric sweeteners. No adverse health effects of noncaloric sweeteners have been consistently demonstrated, but there are concerns that diet beverages may increase calorie consumption by justifying consumption of other caloric foods or by promoting a preference for sweet tastes.[34] At present, we do not propose taxing beverages with noncaloric sweeteners, but we recommend close tracking of studies to determine whether taxing might be justified in the future.

Revenue-Generating Potential

The revenue generated from a tax on sugar-sweetened beverages would be considerable and could be used to help support childhood nutrition programs, obesity-prevention programs, or health care for the uninsured or to help meet general revenue needs. A national tax of 1 cent per ounce on sugar-sweetened beverages would raise $14.9 billion in the first year alone. Taxes at the state level would also generate considerable revenue—for example, $139 million in Arkansas, $183 million in Oregon, $221 million in Alabama, $928 million in Florida, $937 million in New York, $1.2 billion in Texas, and $1.8 billion in California.

A tax calculator that is available online can generate revenue numbers for states and 25 major cities.[35]

Objections, Industry Reaction, Public Support, and Framing

One objection to a tax on sugar-sweetened beverages is that it would be regressive. This argument arose with respect to tobacco taxes but was challenged successfully by proponents of the taxes, who pointed out that the poor face a disproportionate burden of smoking-related illnesses, that nearly all smokers begin to smoke when they are teenagers, and that both groups are sensitive to price changes.[7] In addition, some of the tobacco revenue has been used for programs developed specifically for the poor and for youth. The poor are most affected by illnesses that are related to unhealthful diets, and brand loyalties for beverages tend to be set by the teenage years. In addition, sugar-sweetened beverages are not necessary for survival, and an alternative (i.e., water) is available at little or no cost; hence, a tax that shifted intake from sugar-sweetened beverages to water would benefit the poor both by improving health and by lowering expenditures on beverages. Designating revenues for programs promoting childhood nutrition, obesity prevention, or health care for the uninsured would preferentially help those most in need.

A second objection is that taxing sugar-sweetened beverages will not solve the obesity crisis and is a blunt instrument that affects even those who consume small amounts of such beverages. Seat-belt legislation and tobacco taxation do not eliminate traffic accidents and heart disease but are nevertheless sound policies. Similarly, obesity is unlikely to yield to any single policy intervention, so it is important to pursue multiple opportunities to obtain incremental gains. Reducing caloric intake by 1 to 2% per year would have a marked impact on health in all age groups, and the financial burden on those who consumed small amounts of sugar-sweetened beverages would be minimal.

Opposition to a tax by the beverage industry is to be expected, given the possible effect on sales; opposition has been seen in jurisdictions that have considered such taxes and can be predicted from the behavior of the tobacco industry under similar circumstances.[36] PepsiCo threatened to move its corporate headquarters out of New York when the state considered implementing an 18% sales tax on sugar-sweetened beverages.[37] The tobacco industry fought policy changes by creating front groups with names that suggested community involvement. The beverage industry has created Americans Against Food Taxes.[38] These reactions suggest that the beverage industry believes that a tax would have a substantial impact on consumption.

Public support for food and beverage taxes to address obesity has increased steadily. Questions about taxes in polls have been asked in various ways, and the results are therefore not directly comparable from year to year, but overall trends are clear. Support for food taxes rose from 33% in 2001 to

41% in 2003 and then to 54% in 2004.[39] A 2008 poll of New York State residents showed that 52% of respondents support a soda tax; 72% support such a tax if the revenue is used to support programs for the prevention of obesity in children and adults. The way in which the issue is framed is essential; support is highest when the tax is introduced in the context of promoting health and when the revenues are earmarked for programs promoting childhood nutrition or obesity prevention.

Conclusions

The federal government, a number of states and cities, and some countries (e.g., Mexico[8]) are considering levying taxes on sugar-sweetened beverages. The reasons to proceed are compelling. The science base linking the consumption of sugar-sweetened beverages to the risk of chronic diseases is clear. Escalating health care costs and the rising burden of diseases related to poor diet create an urgent need for solutions, thus justifying government's right to recoup costs.

As with any public health intervention, the precise effect of a tax cannot be known until it is implemented and studied, but research to date suggests that a tax on sugar-sweetened beverages would have strong positive effects on reducing consumption.[5,33] In addition, the tax has the potential to generate substantial revenue to prevent obesity and address other external costs resulting from the consumption of sugar-sweetened beverages, as well as to fund other health-related programs. Much as taxes on tobacco products are routine at both state and federal levels because they generate revenue and they confer a public health benefit with respect to smoking rates, we believe that taxes on beverages that help drive the obesity epidemic should and will become routine.

References

1. Malik VS, Schulze MB, Hu FB. Intake of sugar-sweetened beverages and weight gain: a systematic review. Am J Clin Nutr 2006;84:274–88.

2. Vartanian LR, Schwartz MB, Brownell KD. Effects of soft drink consumption on nutrition and health: a systematic review and meta-analysis. Am J Public Health 2007;97:667–75.

3. Fung TT, Malik V, Rexrode KM, Manson JE, Willett WC, Hu FB. Sweetened beverage consumption and risk of coronary heart disease in women. Am J Clin Nutr 2009;89:1037–42.

4. Brownell KD. Get slim with higher taxes. New York Times. December 15, 1994:A29.

5. Brownell KD, Frieden TR. Ounces of prevention—the public policy case for taxes on sugared beverages. N Engl J Med 2009;360:1805–8.

6. Jacobson MF, Brownell KD. Small taxes on soft drinks and snack foods to promote health. Am J Public Health 2000;90:854–7.

7. Powell LM, Chaloupka FJ. Food prices and obesity: evidence and policy implications for taxes and subsidies. Milbank Q 2009;87:229–57.

8. Barquera S, Hernandez-Barrera L, Tolentino ML, et al. Energy intake from beverages is increasing among Mexican adolescents and adults. J Nutr 2008;138:2454–61.

9. Duffey KJ, Popkin BM. Shifts in patterns and consumption of beverages between 1965 and 2002. Obesity (Silver Spring) 2007;15:2739–47.

10. Forshee RA, Anderson PA, Storey ML. Sugar-sweetened beverages and body mass index in children and adolescents: a meta-analysis. Am J Clin Nutr 2008;87:1662–71. [Erratum, Am J Clin Nutr 2009;89:441–2.]

11. Malik VS, Willett WC, Hu FB. Sugar-sweetened beverages and BMI in children and adolescents: reanalyses of a meta-analysis. Am J Clin Nutr 2009;89:438–9.

12. Ludwig DS, Peterson KE, Gortmaker SL. Relation between consumption of sugar-sweetened drinks and childhood obesity: a prospective, observational analysis. Lancet 2001;357:505–8.

13. Schulze MB, Manson JE, Ludwig DS, et al. Sugar-sweetened beverages, weight gain, and incidence of type 2 diabetes in young and middle-aged women. JAMA 2004;292:927–34.

14. Tordoff MG, Alleva AM. Effect of drinking soda sweetened with aspartame or high-fructose corn syrup on food intake and body weight. Am J Clin Nutr 1990;51:963–9.

15. Raben A, Vasilaras TH, Moller AC, Astrup A. Sucrose compared with artificial sweeteners: different effects on ad libitum food intake and body weight after 10 wk of supplementation in overweight subjects. Am J Clin Nutr 2002;76:721–9.

16. James J, Thomas P, Cavan D, Kerr D. Preventing childhood obesity by reducing consumption of carbonated drinks: cluster randomised controlled trial. BMJ 2004;328:1237. [Erratum, BMJ 2004;328:1236.]

17. Sichieri R, Paula Trotte A, de Souza RA, Veiga GV. School randomised trial on prevention of excessive weight gain by discouraging students from drinking sodas. Public Health Nutr 2009;12:197–202.

18. Ebbeling CB, Feldman HA, Osganian SK, Chomitz VR, Ellen bogen SJ, Ludwig DS. Effects of decreasing sugar-sweetened beverage consumption on body weight in adolescents: a randomized, controlled pilot study. Pediatrics 2006;117:673–80.

19. Albala C, Ebbeling CB, Cifuentes M, Lera L, Bustos N, Ludwig DS. Effects of replacing the habitual consumption of sugar-sweetened beverages with milk in Chilean children. Am J Clin Nutr 2008;88:605–11.

20. Montonen J, Järvinen R, Knekt P, Heliövaara M, Reunanen A. Consumption of sweetened beverages and intakes of fructose and glucose predict type 2 diabetes occurrence. J Nutr 2007;137:1447–54.

21. Palmer JR, Boggs DA, Krishnan S, Hu FB, Singer M, Rosenberg L. Sugar-sweetened beverages and incidence of type 2 diabetes mellitus in African American women. Arch Intern Med 2008;168:1487–92.

22. Appel LJ, Sacks FM, Carey VJ, et al. Effects of protein, mono-unsaturated fat, and carbohydrate intake on blood pressure and serum lipids: results of the OmniHeart randomized trial. JAMA 2005;294:2455–64.

23. Ludwig DS. The glycemic index: physiological mechanisms relating to obesity, diabetes, and cardiovascular disease. JAMA 2002;287:2414–23.

24. Yoshida M, McKeown NM, Rogers G, et al. Surrogate markers of insulin resistance are associated with consumption of sugar-sweetened drinks and fruit juice in middle and older-aged adults. J Nutr 2007;137:2121–7.

25. Mourao DM, Bressan J, Campbell WW, Mattes RD. Effects of food form on appetite and energy intake in lean and obese young adults. Int J Obes (Lond) 2007;31:1688–95.

26. De Castro JM. The effects of the spontaneous ingestion of particular foods or beverages on the meal pattern and overall nutrient intake of humans. Physiol Behav 1993;53:1133–44.

27. Harnack L, Stang J, Story M. Soft drink consumption among US children and adolescents: nutritional consequences. J Am Diet Assoc 1999;99:436–41.

28. Flood JE, Roe LS, Rolls BJ. The effect of increased beverage portion size on energy intake at a meal. J Am Diet Assoc 2006;106:1984–90.

29. Cawley J. An economic framework for understanding physical activity and eating behaviors. Am J Prev Med 2004;27:117–25.

30. Finkelstein EA, Ruhm CJ, Kosa KM. Economic causes and consequences of obesity. Annu Rev Public Health 2005;26:239–57.

31. Finkelstein EA, Trogdon JG, Cohen JW, Dietz W. Annual medical spending attributable to obesity: payer-and-service-specific estimates. Health Aff (Millwood) 2009;28:w822–w831.

32. Chaloupka FJ, Peck RM., Tauras JA, Yurekli A. Cigarette excise taxation: the impact of tax structure on prices, revenues, and cigarettes smoking. Geneva: World Health Organization (in press).

33. Andreyeva T, Long MW, Brownell KD. The impact of food prices on consumption: a systematic review of research on price elasticity of demand for food. Am J Public Health (in press).

34. Mattes RD, Popkin BM. Nonnutritive sweetener consumption in humans: effects on appetite and food intake and their putative mechanisms. Am J Clin Nutr 2009;89:1–14.

35. Rudd Center for Food Policy and Obesity. Revenue calculator for soft drink taxes. (Accessed September 24, 2009, at http://www.yaleruddcenter.org/sodatax .aspx.)

36. Brownell KD, Warner KE. The perils of ignoring history: big tobacco played dirty and millions died: how similar is big food? Milbank Q 2009;87:259–94.

37. Hakim D, McGeehan P. New York vulnerable to poaching in recession. New York Times. March 1, 2009.

38. Americans Against Food Taxes home page. (Accessed September 24, 2009, at http://nofoodtaxes.com.)

39. Brownell KD. The chronicling of obesity: growing awareness of its social, economic, and political contexts. J Health Polit Policy Law 2005;30:955–64.

Daniel Engber    **NO**

Let Them Drink Water! What a Fat Tax Really Means for America

Not long after the attack on Pearl Harbor, in the winter of 1942, physiologist A.J. Carlson made a radical suggestion: If the nation's largest citizens were charged a fee—say, $20 for each pound of overweight—we might feed the war effort overseas while working to subdue an "injurious luxury" at home.

Sixty-seven years later, the "fat tax" is back on the table. We're fighting another war—our second-most-expensive ever—and Congress seems on the verge of spending $1 trillion on health care. Once again, a bloated budget may fall on the backs of the bloated public. Some commentators, following Carlson, have lately called for a tax on fat people themselves (cf. the *Huffington Post* and the *New York Times*); others . . . propose a hefty surcharge on soft drinks instead.

The notion hasn't generated much enthusiasm in Congress, but fat taxes are spreading through state legislatures: Four-fifths of the union now takes a cut on the sales of junk food or soda. Pleas for a federal fat tax are getting louder, too. The *New York Times* recently endorsed a penny-per-ounce soda tax, and Michael Pollan has made a convincing argument for why the insurance industry may soon throw its weight behind the proposal. Even President Obama said he likes the idea in a recent interview with *Men's Health*. (For the record, Stephen Colbert is against the measure: "I do not obey big government; I obey my thirst.")

For all this, the public still has strong reservations about the fat tax. The state-level penalties now in place have turned out to be way too small to make anyone lose weight, and efforts to pass more heavy-handed laws have so far fallen short. But proponents say it's only a matter of time before taxing junk food feels as natural as taxing cigarettes. The latter has been a tremendous success, they argue, in bringing down rates of smoking and death from lung cancer. In theory, a steep tax on sweetened beverages could do the same for overeating and diabetes.

It may take more than an analogy with tobacco to convince voters. As my colleague William Saletan points out, the first step in policing eating habits is to redefine food as something else. If you want to tax the hell out of soda, you need to make people think that it's a drug, not a beverage—that downing a Coke is just like puffing on a cigarette. But is soda as bad as tobacco? Let's ask the neuropundits.

Junk food literally "alters the biological circuitry of our brains," writes David Kessler in this summer's best-seller, *The End of Overeating*. In a previous book, Kessler detailed his role in prosecuting the war on smoking as the head of the FDA; now he's explaining what makes us fat with all the magisterial jargon of cognitive neuroscience. Eating a chocolate-covered pretzel, he says, activates the brain's pleasure system—the dopamine reward circuit, to be exact—and changes the "functional connectivity among important brain regions." Thus, certain foods—the ones concocted by industrial scientists and laden with salt, sugar, and fat—can circumvent our natural inclinations and trigger "action schemata" for mindless eating. Got that? Junk food is engineered to enslave us. Kessler even has a catchphrase to describe these nefarious snacks: They're hyperpalatable.

Try as we might, we're nearly powerless to resist these treats. That's because evolution has us programmed to experience two forms of hunger. The first kicks in when we're low on energy. As an adaptation, its purpose is simple enough—we eat to stay alive. The second, called hedonic hunger, applies even when we're full—it's the urge to eat for pleasure. When food is scarce, hedonic hunger comes in handy, so we can stock up on calories for the hard times ahead. But in a world of cheap food, the same impulse makes us fat.

That's the problem with junk food. Manufacturers have figured out how to prey on man's voluptuous nature. Like the cigarette companies, they lace their products with addictive chemicals and cajole us into wanting things we don't really need. Soda is like a designer drug, layered with seductive elements—sweetness for a burst of dopamine, bubbles to prick the trigeminal nerve.

It's hard to draw a line, though, between foods that are drugs and foods that are merely delicious. Soda and candy aren't the only stimuli that "rewire your brain," of course. Coffee does, too, and so do video games, Twitter, meditation, and just about anything else that might give you pleasure (or pain). That's what brains do—they learn, they rewire. To construe an earthly delight as hyperpalatable—as too good for our own good—we're lashing out at sensuality itself. "Do you design food specifically to be highly hedonic?" Kessler asks an industry consultant at one point in the book. What's the guy going to say? "No, we design food to be bland and nutritious. . . ."

It's ironic that so many advocates for healthy eating are also outspoken gourmands. Alice Waters, the proprietor of Chez Panisse, calls for a "delicious revolution" of low-fat, low-sugar lunch programs. It's a central dogma of the organic movement that you can be a foodie and a health nut at the same time—that what's real and natural tastes better, anyway. Never mind how much fat and sugar and salt you'll get from a Wabash Cannonball and a slice of *pain au levain*. Forget that *cuisiniers* have for centuries been catering to our hedonic hunger—our pleasure-seeking, caveman selves—with a repertoire of batters and sauces. Junk foods are *hyperpalatable*. Whole Foods is *delicious*. Doughnuts are a drug; brioche is a treat.

Some tastes, it seems, are more equal than others.

A fat tax, then, discriminates among the varieties of gustatory experience. And its impact would fall most directly on the poor, nonwhite people who tend to be the most avid consumers of soft drinks and the most sensitive to price. Under an apartheid of pleasure, palatable drinks are penalized while delicious—or even hyperdelicious—products come at no extra charge. What about the folks who can't afford a $5 bottle of POM Wonderful? No big deal, say the academics writing in the *New England Journal of Medicine*; they can always drink from the faucet. Here's how the article puts it: "Sugar-sweetened beverages are not necessary for survival, and an alternative (i.e. water) is available at little or no cost." So much for *Let them eat cake*.

We've known for a long time that any sin tax is likely to be a burden on the poor, since they're most prone to unhealthy behavior. (*James Madison* fought the snuff tax on these grounds way back in 1794.) But you might just as well say that poor people have the most to gain from a sin tax for exactly the same reason. It's also possible that revenues from a fat tax would be spent on obesity prevention—or go back to the community in other ways. There's a knotty argument here about the vexing and reciprocal interactions among health, wealth, and obesity. (I'll try to untangle some of these in my next column.) It's not clear whether, and in what direction, a soda tax might redistribute wealth. Whatever you think of the economics, though, raising the price on soda—and offering water in its place—will redistribute pleasure.

I don't mean to imply that any such regulation is unjust. We have laws against plenty of chemicals and behaviors that are as delightful as they are destructive. These are, for the most part, sensible measures to protect our health. What's disturbing is the thought that the degree of government control should vary according to who's using which drug. In April, the Obama administration called for an end to a long-standing policy that gives dealers of powdered cocaine 100 times more leeway than dealers of crack when it comes to federal prison sentences. Let's not repeat this drug-war injustice in the war on obesity. We may be ready to say that foods are addictive. Are we ready to judge the nature of a delicious high?

CHALLENGE QUESTIONS

Should Government Levy a Fat Tax?

1. List health problems associated with consumption of sugar-sweetened beverages (SSB).
2. Outline the various ways to calculate a tax on SSB as proposed by Brownell and colleagues.
3. Explain why some people think that SSB are addictive.
4. New York's Governor Paterson proposed a penny per ounce tax on SSB but it did not pass. There were several antitax groups who lobbied heavily against the tax proposal. What type of people do you think would be opposed to this form of "fat tax" and what arguments do you think they would have?
5. Many poor, slim people enjoy the taste, and actually benefit from the extra calories from SSB and high fat snacks. What impact could taxation of sugary beverages have on poor, thin people? Design a strategy to ameliorate this problem.

ISSUE 16

Can Michelle Obama's "Let's Move" Initiative Halt Childhood Obesity?

YES: White House Press Release, from "First Lady Michelle Obama Launches *Let's Move*: America's Move to Raise a Healthier Generation of Kids" (February 9, 2010)

NO: Michele Simon, from "Michelle Obama's *Let's Move*—Will It Move Industry?" *AlterNet* (March 14, 2010)

As you read the issue, focus on the following points:

1. The four key objectives of the Task Force on Childhood Obesity.
2. The public and private resources that will work to solve childhood obesity and the role each will play.
3. The early signs outlined by Michele Simon that indicate the initiative is more talk than action.

ISSUE SUMMARY

YES: First Lady Michelle Obama says that the *Let's Move* campaign can correct the health problems of the upcoming generation and realizes that the problem cannot be solved overnight. She thinks that "with everyone working together, it can be solved." The "first ever" Task Force on Childhood Obesity was formed to help implement the campaign.

NO: Public health attorney Michele Simon claims that *Let's Move* is just another task force and there is more talk than action. She questions if it's realistic to be able to reverse the nation's childhood obesity epidemic in a generation.

One of the good things about having a healthy president and first lady is they can speak out about weight problems and lead by example. In February 2010, our physically fit president issued a press release about the formation of the "first ever Task Force on Childhood Obesity" and his equally fit wife's role in the effort. In the release he wrote:

> My Administration is committed to redoubling our efforts to solve the problem of childhood obesity within a generation through a

comprehensive approach that builds on effective strategies, engages families and communities, and mobilizes both public and private sector resources.

Nearly one third of children in America are overweight or obese—a rate that has tripled in adolescents and more than doubled in younger children since 1980. One third of all individuals born in the year 2000 or later will eventually suffer from diabetes over the course of their lifetime, while too many others will face chronic obesity-related health problems such as heart disease, high blood pressure, cancer, and asthma. Without effective intervention, many more children will endure serious illnesses that will put a strain on our health-care system. We must act now to improve the health of our Nation's children and avoid spending billions of dollars treating a preventable disease.

Therefore, I have set a goal to solve the problem of childhood obesity within a generation so that children born today will reach adulthood at a healthy weight. The First Lady will lead a national public awareness effort to tackle the epidemic of childhood obesity.

The Task Force that he mentions will be headed by the Department of Health and Human Services (HHS). The mission and functions of that group are as follow:

The Task Force shall work across executive departments and agencies to develop a coordinated Federal response while also identifying non-governmental actions.... The functions of the Task Force are ... making recommendations to meet the following objectives:

(a) ensuring access to healthy, affordable food;
(b) increasing physical activity in schools and communities;
(c) providing healthier food in schools; and
(d) empowering parents with information and tools to make good choices for themselves and their families.

Is it possible to meet these objectives and to solve the problem of childhood obesity within a generation? First Lady Michelle Obama thinks it is and that people working together through the "Let's Move" campaign is the way it can be accomplished. Public health lawyer Michele Simon says "no." She feels that the "early signs indicate more talk than action."

TIMELINE

1980	Five percent of American children and teens are obese.
1990	Number of obese children and teens doubles.
2000	Obesity in children and teens triples, compared to 1980.
2004	FDA's Obesity Working Group is established.
2007	FCC Task Force on Media and Childhood Obesity is established.
2009	Interagency (FTC, CNPP, CDC, and FDA) Working Group is established.
2010	Task Force on Childhood Obesity is established.
2010	Michelle Obama launches "Let's Move" campaign.
2010	Partnership for a Healthier America is formed.

DEFINITIONS

Obese Having excessive body fat that may have an adverse impact on health; with children and teens, BMI-for-age ≥95th percentile.

Overweight A preobese state, having more body fat than is desirable; with children and teens, BMI-for-age ≥85th to ≤94.9th percentile.

Food Desert An area with little or no access to nutrient-dense foods.

YES

First Lady Michelle Obama Launches *Let's Move*: America's Move to Raise a Healthier Generation of Kids

T he White House, Washington—First Lady Michelle Obama today announced an ambitious national goal of solving the challenge of childhood obesity within a generation so that children born today will reach adulthood at a healthy weight and unveiled a nationwide campaign—*Let's Move*—to help achieve it. The *Let's Move* campaign will combat the epidemic of childhood obesity through a comprehensive approach that builds on effective strategies, and mobilizes public and private sector resources. *Let's Move* will engage every sector impacting the health of children to achieve the national goal, and will provide schools, families and communities simple tools to help kids be more active, eat better, and get healthy. To support *Let's Move* and facilitate and coordinate partnerships with States, communities, and the non-profit and for-profit private sectors, the nation's leading children's health foundations have come together to create a new independent foundation—the Partnership for a Healthier America—which will accelerate existing efforts addressing child-hood obesity and facilitate new commitments toward the national goal of solving childhood obesity within a generation.

Almost a year ago, Mrs. Obama began a national conversation about the health of America's children when she broke ground on the White House Kitchen Garden with students from Bancroft Elementary School in Washington, DC. Through the garden, she began a discussion with kids about proper nutri-tion and the role food plays in living a healthy life. That discussion grew into the *Let's Move* campaign announced today.

Over the past three decades, childhood obesity rates in America have tripled, and today, nearly one in three children in America are overweight or obese. One third of all children born in 2000 or later will suffer from diabe-tes at some point in their lives; many others will face chronic obesity-related health problems like heart disease, high blood pressure, cancer, and asthma. A recent study put the health care costs of obesity-related diseases at $147 billion per year. This epidemic also impacts the nation's security, as obesity is now one of the most common disqualifiers for military service.

"The physical and emotional health of an entire generation and the eco-nomic health and security of our nation is at stake," said Mrs. Obama. "This isn't the kind of problem that can be solved overnight, but with everyone working together, it can be solved. So, *let's move*."

The First Lady launched the *Let's Move* campaign at the White House where she was joined by members of the President's cabinet, including Agriculture Secretary Vilsack, HHS Secretary Sebelius, Education Secretary Duncan, HUD Secretary Donovan, Labor Secretary Solis, and Interior Secretary Salazar, Surgeon General Regina Benjamin, Members of Congress, mayors from across the nation and leaders from the media, medical, sports, entertainment, and business communities who impact the health of children and want to be part of the solution. Program participants included: Tiki Barber, NBC correspondent and former NFL football player; Dr. Judith Palfrey, President of the American Academy of Pediatrics; Will Allen, Founder and CEO of Growing Power; Mayor Curtatone of Somerville, Massachusetts; Mayor Chip Johnson of Hernando, Mississippi; and local students, including a student from DC's Bancroft elementary school, and members of the 2009 National Championship Pee-Wee football team, the Watkins Hornets.

Let's Move is comprehensive, collaborative, and community oriented and will include strategies to address the various factors that lead to childhood obesity. It will foster collaboration among the leaders in government, medicine and science, business, education, athletics, community organizations and more. And it will take into account how life is really lived in communities across the country—encouraging, supporting and pursuing solutions that are tailored to children and families facing a wide range of challenges and life circumstances.

President Barack Obama kicked off the launch by signing a Presidential Memorandum creating the first ever *Task Force on Childhood Obesity* which will include the DPC, Office of the First Lady, Interior, USDA, HHS, Education, NEC and other agencies. Within 90 days, the Task Force will conduct a review of every single program and policy relating to child nutrition and physical activity and develop a national action plan that maximizes federal resources and sets concrete benchmarks toward the First Lady's national goal. While the review is under way, Administration and public and private efforts are already moving to combat obesity and reach the First Lady's national goal.

Helping Parents Make Healthy Family Choices

Parents play a key role in making healthy choices for their children and teaching their children to make healthy choices for themselves. But in today's busy world, this isn't always easy. So *Let's Move* will offer parents the tools, support and information they need to make healthier choices for their families. The Administration, along with partners in the private sector and medical community, will:

Empower Consumers

By the end of this year, the Food and Drug Administration will begin working with retailers and manufacturers to adopt new nutritionally sound and consumer friendly front-of-package labeling. This will put us on a path toward

65 million parents in America having easy access to the information needed to make healthy choices for their children.

Already, the private sector is responding. Today, the American Beverage Association announced that its member companies will voluntarily put a clear, uniform, front-of-pack calorie label on all of their cans, bottles, vending and fountain machines within two years. The label will reflect total calories per container in containers up to 20 oz. in size. For containers greater than 20 oz., the label will reflect a 12-oz. serving size. While more work remains to be done, this marks an important first step in ensuring parents have the information they need to make healthier choices.

Provide Parents with an Rx for Healthier Living

The American Academy of Pediatrics, in collaboration with the broader medical community, will educate doctors and nurses across the country about obesity, ensure they regularly monitor children's BMI, provide counseling for healthy eating early on, and, for the first time ever, will even write a prescription for parents laying out the simple things they can do to increase healthy eating and active play.

Major New Public Information Campaign

Major media companies—including the Walt Disney Company, NBC, Universal and Viacom—have committed to join the First Lady's effort and increase public awareness of the need to combat obesity through public service announcements (PSAs), special programming, and marketing. The Ad Council, Warner Brothers and Scholastic Media have also partnered with the U.S. Department of Health and Human Services (HHS) to run PSAs featuring top professional athletes, Scholastic Media's Maya & Miguel, and Warner Brothers' legendary Looney Tunes characters.

Next Generation Food Pyramid

To help people make healthier food and physical activity choices, the U.S. Department of Agriculture will revamp the famous food pyramid. MyPyramid.gov is one of the most popular Web sites in the federal government, and a 2.0 version of the Web site will offer consumers a host of tools to help them put the Dietary Guidelines into practice.

Empower Change

USDA has created the first-ever interactive database—the Food Environment Atlas—that maps healthy food environments at the local level across the country. It will help people identify the existence of food deserts, high incidences of diabetes, and other conditions in their communities. This information can be used by parents, educators, government and businesses to create change across the country.

LetsMove.gov

To help children, parents, teachers, doctors, coaches, the non-profit and business communities and others understand the epidemic of childhood obesity and take steps to combat it, the Administration has launched a new "one-stop" shopping Web site—LetsMove.gov—to provide helpful tips, step-by-step strategies for parents, and regular updates on how the federal government is working with partners to reach the national goal.

Serving Healthier Food in Schools

Many children consume as many as half of their daily calories at school. As families work to ensure that kids eat right and have active play at home, we also need to ensure our kids have access to healthy meals in their schools. With more than 31 million children participating in the National School Lunch Program and more than 11 million participating in the National School Breakfast Program, good nutrition at school is more important than ever. Together with the private sector and the non-profit community, we will take the following steps to get healthier food in our nation's schools:

Reauthorize the Child Nutrition Act

The Administration is requesting an historic investment of an additional $10 billion over ten years starting in 2011 to improve the quality of the National School Lunch and Breakfast program, increase the number of kids participating, and ensure schools have the resources they need to make program changes, including training for school food service workers, upgraded kitchen equipment, and additional funding for meal reimbursements. With this investment, additional fruits, vegetables, whole grains, and low-fat dairy products will be served in our school cafeterias and an additional one million students will be served in the next five years.

Double the Number of Schools Participating in the Healthier US School Challenge

The Healthier US School Challenge establishes rigorous standards for schools' food quality, participation in meal programs, physical activity, and nutrition education—the key components that make for healthy and active kids—and provides recognition for schools that meet these standards. Over the next school year, the U.S. Department of Agriculture, working with partners in schools and the private sector, will double the number of schools that meet the Healthier US School Challenge and add 1,000 schools per year for two years after that.

We are bringing to the table key stakeholder groups that have committed to work together to improve the nutritional quality of school meals across the country.

New Commitments from Major School Food Suppliers

School food suppliers are taking important first steps to help meet the Healthier US School Challenge goal. Major school food suppliers including Sodexho,

Chartwells School Dining Services, and Aramark have voluntarily committed to meet the Institute of Medicine's recommendations within five years to decrease the amount of sugar, fat and salt in school meals; increase whole grains; and double the amount of produce they serve within 10 years. By the end of the 2010–2011 school year, they have committed to quadruple the number of the schools they serve that meet the Healthier US School Challenge.

School Nutrition Association

The School Nutrition Association (SNA), which represents food service workers in more than 75% of the nation's schools, has joined the *Let's Move* campaign. Working with other education partners, SNA has committed to increasing education and awareness of the dangers of obesity among their members and the students they serve, and ensuring that the nutrition programs in 10,000 schools meet the Healthier US School Challenge standards over the next five years.

School Leadership

Working with school food service providers and SNA, the National School Board Association, the Council of Great City Schools and the American Association of School Administrators Council have all embraced, and committed to meeting, the national *Let's Move* goal. The Council of Great City Schools has also . . . set a goal of having every urban school meet the Healthier US Schools gold standard within five years. The American Association of School Administrators has committed to ensuring that an additional 2,000 schools meet the challenge over the next two years. These combined efforts will touch 50 million students and their families in every school district in America.

Accessing Healthy, Affordable Food

More than 23 million Americans, including 6.5 million children, live in low-income urban and rural neighborhoods that are more than a mile from a supermarket. These communities, where access to affordable, quality, and nutritious foods is limited, are known as *food deserts*. Lack of access is one reason why many children are not eating recommended levels of fruits, vegetables, and whole grains. And food insecurity and hunger among children [are] widespread. A recent USDA report showed that in 2008, an estimated 49.1 million people, including 16.7 million children, lived in households that experienced hunger multiple times throughout the year. The Administration, through new federal investments and the creation of public-private partnerships, will:

Eliminate Food Deserts

As part of the President's proposed FY 2011 budget, the Administration announced the new Healthy Food Financing Initiative—a partnership between the U.S. Departments of Treasury, Agriculture and Health and Human Services that will invest $400 million a year to help bring grocery stores to underserved areas and help places such as convenience stores and bodegas carry healthier food options. Through these initiatives and private sector engagement, the Administration will work to eliminate food deserts across the country within seven years.

Increase Farmers Markets

The President's 2011 Budget proposes an additional $5 million investment in the Farmers Market Promotion Program at the U.S. Department of Agriculture which provides grants to establish, and improve access to, farmers markets.

Increasing Physical Activity

Children need 60 minutes of active play each day. Yet, the average American child spends more than 7.5 hours a day watching TV and movies, using cell phones and computers, and playing video games, and only a third of high school students get the recommended levels of physical activity. Through public–private partnerships, and reforms of existing federal programs, the Administration will address this imbalance by:

Expanding and Modernizing the President's Physical Fitness Challenge

In the coming weeks, the President will be naming new members to the President's Council on Physical Fitness and Sports, housed at the U.S. Department of Health and Human Services. The council will be charged with increasing participation in the President's Challenge and with modernizing and expanding it, so that it is consistent with the latest research and science.

Doubling the Number of Presidential Active Lifestyle Awards

As part of the President's Physical Fitness Council, the President will challenge both children and adults to commit to physical activity five days a week, for six weeks. As part of the First Lady's commitment to solve the problem of childhood obesity in a generation, the Council will double the number of children in the 2010–2011 school year who earn a "Presidential Active Lifestyle Award" for meeting this challenge.

Safe and Healthy Schools

The U.S. Department of Education will be working with Congress on the creation of a Safe and Healthy Schools fund as part of the reauthorization of the Elementary and Secondary School Education Act this year. This fund will support schools with comprehensive strategies to improve their school environment, including efforts to get children physically active in and outside of school, and improve the quality and availability of physical education.

Professional Sports

Professional athletes from twelve leagues including the NFL, MLB, WNBA, and MLS have joined the First Lady on the *Let's Move* campaign and will promote "60 Minutes of Play a Day" through sports clinics, public service announcements, and more to help reach the national goal of solving the problem of childhood obesity in a generation.

Partnership for a Healthier America

Core to the success of this initiative is the recognition that government approaches alone will not solve this challenge. Achieving the goal will require engaging in partnerships with States, communities, and the non-profit and for-profit private sectors. To support this effort, several foundations are coming together to organize and fund a new central foundation—the Partnership for a Healthier America—to serve as a non-partisan convener across the private, non-profit and public sectors to accelerate existing efforts addressing childhood obesity and to facilitate commitments toward the national goal of solving childhood obesity within a generation. The Partnership for a Healthier America is being created by a number of leading health care foundations and childhood obesity non-profits, including the Robert Wood Johnson Foundation, The California Endowment, W.K. Kellogg Foundation, The Alliance for Healthier Generation, Kaiser Permanente, and Nemours, and will seek to add new members in the days and months ahead.

Michele Simon

 **NO**

Michelle Obama's *Let's Move*—Will It Move Industry?

So what's all the fuss over Michelle Obama's *Let's Move* campaign to end childhood obesity, and will it make a difference? Of course, it's too soon to know for sure . . . , but early signs indicate more talk than action and deafening silence on corporate marketing practices.

The most obvious problem is framing the issue around obesity, which implies a couple of troubling assumptions. One, that skinny kids are just fine, no matter what garbage they are being fed, and two, that exercise, which has long been a convenient distraction, will continue to be so.

What Is *Let's Move*?

I highly recommend spending a few minutes perusing the *Let's Move* website, which is simple, but informative in describing the campaign. (For a more detailed description, read the press release.) While the name *Let's Move* implies a program all about exercise, in fact 3 of the 4 components have to do with food, which leads me to wonder why the White House wanted that to be less obvious. According to the home page:

> *Let's Move* will give parents the support they need, provide healthier food in schools, help our kids to be more physically active, and make healthy, affordable food available in every part of our country.

All laudable goals indeed, but notably absent is any criticism of the billions of dollars a year Big Food spends successfully convincing both parents and children to eat highly processed junk food and sugary beverages. Michelle Obama may be able to withstand the call of the Happy Meal, but most parents aren't so lucky to have a White House chef at their disposal.

To her credit, the First Lady is saying many good things about parents needing more support. Also, for the first time I heard the phrase "food desert" uttered on national TV. So she really does seem to understand that it's not all about education or personal responsibility.

But how exactly will Mrs. Obama and her husband attempt to end childhood obesity "within a generation." First is the formation of yet another task force. As the President's memo explains, members of the Task Force on Childhood Obesity are to include the Secretaries of the Interior, Agriculture, Health and Human Services, Education, the Director of the Office of Management and Budget, and the Assistant to the President and Chief of Staff to the First Lady. Heavy hitters yes, but might they have just a few other items already on their to-do list?

Also, in key language, the memo explains that "the functions of the Task Force are *advisory only*," meaning that this body, at the end of the day (or many months), will only make recommendations for another body (Congress?) to then maybe, someday, consider.

Do We Really Need Another Task Force?

The Obama Administration may be surprised (since they are calling it the "first ever") to learn that theirs is not the first federal task force on this issue. The previous administration had a few failed attempts. We already tried the Task Force on Media and Childhood Obesity, which the Federal Communications Commission spearheaded. Perhaps it never really went anywhere thanks to its members, who included the likes of Coca-Cola, McDonald's, and Disney.

Then there was the Food and Drug Administration's Obesity Working Group, which was broader than just childhood obesity, and whose pathetic achievement was the startling discovery (and accompanying silly web-based tool) that "calories count."

But given that we really can't count anything tried under the previous administration, I am willing to wait and see if this task force can come up with something better. It certainly can't be any worse than the lame "Small Steps" program (still online).

And let's not forget the still active Interagency Working Group on Food Marketed to Children, which is comprised of officials from four agencies: the Federal Trade Commission, the Centers for Disease Control and Prevention, the Food and Drug Administration, and the U.S. Department of Agriculture. In December [2009], this body released "tentative proposed nutrition standards" (for food products the government says are A-OK to market to kids) and is planning a final report with recommendations (for voluntary standards) to Congress this July. (Read author and fellow blogger Jill Richardson's excellent description of its public panel and proposed standards.)

This is the historical backdrop into which Michelle Obama now brings us *Let's Move*. It's not as if we haven't been here before; she's building on many failed attempts. But let's take a closer look at one of the four *Let's Move* components—school food.

How to Improve School Nutrition?

Under the "Healthier Schools" tab of the campaign's website, I recognize a few programs that have been out there for some time. For example, the underfunded Healthier US School Challenge and the ineffective Team Nutrition program, both under the U.S. Department of Agriculture, that agency whose number one mission is to prop up Big Agriculture. (The USDA also happens to be in charge of school nutrition and other food assistance programs, which has never proven to be a good combination.)

A few things are new under *Let's Move*, including doubling the number of schools that meet the Healthier US Schools Challenge and adding 1,000 schools per year for two years after that. And the President proposes to increase the federal budget by $1 billion annually to improve the quality of school meals. This sounds impressive, but as school lunch expert and Chef Ann Cooper pointed out in a recent *Washington Post* article, a mere 10 percent increase is a drop in the bucket. Currently, we feed 31 million students a day on $9.3 billion, which amounts to only $2.68 per meal. When was the last time you ate a decent lunch less than 3 bucks? (No, the dollar menu meal doesn't count.)

And nowhere is any mention of the ongoing problem of competitive foods, which is government doublespeak for Coke and Pepsi vending machines in every school hallway, Doritos, Milky Way, and Good Humor sold in school stores, not to mention fast food like Pizza Hut that has taken over many school lunchrooms. Maybe that's because the Obama Administration has decided that the success of *Let's Move* depends in part on "the creation of public private partnerships." That sounds familiar.

Working With Industry?

Since signing up for the *Let's Move* email updates, I haven't been too impressed. Here are two topics that landed in my in-box last week: Attention Techies! Apps for Healthy Kids Launched Yesterday and Paralympic Games Show All Athletes Can Be Champions. Now please don't send hate mail; I have nothing against apps or the Paralympics, I just don't understand how these concepts will solve childhood obesity "within a generation."

In an especially bad sign, Michelle Obama is speaking at a gathering of the Grocery Manufacturers Association this Tuesday. As I chronicled in *Appetite for Profit*, GMA, the lobbying arm of packaged foods conglomerates such as Kraft and PepsiCo has a long history of undermining school nutrition standards, among other positive policies.

As another blogger suggests, Mrs. Obama's own ties to Big Food may explain her deferential treatment of industry. She served on the board of directors of TreeHouse Foods (a spin-off of conglomerate Dean Foods) for two years until 2007, when her husband's presidential campaign became all consuming. This same blogger predicts that at the GMA meeting:

> Mrs. Obama will focus on "the pressing need to pursue comprehensive solutions to combat childhood obesity" and call upon food manufacturers to join these efforts by "providing healthier food options and better information about healthy food choices."

But Kraft, PepsiCo, Kellogg's and others have been all over that idea for several years now with their "smart choices" foods and claims of responsible marketing to children through its bogus Children's Food and Beverage Advertising Initiative.

We won't hear any scolding or warning aimed at industry. Instead, the First Lady will simply ask the major food corporations to jump on the *Let's Move* bandwagon. And they will do so gladly. With no threats looming (for example, that Congress might pass legislation to restrict marketing to kids) Big Food has nothing to fear; quite the contrary, industry gains positive PR in the process. Indeed, not missing a beat, GMA sent the White House a letter of support for the campaign on the *same day* that *Let's Move* launched.

Let's Move the Corporations Out of Washington

The bottom line for me is that while there are many things to like about *Let's Move* and it's certainly encouraging for a First Lady to talk about access to fresh, healthy food as a national priority, much of it is still rhetoric we've heard before.

To turn the talk into real action will take a ton of leadership from President Obama and even more political will from Congress. Most importantly, unless and until the ubiquitous junk food marketing stops, both in schools and out, very little of substance will change and we will be back here once again with the next administration's childhood obesity task force.

Let me know what you think.

I am a public health lawyer whose first book, *Appetite for Profit,* exposed food industry lobbying and deceptive marketing. Visit my website: www.appetiteforprofit.com.

CHALLENGE QUESTIONS

Can Michelle Obama's "Let's Move" Initiative Halt Childhood Obesity?

1. Of the four key objectives outlined in the Task Force on Childhood Obesity, which do you think will have the greatest impact on reducing childhood obesity? Explain your answer.
2. Identify the public and private stakeholders who must work together to solve childhood obesity and summarize the role each will play.
3. Of the stakeholders, which ones do you believe will have the greatest positive impact? Justify your answer.
4. Identify one roadblock that you forecast the stakeholders will have and develop a way to overcome this roadblock.
5. Reflect on your own eating habits and lifestyle when you were in the 4th grade. What one thing (or person) had the greatest impact on your negative food choices or dietary practices? Who could have changed this and how?
6. Increases in childhood obesity have paralleled increases in number of $1 items on fast-food restaurant menus, junk foods allowed in schools, number of mothers in the workforce, decreases in PE teachers in schools, and the number of TVs sold by Sony and Samsung and video games sold by Walmart. At the same time, the government and some private health insurance companies are paying record amounts to care for children who already have been diagnosed with type 2 diabetes and other conditions associated with excessive weight. Who is/are responsible for these trends? And do you think "Let's Move" is moving in the right direction?

Additional Internet Resources

Let's Move—America's Move to Raise a Healthier Generation

A nationwide initiative to promote making healthy choices, improving food quality in schools, increasing access to healthy, affordable food, and increasing physical activity.

http:www.letsmove.gov

Media and Childhood Obesity Web site

Task force Web site created by the Federal Communications Commission designed to promote awareness of the role that media plays in increasing childhood obesity.

http://www.fcc.gov/obesity

Small Step Web site

Web site hosted by the United States Department of Health and Human Services that features stories, newsletter, tips, and recipes geared to helping people manage their weight and improve well-being.

http://www.smallstep.gov

Partnership for a Healthier America

Partner to the *Let's Move* initiative that is linking and mobilizing the private sector, foundations, thought leaders, media, and local communities to action and further the goals of curbing childhood obesity within a generation.

http://www.ahealthieramerica.org/

Internet References . . .

Food Security Institute

The Food Security Institute at Brandeis University provides a frequently updated guide to studies on hunger and food security, demands for food and welfare assistance, and the effects of food insecurity on health.

http://www.centeronhunger.org/FSI/fsiguide.html

The International Baby Food Action Network

The International Baby Food Action Network Web site promotes breastfeeding and monitors the actions of international companies that promote formula feeding and the use of commercial baby food.

http://www.ibfan.org/english/gateenglish.html

Food Safety Information: Irradiation

This Web site concerning food safety information contains links to United States government agencies and their answers to basic questions about food safety.

http://www.foodsafety.gov/

Nutrition Concerns of Pregnant Women and Infants

*M*any *people believe that the phase of life that nutrition has the most critical impact is during periods of development and growth. What should be included in the diet and what should be avoided is the topic of many debates. Issues in this unit begin with the impact alcohol has on pregnancy and continue with the optimal way to feed infants.*

- Is It Necessary for Pregnant Women to Completely Abstain from All Alcoholic Beverages?
- Should Infant Formulas Contain Synthetic ARA and DHA?
- Is Breast-Feeding the Best Way to Feed Babies?

ISSUE 17

Is It Necessary for Pregnant Women to Completely Abstain from All Alcoholic Beverages?

YES: Phyllida Brown, from "Drinking for Two," *New Scientist* (July 1, 2006)

NO: Julia Moskin, from "The Weighty Responsibility of Drinking for Two," *The New York Times* (November 29, 2006)

As you read the issue, focus on the following points:

1. The differences between fetal alcohol syndrome (FAS) and fetal alcohol spectrum disorder (FASD).

2. How Americans drink alcohol and the impact it could have on a developing fetus compared with how European woman consume alcohol and their pregnancy outcomes.

ISSUE SUMMARY

YES: Science writer Phyllida Brown maintains that even a small amount of alcohol can damage a developing fetus and cites new research indicating that any alcohol consumed during pregnancy may be harmful.

NO: Food and nutrition journalist Julia Moskin argues that there are almost no studies on the effects of moderate drinking during pregnancy and that small amounts of alcohol are unlikely to have much effect.

$\mathbf{T}$he impact that alcohol has on a developing fetus was mentioned in the *Old Testament Bible* and by ancient Greeks. However, the scientific studies that support and explain the relationship are relatively new. According to the Fetal Alcohol Spectrum Disorders (FASD) Center for Excellence, the first link dates back to the late 1800s. They provide the following historical perspective:

> . . . a specific medical link [between prenatal alcohol and fetal abnormalities] was not identified until 1899. Dr. William Sullivan compared

the pregnancy outcomes of 120 alcoholic prisoners with 28 of their relatives. The infant mortality rate among the alcoholic women was higher.

In 1957, Jacqueline Rouquette wrote about prenatal alcohol exposure. Then, in 1968, Dr. Paul Lemoine published a study in which he described 127 children with distinctive facial features and other symptoms related to prenatal alcohol exposure. Five years later, researchers in Seattle (K.L. Jones and D.W. Smith) published findings of a similar study. They named the condition "fetal alcohol syndrome" (FAS).

To meet the criteria for a diagnosis of FAS, infants must be born with certain physical and neurological abnormalities. Physically, they have a low birth weight, an extra fold of skin in the inner corner of the eyes, a flattened groove between the mouth and nose, a thin upper lip, and a small head circumference. The small head reflects reduced brain development and lower cognitive abilities. Fortunately, FAS is relatively uncommon, though the United States has one of the highest rates in developed countries. But many infants are exposed to alcohol during pregnancy and are born without these full-blown FAS characteristics. In fact, it is estimated that only a small percentage of the offspring of alcohol-abusing women meet the criteria necessary for a full diagnosis. The term "fetal alcohol effect" has been used to describe the mild problems seen in children whose mothers consumed some alcohol during pregnancy.

In reality, there is a range, or spectrum of abnormalities seen, from the mild effect on social and behavioral problems to severely retarded brain and physical development noted in FAS. To fill in the gap between total FAS and mild problems, the term "fetal alcohol spectrum disorder" (FASD) is used.

It is well established that alcohol causes a range of fetal abnormalities. Some women continue to drink during pregnancy and have a perfectly normal infant while others report only moderate alcohol intake and have a child with some degree of FASD.

The American Pregnancy Association, which promotes reproductive and pregnancy wellness, says, "all drinks that contain alcohol can be harmful to your baby. *There is no safe amount of alcohol* to consume while you are pregnant." The March of Dimes, whose mission is to improve the health of children, concludes:

> Although many women are aware that heavy drinking during pregnancy can cause birth defects, many do not realize that moderate or even light drinking also may harm the fetus. In fact, no level of alcohol use during pregnancy has been proved safe. Therefore, the March of Dimes recommends that pregnant women do not drink any alcohol, including beer, wine, wine coolers, and liquor, throughout their pregnancy and while nursing. In addition, because women often do not know they are pregnant for a few months, women who may be pregnant or those who are attempting to become pregnant should not drink alcohol.

The following articles address whether it is safe for pregnant women to drink during pregnancy. Phyllida Brown argues that even a small amount of alcohol can damage a developing fetus and cites research indicating that even small amounts of alcohol consumed during pregnancy may be harmful. Julia Moskin counters that there are almost no studies on the effects of moderate drinking during pregnancy and that small amounts of alcohol are unlikely to have much harmful effect.

TIMELINE

1899   First medical link between prenatal alcohol consumption and birth abnormalities.

1957   Study of prisoners shows infant mortality higher among alcoholic mothers.

1968   First publication describing distinctive facial features and other symptoms related to prenatal alcohol exposure.

1973   FAS first described in *The Lancet*.

1981   U.S. Surgeon General warns American women about the dangers of alcohol in pregnancy.

DEFINITIONS

Apoptosis   When a cell dies.

Fetal alcohol spectrum disorders (FASD)   Term describing the range of effects that can occur in an individual whose mother drank alcohol during pregnancy.

Fetal alcohol syndrome (FAS)   refers to growth, mental, and physical problems that may occur in a baby when a mother drinks alcohol during pregnancy.

Neuron   A nerve cell that is the basic building block of the nervous system.

Synaptogenesis   Critical time when neurons are rapidly forming synapses, where nerve impulses are transmitted and received.

Neurotransmitter   Chemical substance that transmits a nerve signal across a synapse to another nerve.

Glutamate   An amino acid that may function as a neurotransmitter in fetal development.

Gamma-aminobutyric acid (GABA)   A neurotransmitter that stimulates relaxation and sleep in the brain.

YES

Phyllida Brown

Drinking for Two?

At first, Susie's teachers thought she was a bright child. Her adoptive mother knew different. Give Susie a set of instructions and only a few seconds later she would have forgotten them. She was talkative, with a large vocabulary, but could not seem to form lasting friendships. Then, one day, Susie's adoptive mother heard a lecture that described fetal alcohol syndrome—a condition which affects some children born to heavy drinkers. "Bells went off in my head," she says. "The lecturer described eight traits, and my daughter had seven of them."

Children like Susie could well be just the tip of the iceberg. Fetal alcohol syndrome was once thought to affect only the children of heavy drinkers, such as Susie's biological mother, but a mounting body of research suggests that even a small amount of alcohol can damage a developing fetus—a single binge during pregnancy or a moderate seven small glasses of wine per week.

The new research has already prompted some governments to tighten up their advice on drinking during pregnancy. Others, however, say there is no convincing evidence that modest alcohol intake is dangerous for the fetus. With advice varying wildly from one country to another, the message for pregnant women has never been so confusing.

In 2005 the US Surgeon General revised official advice warning pregnant women to limit their alcohol intake. Now they are told "simply not to drink" alcohol—not only in pregnancy, but as soon as they plan to try for a baby. France also advises abstinence, as does Canada. The UK's Department of Health says that pregnant women should avoid more than "one to two units, once or twice a week," but is finalising a review of the latest evidence, which it will publish within weeks. In Australia, women are advised to "consider" abstinence, but if choosing to drink should limit their intake to less than seven standard Australian drinks a week, with no more than two standard drinks on any one day. . . .

Whichever guidelines women choose to follow, some level of drinking during pregnancy is common in many countries. The last time pregnant women in the UK were asked, in 2002, 61 per cent admitted to drinking some alcohol. Even in the US, where abstinence is expected, and where pregnant women in some states have been arrested for drinking, 13 per cent still admit to doing it.

Children with fetal alcohol syndrome (FAS) are generally smaller than average and have a range of developmental and behavioural problems such as an inability to relate to others and a tendency to be impulsive. They also have distinctive facial features such as a thin upper lip, an extra fold of skin in the inner corners of the eyes and a flattening of the groove between the nose and upper lip.

In recent years researchers investigating the effects of alcohol in pregnancy have begun to widen their definition of antenatal alcohol damage beyond the diagnosis of FAS. They now talk of fetal alcohol spectrum disorders, or FASD, an umbrella term that covers a range of physical, mental and behavioural effects which can occur without the facial features of FAS. Like children with FAS, those with FASD may have problems with arithmetic, paying attention, working memory and the planning of tasks. They may be impulsive, find it difficult to judge social situations correctly and relate badly to others, or be labelled as aggressive or defiant. In adulthood they may find it difficult to lead independent lives, be diagnosed with mental illnesses, or get into trouble with the law. Some have damage to the heart, ears or eyes.

While some children with FASD have been exposed to as much alcohol before birth as those with FAS, others may be damaged by lower levels, says Helen Barr, a statistician at the University of Washington, Seattle. Barr has spent 30 years tracking children exposed to alcohol before birth and comparing them with non-exposed children. The less alcohol, in general, says Barr, the milder the effects, such as more subtle attention problems or memory difficulties. Other factors that can affect the type of damage include the fetus's stage of development when exposed to alcohol and the mother's genetic make-up.

Although FASD is not yet an official medical diagnosis, some researchers estimate that it could be very common indeed. While FAS is thought to account for 1 in 500 live births, Ann Streissguth and her colleagues at the University of Washington believe that as many as 1 in every 100 babies born in the US are affected by FASD. Others put the figure at about 1 in 300. Whichever figure is more accurate, it would still make the condition far more common than, say, Downs syndrome, which affects 1 in 800 babies born in the US.

Streissguth was among the first to study the long-term effects of moderate drinking in pregnancy. In 1993 she reported that a group of 7-year-olds whose mothers had drunk 7 to 14 standard drinks per week in pregnancy tended to have specific problems with arithmetic and attention. Compared with children of similar IQ whose mothers had abstained during pregnancy, they struggled to remember strings of digits or the details of stories read to them, and were unable to discriminate between two rhythmic sound patterns.

When Streissguth's team followed the alcohol-exposed children through adolescence and into their early twenties they found them significantly more likely than other individuals of similar IQ and social background to be labelled as aggressive by their teachers. According to their parents, these children were unable to consider the effects of their actions on others, and unable to take hints or understand social cues. As young adults, they were more likely to drink heavily and use drugs than their peers.

These findings were borne out by similar studies later in the 1990s by Sandra Jacobson and Joseph Jacobson, both psychologists at Wayne State University in Detroit, Michigan. To try and work out what dose of alcohol might be harmful, the Jacobsons ran a study of children born to 480 women in Detroit. In it, they compared the children born to women who, at their first antenatal appointment, said they drank seven or more standard US drinks a week with the babies of women who drank less than seven, and with those whose mothers abstained altogether. The psychologists then tested the children's mental function in infancy and again at 7 years old. In the children whose mothers had seven drinks or more, the pair found significant deficits in their children's mental function in infancy, and again at age 7, mainly in arithmetic, working memory and attention (*Alcoholism: Clinical and Experimental Research*, vol. 28, p. 1732). Where the mother drank less than that they found no effect.

Spread It Out

Seven drinks a week may be more than many pregnant women manage, but according to the Jacobsons, what's important is when you are drinking them, whether you have eaten, and how quickly your body metabolises alcohol. In their study, only one woman of the 480 drank daily; most of the others restricted their drinking to a couple of weekend evenings. If a woman is drinking seven standard drinks on average across the week, but having them all on two nights, she must be reaching four drinks on one night. That constitutes a binge. "Women don't realise that if they save up their alcohol 'allowance' to the end of the week, they are concentrating their drinking in a way that is potentially harmful," she says. This means that even women who have fewer than seven glasses per week could potentially be putting their babies at risk if they drink them all on one night.

There is also some evidence that fewer than seven drinks a week could have measurable effects on an unborn baby. Peter Hepper at Queen's University, Belfast, UK, examined the movements of fetuses scanned on ultrasound in response to a noise stimulus. Having asked women about their drinking habits, they compared the responses of fetuses exposed to low levels of alcohol— between 1 and 6 British units per week, each containing 10 millilitres of alcohol—and those exposed to none. When tested between 20 and 35 weeks, the fetuses exposed to alcohol tended to show a "startle response" usually found only in the earlier stages of pregnancy, when the nervous system is less developed. Five months after birth, the same babies showed different responses to visual stimuli from the babies whose mothers had abstained. Hepper interprets these findings as evidence that a low dose of alcohol has some as yet unexplained effect on the developing nervous system. Whether or not these differences will translate into behaviour problems in later life is as yet unknown.

When Ed Riley and colleagues at San Diego State University in California looked at children's brains using magnetic resonance imaging, they found obvious changes in the brain structure of children whose mothers drank very heavily, but also some changes in children born to moderate drinkers. For example, there were abnormalities in the corpus callosum, the tract of fibres connecting the right and left hemispheres of the brain. The greater the abnormality, the worse the children performed on a verbal learning task.

Despite these recent studies, the link between alcohol and fetal development is far from clear. Not all babies born to alcoholic women have FAS, yet other babies appear to be damaged by their mothers indulging in just a single binge. And if 61 percent of British women drink while pregnant, how come there are not hundreds of thousands of British children with FASD? Wouldn't we notice if 1 in 100 children being born were affected?

Hepper argues that few teachers would raise an eyebrow if they had two or three children in a class of 30 with marked behaviour difficulties, and several more with milder, manageable problems. He therefore thinks it is plausible to suggest that 1 in 100 children could have alcohol-related problems of some sort.

Hepper's research is widely quoted by anti-drinking campaigners such as FAS Aware, an international organisation which advertises in the women's bathrooms of bars to encourage pregnant women not to drink. The posters warn that "drinking in pregnancy could leave you with a hangover for life" and that "everything you drink goes to your baby's head."

Critics of these tactics point out that trying to scare women into abstinence is not helpful. There are reports in North America of women rushing off for an abortion because they had one drink before they knew they were pregnant or being racked with guilt about past drinking if they have a child with a mild disability.

Researchers like the Jacobsons acknowledge that it is hard to be certain about how alcohol affects a developing fetus on the basis of epidemiological studies, especially when they measure the notoriously messy subject of human behaviour. Any effect on the developing brain would vary depending on exactly when the fetus was exposed, and since some behavioural effects may not become apparent until several years after birth, it is difficult to pin down specific disabilities to specific antenatal exposure to alcohol.

To try and get around the epidemiological problem, John Olney, a neuroscientist at Washington University in St Louis, Missouri, has examined the impact of alcohol on developing rodent brains as a model for what happens in humans. Ten years ago Olney and others showed that alcohol causes neurons in the developing rat brain to undergo programmed cell death, or apoptosis (*Science*, vol. 287, p. 1056).

Olney found that alcohol does the most serious damage if exposure happens during synaptogenesis, a critical time in development when neurons are rapidly forming connections. In rats, this happens just after birth, but in humans it begins in the second half of pregnancy and continues for two or more years. In the *Science* study, the team found that exposure to alcohol for baby rats during this developmental stage, at levels equivalent to a binge lasting several hours, could trigger the suicide of millions of neurons, damaging the structure of the animals' forebrains. The alcohol seems to interfere with the action of receptors for two chemical signals or neurotransmitters, glutamate and GABA (gamma amino butyric acid), that must function normally for connections to form.

Lost Neurons

The changes to brain development in rodents, Olney believes, could explain some of the behavioural problems seen in children with FASD, including attention deficit, learning and memory problems. For example, in the rat study, large numbers of neurons were lost in the brain regions that comprise the extended hippocampal circuit, which is disrupted in other disorders of learning and memory (*Addiction Biology*, vol. 9, p. 137). Loss of cells in the thalamus, which is thought to play a role in "filtering" irrelevant stimuli, may partly explain why FASD children are easily distracted.

The timing of alcohol exposure during pregnancy dictates what type of damage will occur, Olney says: if it is early on, when facial structures are forming, the facial characteristics of FAS may be obvious. Later, when synapses are forming, mental function may be affected. This runs counter to the popular view that the fetus is only vulnerable in the first trimester; in fact, different stages may be vulnerable in different ways.

Olney has recently tried to find out exactly how much alcohol is enough to trigger apoptosis. In 2006 he reported that, in infant mice whose brains are at the equivalent stage of development to a third-trimester fetus, some 20,000 neurons are deleted when they are exposed to only mildly raised blood alcohol levels, for periods as short as 45 minutes. In humans, he says, this is equivalent to deleting 20 million neurons with a 45-minute exposure to blood alcohol levels of just 50 milligrams per 100 millilitres of blood—which is well below the legal limit for driving, and easily achieved in "normal social" drinking (*Neurobiology of Disease*, DOI: 10.1016/j.nbd.2005.12.015). At blood alcohol levels below this, the team found no apoptosis.

Olney is quick to stress that, alarming as 20 million neurons sounds, it is "a very small amount of brain damage" in the context of the human brain, which is estimated to have trillions of neurons. He has no evidence that such small-scale damage would translate into any detectable effects on a child's cognitive abilities. "But if a mother is advised that one or two glasses of wine with dinner is OK, and if she then has two glasses with dinner three times a week, this is exposing the fetus to a little bit of damage three times a week," he says.

The bottom line is that, as yet, it's impossible to translate these findings into blanket advice for women about how many drinks they can or can't have when pregnant. A drink before food will raise blood alcohol concentrations faster than a drink with a meal; two drinks downed quickly will raise it more sharply than two drinks spread over 3 hours. Because of this uncertainty, some researchers—and some authorities—would rather take no chances. "The best possible advice I can give mothers is to totally abstain from alcohol the moment they know they are pregnant," Olney says.

Julia Moskin  **NO**

The Weighty Responsibility of Drinking for Two

It happens at coffee bars. It happens at cheese counters. But most of all, it happens at bars and restaurants. Pregnant women are slow-moving targets for strangers who judge what we eat—and, especially, drink.

"Nothing makes people more uncomfortable than a pregnant woman sitting at the bar," said Brianna Walker, a bartender in Los Angeles. "The other customers can't take their eyes off her."

Drinking during pregnancy quickly became taboo in the United States after 1981, when the Surgeon General began warning women about the dangers of alcohol. The warnings came after researchers at the *University of Washington* identified Fetal Alcohol Syndrome, a group of physical and mental birth defects caused by alcohol consumption, in 1973. In its recommendations, the government does not distinguish between heavy drinking and the occasional beer: all alcohol poses an unacceptable risk, it says.

So those of us who drink, even occasionally, during pregnancy face unanswerable questions, like why would anyone risk the health of a child for a passing pleasure like a beer?

"It comes down to this: I just don't buy it," said Holly Masur, a mother of two in Deerfield, Ill., who often had half a glass of wine with dinner during her pregnancies, based on advice from both her mother and her obstetrician. "How can a few sips of wine be dangerous when women used to drink martinis and smoke all through their pregnancies?"

Many American obstetricians, skeptical about the need for total abstinence, quietly tell their patients that an occasional beer or glass of wine—no hard liquor—is fine.

"If a patient tells me that she's drinking two or three glasses of wine a week, I am personally comfortable with that after the first trimester," said Dr. Austin Chen, an obstetrician in TriBeCa. "But technically I am sticking my neck out by saying so."

Americans' complicated relationship with food and drink—in which everything desirable is also potentially dangerous—only becomes magnified in pregnancy.

When I was pregnant with my first child in 2001 there was so much conflicting information that doubt became a reflexive response. Why was tea allowed but not coffee? How could all "soft cheeses" be forbidden if cream cheese was recommended? What were the real risks of having a glass of wine on my birthday?

Pregnant women are told that danger lurks everywhere: listeria in soft cheese, mercury in canned tuna, *salmonella* in fresh-squeezed orange juice. Our responsibility for minimizing risk through perfect behavior feels vast.

Eventually, instead of automatically following every rule, I began looking for proof.

Proof, it turns out, is hard to come by when it comes to "moderate" or "occasional" drinking during pregnancy. Standard definitions, clinical trials and long-range studies simply do not exist.

"Clinically speaking, there is no such thing as moderate drinking in pregnancy," said Dr. Ernest L. Abel, a professor at Wayne State University Medical School in Detroit, who has led many studies on pregnancy and alcohol. "The studies address only heavy drinking"—defined by the *National Institutes of Health* as five drinks or more per day—"or no drinking."

Most pregnant women in America say in surveys that they do not drink at all—although they may not be reporting with total accuracy. But others make a conscious choice not to rule out drinking altogether.

For me, the desire to drink turned out to be all tied up with the ritual of the table—sitting down in a restaurant, reading the menu, taking that first bite of bread and butter. That was the only time, I found, that sparkling water or nonalcoholic beer didn't quite do it. And so, after examining my conscience and the research available, I concluded that one drink with dinner was an acceptable risk.

My husband, frankly, is uncomfortable with it. But he recognizes that there is no way for him to put himself in my position, or to know what he would do under the same circumstances.

While occasional drinking is not a decision I take lightly, it is also a decision in which I am not (quite) alone. Lisa Felter McKenney, a teacher in Chicago whose first child was due in January 2007, said she feels comfortable at her current level of three drinks a week, having been grudgingly cleared by her obstetrician. "Being able to look forward to a beer with my husband at the end of the day really helps me deal with the horrible parts of being pregnant," she said. "It makes me feel like myself: not the alcohol, but the ritual. Usually I just take a few sips and that's enough."

Ana Sortun, a chef in Cambridge, Mass., who gave birth in 2005, said that she (and the nurse practitioner who delivered her baby) both drank wine during their pregnancies. "I didn't do it every day, but I did it often," she said. "Ultimately I trusted my own instincts, and my doctor's, more than anything else. Plus, I really believe all that stuff about the European tradition."

Many women who choose to drink have pointed to the habits of European women who legendarily drink wine, eat raw-milk cheese and quaff Guinness to improve breast milk production, as justification for their own choices in pregnancy.

Of course, those countries have their own taboos. "Just try to buy unpasteurized cheese in England, or to eat salad in France when you're pregnant," wrote a friend living in York, England. (Many French obstetricians warn patients that raw vegetables are risky.) However, she said, a drink a day is taken for granted. In those cultures, wine and beer are considered akin to food, part of daily life; in ours, they are treated more like drugs.

But more European countries are adopting the American stance of abstinence. In October 2006, France passed legislation mandating American-style warning labels on alcohol bottles, beginning in October 2007.

If pregnant Frenchwomen are giving up wine completely (although whether that will happen is debatable—the effects of warning labels are far from proven), where does that leave the rest of us?

"I never thought it would happen," said Jancis Robinson, a prominent wine critic in Britain, one of the few countries with government guidelines that still allow pregnant women any alcohol—one to two drinks per week. Ms. Robinson, who spent three days tasting wine for her Masters of Wine qualification in 1990 while pregnant with her second child, said that she studied the research then available and while she was inclined to be cautious, she didn't see proof that total abstinence was the only safe course.

One thing is certain: drinking is a confusing and controversial choice for pregnant women, and among the hardest areas in which to interpret the research.

Numerous long-term studies, including the original one at the University of Washington at Seattle, have established beyond doubt that heavy drinkers are taking tremendous risks with their children's health.

But for women who want to apply that research to the question of whether they must refuse a single glass of Champagne on New Year's Eve or a serving of rum-soaked Christmas pudding, there is almost no information at all.

My own decision came down to a stubborn conviction that feels like common sense: a single drink—sipped slowly, with food to slow the absorption—is unlikely to have much effect.

Some clinicians agree with that instinct. Others claim that the threat at any level is real.

"Blood alcohol level is the key," said Dr. Abel, whose view, after 30 years of research, is that brain damage and other alcohol-related problems most likely result from the spikes in blood alcohol concentration that come from binge drinking—another difficult definition, since according to Dr. Abel a binge can be as few as two drinks, drunk in rapid succession, or as many as 14, depending on a woman's physiology.

Because of ethical considerations, virtually no clinical trials can be performed on pregnant women.

"Part of the research problem is that we have mostly animal studies to work with," Dr. Abel said. "And who knows what is two drinks, for a mouse?"

Little attention has been paid to pregnant women at the low end of the consumption spectrum because there isn't a clear threat to public health there, according to Janet Golden, a history professor at Rutgers who has written about Americans' changing attitudes toward drinking in pregnancy.

The research—and the public health concern—is focused on getting pregnant women who don't regulate their intake to stop completely.

And the public seems to seriously doubt whether pregnant women can be trusted to make responsible decisions on their own.

"Strangers, and courts, will intervene with a pregnant woman when they would never dream of touching anyone else," Ms. Golden said.

Ms. Walker, the bartender, agreed. "I've had customers ask me to tell them what the pregnant woman is drinking," she said. "But I don't tell them. Like with all customers, unless someone is drunk and difficult it's no one else's business—or mine."

CHALLENGE QUESTIONS ↻

Is It Necessary for Pregnant Women to Completely Abstain from All Alcoholic Beverages?

1. List the problems seen in children whose mothers consumed alcohol during pregnancy.
2. Compare the European attitude about alcohol consumption to the American attitude.
3. Explain how Julia Moskin concludes that one drink with dinner is an "acceptable risk."
4. Write a one-page article for a student newspaper to be published during "Alcohol Awareness Week" about alcohol consumption of sexually active women of childbearing age.
5. Phyllida Brown points out some tactics that try to scare women into abstinence such as "drinking in pregnancy could leave you with a hangover for life" and that "everything you drink goes to your baby's head." She cites reports that say the messages may cause women to rush into an abortion because of one drink. Design a poster to convey an accurate message to college students about the effects of alcohol during early pregnancy.

Additional Internet Resources

The Fetal Alcohol Spectrum Disorders Center for Excellence

Web site for the federal initiative devoted to preventing and treating FASD. The Web site provides information and resources about FASD that will raise awareness about FASD.

http://www.fasdcenter.samhsa.gov

American Pregnancy Association

The national health organization committed to promoting reproductive and pregnancy wellness through education, research, advocacy, and community awareness. Web site provides statistics and information on all aspects of pregnancy health.

http://www.americanpregnancy.org

The March of Dimes

The nonprofit organization works to improve the health of babies by preventing birth defects, premature birth, and infant mortality. Their Web site features educational resources on ways to prevent birth defects and improve infant health.

http://www.marchofdimes.com/

ISSUE 18

Should Infant Formulas Contain Synthetic ARA and DHA?

YES: Haley C. Stevens and Mardi K. Mountford, MPH, from "Infant Formula and DHA/ARA," International Formula Council (IFC) Statement on DHA/ARA and Infant Formula, (http://www.infantformula.org/news-room/press-releases-and-statements/infant-formula-and-dha/ara) (Press release, March 1, 2008)

NO: Ari LeVaux, from "Dangerous Hype: Infant Formula Companies Claim They Can Make Babies 'Smarter,'" *AlterNet* (http://www.alternet.org/health/143369) (October 20, 2009)

As you read the issue, focus on the following points:

1. Why infant formulas contain added docosahexaenoic acid (DHA) and arachidonic acid (ARA).
2. Comments from various health and consumer agencies about DHA and ARA added to formulas.
3. Health concerns surrounding lab-grown DHA and ARA.

ISSUE SUMMARY

YES: Haley Stevens and Mardi Mountford, representing the International Formula Council (IFC), point out that "the available evidence strongly supports benefits of adding DHA and ARA to infant formula." They point out that "a large database exists concerning not only the safety but also the efficacy of infant formula containing both ARA and DHA. These facts, together, support the addition of both ARA and DHA when LC-PUFAs [long-chain polyunsaturated fatty acids] are added to formula."

NO: Food writer Ari LeVaux is more skeptical. He says the oils are produced from lab-grown algae and fungi and extracted with the neurotoxin hexane. He also is concerned that some "parents and medical professionals believe these additives are causing severe reactions in some babies, and it has been repeatedly shown that taking affected babies off DHA/ARA formula makes the problems go away almost immediately."

Infant formulas have come a long way since they became popular after World War II. Federal regulations for making infant formulas went into effect in 1941. The first formulas used a simple base of modified cow's milk protein. In 1959, iron-fortified formulas were introduced; a few years later, formulas made with isolated soy protein became available. Each time significant changes are made, the formula manufacturer must notify the FDA, the federal agency that monitors the safety of America's food supply.

The American Academy of Pediatrics considers human milk the "gold standard" when it comes to infant feeding. Formula companies continue to examine nutrients in breast milk and try to imitate them in their artificially made products. In the 1990s, many studies reported that the intellectual and visual superiority of infants who were breast-fed is linked to the long-chain fatty acid docosahexaenoic acid (DHA) and arachidonic acid (ARA) that are abundant in mother's milk.

In 2002, Mead Johnson Nutritionals, the leading infant formula manufacturer, introduced Enfamil LIPIL Soon after, other companies began adding them to their products.

So why is it added to formula? Mead Johnson claims DHA and ARA "*may help to support babies' mental and visual development.*" In her June 10, 2010, *Food Politics* blog, Marion Nestle says that DHA is added to formula as a marketing ploy. She writes:

> DHA (an omega-3 fatty acid) came first. As I discuss in my book, *What to Eat*, infant formula companies could not wait to add it. They knew they could market it on the basis of preliminary evidence associating DHA with visual and cognitive benefits in young infants. Although evidence for long-term benefits is scanty, the companies also knew that they could charge higher prices for formulas containing DHA.

The FDA approved the use of DHA in infant formulas on the grounds that it is safe, but did not require the companies to establish that DHA makes any difference to infant health after the first year. Because of its marketing advantage, virtually all infant formulas now contain DHA. Surprise! They also cost more.

But more importantly, are they safe for the infants who consume them? The Cornucopia Institute, a farming advocacy group from Wisconsin, says "No." They question the safety and value of adding synthetically made DHA and ARA to infant formula. The group also wonders if the addition is a "risky marketing gimmick" by the formula industry. Their 2008 report points out that the DHA and ARA are "extracted from laboratory-grown fermented algae and fungi and processed utilizing the toxic chemical, hexane." DHA is from the alga *Crypthecodinium cohnii* and ARA is from the fungus *Mortierella alpina*. On infant formula ingredient labels, you may see the terms "Mortierella alpina oil" and "Crypthecodinium cohnii oil." They also cite evidence from laboratory studies that link the synthetic fat to increases in liver weight in lab animals and diarrhea in children. (Baby food manufacturers use tuna oil for their source of added DHA.)

After reading the two selections, decide what you think about the safety of added DHA/ARA to formulas. Haley Stevens and Marisa Salcines speak for the International Formula Council and point out that "the available evidence strongly supports benefits of adding DHA and ARA to infant formula." Ari LeVaux is more skeptical and agrees with Cornucopia's concern about the toxic potential of the hexane used to manufacture the oils.

DEFINITIONS

Arachidonic acid (ARA)   The 20-carbon, omega-6 fatty acid that is involved in brain and visual development.

Crypthecodinium cohnii   Algae used to produce DHA.

Docosahexaenoic acid (DHA)   The 22-carbon, omega-3 fatty acid that is involved in brain and visual development.

Hexane   A known neurotoxin and possible carcinogen used as an organic solvent in DHA/ARA production.

Long-chain polyunsaturated fatty acid (LC-PUFA)   A fatty acid with 12 or more carbons and two double bonds.

Mortierella alpina   Fungus used to produce ARA.

YES ↵

**Haley C. Stevens and
Mardi K. Mountford, MPH**

Infant Formula and DHA/ARA

U.S. infant formula manufacturers currently offer formulas containing docosahexaenoic acid (DHA) and arachidonic acid (ARA). Formulas containing DHA and ARA have been shown to provide visual and mental development similar to that of the breastfed infant. The decision to supplement formulas with these nutritional long-chain polyunsaturated fatty adds (LCPUFAs) was made following years of research studying the clinical effects of both DHA and ARA in infants. The use of LCPUFAs in infant formulas has been reviewed and supported by the U.S. Food and Drug Administration, the European Food Safety Authority, the Food and Agriculture Organization and World Health Organization, the Codex Alimentarius Commission, the Agence Francaise De Securite Sanitaire Des Aliments, the American Dietetic Association and the Dietitians of Canada, the European Society for Paediatric Gastroenterology and Nutrition, the World Association of Perinatal Medicine and Child Health Foundation, the Commission of European Communities and the National Academy of Sciences.

DHA and ARA are considered to be "building blocks" for the development of brain and eye tissue. Research has demonstrated that DHA and ARA, both present in human milk, are physiologically important in prenatal and postnatal life during the period of rapid brain and eye development and throughout life as well. DHA and ARA have been shown to rapidly accumulate in the brain during the last trimester prenatally and the first two years postnatally, and preclinical studies have also demonstrated their importance in visual and neural systems.

The IFC supports breastfeeding and the position of the World Health Organization, the American Academy of Pediatrics and other leading health organizations that breastfeeding is ideal, and offers specific child and maternal benefits. However, for those mothers who cannot or choose not to breastfeed, infant formula is recommended. Years of product development and careful clinical research have resulted in commercially available infant formulas that provide the appropriate levels of protein, fat, carbohydrate, vitamins, and minerals for a baby to sustain a rapid rate of growth and development without stressing the infant's delicate and developing organ systems. With the addition of DHA and ARA to infant formulas, the industry continues its commitment to provide the best nutrition for infants whose mothers cannot or choose not to breastfeed.

The International Formula Council (IFC) is an association of manufacturers and marketers of formulated nutrition products, e.g., infant formulas and adult nutritionals, whose members are based predominantly in North America. IFC members are Abbott Nutrition, Mead Johnson Nutrition, Nestlé Infant Nutrition, PBM Nutritionals and Pfizer Nutrition. Copyright © 2008 by International Formula Council. Reprinted by permission.

After reviewing the recent literature and current recommendations regarding LC-PUFA for term infant nutrition during the first months of life, a 2008 international expert working group on LC-PUFAs in perinatal practice led by B. Koletzko concluded that "the available evidence strongly supports benefits of adding DHA and ARA to infant formula." The panel stated that the addition of DHA and ARA to infant formula "appears appropriate." Furthermore, the authors stated that, "a large database exists concerning not only the safety, but also the efficacy, of infant formula containing both ARA and DHA. These facts, together, support the addition of both ARA and DHA when LC-PUFAs are added to formula."

Parents and health professionals can be assured infant formula is safe and nutritious. Worldwide Regulatory Bodies Who Support DHA and ARA for Infants.

U.S. Food and Drug Administration (FDA)

In May 2001, following [is] an extensive review of the available scientific data supporting the safety of DHA and ARA, the FDA agreed that oils containing DHA and ARA are generally recognized as safe (GRAS) for use in infant formula. Additionally, in accordance with the requirements of the Infant Formula Act of 1980 and its subsequent amendments, any manufacturer wishing to add these oils to a specific infant formula was required to notify the FDA 90 days prior to the introduction of such a new formula, so that the agency could conduct an appropriate review of the scientific literature and testing that has been assembled by the manufacturer to demonstrate the formula's ability to support growth as a substitute for breast milk.

European Food Safety Authority (EFSA)

In March 2010, the scientific opinion of the EFSA Panel on Dietetic Products, Nutrition, and Allergies (NDA) regarding Dietary Reference Values (DRVs) for fats, including saturated fatty acids, polyunsaturated fatty acids, monounsaturated fatty acids, trans fatty adds, and cholesterol was published. The opinion set an Adequate Intake (AI) level for DHA for infants and young children, and stated "small amounts of DHA may be needed for optimal growth and development of infants and children," including 20–50 mg/day for infants 0–6 months of age.

Food Agriculture Organization (FAO) and the World Health Organization (WHO)

FAO and WHO have recommended the addition of DHA and ARA to infant formula at the levels found in human breast milk. In October 1993, a joint expert consultation concluded: "In view of the evidence on the higher efficiency of long-chain polyunsaturated fatty acids for neural development . . . and the data on premature infants . . . the long-chain polyunsaturated fatty acids should be included in infant formula." Additionally, in 2008 the WHO restated its views about the importance of DHA and ARA for infants.

Codex Alimentarius Commission (CAC)

The CAC, a global body formed by the FAO and the WHO, adopted in July 2007 the Revised Standard for Infant Formula and Formula for Special Medical Purposes Intended for Infants, which upholds the safety and provides for the optional addition of LCPUFAs to infant formulas.

Agence Francaise De Securite Sanitaire Des Aliments (AFSSA)

In March 2010, AFSSA published Dietary Reference Intakes (DRIs) for Fatty Acids, including DRIs for infants 0–6 months and infants and young children 6–36 months. AFSSA also recognized DHA as an essential fatty acid for its role in structure and function of the brain and eye.

American Dietetic Association (ADA) and the Dietitians of Canada (DC)

The ADA and the DC have recommended the inclusion of DHA and ARA in infant formula and have highlighted the importance of DHA and ARA to infant health. In their position statement on dietary fatty acids, the ADA/DC note "no adverse effects of feeding marketed infant formula containing both ARA and DHA in amounts found in human milk are known. Because of possible benefits and lack of adverse effects, it is recommended that all infants who are not breastfed be fed a formula containing both ARA and DHA through at least the first year of life."

European Society for Pediatric Gastroenterology, Hepatology and Nutrition (ESPGHAN)

ESPGHAN recommends the addition of LCPUFAs to infant formulas. In 2005, an ESPGHAN-coordinated International Expert Group supported the addition of DHA and ARA to infant formulas. In 2006, the ESPGHAN Committee on Nutrition concluded that preterm infants, when formula fed, should receive infant formula with provision of LCPUFAs.

World Association of Perinatal Medicine (WAPM) and the Child Health Foundation

In 2001, the Child Health Foundation, under guidance from the WAPM, asked investigators in the field of LCPUFAs to review available scientific data and form a recommendation. That working group supported the addition of DHA and ARA to infant formulas for term and premature infants. Further, a recommendation from the 2001 workshop was that investigators update its recommendation as additional data became available. Therefore, in 2008, the same group of investigators reviewed the available scientific literature and endorsed its previous position.

Commission of the European Communities (EC)

The EC states that DHA and ARA are considered safe for use as an optional ingredient for infant formulas.

National Academy of Sciences (NAS)

In 2005, a panel organized by NAS developed a report on dietary reference intakes for various macronutrients, including dietary fatty acids like LCPUFAs, and supports the addition of DHA to infant formula in the amounts found in breast milk. According to NAS, "n-3 polyunsaturated fatty acids provide DHA that is important for developing brain and retina."

Background

DHA is particularly required for the development of the cerebral cortex, the region of the brain responsible for language development and information processing, and plays a vital function in developing visual sharpness (acuity). ARA is an important precursor for modulators/mediators of a variety of essential biological processes (e.g., the inflammatory response, regulation of blood pressure, regulation of sleep/wake cycle). DHA and ARA are synthesized in the body from the precursor essential fatty acids, α-linolenic acid (ALA) and linoleic acid (LA), respectively, that are also present in human milk and infant formula.

Evidence that blood levels of DHA and ARA are typically higher in breast-fed infants than in infants fed formulas not containing these LCPUFAs provided a basis for investigating the addition of DHA and ARA to infant formulas. Studies suggest that premature infants may benefit the most from direct consumption of DHA and ARA. Throughout the third trimester, a mother passes DHA and ARA to the baby through the placenta. Postnatally, these nutrients are passed through human milk. In the event that a baby is born prematurely, placental transport of DHA and ARA is interrupted, thereby reducing the baby's total accumulation of ARA and DHA prior to birth. Addition of the GRAS sources of DHA and ARA to preterm formula provides these important nutrients safely. Studies show that formulas containing added DHA and ARA are safe and support visual and cognitive development.

U.S. infant formula manufacturers continue to evaluate the potential benefits of adding nutritional fatty acids to infant formulas. They also take very seriously their responsibility to provide safe and nutritious infant formulas to the millions of infants fed infant formula, often as the sole source of nutrition. Millions of infants in the U.S. and worldwide have safely been fed infant formula with DHA and ARA and millions more continue to be fed every day. The addition of DHA and ARA to infant formula is modeled on the levels present in breast milk. Clinical studies did not find more adverse events in subjects fed DHA and ARA containing infant formulas. There has not been an increase in diarrhea and vomiting complaints, as alleged by recent media reports, since introduction of these ingredients into infant formulas.

Ari LeVaux  **NO**

Dangerous Hype: Infant Formula Companies Claim They Can Make Babies 'Smarter'

If you believed a certain baby formula would make your child smarter, would you buy it?

Infant formula manufacturers are banking that you would. That's why, since 2002, several companies have fortified their products with synthetic versions of DHA and ARA, long-chain fatty acids that occur naturally in breast milk and have been associated with brain development.

The oils are produced by Martek Biosciences Corp. from lab-grown algae and fungus and extracted with hexane, according to the company's patent application. Hexane is a neurotoxin.

A growing number of parents and medical professional believe these additives are causing severe reactions in some babies, and it has been repeatedly shown that taking affected babies off DHA/ARA formula makes the problems go away almost immediately. The FDA has received hundreds of letters to this effect by upset parents, even as products containing the additives are being marketed as better than breast milk.

Karen Jensen says that due to health complications she was unable to breastfeed her daughter, and so fed her daughter Neocate, a formula with DHA/ARA.

"At two weeks, my daughter would often stop breathing in her sleep and was having various other serious health conditions. She cried constantly and couldn't sleep due to gastrointestinal upset."

After many trips to the hospital, a CT scan, an EEG, time on an apnea monitor and thousands of dollars in bills, "we tried the Neocate without the DHA/ARA in it. Within 24 hours, we had a brand-new, entirely different baby. She had no abdominal distress, no gas, she smiled and played, and for the first time ever we heard her laugh."

Jensen's story is echoed many times over in similar letters urging the FDA to ban DHA and ARA from baby foods, or at the very least to put warning labels on the product advising that some babies may experience adverse reactions like bloating, gastrointestinal distress, vomiting, and diarrhea.

From *Alternet*, October 20, 2009. Copyright © 2009 by Ari LeVaux. Reprinted by permission of the author.

While only a fraction of babies seem to react in this way, it's a common enough occurrence to have earned DHA/ARA baby formula the nickname "the diarrhea formula" in the neonatal unit of an Ohio hospital.

In 2001, the FDA expressed concerns about the safety of adding DHA and ARA to infant-formula additives and notified Martek of the agency's plans to convene a group of scientists to study these concerns.

Martek wrote back: ". . . convening a group of scientific experts to answer such hypothetical concerns would not be productive." Within months, the FDA wrote to Martek that it would allow DHA and ARA in infant formula, without any scientific review of its own.

While quick to protest hypothetical safety concerns about DHA/ARA, Martek was ready to pounce on the hypothetical benefits of its oils.

In a 1996 investment brief, Martek explained, "Even if [the DHA/ARA blend] has no benefit, we think it would be widely incorporated into formulas as a marketing tool and to allow companies to promote their formula as 'closest to human milk.'"

Mead Johnson Nutritionals took this opportunity to heart, drawing the ire of breastfeeding advocates when it began promoting its DHA/ARA Enfamil Lipil as "The Breast Milk Formula."

Mead Johnson was also involved with a report in current issue of the journal *Child Development*, in which a Dallas team of scientists provided evidence that DHA and ARA in baby food improves brain development. Several members of the team have received Mead Johnson money in the form of research funding, as well as the coveted currency known as "consulting fees."

The report claims that infants fed DHA/ARA baby formula (supplied for free by Mead Johnson) showed greater ability to solve certain problems, like pulling a blanket with a ball on it toward them. The researchers say this problem-solving ability correlates with enhanced IQ and vocabulary development.

"New evidence favors baby formula," announced the *Los Angeles Times*, in an ambiguously worded headline that begs the question: Over what is baby formula favored?

Breastfeeding advocates went on the warpath over the suggestion that formula could be better for babies than breast milk.

"Parents will be encouraged to forgo breastfeeding in favor of a hyped-up infant formula," complained Barbara Moore, president and CEO of Shape Up America. "Breast milk has other benefits not related to mental development. It confers protection against infection, including viral infections, and the CDC promotes breastfeeding to confer maximal protection against swine flu and other infections."

Charlotte Vallaeys, a researcher for the Cornucopia Institute, wrote a substantial report on the risks and benefits of DHA/ARA in baby formula. She says the Mead Johnson-funded team behind the *Child Development* story is "the only group that has found real differences in cognitive development" resulting from the addition of DHA and ARA to formula.

Not that other research teams haven't looked. To make sense of the growing body of research on the subject, a team of scientists led by Karen Simmer compiled a review, published in January 2008, of all available literature. The team found "feeding term infants with milk formula enriched with [DHA and ARA] had no proven benefit regarding vision, cognition or physical growth."

A March 2009 review by the European Food Safety Authority also found the available data "insufficient to establish a cause-and-effect relationship" between DHA, ARA and brain development.

Nonetheless, the use of DHA and ARA has grown, and has even won approval for use in organic baby formula, as well as in organic milk.

In an article for the *Washington Post* on the eroding integrity of the "certified organic" label, Kimberly Kindy described how these laboratory produced oils received organic approval.

> . . . in 2006, [USDA] staff members concluded that the fatty acids could not be added to organic baby formula because they are synthetics that are not on the standards board's approved list. . . . Barbara Robinson, who administers the organics program and is a deputy USDA administrator, overruled the staff decision after a telephone call and an e-mail exchange with William J. Friedman, a lawyer who represents the formula makers.

While the FDA has raised serious questions regarding the safety of DHA/ARA, the issue remains in limbo, with concerned parents, medical professionals and advocacy groups pushing one way, and the deep-pocketed corporations pushing the other.

The FDA did instruct Martek and the formula companies to conduct post-market surveillance of its DHA and ARA products, but after seven years none has been submitted.

Until conclusive proof emerges on the safety and/or benefit of DHA and ARA in baby formula, it's buyer beware for parents of newborns. And last I checked, breast milk—the product of millions of years of evolutionary shaping into the perfect food for babies—remains widely available and free of charge. . . .

CHALLENGE QUESTIONS

Should Infant Formulas Contain Synthetic ARA and DHA?

1. List the benefits that DHA and ARA may provide to growing infants.
2. List two reasons why formula manufacturers add DHA and ARA to infant formulas.
3. Prepare a table that includes the positions of various infant and health care agencies around the world regarding LC-PUFA added to infant formula. Include the date of the statement, the type of oils mentioned, and their rationale behind their positions.
4. Write a letter to the FDA requesting that they develop a warning label for infant formula about the risk of added ARA and DHA. The letter should be limited to one page in length.
5. Your best friend has decided to formula feed the infant she is expecting in a month. She asks for your opinion on which type of formula she should use. What advice would you give her and why would you give her this advice?

ISSUE 19

Is Breast-Feeding the Best Way to Feed Babies?

YES: Pat Thomas, from "Suck on This," *The Ecologist* (May 2006)

NO: Hanna Rosin, from "The Case Against Breast-Feeding," *The Atlantic* (April 2009)

As you read the issue, focus on the following points:

1. Science-based benefits of breast-feeding and negative aspects of breast-feeding that some infants and/or mothers experience.
2. Changes in modern society and health care that resulted in less women breast-feeding.
3. The steps various national and international health organizations are taking to increase breast-feeding.

ISSUE SUMMARY

YES: Pat Thomas, the editor of the London-based *The Ecologist*, believes that breast-feeding is the best and healthiest way to feed babies and contends that advertisements from formula companies are jeopardizing the health of infants and children around the world.

NO: *The Atlantic* editor Hanna Rosin claims the scientific data on benefits of breast-feeding are inconclusive and, as an experienced mother of three, suggests a more relaxed approach to the issue.

For centuries, breast-feeding was the only way to feed babies. If a mother died at birth, either family members found a wet-nurse to feed the newborn or the infant died. (A wet-nurse is a woman hired to breast-feed someone else's baby.) During the 1800s, a homemade "formula" that consisted of raw cow's milk diluted with water and honey was introduced, but there were problems with it. The milk was not pasteurized and it lacked vitamins C and D, which resulted in a very high incidence of death in the infants who were given the homemade formula.

In the early 1900s, use of evaporated milk became popular, and many babies were fed bottles filled with diluted evaporated milk. In the 1950s, commercially prepared infant formulas hit the market. Two of the earliest brands were SMA (simulated milk adapted) and Similac (similar to lactation). Companies who made formula spent millions on marketing campaigns to hospitals and physicians. They provided hospitals with formula for newborns while in the hospital and cans of formula (with free bottles) to send home with new mothers. Since most infants are fed the same brand of infant formula for the first 12 months of life, the formula manufacturer who initially provides the formula profits tremendously.

In America, by the 1970s, formula was so popular that almost 80 percent of infants were bottle-fed from birth. And many of the women who began breast-feeding, quickly switched to bottles since they had the free formula (and bottles) they brought home from the hospital.

Things began changing in the mid-1970s and have continued until today. Most doctors, scientists, and child advocacy groups began to promote that human milk is the most healthful form of milk for babies. International groups developed recommendations and policies that encouraged the return to breast-feeding. In 1974, the World Health Organization (WHO) urged: "member countries to review sales promotion activities on baby foods to introduce appropriate remedial measures, including advertisement codes and legislation where necessary."

Since that time, numerous studies have found that breast milk makes healthier and happier babies and smarter children and teens. And not only is breast-feeding easier and cheaper than bottle feeding, it also provides numerous health benefits to the mother, such as lower risk of breast and ovarian cancers, type 2 diabetes, and osteoporosis.

The American Dietetic Association (ADA), the American Academy of Pediatrics (AAP), the United Nations Children's Fund (UNICEF), and the WHO all recommend exclusive breast-feeding for the first 6 months of life. ADA and AAP recommend introduction of complementary foods at 6 months, and to continue breast-feeding until at least 12 months of age. WHO and UNICEF go a little further and recommend breast-feeding until 2 years or beyond.

There's a difference between "exclusive breast-feeding" and simply "breast-feeding." "Exclusive" means the infant only has breast milk with no added formula or other foods. Based on a 2005 study of over 15,000 U.S. infants, of the 75 percent of women who initiated breast-feeding at birth, only 32 percent were exclusively breast-feeding when the infant was 3 months and 12 percent at 6 months. So most women do begin with good intentions, but quickly begin giving some infant formula or stop nursing all together. Today's new mothers are far from meeting the recommended "exclusive breast-feeding until 6 months."

While there are significant benefits to breast-feeding, most bottle-fed children grow up to be perfectly healthy. Most people who were born during the bottle-feeding revolution (1950–1975) are currently between ages 40 and 65 years and most of us are healthy, thriving adults.

After reading the following articles, you decide if breast-feeding is really superior to bottle-feeding. Pat Thomas argues that the health benefits of breast-feeding are enormous and that formula companies promote their products at the expense of infant health. Hanna Rosin, a mother who nursed her three children, discusses the inconsistent results from the scientific studies on the benefits of breast-feeding.

TIMELINE

1800s A few women use homemade "formula" but many infants die.

1900s Evaporated milk is introduced and used to feed infants.

1950s Commercially prepared infant formulas are prevalent on the market.

1970s 80 percent of American infants are formula-fed.

1974 WHO urges countries to develop legislation to promote breast-feeding.

DEFINITIONS

Iatrogenic Medically induced adverse effect.

£ British pound; £1=$1.50

p British pence; £1=100

YES

Pat Thomas

Suck on This

The human species has been breastfeeding for nearly half a million years. It's only in the last 60 years that we have begun to give babies the highly processed convenience food called "formula." The health consequences—twice the risk of dying in the first six weeks of life, five times the risk of gastroenteritis, twice the risk of developing eczema and diabetes and up to eight times the risk of developing lymphatic cancer—are staggering. With UK formula manufacturers spending around £20 per baby promoting this 'baby junk food', compared to the paltry 14 pence per baby the government spends promoting breastfeeding, can we ever hope to reverse the trend? Pat Thomas uncovers a world where predatory baby milk manufacturers, negligent health professionals and an ignorant, unsympathetic public all conspire to keep babies off the breast and on the bottle.

All mammals produce milk for their young, and the human species has been nurturing its babies at the breast for at least 400,000 years. For centuries, when a woman could not feed her baby herself, another lactating woman, or 'wet nurse', took over the job. It is only in the last 60 years or so that we have largely abandoned our mammalian instincts and, instead, embraced a bottle-feeding culture that not only encourages mothers to give their babies highly processed infant formulas from birth, but also to believe that these breastmilk substitutes are as good as, if not better than, the real thing.

Infant formulas were never intended to be consumed on the widespread basis that they are today. They were conceived in the late 1800s as a means of providing necessary sustenance for foundlings and orphans who would otherwise have starved. In this narrow context—where no other food was available—formula was a lifesaver.

However, as time went on, and the subject of human nutrition in general—and infant nutrition, in particular—became more "scientific," manufactured breastmilk substitutes were sold to the general public as a technological improvement on breastmilk.

"If anybody were to ask 'which formula should I use?' or 'which is nearest to mother's milk?', the answer would be 'nobody knows' because there is not one single objective source of that kind of information provided by anybody," says Mary Smale, a breastfeeding counsellor with the National Childbirth

Trust (NCT) for 28 years. "Only the manufacturers know what's in their stuff, and they aren't telling. They may advertise special 'healthy' ingredients like oligosaccharides, long-chain fatty acids or, a while ago, beta-carotene, but they never actually tell you what the basic product is made from or where the ingredients come from."

The known constituents of breastmilk were and are used as a general reference for scientists devising infant formulas. But, to this day, there is no actual "formula" for formula. In fact, the process of producing infant formulas has, since its earliest days, been one of trial and error.

Within reason, manufacturers can put anything they like into formula. In fact, the recipe for one product can vary from batch to batch, according to the price and availability of ingredients. While we assume that formula is heavily regulated, no transparency is required of manufacturers: they do not, for example, have to log the specific constituents of any batch or brand with any authority.

Most commercial formulas are based on cow's milk. But before a baby can drink cow's milk in the form of infant formula, it needs to be severely modified. The protein and mineral content must be reduced and the carbohydrate content increased, usually by adding sugar. Milk fat, which is not easily absorbed by the human body, particularly one with an immature digestive system, is removed and substituted with vegetable, animal or mineral fats.

Vitamins and trace elements are added, but not always in their most easily digestible form. (This means that the claims that formula is 'nutritionally complete' are true, but only in the crudest sense of having had added the full complement of vitamins and mineral to a nutritionally inferior product.)

Many formulas are also highly sweetened. While most infant formulas do not contain sugar in the form of sucrose, they can contain high levels of other types of sugar such as lactose (milk sugar), fructose (fruit sugar), glucose (also known as dextrose, a simple sugar found in plants) and maltodextrose (malt sugar). Because of a loophole in the law, these can still be advertised as "sucrose free."

Formula may also contain unintentional contaminants introduced during the manufacturing process. Some may contain traces of genetically engineered soya and corn.

The bacteria *Salmonella* and aflatoxins—potent toxic, carcinogenic, mutagenic, immunosuppressive agents produced by species of the fungus *Aspergillus*—have regularly been detected in commercial formulas, as has *Enterobacter sakazakii*, a devastating foodborne pathogen that can cause sepsis (overwhelming bacterial infection in the bloodstream), meningitis (inflammation of the lining of the brain) and necrotising enterocolitis (severe infection and inflammation of the small intestine and colon) in newborn infants.

The packaging of infant formulas occasionally gives rise to contamination with broken glass and fragments of metal as well as industrial chemicals such as phthalates and bisphenol A (both carcinogens) and, most recently, the packaging constituent isopropyl thioxanthone (ITX; another suspected carcinogen).

Infant formulas may also contain excessive levels of toxic or heavy metals, including aluminum, manganese, cadmium and lead.

Soya formulas are of particular concern due to the very high levels of plant-derived oestrogens (phytoestrogens) they contain. In fact, concentrations of phytoestrogens detected in the blood of infants receiving soya formula can be 13,000 to 22,000 times greater than the concentrations of natural oestrogens. Oestrogen in doses above those normally found in the body can cause cancer.

Killing Babies

For years, it was believed that the risks of illness and death from bottlefeeding were largely confined to children in developing countries, where the clean water necessary to make up formula is sometimes scarce and where poverty-stricken mothers may feel obliged to dilute formula to make it stretch further, thus risking waterborne illnesses such as diarrhoea and cholera as well as malnutrition in their babies. But newer data from the West clearly show that babies in otherwise affluent societies are also falling ill and dying due to an early diet of infant convenience food.

Because it is not nutritionally complete, because it does not contain the immune-boosting properties of breastmilk and because it is being consumed by growing babies with vast, ever-changing nutritional needs—and not meeting those needs—the health effects of sucking down formula day after day early in life can be devastating in both the short and long term.

Bottlefed babies are twice as likely to die from any cause in the first six weeks of life. In particular, bottlefeeding raises the risk of SIDS (sudden infant death syndrome) by two to five times. Bottlefed babies are also at a significantly higher risk of ending up in hospital with a range of infections. They are, for instance, five times more likely to be admitted to hospital suffering from gastroenteritis.

Even in developed countries, bottlefed babies have rates of diarrhoea twice as high as breastfed ones. They are twice as likely (20 per cent vs 10 per cent) to suffer from otitis media (inner-ear infection), twice as likely to develop eczema or a wheeze if there is a family history of atopic disease, and five times more likely to develop urinary tract infections. In the first six months of life, bottlefed babies are six to 10 times more likely to develop necrotising enterocolitis—a serious infection of the intestine, with intestinal tissue death—a figure that increases to 30 times the risk after that time.

Even more serious diseases are also linked with bottlefeeding. Compared with infants who are fully breastfed even for only three to four months, a baby drinking artificial milk is twice as likely to develop juvenile-onset insulin-dependent (type 1) diabetes. There is also a five- to eightfold risk of developing lymphomas in children under 15 who were formulated, or breastfed for less than six months.

In later life, studies have shown that bottlefed babies have a greater tendency towards developing conditions such as childhood inflammatory bowel disease, multiple sclerosis, dental malocclusion, coronary heart disease, diabetes, hyperactivity, autoimmune thyroid disease and coeliac disease.

BREASTMILK VS FORMULA: NO CONTEST

Breastmilk is a "live" food that contains living cells, hormones, active enzymes, antibodies and at least 400 other unique components. It is a dynamic substance, the composition of which changes from the beginning to the end of the feed and according to the age and needs of the baby. Because it also provides active immunity, every time a baby breastfeeds it also receives protection from disease.

Compared to this miraculous substance, the artificial milk sold as infant formula is little more than junk food. It is also the only manufactured food that humans are encouraged to consume exclusively for a period of months, even though we know that no human body can be expected to stay healthy and thrive on a steady diet of processed food.

Breastmilk	Formula	Comments
Fats		
Rich in brain-building omega-3s, namely, DHA and AA. Automatically adjusts to infant's needs; levels decline as baby gets older. Rich in cholesterol; nearly completely absorbed. Contains the fat-digesting enzyme lipase	No DHA Doesn't adjust to infant's needs No cholesterol Not completely absorbed No lipase	The most important nutrient in breastmilk; the absence of cholesterol and DHA may predispose a child to adult heart and CNS diseases. Leftover, unabsorbed fat accounts for unpleasant smelling stools in formula-fed babies
Protein		
Soft, easily digestible whey. More completely absorbed; higher in the milk of mothers who deliver preterm. Lactoferrin for intestinal health. Lysozyme, an antimicrobial. Rich in brain- and body-building protein components. Rich in growth factors. Contains sleep-inducing proteins	Harder-to-digest casein curds Not completely absorbed, so more waste, harder on kidneys Little or no lactoferrin No lysozyme. Deficient or low in some brain and body-building proteins Deficient in growth factors Contains fewer sleep-inducing proteins	Infants aren't allergic to human milk proteins
Carbohydrates		
Rich in oligosaccharides, which promote intestinal health	No lactose in some formulas Deficient in oligosaccharides	Lactose is important for brain development
Immune-boosters		
Millions of living white blood cells, in every feeding Rich in immunoglobulins	No live white blood cells or any other cells. Has no immune benefit	Breastfeeding provides active and dynamic protection from infections of all kinds. Breastmilk can be used to alleviate a range of external health problems such as nappy rash and conjunctivitis

(Continued)

Breastmilk	Formula	Comments
Vitamins & Minerals		
Better absorbed	Not absorbed as well	Nutrients in formula are poorly
Iron is 50–75 per cent absorbed	Iron is 5–10 per cent absorbed	absorbed. To compensate, more nutrients are added to
Contains more selenium (an antioxidant)	Contains less selenium (an antioxidant)	formula, making it harder to digest
Enzymes & Hormones		
Rich in digestive enzymes such as lipase and amylase. Rich in many hormones such as thyroid, prolactin and oxytocin. Taste varies with mother's diet, thus helping the child acclimatise to the cultural diet	Processing kills digestive enzymes
Processing kills hormones, which are not human to begin with
Always tastes the same	Digestive enzymes promote intestinal health; hormones contribute to the biochemical balance and wellbeing of the baby
Cost		
Around £350/year in extra food for mother if she was on a very poor diet to begin with	Around £650/year. Up to £1300/year for hypoallergenic formulas. Cost for bottles and other supplies. Lost income when parents must stay home to care for a sick baby	In the UK, the NHS spends £35 million each year just treating gastroenteritis in bottlefed babies. In the US, insurance companies pay out $3.6 billion for treating diseases in bottlefed babies

For all of these reasons, formula cannot be considered even 'second best' compared with breastmilk. Officially, the World Health Organization (WHO) designates formula milk as the last choice in infant-feeding: Its first choice is breastmilk from the mother; second choice is the mother's own milk given via cup or bottle; third choice is breastmilk from a milk bank or wet nurse and, finally, in fourth place, formula milk.

And yet, breastfed babies are becoming an endangered species. In the UK, rates are catastrophically low and have been that way for decades. Current figures suggest that only 62 per cent of women in Britain even attempt to breastfeed (usually while in hospital). At six weeks, just 42 per cent are breastfeeding. By four months, only 29 per cent are still breastfeeding and, by six months, this figure drops to 22 per cent.

These figures could come from almost any developed country in the world and, it should be noted, do not necessarily reflect the ideal of 'exclusive' breastfeeding. Instead, many modern mothers practice mixed feeding—combining breastfeeding with artificial baby milks and infant foods. Worldwide, the WHO estimates that only 35 per cent of infants are getting any breastmilk at all by age four months and, although no one can say for sure because research into exclusive breastfeeding is both scarce and incomplete, it is estimated that only 1 per cent are exclusively breastfed at six months.

Younger women in particular are the least likely to breastfeed, with over 40 per cent of mothers under 24 never even trying. The biggest gap, however, is a socioeconomic one. Women who live in low-income households or who are poorly educated are many times less likely to breastfeed, even though it can make an enormous difference to a child's health.

In children from socially disadvantaged families, exclusive breastfeeding in the first six months of life can go a long way towards cancelling out the health inequalities between being born into poverty and being born into affluence. In essence, breastfeeding takes the infant out of poverty for those first crucial months and gives it a decent start in life.

So Why Aren't Women Breastfeeding?

Before bottles became the norm, breastfeeding was an activity of daily living based on mimicry, and learning within the family and community. Women became their own experts through the trial and error of the experience itself. But today, what should come more or less naturally has become extraordinarily complicated—the focus of global marketing strategies and politics, lawmaking, lobbying support groups, activists and the interference of a well-intentioned, but occasionally ineffective, cult of experts.

According to Mary Smale, it's confidence and the expectation of support that make the difference, particularly for socially disadvantaged women.

"The concept of 'self efficacy'—in other words, whether you think you can do something—is quite important. You can say to a woman that breastfeeding is really a good idea, but she's got to believe various things in order for it to work. First of all, she has to think it's a good idea—that it will be good for her and her baby. Second, she has to think: 'I'm the sort of person who can do that"; third—and maybe the most important thing—is the belief that if she does have problems, she's the sort of person who, with help, will be able to sort them out.

"Studies show, for example, that women on low incomes often believe that breastfeeding hurts, and they also tend to believe that formula is just as good. So from the start, the motivation to breastfeed simply isn't there. But really, it's the thought that if there were any problems, you couldn't do anything about them; that, for instance, if it hurts, it's just the luck of the draw. This mindset is very different from that of a middle-class mother who is used to asking for help to solve things, who isn't frightened of picking up the phone, or saying to her midwife or health visitor, 'I want you to help me with this'."

Nearly all women—around 99 per cent—can breastfeed successfully and make enough milk for their babies to not simply grow, but to thrive. With encouragement, support and help, almost all women are willing to initiate breastfeeding, but the drop-off rates are alarming: 90 per cent of women who give up in the first six weeks say that they would like to have continued. And it seems likely that long-term exclusive breastfeeding rates could be improved if consistent support were available, and if approval within the family and the wider community for breastfeeding, both at home and in public, were more obvious and widespread.

Clearly, this social support isn't there, and the bigger picture of breastfeeding vs bottlefeeding suggests that there is, in addition, a confluence of complex factors—medical, socioeconomic, cultural and political—that regularly undermine women's confidence, while reinforcing the notion that feeding their children artificially is about lifestyle rather than health, and that the modern woman's body is simply not up to the task of producing enough milk for its offspring.

"Breastfeeding is a natural negotiation between mother and baby and you interfere with it at your peril," says Professor Mary Renfrew, Director of the Mother and Infant Research Unit, University of York. "But, in the early years of the last century, people were very busy interfering with it. In terms of the ecology of breastfeeding, what you have is a natural habitat that has been disturbed. But it's not just the presence of one big predator—the invention of artificial milk—that is important. It is the fact that the habitat was already weakened by other forces that made it so vulnerable to disaster.

"If you look at medical textbooks from the early part of the 20th century, you'll find many quotes about making breastfeeding scientific and exact, and it's out of these that you can see things beginning to fall apart." This falling apart, says Renfrew, is largely due to the fear and mistrust that science had of the natural process of breastfeeding. In particular, the fact that a mother can put a baby on the breast and do something else while breastfeeding, and have the baby naturally come off the breast when it's had enough, was seen as disorderly and inexact. The medical/scientific model replaced this natural situation with precise measurements—for instance, how many millilitres of milk a baby should ideally have at each sitting—which skewed the natural balance between mother and baby, and established bottlefeeding as a bio-logical norm.

Breastfeeding rates also began to decline as a consequence of women's changed circumstances after World War I, as more women left their children behind to go into the workplace as a consequence of women's emancipation—and the loss of men in the "killing fields"—and to an even larger extent with the advent of World War II, when even more women entered into employ-ment outside of the home.

"There was also the first wave of feminism," says Renfrew, "which stamped into everyone's consciousness in the 60s, and encouraged women get away from their babies and start living their lives. So the one thing that might have helped—women supporting each other—actually created a situation where even the intellectual, engaged, consciously aware women who might have questioned this got lost for a while. As a consequence, we ended up with a widespread and declining confidence in breastfeeding, a declining understand-ing of its importance and a declining ability of health professionals to support it. And, of course, all this ran along the same timeline as the technological development of artificial milk and the free availability of formula."

Medicalised Birth

Before World War II, pregnancy and birth—and, by extension, breastfeeding—were part of the continuum of normal life. Women gave birth at home with the assistance and support of trained midwives, who were themselves part of the community, and afterwards they breastfed with the encouragement of family and friends.

Taking birth out of the community and relocating it into hospitals gave rise to the medicalisation of women's reproductive lives. Life events were transformed into medical problems, and traditional knowledge was replaced with scientific and technological solutions. This medicalisation resulted in a cascade of interventions that deeply undermined women's confidence in their abilities to conceive and grow a healthy baby, give birth to it and then feed it.

The cascade falls something like this: Hospitals are institutions; they are impersonal and, of necessity, must run on schedules and routines. For a hospital to run smoothly, patients must ideally be sedate and immobile. For the woman giving birth, this meant lying on her back in a bed, an unnatural position that made labour slow, unproductive and very much more painful.

To "fix" these iatrogenically dysfunctional labours, doctors developed a range of drugs (usually synthetic hormones such as prostaglandins or syntocinon), technologies (such as forceps and vacuum extraction) and procedures (such as episiotomies) to speed the process up. Speeding up labour artificially made it even more painful and this, in turn, led to the development of an array of pain-relieving drugs. Many of these were so powerful that the mother was often unconscious or deeply sedated at the moment of delivery and, thus, unable to offer her breast to her newborn infant.

All pain-relieving drugs cross the placenta, so even if the mother were conscious, her baby may not have been, or may have been so heavily drugged that its natural rooting instincts (which help it find the nipple) and muscle coordination (necessary to latch properly onto the breast) were severely impaired.

While both mother and baby were recovering from the ordeal of a medicalised birth, they were, until the 1970s and 1980s, routinely separated. Often, the baby wasn't "allowed" to breastfeed until it had a bottle first, in case there was something wrong with its gastrointestinal tract. Breastfeeding, when it took place at all, took place according to strict schedules. These feeding schedules—usually on a three- or four-hourly basis—were totally unnatural for human newborns, who need to feed 12 or more times in any 24-hour period. Babies who were inevitably hungry between feeds were routinely given supplements of water and/or formula.

"There was lots of topping up," says Professor Renfrew. "The way this 'scientific' breastfeeding happened in hospital was that the baby would be given two minutes on each breast on day one, then four minutes on each breast on day two, seven minutes on each on day three, and so on. This created enormous anxiety since the mother would then be watching the clock instead of the baby. The babies would then get topped-up after every feed, then topped-up again throughout the night rather than brought to their mothers to feed. So you had a situation where the babies were crying in the nursery, and the mothers were crying in the postnatal ward. That's what we called 'normal' all throughout the 60s and 70s."

Breastmilk is produced on a supply-and-demand basis, and these topping-up routines, which assuaged infant hunger and lessened demand, also reduced the mother's milk supply. As a result, women at the mercy of institutionalised birth experienced breastfeeding as a frustrating struggle that was often painful and just as often unsuccessful.

When, under these impossible circumstances, breastfeeding "failed," formula was offered as a "nutritionally complete solution" that was also more "modern," "cleaner" and more "socially acceptable."

At least two generations of women have been subjected to these kinds of damaging routines and, as a result, many of today's mothers find the concept of breastfeeding strange and unfamiliar, and very often framed as something that can and frequently does not "take," something they might "have a go" at but, equally, something that they shouldn't feel too badly about if it doesn't work out.

Professional Failures

The same young doctors, nurses and midwives who were pioneering this medical model of reproduction are now running today's health services. So, perhaps not surprisingly, modern hospitals are, at heart, little different from their predecessors. They may have TVs and CD players, and prettier wallpaper, and the drugs may be more sophisticated, but the basic goals and principles of medicalised birth have changed very little in the last 40 years—and the effect on breastfeeding is still as devastating.

In many cases, the healthcare providers' views on infant-feeding are based on their own, highly personal experiences. Surveys show, for instance, that the most important factor influencing the effectiveness and accuracy of a doctor's breastfeeding advice is whether the doctor herself, or the doctor's wife, had breastfed her children. Likewise, a midwife, nurse or health visitor formulated her own children is unlikely to be an effective advocate for breastfeeding.

More worrying, these professionals can end up perpetuating damaging myths about breastfeeding that facilitate its failure. In some hospitals, women are still advised to limit the amount of time, at first, that a baby sucks on each breast, to "toughen up" their nipples. Or they are told their babies get all the milk they "need" in the first 10 minutes and sucking after this time is unnecessary. Some are still told to stick to four-hour feeding schedules. Figures from the UK's Office of National Statistics show that we are still topping babies up. In 2002, nearly 30 per cent of babies in UK hospitals were given supplemental bottles by hospital staff, and nearly 20 percent of all babies were separated from their mothers at some point while in hospital.

Continued inappropriate advice from medical professionals is one reason why, in 1991, UNICEF started the Baby Friendly Hospital Initiative (BFHI)—a certification system for hospitals meeting certain criteria known to promote successful breastfeeding. These criteria include: training all healthcare staff on how to facilitate breastfeeding; helping mothers start breastfeeding within one hour of birth; giving newborn infants no food or drink other than breastmilk, unless medically indicated; and the hospital not accepting free or heavily discounted formula and supplies. In principle, it is an important step in the promotion of breastfeeding, and studies show that women who give birth in Baby Friendly hospitals do breastfeed for longer.

In Scotland, for example, where around 50 per cent of hospitals are rated Baby Friendly, breastfeeding initiation rates have increased dramatically in recent years. In Cuba, where 49 of the country's 56 hospitals and maternity facilities are Baby Friendly, the rate of exclusive breastfeeding at four months almost tripled in six years—from 25 per cent in 1990 to 72 per cent in 1996. Similar increases have been found in Bangladesh, Brazil and China.

Unfortunately, interest in obtaining BFHI status is not universal. In the UK, only 43 hospitals (representing just 16 per cent of all UK hospitals) have achieved full accreditation—and none are in London. Out of the approximately 16,000 hospitals worldwide that have qualified for the Baby Friendly designation, only 32 are in the US. What's more, while Baby Friendly hospitals achieve a high initiation rate, they cannot guarantee continuation of breastfeeding once the woman is back in the community. Even among women who give birth in Baby Friendly hospitals, the number who exclusively breastfeed for six months is unacceptably low.

The Influence of Advertising

Baby Friendly hospitals face a daunting task in combatting the laissez-faire and general ignorance of health professionals, mothers and the public at large. They are also fighting a difficult battle with an acquiescent media which, through politically correct editorialising aimed at assuaging mothers' guilt if they bottlefeed and, more influentially, through advertising, has helped redefine formula as an acceptable choice.

Although there are now stricter limitations on the advertising of infant formula, for years, manufacturers were able, through advertising and promotion, to define the issue of infant-feeding in both the scientific world (for instance, by providing doctors with growth charts that established the growth patterns of bottlefed babies as the norm) and in its wider social context, reframing perceptions of what is appropriate and what is not.

As a result, in the absence of communities of women talking to each other about pregnancy, birthing and mothering, women's choices today are more directly influenced by commercial leaflets, booklets and advertising than almost anything else.

Baby-milk manufacturers spend countless millions devising marketing strategies that keep their products at the forefront of public consciousness. In the UK, formula companies spend at least £12 million per year on booklets, leaflets and other promotions, often in the guise of "educational materials." This works out at approximately £20 per baby born. In contrast, the UK government spends about 14 pence per newborn each year to promote breastfeeding.

It's a pattern of inequity that is repeated throughout the world—and not just in the arena of infant-feeding. The food-industry's global advertising budget is $40 billion, a figure greater than the gross domestic product (GDP) of 70 per cent of the world's nations. For every $1 spent by the WHO on preventing the diseases caused by Western diets, more than $500 is spent by the food industry to promote such diets.

Since they can no longer advertise infant formulas directly to women (for instance, in mother and baby magazines or through direct leafleting), or hand out free samples in hospitals or clinics, manufacturers have started to exploit other outlets, such as mother and baby clubs, and Internet sites that purport to help busy mothers get all the information they need about infant-feeding. They also occasionally rely on subterfuge. Manufacturers are allowed to advertise follow-on milks, suitable for babies over six months, to parents. But, sometimes, these ads feature a picture of a much younger baby, implying the product's suitability for infants.

The impact of these types of promotions should not be underestimated. A 2005 NCT/UNICEF study in the UK determined that one third of British mothers who admitted to seeing formula advertisements in the previous six months believed that infant formula was as good or better than breastmilk. This revelation is all the more surprising since advertising of infant formula to mothers has been banned for many years in several countries, including the UK.

To get around restrictions that prevent direct advertising to parents, manufacturers use a number of psychological strategies that focus on the natural worries that new parents have about the health of their babies. Many of today's formulas, for instance, are conceived and sold as solutions to the "medical" problems of infants such as lactose intolerance, incomplete digestion and being "too hungry"—even though many of these problems can be caused by inappropriately giving cow's milk formula in the first place.

The socioeconomic divide among breastfeeding mothers is also exploited by formula manufacturers, as targeting low-income women (with advertising as well as through welfare schemes) has proven very profitable.

When presented with the opportunity to provide their children with the best that science has to offer, many low-income mothers are naturally tempted by formula. This is especially true if they receive free samples, as is still the case in many developing countries.

But the supply-and-demand nature of breastmilk is such that, once a mother accepts these free samples and starts her baby on formula, her own milk supply will quickly dry up. Sadly, after these mothers run out of formula samples and money-off coupons, they will find themselves unable to produce breastmilk and have no option but to spend large sums of money on continuing to feed their child with formula.

Even when manufacturers "promote" breastfeeding, they plant what Mary Smale calls "seeds of conditionality" that can lead to failure. Several years ago, manufacturers used to produce these amazing leaflets for women, encouraging women to breastfeed and reassuring them that they only need a few extra calories a day. You couldn't fault them on the words, but the pictures which were of things like Marks & Spencer yoghurt and whole fish with their heads on, and wholemeal bread—but not the sort of wholemeal bread that you buy in the corner shop, the sort of wholemeal bread you buy in specialist shops.

The underlying message was clear: a healthy pregnancy and a good supply of breastmilk are the preserve of the middle classes, and that any women who doesn't belong to that group will have to rely on other resources to provide for her baby.

A quick skim through any pregnancy magazine or the "Bounty" pack—the glossy information booklet with free product samples given to new mothers in the UK—shows that these subtle visual messages, which include luxurious photos of whole grains and pulses, artistically arranged bowls of muesli, artisan loaves of bread and wedges of deli-style cheeses, exotic mangoes, grapes and kiwis, and fresh vegetables artistically arranged as crudités, are still prevalent.

Funding Research

Manufacturers also ply their influence through contact with health professionals (to whom they can provide free samples for research and "educational purposes") as middlemen. Free gifts, educational trips to exotic locations and funding for research are just some of the ways in which the medical profession becomes "educated" about the benefits of formula.

According to Patti Rundall, OBE, policy director for the UK's Baby Milk Action group, which has been lobbying for responsible marketing of baby food for over 20 years, "Throughout the last two decades, the baby-feeding companies have tried to establish a strong role for themselves with the medical profession, knowing that health and education services represent a key marketing opportunity. Companies are, for instance, keen to fund the infant-feeding research on which health policies are based, and to pay for midwives, teachers, education materials and community projects."

They are also keen to fund "critical" NGOs—that is, lay groups whose mandate is to inform and support women. But this sort of funding is not allowed by the International Code of Marketing of Breastmilk Substitutes (see below) because it prejudices the ability of these organisations to provide mothers with independent information about infant feeding. Nevertheless, such practices remain prevalent—if somewhat more discreet than in the past—and continue to weaken health professionals' advocacy for breastfeeding.

Fighting Back

When it became clear that declining breastfeeding rates were affecting infant health and that the advertising of infant formula had a direct effect on a woman's decision not to breastfeed, the International Code of Marketing of Breastmilk Substitutes was drafted and eventually adopted by the World Health Assembly (WHA) in 1981. The vote was near-unanimous, with 118 member nations voting in favour, three abstaining and one—the US—voting against. (In 1994, after years of opposition, the US eventually joined every other developed nation in the world as a signatory to the Code.)

The Code is a unique instrument that promotes safe and adequate nutrition for infants on a global scale by trying to protect breastfeeding and ensuring the appropriate marketing of breastmilk substitutes. It applies to all products marketed as partial or total replacements for breastmilk, including infant formula, follow-on formula, special formulas, cereals, juices, vegetable mixes and baby teas, and also applies to feeding bottles and teats. In addition, it maintains that no infant food may be marketed in ways that undermine breastfeeding. Specifically, the Code:

- Bans all advertising or promotion of these products to the general public
- Bans samples and gifts to mothers and health workers
- Requires information materials to advocate for breastfeeding, to warn against bottlefeeding and to not contain pictures of babies or text that idealises the use of breastmilk substitutes
- Bans the use of the healthcare system to promote breastmilk substitutes
- Bans free or low-cost supplies of breastmilk substitutes
- Allows health professionals to receive samples, but only for research purposes
- Demands that product information be factual and scientific
- Bans sales incentives for breastmilk substitutes and direct contact with mothers
- Requires that labels inform fully on the correct use of infant formula and the risks of misuse
- Requires labels not to discourage breastfeeding.

This document probably couldn't have been created today. Since the founding of the World Trade Organization (WTO) and its "free trade" ethos in 1995, the increasing sophistication of corporate power strategies and aggressive lobbying of health organisations has increased to the extent that the Code would have been binned long before it reached the voting stage.

However, in 1981, member states, corporations and NGOs were on a somewhat more equal footing. By preventing industry from advertising infant formula, giving out free samples, promoting their products in healthcare facilities or by way of mother-and-baby "goody bags," and insisting on better labelling, the Code acts to regulate an industry that would otherwise be given a free hand to peddle an inferior food product to babies and infants.

Unfortunately . . .

Being a signatory to the Code does not mean that member countries are obliged to adopt its recommendations wholesale. Many countries, the UK included, have adopted only parts of it—for instance, the basic principle that breastfeeding is a good thing—while ignoring the nuts-and-bolts strategies that limit advertising and corporate contact with mothers. So, in the UK, infant formula for "healthy babies" can be advertised to mothers through hospitals and clinics, though not via the media.

What's more, formula manufacturers for their part continue to argue that the Code is too restrictive and that it stops them from fully exploiting their target markets. Indeed, Helmut Maucher, a powerful corporate lobbyist and honorary chairman of Nestlé—the company that claims 40 per cent of the global baby-food market—has gone on record as saying: "Ethical decisions that injure a firm's ability to compete are actually immoral."

And make no mistake, these markets are big. The UK baby milk market is worth £150 million per year and the US market around $2 billion. The world-wide market for baby milks and foods is a staggering $17 billion and growing by 12 per cent each year. From formula manufacturers' point of view, the more women breastfeed, the more profit is lost. It is estimated that, for every child exclusively breastfed for six months, an average of $450 worth of infant food will not be bought. On a global scale, that amounts to billions of dollars in lost profits.

What particularly worries manufacturers is that, if they accept the Code without a fight, it could set a dangerous precedent for other areas of international trade—for instance, the pharmaceutical, tobacco, food and agriculture industries, and oil companies. This is why the focus on infant-feeding has been diverted away from children's health and instead become a symbolic struggle for a free market.

While most manufacturers publicly agree to adhere to the Code, privately, they deploy enormous resources in constructing ways to reinterpret or get round it. In this endeavour, Nestlé has shown a defiance and tenacity that beggars belief.

In India, for example, Nestlé lobbied against the Code being entered into law and when, after the law was passed, it faced criminal charges over its labelling, it issued a writ petition against the Indian government rather than accept the charges.

Years of aggressive actions like this, combined with unethical advertising and marketing practices, has led to an ongoing campaign to boycott the company's products that stretches back to 1977.

The Achilles' heel of the Code is that it does not provide for a monitoring office. This concept was in the original draft, but was removed from subsequent drafts. Instead, monitoring of the Code has been left to "governments acting individually and collectively through the World Health Organization."

But, over the last 25 years, corporate accountability has slipped lower down on the UN agenda, far behind free trade, self-regulation and partnerships. Lack of government monitoring means that small and comparatively poorly funded groups like the International Baby Food Action Network (IBFAN), which has 200 member groups working in over 100 countries, have taken on the job of monitoring Code violations almost by default. But while these watchdog groups can monitor and report Code violations to the health authorities, they cannot stop them.

In 2004, IBFAN's bi-annual report *Breaking the Rules, Stretching the Rules*, analysed the promotional practices of 16 international baby-food companies, and 14 bottle and teat companies, between January 2002 and April 2004. The researchers found some 2,000 violations of the Code in 69 countries.

On a global scale, reinterpreting the Code to suit marketing strategies is rife, and Nestlé continues to be the leader of the pack. According to IBFAN, Nestlé believes that only one of its products—infant formula—comes within the scope of the Code. The company also denies the universality of the Code, insisting that it only applies to developing nations. Where Nestlé, and the Infant Food Manufacturers Association that it dominates, leads, other companies have followed, and when companies like Nestlé are caught breaking the

Code, the strategy is simple, but effective—initiate complex and boring discussions with organisations at WHO or WHA level about how best to interpret the Code in the hopes that these will offset any bad publicity and divert attention from the harm caused by these continual infractions.

According to Patti Rundall, it's important not to let such distractions divert attention from the bottom line: "There can be no food more locally produced, more sustainable or more environmentally friendly than a mother's breastmilk, the only food required by an infant for the first six months of life. It is a naturally renewable resource, which requires no packaging or transport, results in no wastage and is free. Breastfeeding can also help reduce family poverty, which is a major cause of malnutrition."

So perhaps we should be further simplifying the debate by asking: Are the companies who promote infant formula as the norm simply clever entrepreneurs doing their jobs or human-rights violators of the worst kind?

Not Good Enough

After more than two decades, it is clear that a half-hearted advocacy of breast-feeding benefits multinational formula manufacturers, not mothers and babies, and that the baby-food industry has no intention of complying with UN recommendations on infant-feeding or with the principles of the International Code for Marketing of Breastmilk Substitutes—unless they are forced to do so by law or consumer pressure or, more effectively, both.

Women do not fail to breastfeed. Health professionals, health agencies and governments fail to educate and support women who want to breastfeed.

Without support, many women will give up when they encounter even small difficulties. And yet, according to Mary Renfrew, "Giving up breastfeeding is not something that women do lightly. They don't just stop breastfeeding and walk away from it. Many of them fight very hard to continue it and they fight with no support. These women are fighting society—a society that is not just bottle-friendly, but is deeply breastfeeding-unfriendly."

To reverse this trend, governments all over the world must begin to take seriously the responsibility of ensuring the good health of future generations. To do this requires deep and profound social change. We must stop harassing mothers with simplistic "breast is best" messages and put time, energy and money into reeducating health professionals and society at large.

We must also stop making compromises. Government health policies such as, say, in the UK and US, which aim for 75 per cent of women to be breastfeeding on hospital discharge, are little more than paying lip service to the importance of breastfeeding.

Most of these women will stop breastfeeding within a few weeks, and such policies benefit no one except the formula manufacturers, who will start making money the moment breastfeeding stops.

To get all mothers breastfeeding, we must be prepared to:

- Ban all advertising of formula including follow-on milks
- Ban all free samples of formula, even those given for educational or study purposes

- Require truthful and prominent health warnings on all tins and cartons of infant formula
- Put substantial funding into promoting breastfeeding in every community, especially among the socially disadvantaged, with a view to achieving 100-per-cent exclusive breastfeeding for the first six months of life
- Fund advertising and education campaigns that target fathers, mothers-in-law, schoolchildren, doctors, midwives and the general public
- Give women who wish to breastfeed in public the necessary encouragement and approval
- Make provisions for all women who are in employment to take at least six months paid leave after birth, without fear of losing their jobs.

Such strategies have already proven their worth elsewhere. In 1970, breast-feeding rates in Scandinavia were as low as those in Britain. Then, one by one, the Scandinavian countries banned all advertising of artificial formula milk, offered a year's maternity leave with 80 per cent of pay and, on the mother's return to work, an hour's breastfeeding break every day. Today, 98 per cent of Scandinavian women initiate breastfeeding, and 94 per cent are still breastfeeding at one month, 81 per cent at two months, 69 per cent at four months and 42 per cent at six months. These rates, albeit still not optimal, are nevertheless the highest in the world, and the result of a concerted, multifaceted approach to promoting breastfeeding.

Given all that we know of the benefits of breastfeeding and the dangers of formula milk, it is simply not acceptable that we have allowed breastfeeding rates in the UK and elsewhere in the world to decline so disastrously.

The goal is clear—100 per cent of mothers should be exclusively breast-feeding for at least the first six months of their babies' lives.

Hanna Rosin

The Case Against Breast-Feeding

One afternoon at the playground last summer, shortly after the birth of my third child, I made the mistake of idly musing about breast-feeding to a group of new mothers I'd just met. This time around, I said, I was considering cutting it off after a month or so. At this remark, the air of insta-friendship we had established cooled into an icy politeness, and the mothers shortly wandered away to chase little Emma or Liam onto the slide. Just to be perverse, over the next few weeks I tried this experiment again several more times. The reaction was always the same: circles were redrawn such that I ended up in the class of mom who, in a pinch, might feed her baby mashed-up Chicken McNuggets.

In my playground set, the urban moms in their tight jeans and over-size sunglasses size each other up using a whole range of signifiers: organic content of snacks, sleekness of stroller, ratio of tasteful wooden toys to plastic. But breast-feeding is the real ticket into the club. My mother friends love to exchange stories about subversive ways they used to sneak frozen breast milk through airline security (it's now legal), or about the random brutes on the street who don't approve of breast-feeding in public. When Angelina Jolie wanted to secure her status as America's ur-mother, she posed on the cover of *W* magazine nursing one of her twins. Alt-rocker Pete Wentz recently admitted that he tasted his wife, Ashlee Simpson's, breast milk ("soury" and "weird"), after bragging that they have a lot of sex—both of which must have seemed to him markers of a cool domestic existence.

From the moment a new mother enters the obstetrician's waiting room, she is subjected to the upper-class parents' jingle: "Breast Is Best." Parenting magazines offer "23 Great Nursing Tips," warnings on "Nursing Roadblocks," and advice on how to find your local lactation consultant (note to the child-less: yes, this is an actual profession, and it's thriving). Many of the stories are accompanied by suggestions from the ubiquitous parenting guru Dr. William Sears, whose Web site hosts a comprehensive list of the benefits of mother's milk. "Brighter Brains" sits at the top: "I.Q. scores averaging seven to ten points higher!" (Sears knows his audience well.) The list then moves on to the dangers averted, from infancy on up: fewer ear infections, allergies, stomach illnesses; lower rates of obesity, diabetes, heart disease. Then it adds, for good measure, stool with a "buttermilk-like odor" and "nicer skin"—benefits, in short, "more far-reaching than researchers have even dared to imagine."

In 2005, *Babytalk* magazine won a National Magazine Award for an article called "You *Can* Breastfeed." Given the prestige of the award, I had hoped the article might provide some respite from the relentlessly cheerful tip culture of the parenting magazines, and fill mothers in on the real problems with nursing. Indeed, the article opens with a promisingly realistic vignette, featuring a theoretical "You" cracking under the strain of having to breast-feed around the clock, suffering "crying jags" and cursing at your husband. But fear not, You. The root of the problem is not the sudden realization that your ideal of an equal marriage, with two parents happily taking turns working and raising children, now seems like a farce. It turns out to be quite simple: You just haven't quite figured out how to fit "Part A into Part B." Try the "C-hold" with your baby and some "rapid arm movement," the story suggests. Even Dr. Sears pitches in: "Think 'fish lips,'" he offers.

In the days after my first child was born, I welcomed such practical advice. I remember the midwife coming to my hospital bed and shifting my arm here, and the baby's head there, and then everything falling into place. But after three children and 28 months of breast-feeding (and counting), the insistent cheerleading has begun to grate. Buttermilk-like odor? Now Dr. Sears is selling me too hard. I may have put in fewer parenting years than he has, but I do have *some* perspective. And when I look around my daughter's second-grade class, I can't seem to pick out the unfortunate ones: "Oh, poor little Sophie, whose mother couldn't breast-feed. What dim eyes she has. What a sickly pallor. And already sprouting acne!"

I dutifully breast-fed each of my first two children for the full year that the American Academy of Pediatrics recommends. I have experienced what the *Babytalk* story calls breast-feeding-induced "maternal nirvana." This time around, *nirvana* did not describe my state of mind; I was launching a new Web site and I had two other children to care for, and a husband I would occasionally like to talk to. Being stuck at home breast-feeding as he walked out the door for work just made me unreasonably furious, at him and everyone else.

In Betty Friedan's day, feminists felt shackled to domesticity by the unreasonably high bar for housework, the endless dusting and shopping and pushing the Hoover around—a vacuum cleaner being the obligatory prop for the "happy housewife heroine," as Friedan sardonically called her. When I looked at the picture on the cover of Sears's *Breastfeeding Book*—a lady lying down, gently smiling at her baby and *still in her robe*, although the sun is well up—the scales fell from my eyes: it was not the vacuum that was keeping me and my 21st-century sisters down, but another sucking sound.

Still, despite my stint as the postpartum playground crank, I could not bring myself to stop breast-feeding—too many years of Sears's conditioning, too many playground spies. So I was left feeling trapped, like many women before me, in the middle-class mother's prison of vague discontent: surly but too privileged for pity, breast-feeding with one hand while answering the cell phone with the other, and barking at my older kids to get their own organic, 100 percent juice—the modern, multitasking mother's version of Friedan's "problem that has no name."

And in this prison I would have stayed, if not for a chance sighting. One day, while nursing my baby in my pediatrician's office, I noticed a 2001 issue of the *Journal of the American Medical Association* open to an article about breast-feeding: "Conclusions: There are inconsistent associations among breastfeeding, its duration, and the risk of being overweight in young children." Inconsistent? There I was, sitting half-naked in public for the tenth time that day, the hundredth time that month, the millionth time in my life—and the associations were *inconsistent*? The seed was planted. That night, I did what any sleep-deprived, slightly paranoid mother of a newborn would do. I called my doctor friend for her password to an online medical library, and then sat up and read dozens of studies examining breast-feeding's association with allergies, obesity, leukemia, mother-infant bonding, intelligence, and all the Dr. Sears highlights.

After a couple of hours, the basic pattern became obvious: the medical literature looks nothing like the popular literature. It shows that breast-feeding is probably, maybe, a *little* better; but it is far from the stampede of evidence that Sears describes. More like tiny, unsure baby steps: two forward, two back, with much meandering and bumping into walls. A couple of studies will show fewer allergies, and then the next one will turn up no difference. Same with mother-infant bonding, IQ, leukemia, cholesterol, diabetes. Even where consensus is mounting, the meta studies—reviews of existing studies—consistently complain about biases, missing evidence, and other major flaws in study design. "The studies do not demonstrate a universal phenomenon, in which one method is superior to another in all instances," concluded one of the first, and still one of the broadest, meta studies, in a 1984 issue of *Pediatrics*, "and they do not support making a mother feel that she is doing psychological harm to her child if she is unable or unwilling to breastfeed." Twenty-five years later, the picture hasn't changed all that much. So how is it that every mother I know has become a breast-feeding fascist?

Like many babies of my generation, I was never breast-fed. My parents were working-class Israelis, living in Tel Aviv in the '70s and aspiring to be modern. In the U.S., people were already souring on formula and passing out No NESTLÉ buttons, but in Israel, Nestlé formula was the latest thing. My mother had already ditched her fussy Turkish coffee for Nescafé (just mix with water), and her younger sister would soon be addicted to NesQuik. Transforming soft, sandy grains from solid to magic liquid must have seemed like the forward thing to do. Plus, my mom believed her pediatrician when he said that it was important to precisely measure a baby's food intake and stick to a schedule. (To this day she pesters me about whether I'm *sure* my breast-fed babies are getting enough to eat; the parenting magazines would classify her as "unsupportive" and warn me to stay away.) Formula grew out of a late-19th-century effort to combat atrocious rates of infant mortality by turning infant feeding into a controlled science. Pediatrics was then a newly minted profession, and for the next century, the men who dominated it would constantly try to get mothers to welcome "enlightenment from the laboratory," writes Ann Hulbert in *Raising America*. But now and again, mothers would fight back. In the U.S., the rebellion against formula began in the late '50s, when a group of moms from the Chicago suburbs got together to form a breast-feeding support group they called La Leche League. They were Catholic mothers, influenced by the Christian Family Movement, who spoke of breast-feeding as "God's plan for mothers and babies." Their role model was the biblical Eve ("Her baby came. The milk came. She nursed her baby," they wrote in their first, pamphlet edition of *The Womanly Art of Breastfeeding*, published in 1958).

They took their league's name, La Leche, from a shrine to the Madonna near Jacksonville, Florida, called Nuestra Señora de La Leche y Buen Parto, which loosely translates into "Our Lady of Happy Delivery and Plentiful Milk." A more forthright name was deemed inappropriate: "You didn't mention *breast* in print unless you were talking about Jean Harlow," said co-founder Edwina Froehlich. In their photos, the women of La Leche wear practical pumps and high-neck housewife dresses, buttoned to the top. They saw themselves as a group of women who were "kind of thinking crazy," said co-founder Mary Ann Cahill. "Everything we did was radical."

La Leche League mothers rebelled against the notion of mother as lab assistant, mixing formula for the specimen under her care. Instead, they aimed to "bring mother and baby together again." An illustration in the second edition shows a woman named Eve—looking not unlike Jean Harlow—exposed to the waist and caressing her baby, with no doctor hovering nearby. Over time the group adopted a feminist edge. A 1972 publication rallies mothers to have "confidence in themselves and their sisters rather than passively following the advice of licensed professionals." As one woman wrote in another league publication, "Yes, I want to be liberated! I want to be free! I want to be free to be a woman!"

In 1971, the Boston Women's Health Book Collective published *Our Bodies, Ourselves*, launching a branch of feminism known as the women's-health movement. The authors were more groovy types than the La Leche League moms; they wore slouchy jeans, clogs, and bandanas holding back waist-length hair. But the two movements had something in common; *Our Bodies* also grew out of "frustration and anger" with a medical establishment that was "condescending, paternalistic, judgmental and non-informative." Teaching women about their own bodies would make them "more self-confident, more autonomous, stronger," the authors wrote. Breasts were not things for men to whistle and wink at; they were made for women to feed their babies in a way that was "sensual and fulfilling." The book also noted, in passing, that breast-feeding could "strengthen the infant's resistance to infection and disease"—an early hint of what would soon become the national obsession with breast milk as liquid vaccine.

Pediatricians have been scrutinizing breast milk since the late 1800s. But the public didn't pay much attention until an international scandal in the '70s over "killer baby bottles." Studies in South America and Africa showed that babies who were fed formula instead of breast milk were more likely to die. The mothers, it turned out, were using contaminated water or rationing formula because it was so expensive. Still, in the U.S., the whole episode turned breast-feeding advocates and formula makers into Crips and Bloods, and introduced the take-no-prisoners turf war between them that continues to this day.

Some of the magical thinking about breast-feeding stems from a common misconception. Even many doctors believe that breast milk is full of maternal antibodies that get absorbed into the baby's bloodstream, says Sydney Spiesel, a clinical professor of pediatrics at Yale University's School of Medicine. That is how it works for most mammals. But in humans, the process is more pedestrian, and less powerful. A human baby is born with antibodies already in place, having absorbed them from the placenta. Breast milk dumps another layer of antibodies, primarily secretory IgA, directly into the baby's gastrointestinal tract. As the baby is nursing, these extra antibodies provide some added protection against infection, but they never get into the blood.

Since the identification of sIgA, in 1961, labs have hunted for other marvels. Could the oligosaccharides in milk prevent diarrhea? Do the fatty acids boost brain development? The past few decades have turned up many promising leads, hypotheses, and theories, all suggestive and nifty but never confirmed in the lab. Instead, most of the claims about breast-feeding's benefits lean on research conducted outside the lab: comparing one group of infants being breast-fed against another being breast-fed less, or not at all. Thousands of such studies have been published, linking breast-feeding with healthier, happier, smarter children. But they all share one glaring flaw.

An ideal study would randomly divide a group of mothers, tell one half to breast-feed and the other not to, and then measure the outcomes. But researchers cannot ethically tell mothers what to feed their babies. Instead they have to settle for "observational" studies. These simply look for differences in two populations, one breast-fed and one not. The problem is, breast-fed infants are typically brought up in very different families from those raised on the bottle. In the U.S., breast-feeding is on the rise—69 percent of mothers initiate the practice at the hospital, and 17 percent nurse exclusively for at least six months. But the numbers are much higher among women who are white, older, and educated; a woman who attended college, for instance, is roughly twice as likely to nurse for six months. Researchers try to factor out all these "confounding variables" that might affect the babies' health and development. But they still can't know if they've missed some critical factor. "Studies about the benefits of breast-feeding are extremely difficult and complex because of who breast-feeds and who doesn't," says Michael Kramer, a highly respected researcher at McGill University. "There have been claims that it prevents everything—cancer, diabetes. A reasonable person would be cautious about every new amazing discovery."

The study about obesity I saw in my pediatrician's office that morning is a good example of the complexity of breast-feeding research—and of the pitfalls it contains. Some studies have found a link between nursing and slimmer kids, but they haven't proved that one causes the other. This study surveyed 2,685 children between the ages of 3 and 5. After adjusting for race, parental education, maternal smoking, and other factors—all of which are thought to affect a child's risk of obesity—the study found little correlation between breast-feeding and weight. Instead, the strongest predictor of the child's weight was the mother's. Whether obese mothers nursed or used formula, their children were more likely to be heavy. The breast-feeding advocates' dream—that something in the milk somehow reprograms appetite—is still a long shot.

In the past decade, researchers have come up with ever more elaborate ways to tease out the truth. One 2005 paper focused on 523 sibling pairs who were fed differently, and its results put a big question mark over all the previous research. The economists Eirik Evenhouse and Siobhan Reilly compared rates of diabetes, asthma, and allergies; childhood weight; various measures of mother-child bonding; and levels of intelligence. Almost all the differences turned out to be statistically insignificant. For the most part, the "long-term effects of breast feeding have been overstated," they wrote.

Nearly all the researchers I talked to pointed me to a series of studies designed by Kramer, published starting in 2001. Kramer followed 17,000 infants born in Belarus throughout their childhoods. He came up with a clever way to randomize his study, at least somewhat, without doing anything unethical. He took mothers who had already started nursing, and then subjected half of them to an intervention strongly encouraging them to nurse exclusively for several months. The intervention worked: many women nursed longer as a result. And extended breast-feeding did reduce the risk of a gastrointestinal infection by 40 percent. This result seems to be consistent with the protection that sIgA provides; in real life, it adds up to about four out of 100 babies having one less incident of diarrhea or vomiting. Kramer also noted some reduction in infant rashes. Otherwise, his studies found very few significant differences: none, for instance, in weight, blood pressure, ear infections, or allergies—some of the most commonly cited benefits in the breast-feeding literature.

Both the Kramer study and the sibling study did turn up one interesting finding: a bump in "cognitive ability" among breast-fed children. But intelligence is tricky to measure, because it's subjective and affected by so many factors. Other recent studies, particularly those that have factored out the mother's IQ, have found no difference at all between breast-fed and formula-fed babies. In Kramer's study, the mean scores varied widely and mysteriously from clinic to clinic. What's more, the connection he found "could be banal," he told me—simply the result of "breast-feeding mothers' interacting more with their babies, rather than of anything in the milk."

The IQ studies run into the central problem of breast-feeding research: it is impossible to separate a mother's decision to breast-feed—and everything that goes along with it—from the breast-feeding itself. Even sibling studies can't get around this problem. With her first child, for instance, a mother may be extra cautious, keeping the neighbor's germy brats away and slapping the nurse who gives out the free formula sample. By her third child, she may no longer breast-feed—giving researchers the sibling comparison that they crave—but many other things may have changed as well. Maybe she is now using day care, exposing the baby to more illnesses. Surely she is not noticing that kid No.2 has the baby's pacifier in his mouth, or that the cat is sleeping in the crib (trust me on this one). She is also not staring lovingly into the baby's eyes all day, singing songs, reading book after infant book, because she has to make sure that the other two kids are not drowning each other in the tub. On paper, the three siblings are equivalent, but their experiences are not.

What does all the evidence add up to? We have clear indications that breast-feeding helps prevent an extra incident of gastrointestinal illness in some kids—an unpleasant few days of diarrhea or vomiting, but rarely life-threatening in developed countries. We have murky correlations with a whole bunch of long-term conditions. The evidence on IQs is intriguing but not all that compelling, and at best suggests a small advantage, perhaps five points; an individual kid's IQ score can vary that much from test to test or day to day. If a child is disadvantaged in other ways, this bump might make a difference. But for the kids in my playground set, the ones whose mothers obsess about breast-feeding, it gets lost in a wash of Baby Einstein videos, piano lessons, and the rest. And in any case, if a breast-feeding mother is miserable, or stressed out, or alienated by nursing, as many women are, if her marriage is under stress and breast-feeding is making things worse, surely that can have a greater effect on a kid's future success than a few IQ points.

So overall, yes, breast is probably best. But not so much better that formula deserves the label of "public health menace," alongside smoking. Given what we know so far, it seems reasonable to put breast-feeding's health benefits on the plus side of the ledger and other things—modesty, independence, career, sanity—on the minus side, and then tally them up and make a decision. But in this risk-averse age of parenting, that's not how it's done.

In the early '90s, a group of researchers got together to revise the American Academy of Pediatrics' policy statement on breast-feeding. They were of the generation that had fought the formula wars and had lived through the days when maternity wards automatically gave women hormone shots to stop the flow of breast milk. The academy had long encouraged mothers to make "every effort" to nurse their newborns, but the researchers felt the medical evidence justified a stronger statement. Released in 1997, the new policy recommended exclusive breast-feeding for six months, followed by six more months of partial breast-feeding, supplemented with other foods. The National Organization for Women complained that this would tax working mothers, but to no avail. "The fact that the major pediatric group in the country was taking a definitive stance made all the difference," recalls Lawrence Gartner, a pediatrician and neonatologist at the University of Chicago, and the head of the committee that made the change. "After that, every major organization turned the corner, and the popular media changed radically."

In 2004, the Department of Health and Human Services launched the National Breastfeeding Awareness Campaign. The ads came out just after my second child was born, and were so odious that they nearly caused me to wean him on the spot. One television ad shows two hugely pregnant women in a logrolling contest, with an audience egging them on. "You wouldn't take risks before your baby is born," reads the caption. "Why start after?" The screen then flashes: "Breastfeed exclusively for 6 months." A second spot shows a pregnant woman—this time African American—riding a mechanical bull in a bar while trying to hold on to her huge belly. She falls off the bull and the crowd moans.

To convey the idea that failing to breast-feed is harmful to a baby's health, the print ads show ordinary objects arranged to look like breasts: two dandelions (respiratory illness), two scoops of ice cream with cherries on top (obesity), two otoscopes (ear infections). Plans were made to do another ad showing rubber nipples on top of insulin syringes (suggesting that bottle-feeding causes diabetes), but then someone thought better of it. The whole campaign is so knowing, so dripping with sexual innuendo and condescension, that it brings to mind nothing so much as an episode of *Mad Men*, where Don Draper and the boys break out the whiskey at day's end to toast another victory over the enemy sex.

What's most amazing is how, 50 years after La Leche League's founding, "enlightenment from the laboratory"—judgmental and absolutist—has triumphed again. The seventh edition of *The Womanly Art*, published in 2004, has ballooned to more than 400 pages, and is filled with photographs in place of the original hand drawings. But what's most noticeable is the shift in attitude. Each edition of the book contains new expert testimony about breast milk as an "arsenal against illness." "The resistance to disease that human milk affords a baby cannot be duplicated in any other way," the authors scold. The experience of reading the 1958 edition is like talking with your bossy but charming neighbor, who has some motherly advice to share. Reading the latest edition is like being trapped in the office of a doctor who's haranguing you about the choices you make.

In her critique of the awareness campaign, Joan Wolf, a women's-studies professor at Texas A&M University, chalks up the overzealous ads to a new ethic of "total motherhood." Mothers these days are expected to "optimize every dimension of children's lives," she writes. Choices are often presented as the mother's selfish desires versus the baby's needs. As an example, Wolf quotes *What to Expect When You're Expecting*, from a section called the "Best-Odds Diet," which I remember quite well: "Every bite counts. You've got only nine months of meals and snacks with which to give your baby the best possible start in life. . . . Before you close your mouth on a forkful of food, consider, 'Is this the best bite I can give my baby?' If it will benefit your baby, chew away. If it'll only benefit your sweet tooth or appease your appetite put your fork down." To which any self-respecting pregnant woman should respond: "I am carrying 35 extra pounds and my ankles have swelled to the size of a life raft, and now I would like to eat some coconut-cream pie. So you know what you can do with this damned fork."

About [eight] years ago, I met a woman from Montreal, the sister-in-law of a friend, who was young and healthy and normal in every way, except that she refused to breast-feed her children. She wasn't working at the time. She just felt that breast-feeding would set up an unequal dynamic in her marriage—one in which the mother, who was responsible for the very sustenance of the infant, would naturally become responsible for everything else as well. At the time, I had only one young child, so I thought she was a kooky Canadian—and selfish and irresponsible. But of course now I know she was right. I recalled her with sisterly love a few months ago, at three in the morning, when I was propped up in bed for the second time that night with my new baby (note the *my*). My husband acknowledged the ripple in the nighttime peace with a grunt, and that's about it. And why should he do more? There's no use in both of us being a wreck in the morning. Nonetheless, it's hard not to seethe.

The Bitch in the House, published in 2002, reframed *The Feminine Mystique* for my generation of mothers. We were raised to expect that co-parenting was an attainable goal. But who were we kidding? Even in the best of marriages, the domestic burden shifts, in incremental, mostly unacknowledged ways, onto the woman. Breast-feeding plays a central role in the shift. In my set, no husband tells his wife that it is her womanly duty to stay home and nurse the child. Instead, both parents together weigh the evidence and then make a rational, informed decision that she should do so. Then other, logical decisions follow: she alone fed the child, so she naturally knows better how to comfort the child, so she is the better judge to pick a school for the child and the better nurse when the child is sick, and so on. Recently, my husband and I noticed that we had reached the age at which friends from high school and college now hold positions of serious power. When we went down the list, we had to work hard to find any women. Where had all our female friends strayed? Why had they disappeared during the years they'd had small children?

The debate about breast-feeding takes place without any reference to its actual context in women's lives. Breast-feeding exclusively is not like taking a prenatal vitamin. It is a serious time commitment that pretty much guarantees that you will not work in any meaningful way. Let's say a baby feeds seven times a day and then a couple more times at night. That's nine times for about a half hour each, which adds up to more than half of a working day, every day, for at least six months. This is why, when people say that breast-feeding is "free," I want to hit them with a two-by-four. It's only free if a woman's time is worth nothing.

That brings us to the subject of pumping. Explain to your employer that while you're away from your baby, "you will need to take breaks throughout the day to pump your milk," suggest the materials from the awareness campaign. Demand a "clean, quiet place" to pump, and a place to store the milk. A clean, quiet place. So peaceful, so spa-like. Leave aside the preposterousness of this advice if you are, say, a waitress or a bus driver. Say you are a newspaper reporter, like I used to be, and deadline is approaching. Your choices are (a) leave your story to go down to the dingy nurse's office and relieve yourself; or (b) grow increasingly panicked and sweaty as your body continues on its merry, milk-factory way, even though the plant shouldn't be operating today and the pump is about to explode. And then one day, the inevitable will happen. You will be talking to a male colleague and saying to yourself, "Don't think of the baby. Please don't think of the baby." And then the pump *will* explode, and the stigmata will spread down your shirt as you rush into the ladies' room.

[In 2009] I had two friends whose babies could not breast-feed for one reason or another, so they mostly had to pump. They were both first-time mothers who had written themselves dreamy birth plans involving hot baths followed by hours of intimate nursing. When that didn't work out, they panicked about their babies' missing out on the milky elixir. One of them sat on my couch the other day hooked up to tubes and suctions and a giant deconstructed bra, looking like some fetish ad, or a footnote from the Josef Mengele years. Looking as far as humanly possible from Eve in her natural, feminine state.

In his study on breast-feeding and cognitive development, Michael Kramer mentions research on the long-term effects of mother rats' licking and grooming their pups. Maybe, he writes, it's "the physical and/or emotional act of breastfeeding" that might lead to benefits. This is the theory he prefers, he told me, because "it would suggest something the formula companies can't reproduce." No offense to Kramer, who seems like a great guy, but this gets under my skin. If the researchers just want us to lick and groom our pups, why don't they say so? We can find our own way to do that. In fact, by insisting that milk is some kind of vaccine, they make it less likely that we'll experience nursing primarily as a loving maternal act—"pleasant and relaxing," in the words of *Our Bodies, Ourselves* and more likely that we'll view it as, well, dispensing medicine.

I continue to breast-feed my new son some of the time—but I don't do it slavishly. When I am out for the day working, or out with friends at night, he can have all the formula he wants, and I won't give it a second thought. I'm not really sure why I don't stop entirely. I know it has nothing to do with the science; I have no grandiose illusions that I'm making him lean and healthy and smart with my milk. Nursing is certainly not pure pleasure, either; often I'm tapping my foot impatiently, waiting for him to finish. I do it partly because I can get away with breast-feeding part-time. I work at home and don't punch a clock, which is not the situation of most women. Had I been more closely tied to a workplace, I would have breast-fed during my maternity leave and then given him formula exclusively, with no guilt.

My best guess is something I can't quite articulate. Breast-feeding does not belong in the realm of facts and hard numbers; it is much too intimate and elemental. It contains all of my awe about motherhood, and also my ambivalence. Right now, even part-time, it's a strain. But I also know that this is probably my last chance to feel warm baby skin up against mine, and one day I will miss it.

CHALLENGE QUESTIONS

Is Breast-Feeding the Best Way to Feed Babies?

1. List reasons why breast-feeding is the best way to feed infants and reasons that formula feeding is just a good way.
2. Explain how marketing by formula companies and hospitals have influenced breast-feeding.
3. After deciding which stand you take on breast-feeding, write a public service announcement to be aired on local radio stations about your position on breast-feeding.
4. Compare the views of both authors on how society as a whole can impact breast-feeding rate.
5. Evaluate the "breast-feeding friendliness" of your college, university, or place of employment.

Additional Internet Resources

La Leche League International (LLLI)

An international, nonprofit organization dedicated to providing education, information, support, and encouragement to women who want to breast-feed. The "Answer Pages" contains information on questions women frequently have, such as the impact of alcohol and drugs on breast milk, feeding with the adopted baby, the impact of breast implants on lactation, and many more.

http://www.llli.org/

World Health Organization (WHO)

WHO is the directing and coordinating authority for health within the United Nations system. It is responsible for providing leadership on global health matters, shaping the health research agenda, setting norms and standards, articulating evidence-based policy options, and monitoring and assessing health trends.

http://www.who.int/en/

Supplemental Nutrition Program for Women, Infants, and Children (WIC)

WIC provides supplemental foods, health care referrals, and nutrition education for low-income pregnant, breast-feeding, and non-breast-feeding postpartum women, and to infants and children up to age 5. In 1992, the national breast-feeding promotion program began to promote breast-feeding as the best method of infant nutrition and to provide breast pumps to WIC mothers who were breast-feeding.

http://www.fns.usda.gov/wic/

United Nations Children's Fund (UNICEF)

International organization that provides emergency food and health care to children in developing countries. Working with WHO, they created the "Baby-Friendly Hospital Initiative." This is also known as "Breastfeeding Friendly Hospitals."

http://www.unicef.org/programme/breastfeeding/baby.htm

Contributors to This Volume

EDITOR

JANET M. COLSON is an associate professor in the Nutrition and Food Science Program at Middle Tennessee State University. She earned her Ph.D. in Nutrition and Food Science from Florida State University, Tallahassee, Florida. Earlier degrees include the B.S. in Home Economics Education from Mississippi College, Clinton, Mississippi, and the M.S. in Home Economics Education from the University of Southern Mississippi. Dr. Colson has spoken nationally on school health and promotion. She is currently involved in research with immigrant populations to determine changes in lifestyle that lead to nutrition and health problems. She has developed ancillaries for publication with McGraw-Hill, Pearson, and Wadsworth publishing.

AUTHORS

MARK ANSLOW is the editor of the *Ecologist* magazine, one of the world's leading environmental publication.

PETA BEE is a health and fitness journalist in the United Kingdom. She has written for *Athletics Today, Rugby World,* and *Today's Runner* magazines. She has a B.S. degree in sports science and graduate degree in nutrition.

JOEL BERG is executive director of the "http://www.huffingtonpost.com/joel-berg/%20www.nyccah.org" New York City Coalition Against Hunger and author of *All You Can Eat: How Hungry is America?* He served for eight years in the Clinton Administration in senior executive service positions at USDA and worked as USDA Community Coordinator of Community Food Security. He is a graduate of Columbia University.

MARK BITTMAN is a food journalist and author. He writes a weekly column for *The New York Times* dining section called *The Minimalist.* He has authored over 10 books on food and cooking.

JANE BRODY is an award-winning author and health columnist for *The New York Times*. She has degrees in biochemistry from Cornell and science writing from the University of Wisconsin. She has authored over a dozen books including two best-sellers, *Jane Brody's Nutrition Book* and *Jane Brody's Good Food Book.*

PHYLLIDA BROWN is a science writer from the United Kingdom. She has worked with UNICEFF and the Centre for Global Health Research in Delhi.

KELLY D. BROWNELL is the director of the Rudd Center for Food Policy and Obesity at Yale. His research deals primarily with obesity and the intersection of behavior, environment, and health with public policy. He was named in 2006 as one of "The World's 100 Most Influential People" by *Time* magazine. His undergraduate work was at Purdue and he received his Ph.D. in clinical psychology from Rutgers.

PAUL CAMPOS is a law professor at University of Colorado in Boulder. He has written extensively on the role of law in American society but is best known for his book *The Diet Myth: Why America's Obsessions with Weight Is Hazardous to Your Health.* He received his law degree from the University of Michigan.

FRANK J. CHALOUPKA is a professor of economics at the University of Illinois at Chicago and affiliate of the National Bureau of Economic Research. His research focuses on the economic analysis of substance use and abuse, and on the effect of prices and substance control policies in affecting the demands for tobacco, alcohol, and illicit drugs.

ELLEN COLEMAN is a nutrition consultant for The Sport Clinic in Riverside, California, and has consulted for the Los Angeles Lakers and other professional teams. She has been the nutrition columnist for *Sports Medicine Digest* for over 20 years. She received her master's in nutrition from Loma

Linda University and master's in physical education from the University of California at Davis. She is a registered dietitian.

GREGORY CONKO is the director of food safety policy at the Competitive Enterprise Institute. His research focuses on issues of food and pharmaceutical drug safety regulation and on health risks in public policy. He graduated from the American University with a degree in Political Science and History.

CORN REFINERS ASSOCIATION is the national trade association representing the corn refining industry of the United States since 1913.

CORNUCOPIA INSTITUTE is the Wisconsin-based advocacy group that supports sustainable and organic agriculture. They conduct research and investigations and provide needed information to consumers, family farmers, and the media.

KEITH DEVLIN is a senior researcher for the Center for the Study of Language and Information and was founder and currently executive director of H-STAR Institute at Stanford. He received his Ph.D. in Mathematics from University of Bristol, U.K.

SAM DOLNICK wrote for the Associated Press before joining *The New York Times* in 2009. He is a graduate of Columbia University.

DANIEL ENGBER is the science editor of *Slate* magazine and finalist for the James Beard Award for reporting on health and nutrition. He received his bachelor's in literature from Harvard and master's in neurobiology from Columbia.

THOMAS FARLEY is currently the New York City Health Commissioner. His research interests include prevention of HIV/STDs, infant mortality, and obesity. He is coauthor of *Prescription for a Healthy Nation*. He received his medical degree from Tulane University.

JEANNE FREELAND-GRAVES is the Bess Heflin Professor in the College of Natural Sciences at the University of Texas at Austin. Her research focuses on mineral metabolism in health and disease and nutrient regulation of gene expression and obesity. She received her doctorate from Rutgers and is a registered dietitian.

LINDSEY GETZ is a full-time freelance writer who has written for dozens of magazines both local and national, as well as many trade publications for a variety of industries. She is a graduate of Muhlenberg College.

ROLAND R. GRIFFITHS is a professor of Behavioral Biology and Neuroscience at Johns Hopkins Bayview Medical Center. His areas of specialization include behavioral pharmacology, drug self-administration, sedatives, caffeine, and hallucinogens. He completed his Ph.D. in psychology from the University of Minnesota.

ED HAMER is a freelance journalist specializing in agricultural globalization issues. He is from the United Kingdom.

SUZANNE HAVALA is a professor and the director of the doctoral program in health leadership at the University of North Carolina, Chapel Hill. Her research interests are food and nutrition policy and alternative and complementary health and nutrition services. She received her doctorate from that university and is a registered dietitian.

INSTITUTE OF MEDICINE (IOM) is an independent, nonprofit organization that works outside of government to provide unbiased and authoritative advice to decision makers and the http://resources.iom.edu/widgets/timeline/index.html public. It is the health arm of the National Academy of Sciences.

INTERNATIONAL FORMULA COUNCIL is an international association of manufacturers and marketers of formulated nutrition products (e.g., infant formulas and adult nutritionals) whose members are predominantly based in North America.

ARI LEVAUX writes "Flash in the Pan," a syndicated weekly food column and contributor to *AlterNet*. He received his master's from the University of Montana.

DAVID S. LUDWIG is a pediatric endocrinologist and professor at Harvard Medical School. His research focuses on the effects of dietary intake on hormones, metabolism, and body weight regulation. He is the founding director of the Optimal Weight for Life clinic at Children's Hospital. He received his medical degree from Stanford.

JOSEPH MERCOLA is an osteopathic physician, health activist, and author practicing in Hoffman Estates, Illinois. He advocates dietary and lifestyle approaches to health and says that his passion is "to transform the traditional medical paradigm in the United States." Dr. Mercola received his medical degree from Chicago College of Osteopathic Medicine.

HENRY I. MILLER is a medical doctor and currently a research fellow at the Hoover Institution at Stanford where his research focuses on public policy toward science and technology. He was the medical reviewer for the first genetically engineered drug evaluated by the FDA and was the founding director of the FDA's Office of Biotechnology.

JULIA MOSKIN writes for *The New York Times'* "Dining In/Dining Out" section, *New Yorker, Saveur,* and *Metropolitan Home* magazines and is a coauthor of nine cookbooks.

MICHAEL MOSS is a reporter with *The New York Times*. In 2010, he won the Pulitzer Prize for Explanatory Reporting for his investigation of the dangers of contaminated meat. He has been an adjunct professor at the Columbia's Graduate School of Journalism and attended San Francisco State University.

SUSAN NITZKE is a professor and extension specialist of nutritional sciences at the University of Wisconsin-Madison where her research focuses on development and evaluation of techniques to improve the effectiveness of nutrition education. She received her doctorate from that university and is a registered dietitian.

CONTRIBUTORS

BARRY M. POPKIN is a professor and the head of nutrition epidemiology at the University of North Carolina, Chapel Hill. His research deals with dynamic changes in diet, physical activity and inactivity, and body composition. He received his doctorate in Agricultural Economics from Cornell.

SAMUEL H. PRESTON is the Fredrick J. Warren Professor of Demography at the University of Pennsylvania and member of the National Academy of Sciences. He received his doctorate in economics from Princeton and is one of the leading demographers in the United States. He was first to describe the relationship between life expectancy and income, which is considered the "Preston Curve."

CHAD J. REISSIG is a pharmacologist with the controlled substance staff at the FDA. He received his doctorate from the University of Buffalo and was a postdoctoral fellow at Johns Hopkins Bayview Medical Center. His research interests include human behavioral pharmacology studies, preclinical rodent research, and in vitro studies examining the mechanisms of action of a variety of psychoactive drugs and drugs of abuse.

HANNA ROSIN is a cofounder of DoubleX, a women's site connected to *Slate*. She is also a contributing editor at the *Atlantic*. She has written for the *Washington Post, The New Yorker, GQ, New York*, and *The New Republic*.

ANNELI RUFUS is an award-winning author who is literary editor for the *East Bay Express*. She graduated from Berkley with a degree in English. Rufus is author of *The Scavengers' Manifesto* (2009), *The Farewell Chronicles: How We Really Respond to Death* (2005) and *Party of One: The Loners' Manifesto* (2002).

SILK SOY NUTRITION CENTER is an education and research initiative promoting a better understanding of soy nutrition among healthcare professionals and the general population.

MICHELE SIMON, a public-health attorney who teaches health policy at University of California Hastings College of the Law, is the director of the Center for Informed Food Choices, a nonprofit in Oakland, California. She received her law degree from Hastings and master's from Yale.

JEREMY SINGER-VINE is a journalist and computer programmer with the New York City-based *Slate* and writes the "Research Report" for the *The Wall Street Journal*. He also develops multimedia projects and edits *Slate's* environmental coverage.

ERIC C. STRAIN is a professor and the section head of the Psychiatry Substance Abuse Programs at Johns Hopkins Bayview Medical Center. Dr. Strain received his medical degree from the Ohio State University School of Medicine and completed an internship and residency at Johns Hopkins.

PAT THOMAS is the editor for *The Ecologist*. She is an American psychotherapist, who specializes in healthcare and environmental issues. She is the author of a variety of books including *What's in This Stuff?*

JOSEPH W. THOMPSON is the surgeon general for Arkansas and a professor of medicine and public health at the University of Arkansas. He earned his medical degree from University of Arkansas and his MPH from the University of North Carolina at Chapel Hill.

THE WHITE HOUSE PRESS RELEASE is responsible for gathering and disseminating information from the president and the White House staff.

WALTER C. WILLETT is the Fredrick John Stare Professor of Epidemiology and Nutrition, and the chair of the Department of Nutrition at Harvard. He is the principal investigator of the second Nurses' Health Study and has published over 1,000 articles regarding various aspects of diet and disease and is the author of *Eat, Drink and Be Healthy*.

DAVID G. WILLIAMS founded the largest noninvasive medical facility, the Williams Chiropractic Clinic, in central Texas. He has worked clinically with many college and professional athletes, including the Houston Oilers. He graduated from the Texas Chiropractic College.

CHIRS WOOLSTON is a freelance health, science and travel writer from Billings, Montana. He writes "The Healthy Skeptic" column in the *Los Angeles Times* and has articles in *Prevention, Health,* and *Reader's Digest*. He received a degree in biology and completed the science writing program at UC Santa Cruz.